Theodosius II

Theodosius II (AD 408–450) is the longest reigning Roman emperor. Ever since Edward Gibbon, he has been dismissed as mediocre and ineffectual. Yet Theodosius ruled an empire which retained its integrity while the West was broken up by barbarian invasions. This book explores Theodosius' challenges and successes. Ten essays by leading scholars of late antiquity provide important new insights into the court at Constantinople, the literary and cultural vitality of the reign, and the presentation of imperial piety and power. Much attention has been directed towards the changes promoted by Constantine at the beginning of the fourth century; much less to their crystallisation under Theodosius II. This volume explores the working out of new conceptions of the Roman empire – its history, its rulers and its God. A substantial introduction offers a new framework for thinking afresh about the long transition from the classical world to Byzantium.

CHRISTOPHER KELLY is a Fellow of Corpus Christi College, Cambridge. His publications include *Ruling the Later Roman Empire* (2004), *The Roman Empire: A Very Short Introduction* (2006), *The End of Empire: Attila the Hun and the Fall of Rome* (2009).

CAMBRIDGE CLASSICAL STUDIES

General editors
R. L. HUNTER, R. G. OSBORNE,
M. MILLETT, D. N. SEDLEY, G. C. HORROCKS,
S. P. OAKLEY, W. M. BEARD

THEODOSIUS II

Rethinking the Roman Empire in late Antiquity

Edited by

CHRISTOPHER KELLY

CAMBRIDGE
UNIVERSITY PRESS

University Printing House, Cambridge CB2 8BS, United Kingdom

Published in the United States of America by Cambridge University Press, New York

Cambridge University Press is part of the University of Cambridge.

It furthers the University's mission by disseminating knowledge in the pursuit of education, learning and research at the highest international levels of excellence.

www.cambridge.org
Information on this title: www.cambridge.org/9781107038585

© Faculty of Classics, University of Cambridge 2013

This publication is in copyright. Subject to statutory exception and to the provisions of relevant collective licensing agreements, no reproduction of any part may take place without the written permission of Cambridge University Press.

First published 2013

Printed in the United Kingdom by Clays, St Ives plc

A catalogue record for this publication is available from the British Library

Library of Congress Cataloguing in Publication data
Theodosius II : rethinking the Roman empire in late antiquity / edited by Christopher Kelly.
pages cm. – (Cambridge classical studies)
Includes bibliographical references and index.
ISBN 978-1-107-03858-5 (hardback)
1. Theodosius II, Emperor of Rome, 401-450. 2. Rome – History – Theodosians, 379-455. I. Kelly, Christopher, 1964- author, editor of compilation.
DF562.T44 2013
949.5'013–dc23
2013013492

ISBN 978-1-107-03858-5 Hardback

Cambridge University Press has no responsibility for the persistence or accuracy of URLs for external or third-party internet websites referred to in this publication, and does not guarantee that any content on such websites is, or will remain, accurate or appropriate.

CONTENTS

List of contributors	page vii
Preface	ix
Frequently cited texts	x
Chronological table	xiii
List of abbreviations	xv

Part I	**Introduction**	**1**
1	Rethinking Theodosius *Christopher Kelly*	3
Part II	***Arcana imperii***	**65**
2	Men without women: Theodosius' consistory and the business of government *Jill Harries*	67
3	Theodosius and his generals *Doug Lee*	90
4	Theodosius II and the politics of the first Council of Ephesus *Thomas Graumann*	109
5	Olympiodorus of Thebes and eastern triumphalism *Peter Van Nuffelen*	130
Part III	**Past and present**	**153**
6	Mapping the world under Theodosius II *Giusto Traina*	155
7	'The insanity of heretics must be restrained': heresiology in the *Theodosian Code* *Richard Flower*	172

8 Writing in Greek: classicism and compilation,
   interaction and transformation   195
   Mary Whitby

Part IV   *Pius princeps*   219
 9 Stooping to conquer: the power of imperial humility   221
   Christopher Kelly
10 The imperial subject: Theodosius II and
   panegyric in Socrates' *Church History*   244
   Luke Gardiner
11 Theodosius II and his legacy in anti-Chalcedonian
   communal memory   269
   Edward Watts

Bibliography   285
Index   315

CONTRIBUTORS

Richard Flower: Lecturer in Classics and Ancient History, University of Exeter

Luke Gardiner: Gaylord and Dorothy Donnelley Research Fellow, University of Chicago

Thomas Graumann: Senior Lecturer in Early Church History, University of Cambridge and Fellow of Homerton College

Jill Harries: Professor of Ancient History, University of St Andrews

Christopher Kelly: Fellow of Corpus Christi College, Cambridge

Doug Lee: Professor of Ancient History, University of Nottingham

Giusto Traina: Professor of Roman History, University of Paris-Sorbonne

Peter Van Nuffelen: Research Professor in Ancient History, Ghent University

Edward Watts: Alkiviadis Vassiliadis Endowed Chair and Professor of History, University of California, San Diego

Mary Whitby: Lector in the Faculty of Classics and Lecturer in Ancient Greek, Merton College, Oxford

PREFACE

This volume has its origins in a conference 'Theodosius II and the making of late antiquity' (organised by Richard Flower and Christopher Kelly) held in Cambridge in March 2011. In addition to those published here, papers were also given by Riccardo Bof, Gillian Clark, Atsuko Gotoh, Boudewijn Sirks and Philip Wood. The discussion was both enlivened and sharpened by the valuable comments of Kate Cooper. Particular thanks are due to Gillian Clark for her unstinting enthusiasm for this project; to Richard Flower, conference organiser extraordinaire; to Robin Whelan, who discharged his task as editorial assistant with peerless proficiency; to Mike Humphreys for compiling an accurate and intelligent index; to Judith Nadler (University Librarian, University of Chicago), whose unfailing courtesy and assistance made it possible for this volume to be completed in America; to Robin Osborne, who (always attentive midst a myriad of other pressing responsibilities) ensured that this project kept moving steadily forwards; and to Michael Sharp and Gillian Dadd, who oversaw all with unfailing courtesy. I am also most grateful to Patrick Gautier Delaché for his help with the illustration of the Carolingian map from Santa María de Ripoll.

Both the conference and editorial assistance for the preparation of this volume were generously supported by the Faculty of Classics, University of Cambridge, and the Henry Arthur Thomas Fund.

FREQUENTLY CITED TEXTS

There are helpful guides to texts and translations in Millar 2006: xxiii–xxvi and Schor 2011: 275–301. For abbreviations, see Jones 1964: III 394–406. On the complexities of the conciliar *acta*, see the useful 'The *acta* of the fifth-century Councils: a brief guide for historians' in Millar 2006: 235–46. The *Acts of the Council of Chalcedon* are translated in Price and Gaddis 2005.

Chron. Pasch.	*Chronicon Paschale*, L. Dindorf (ed.), 2 vols., *CSHB* 4, Bonn, 1832 (trans. Whitby and Whitby 1989).
Const. Porph. *Cer.*	Constantine VII Porphyrogenitus, *On the ceremonies of the Byzantine court*, J. J. Reiske (ed.), *CSHB*, Bonn, 1829.
Cyr. Scyth. *V. Sabae*	Cyril of Scythopolis, *Life of Sabas*, E. Schwartz (ed.), *TU* 49.2, Leipzig, 1939 (trans. R. M. Price, Cistercian Studies series 114, Kalamazoo, MI, 1991).
Eunapius	Eunapius, *History*, Blockley 1983: 1–127 (ed. and trans.).
Eus. *V. Const.*	Eusebius, *Life of Constantine*, F. Winkelmann (ed.), *GCS* 7/1, *Eusebius Werke* I/1, 2nd edn, Berlin, 1991 (trans. Cameron and Hall 1999).
Evagrius	Evagrius (Scholasticus), *Church History*, J. Bidez and L. Parmentier (eds.), London, 1898 (trans. Michael Whitby 2000).
Joh. Lydus, *Mag.*	John Lydus, *On the Magistracies*, A. C. Bandy (ed. and trans.), Memoirs of the American Philosophical Society 149, Philadelphia, PA, 1983.

John of Antioch	U. Roberto (ed. and trans.), *Ioannis Antiocheni Fragmenta ex Historia chronica*, TU 154, Berlin, 2005; also D. Mariev (ed. and trans.), *Ioannis Antiocheni Fragmenta quae supersunt omnia*, CFHB (Series Berolinensis) 47, Berlin, 2008.
John Rufus, *Pler.*	John Rufus, *Plerophoriae*, F. Nau (ed. and French trans.), *PO* 8.1, Paris, 1911.
Malalas	John Malalas, *Chronicle*, H. Thurn (ed.), CFHB (Series Berolinensis) 35, Berlin, 2000 (trans. E. Jeffreys, M. Jeffreys and R. Scott, Australian Association for Byzantine Studies, Byzantina Australiensia 4, Melbourne, 1986).
Marcell. com.	Marcellinus comes, *Chronicle*, T. Mommsen (ed.), *MGH (AA)* 11: 37–108 (Berlin, 1894) (trans. Croke 1995).
Nonnus, *Dion.*	Nonnus, *Dionysiaca*, F. Vian (ed. and French trans.), 19 vols., Paris, 1976–2006 (English trans. W. H. D. Rouse, Loeb Classical Library, 3 vols., Cambridge, MA, 1940–2).
Olymp.	Olympiodorus, *History*, Blockleys 1983: 151–209 (ed. and trans.).
Pan. Lat.	*Panegyrici Latini*, R. A. B. Mynors (ed.), Oxford, 1964 (trans. Nixon and Rodgers 1994).
Philostorgius	Philostorgius, *Church History*, J. Bidez and F. Winkelmann (eds.), *GCS* 21, 3rd edn, Berlin, 1981 (trans. P. R. Amidon, Writings from the Greco-Roman world 23, Leiden, 2007).
Phot. *Bibl.*	Photius, *Bibliotheca*, R. Henry (ed. and French trans.), 9 vols., Paris, 1959–91 (selected English trans. Wilson 1994).
Priscus	Priscus of Panium, *History*, Blockley 1983: 221–377 (ed. and trans.).
Soc.	Socrates, *Church History*, G. C. Hansen (ed.), *GCS (n.F.)* 1, Berlin, 1995 (trans. A. C. Zenos, *NPNF* (2nd series) 2, Oxford, 1891).

FREQUENTLY CITED TEXTS

Soz.	Sozomen, *Church History*, J. Bidez and G. C. Hansen (eds.), *GCS (n.F.)* 4, 2nd edn, Berlin, 1995 (trans. C. D. Hartranft, *NPNF* (2nd series) 2, Oxford, 1891).
Theod. *Ep.* I–XLV	Theodoret, *Letters (Collectio Patmensis)*, Y. Azéma (ed. and French trans.), *SC* 40, Paris, 1955.
Theod. *Ep.* 1–147	Theodoret, *Letters (Collectio Sirmondiana)*, Y. Azéma (ed. and French trans.), *SC* 98 and 111, Paris, 1964–5.
Theod. *HE*	Theodoret, *Church History*, L. Parmentier and G. C. Hansen (eds.), *GCS (n.F.)* 5, Berlin, 1998 (trans. B. Jackson, *NPNF* (2nd series) 3, Oxford, 1892).
Theodore Lector	Theodorus Anagnostes, *Church History*, G. C. Hansen (ed.), *GCS (n.F.)* 3, 2nd edn, Berlin, 1995.
Theophanes	Theophanes Confessor, *Chronicle*, C. de Boor (ed.), Leipzig, 1883 (trans. Mango and Scott 1997).
Zonaras	Zonaras, *Epitome Historiarum*, L. Dindorf (ed.), 6 vols., Leipzig, 1868–75.
Zos.	Zosimus, *New History*, F. Paschoud (ed. and French trans.), *Zosime, Histoire Nouvelle*, 3 vols. in 5, Paris, 1971–89 (vol. 1, 2nd edn, 2000) (English trans. R. T. Ridley, Australian Association for Byzantine Studies, Byzantina Australiensia 2, Sydney, 1982).

CHRONOLOGICAL TABLE

395–423	**Honorius** (western Roman emperor)
395–408	**Arcadius** (eastern Roman emperor)
399–420	Yazdegerd I (shah of Persia)
401	birth of Theodosius II
402	Theodosius II proclaimed Augustus
406	Vandals invade Gaul
408–450	**Theodosius II** (eastern Roman emperor)
410	sack of Rome by Goths under Alaric
412–444	Cyril, bishop of Alexandria
413	completion of Theodosian Walls in Constantinople
414	Pulcheria proclaimed Augusta and takes vow of virginity
418	Goths settled in southern Gaul
421	**Constantius III** (western Roman co-emperor with Honorius); Theodosius marries Aelia Eudocia
421–422	Roman campaign against Persia
425	western usurper John defeated in Ravenna
425–455	**Valentinian III** (western Roman emperor)
428	withdrawal of Roman protection of Armenia
428–431	Nestorius, bishop of Constantinople
429	Vandal invasion of North Africa
430	death of Augustine of Hippo
431	First Council of Ephesus
431–434	Maximianus, bishop of Constantinople
434–446	Proclus, bishop of Constantinople
437	Valentinian III marries Licinia Eudoxia (daughter of Theodosius II) in Constantinople; *Theodosian Code* issued
438	Aelia Eudocia makes Holy Land pilgrimage; *Theodosian Code* received by Senate in Rome; relics of John Chrysostom arrive in Constantinople

CHRONOLOGICAL TABLE

439	Vandals occupy Carthage and provinces of Africa Proconsularis and Byzacena
441–442	Roman expeditionary force to Sicily (to recapture North Africa) withdrawn for defence of Balkans in face of Hun incursions
445–453	Attila sole ruler of Huns
446–449	Flavian, bishop of Constantinople
447	severe earthquake in Constantinople; Huns' most destructive Balkan offensive
449	Second Council of Ephesus
450	death of Theodosius II in riding accident
450–457	**Marcian** (eastern Roman emperor); marries Pulcheria
451	Council of Chalcedon; Attila invades Gaul and retreats after Battle of Catalaunian Plains
452	Attila invades Italy and withdraws
453	death of Attila; death of Pulcheria
455	murder of Valentinian III; Vandals sack Rome

ABBREVIATIONS

ACO	*Acta Conciliorum Oecumenicorum*, ed. E. Schwartz and J. Straub, Berlin, 1914–71.
CCSG	*Corpus Christianum series Graeca*
CCSL	*Corpus Christianum series Latina*
CFHB	*Corpus Fontium Historiae Byzantinae*
CPG	*Clavis Patrum Graecorum*
CSEL	*Corpus Scriptorum Ecclesiasticorum Latinorum*
CSHB	*Corpus Scriptorum Historiae Byzantinae*
CTh	*Codex Theodosianus*
GCS	*Die griechischen christlichen Schriftsteller*
HE	*Historia ecclesiastica*
IGLS	*Inscriptions greques et latines de la Syrie*
MGH (AA)	*Monumenta Germaniae Historica, Auctores Antiquissimi*
NPNF	*A Select Library of Nicene and Post-Nicene Fathers of the Christian Church*
NTh	*Novellae* of Theodosius II
NVal	*Novellae* of Valentinian III
PG	*Patrologia Graeca*, ed. J.-P. Migne
PLRE	*Prosopography of the later Roman empire*, vol. 1: AD *260–395* (ed. A. H. M. Jones, J. R. Martindale and J. Morris, Cambridge, 1971); vol. II: AD *395–527* (ed. J. R. Martindale, Cambridge, 1980).
PO	*Patrologia Orientalia*
SC	*Sources chrétiennes*
SEG	*Supplementum Epigraphicum Graecum*
TU	*Texte und Untersuchungen zur Geschichte der altchristliche Literatur*

Journal abbreviations follow *L'Année Philologique*.

PART I
INTRODUCTION

CHAPTER I

RETHINKING THEODOSIUS

Christopher Kelly

Dramatic interventions in court politics require careful planning. In their celebratory narration they acquire a certain faultless precision. Mark the Deacon's biography of Porphyry, bishop of Gaza (in Palestine), applauded that holy man's achievement in presenting the first petition to be approved by Theodosius II – a feat all the more remarkable as the emperor was not yet one year old. The story (here much abbreviated) runs as follows.[1] Mark, Porphyry and a group of committed Christians journeyed to Constantinople in the hope of convincing the Emperor Arcadius (Theodosius' father) to order the demolition of the temple of Zeus Marnas in their home town. Through court and church connections, they obtained the support of Arcadius' wife, Eudoxia; in return, Porphyry promised the pregnant empress a son. But the emperor was not persuaded; fearing the disruption of tax revenue, he preferred a more gradualist approach (the shutting of the temple and the withdrawal of civic privileges from professed pagans), 'For a sudden change would be troublesome for the people.'[2] As Porphyry had predicted, Eudoxia gave birth to a prince: Theodosius. She then renewed her efforts on Porphyry's behalf. On the day of Theodosius' baptism, as the

---

[1] *V. Porph.* 33–50 (eds. Grégoire and Kugener 1930) with discussion in Jones 1964: 1 344–6; Holum 1982: 54–5; Elton 2009: 136; Van Nuffelen 2010: 237–8, 2012: 191–3. This retelling of Mark's tale conceals some of the inaccuracies which pockmark the text; not least, the entirely wayward chronology of Theodosius' birth (correctly, April 401), baptism (not otherwise attested, see Barnes 1989a) and elevation to *augustus* (10 January 402). Those claiming that the core of the text preserves Mark's eyewitness account argue that the narrative which survives is a later version 'expanded somewhat and dramatized, introducing chronological inaccuracies' (Holum 1982: 55 n. 31 following Grégoire and Kugener 1930: especially xxix–xlv, ciii–cix). Barnes 2010: 260–83 – much less forgiving of these errors – argues strongly for a composition in the mid sixth century (at the earliest); for further debate and comment, see usefully Trombley 2001: 1 246–82; Millar 2006: 26 n. 58.

[2] *V. Porph.* 41.12–13.

3

imperial party emerged from church – the high-ranking dignitaries dressed in white 'as if covered in snow', all carrying candles 'so it seemed that stars were shining on the earth'[3] – Porphyry (as instructed by Eudoxia) rushed forward and presented the courtier carrying the baby boy with a petition for the demolition of the temples in Gaza. The courtier (fully briefed) 'placed his hand under the infant's head causing it to nod, and proclaimed before all: "His Majesty has commanded that the matters requested in the petition shall be carried out."'[4] Under renewed pressure from Eudoxia, Arcadius gave way: "This is a tough request, but much tougher to refuse, since it is our son's first ruling."[5]

For those critical of Theodosius II, the dazzling tableau of Porphyry's staged intervention at the infant emperor's baptism might serve as a poster for the next four decades of the reign: an image of a passive ruler swaddled in ceremony, surrounded by self-interested courtiers and manipulative bishops, and agreeing to a proposition adroitly promoted by a pious empress. The vignettes of Theodosius preserved (elaborated or invented) by Byzantine chroniclers have reinforced a view of an ineffectual ruler who, careless of matters of state, preferred his faith, his hobbies and his horses. Here is a studious emperor with an aptitude for mathematics and astronomy; an avid bibliophile with remarkably neat handwriting (who even in the theatre preferred to practise his calligraphy rather than watch the show); an accomplished modeller in clay; a keen sportsman, archer and experienced equestrian who so enjoyed a competitive chukka that he had a polo field laid out in the grounds of the Great Palace at Constantinople.[6] Here too is an emperor dominated by the eunuchs of the palace household, all too easily distracted from serious matters, 'just like children with toys'; a ruler so negligently uninterested in reading his official

---

[3] *V. Porph.* 47.15, 17–18.
[4] *V. Porph.* 48.11.
[5] *V. Porph.* 49.9–10.
[6] Zonaras 13.23 (III 244B); Cedrenus 586 (*PG* 121: 637B); Nicephorus Callistus, *HE* 14.3 (*PG* 146: 1064A–C); for Theodosius the Calligrapher, see George the Monk II 604.8–9 (eds. C. de Boor and P. Wirth, Stuttgart, 2 vols., 1978); Glykas, *Annales* 4.260–1 (*PG* 158: 488C and 489C) with Lippold 1973: 967; Alan Cameron 2002: 126, 2011: 434; on the polo field (the Tzykanisterion), see Janin 1964: 118–19; Horn 2006: 64; Canepa 2009: 180.

papers before signing them that he once mistakenly authorised his wife to be sold into slavery.[7] Here is a hen-pecked monarch pushed around by his eldest sister, the Empress Pulcheria, who as a teenager publicly proclaimed her perpetual virginity. Even contemporaries were struck by the piety of the imperial court, which was said to resemble a monastery, Theodosius and his three sisters rising early each morning to pray together and fasting twice a week.[8] Monks who visited Constantinople in the late 440s reported that the emperor wore a hair shirt concealed under his purple robes – and had done so for thirty years.[9]

Modern scholarship (until quite recently) has been dismissive of Theodosius: 'a man of intelligence and sincerity but little backbone'.[10] The dislike is deep-rooted in Enlightenment disapproval. Tillemont, although appreciating Theodosius' artistic enthusiasms, sets the disparaging tone.

> Mais il manquoit de cette grandeur d'ame & de ce courage nécessaire à un Souverain pour gouverner par lui-même, & du discernement ou de la force qu'il faut qu'ait un Prince pour choiser ceux qui sont dignes de lui donner conseil, & sur qui il peut décharger d'une partie de ses soins.[11]

Edward Gibbon followed closely (though with markedly less sympathy for the emperor's liberal pursuits).

> The unfortunate prince, who is born in the purple, must remain a stranger to the voice of truth; and the son of Arcadius was condemned to pass his perpetual infancy, encompassed only by a servile train of women and eunuchs. The ample leisure, which he acquired by neglecting the essential duties of his high office, was filled by idle amusements, and unprofitable studies ... Theodosius was never excited to support the weight and glory of an illustrious name.[12]

The claim of a significant weakening in imperial authority is sharpened by comparison between Theodosius II and his imperial grandfather. Theodosius I (379–395) was an experienced officer

---

[7] John of Antioch 288 (= Priscus [3]) quoting 10–11; Theophanes 5941 (101.13–17); Theodore Lector 352; John of Nikiu 87.29–33 (trans. Charles 1916: 107).
[8] Soc. 7.22.3–4.
[9] John Rufus, *Pler.* 99 (*PO* 8.1: 173.12–13) with Brown 2002: 143 n. 89.
[10] Holum 1982: 130.
[11] Tillemont 1738: 22–6 quoting 26.
[12] Gibbon 1781b: 317; brief surveys of modern scholarly censure in Wessel 2001: 285–6; Zecchini 2002: 529–30; Ilski 2005: 3–7; Meier 2007: 135–6.

who had fought in Britain and on the Danube frontier before he became emperor in his early thirties.[13] His military successes included taking armies across the Balkans in 388 and 394 to suppress two rebellions in the West. Theodosius II – 'born in the purple' in April 401 and proclaimed co-emperor by his father, Arcadius, when he was nine months old – is the longest reigning emperor in the history of the Roman empire. Arcadius died when his son was seven. For the next forty-two years (408–450), Theodosius was largely confined to Constantinople: he never saw most of the empire over which he ruled; he never fought on campaign; he never commanded troops in the field.[14] When Theodosius I died in 395, he could fairly claim to have secured the political integrity of the Roman empire which then passed to his sons: Honorius in the West and Arcadius in the East. Over five decades later, when Theodosius II (still without a male heir) was unexpectedly killed in a hunting accident, Roman rule in the West had been significantly compromised by the emergence of independent states in Gothic France and Vandal North Africa. On these quickly sketched criteria, the 'effete, bookish, and ... palace-bound'[15] grandson seems to fall far short of the grandfather. To quote A. H. M. Jones (rarely so tartly epigrammatic): 'none of the male descendants of Theodosius the Great inherited his ability or force of character: they reigned rather than ruled the empire.'[16]

This volume does not attempt a full-scale revision of Theodosius' reputation. It neither comes to praise him nor to bury him beneath the weight of ancient or modern disapprobation. Rather, it aims to build on recent important re-evaluations of key aspects of the eastern Roman empire in the first half of the fifth century. The ten chapters which follow this introduction (Part I) concentrate on three principal areas of interest: the wider circumstances that informed the workings of the court (Part II), literary and cultural

---

[13] *PLRE* I 904 (Theodosius 4); Leppin 2003a: 29–33.
[14] For Theodosius' journeys (for the most part to seaports on the Bosphorus or Sea of Marmara), see Dagron 1974b: 85–6, 97–8; Lee 2000: 35; Millar 2006: 9–10; Elton 2009: 135.
[15] Holum 1982: 101.   [16] Jones 1964: I 173.

activity under Theodosius (Part III), and the presentation of imperial piety and power (Part IV). The four chapters in Part II (*Arcana imperii*) – Jill Harries on imperial decision-making, Doug Lee on military commanders, Thomas Graumann on the procedural framework for the first Council of Ephesus and Peter Van Nuffelen on the contemporary historian Olympiodorus – put pressure on the problems of constructing a satisfactory account of the complex political dynamics of the reign, in particular the role and influence of competing groups at court in Constantinople. Part III (Past and present) – Giusto Traina on cartography, Richard Flower on heresiology and Mary Whitby on Greek literature – focuses on the institutional and textual organisation of knowledge. It exposes some of the contemporary concerns of Theodosian authors, most pressingly an insistence that the empire (whatever the political fragmentation in the West) could still plausibly be presented as a unity. Lastly, Part IV (*Pius princeps*) – Christopher Kelly on imperial ceremonial, Luke Gardiner on the literary tactics of the contemporary church historian Socrates and Edward Watts on the enduring reputation of fifth-century emperors in Christian communities in Egypt – explores the difficulties of presenting, praising and remembering Theodosius II as a pious Christian ruler.

Arcana imperii

In late summer 431, in the immediate and muddy aftermath of the church council held at Ephesus, Theodosius invited two opposing delegations of eight bishops to a series of five formal hearings at the Rufinianae palace in Chalcedon (just across the Bosphorus from Constantinople). In their written briefs and in person before the emperor and his entourage – most importantly, the *consistorium*, the emperor's inner circle of advisers drawn from high-ranking officials and military commanders[17] – both sides had

---

[17] The formal criteria for membership of the *consistorium* are not known; nor how many members would be expected to be present; nor how easily those unused to court protocol could distinguish *consistoriani* from the imperial household. It was not simply a matter of spotting the eunuchs. For discussion, see Jones 1964: I 333–41; Harries 1999: 38–42; Millar 2006: 192–207, especially 193, 204, 221; Elton 2009: 134.

an unparalleled opportunity: one to press the case against Cyril of Alexandria (accused of blatantly perverting the Council's deliberations) and to declare continuing solidarity with Nestorius, bishop of Constantinople, and his disputed Christology; their opponents to demonstrate that Cyril's theology was orthodox, to argue that there had been no breach of protocol in his running of the Council and to persuade the emperor to remove Nestorius from his see. The efforts of Nestorius' supporters can be followed in a letter written to their episcopal colleagues (still in Ephesus) and in the lengthy description by Theodoret, bishop of Cyrrhus (in Syria), a pivotal player in mustering and maintaining the opposition to Cyril.[18]

Initial impressions were favourable. 'To date we have prevailed in these contests against those holding opposing views; and so successfully that all our arguments have proved acceptable to our Christ-loving emperor.' One memorable moment (to the satisfaction of emperor-watchers) came when Theodosius II demonstrated his own hostility to a theological proposition advanced by one of Cyril's advocates: 'our pious emperor was so vexed that he shook his purple robe and stepped back because of the magnitude of the blasphemy. And we saw that the whole *consistorium* made it abundantly clear to us that we were fighting on behalf of piety.'[19] But that initial advantage slipped away. Theodoret's account is much less optimistic: the emperor's advisers seemingly shifted ground, sneering whenever Nestorius' name was mentioned. Theodoret suspected bribery.[20] The outbreak of violence at a public gathering of Nestorius' supporters led to a direct exchange of views between Theodoret and the emperor.

---

[18] *Coll. Ath.* 66 (*ACO* 1 1.7, p. 77) for the communication to Ephesus; *Coll. Ath.* 69 (*ACO* 1 1.7, pp. 79–80) for Theodoret's account (a letter to Alexander, bishop of Hierapolis); for admirably lucid – and attractively concise – accounts of the issues surrounding the Council, see Millar 2006: 158–60; Schor 2011: 85–90; for the imperial audiences at the Rufinianae, Holum 1982: 171–2; McGuckin 1994: 103–7; Wessel 2001: 295–8, 2004: 255–62; Caner 2002: 220–2; Millar 2006: 205–7, 232; Schor 2011: 88–90. Schor 2011 amply answers Millar's call (2006: 146) for a sophisticated account of Theodoret's role in the development and maintenance of a set of complex networks of support.

[19] *Coll. Ath.* 66 (*ACO* 1 1.7, p. 77.18–20 and 24–7).

[20] *Coll. Ath.* 69 (*ACO* 1 1.7, p. 80.8 and 13); on the allegations of a bankrupting campaign of gift-giving by Cyril, see Jones 1964: 1 346; Brown 1992: 15–17; C. M. Kelly 2004: 171–2; Millar 2006: 219–21.

The most pious emperor ... said, 'I know that you are holding your own meetings.' Then I said to him, 'Since you have given me the right to speak freely, listen with understanding. Is it fair that heretics and those who have been excommunicated can conduct church services, but that we who fight for the faith ... cannot enter a church?' He said, 'And what am I to do?' So I responded to him. 'What [your officials] did in Ephesus ... it was right that you gave orders to the bishop there not to allow either them or us to gather until we reached an accord.' ... And to these things he said, 'I cannot give orders to a bishop.' So I replied, 'Do not then give an order to us.'[21]

This frank discussion resulted in imperial permission for public prayer (but with no reading of Scripture or celebration of the Eucharist). For Theodoret, that was a negligible achievement for five formal hearings which had ended in failure. The emperor invited Cyril's backers to consecrate a new bishop of Constantinople. Theodoret and his seven colleagues were sent home.

The delight is in the detail. There are very few records of apparently verbatim exchanges with Roman emperors.[22] Fewer still (outside the imaginary dialogues of Christian martyrs) are the accounts of those who proved unpersuasive. The meetings at the Rufinianae (only briefly outlined here) were part of a protracted series of negotiations in the latter months of 431 whose complex course can be traced in the papers of the Council of Ephesus. It is but one example of the mass of data provided by the *acta* of three church councils (Ephesus in 431 and 449, and Chalcedon in 451). In his *A Greek Roman empire: power and belief under Theodosius II (408–450)* (2006), Fergus Millar has deftly illustrated how much can be done with this 'dense array' of often highly partisan evidence to expose 'the workings of persuasion, command, reaction, and defiance'[23] across a remarkably broad range of intermediaries and interest-groups (sometimes competing, sometimes convergent, sometimes hostile), and the ebb and flow of influence in the more formally constituted advisory bodies in Constantinople (the *consistorium* and the Senate) whose support could be crucial in convincing an emperor to act.[24] The bulky conciliar dossiers, together with letter-collections, doctrinal tracts and the laws collected in both the *Theodosian Code* and the post-*Code Novellae* – that is,

---

[21] *Coll. Ath.* 69 (*ACO* I 1.7, p. 80.23–34), translation following Schor 2011: 90.
[22] Millar 2006: 249. [23] Millar 2006: 217, 131. [24] Millar 2006: 130–234.

"new" laws – of Theodosius II (which concentrate on 438–441), offer an extraordinary resource for understanding the inner workings of imperial government. This is nothing short of an information revolution. 'It is this combination of the *Acta* with the rich material in legal sources which makes this reign, at the level of public persuasive discourse, by far the most fully attested period of antiquity.'[25]

In the opening chapter in Part II of this volume – 'Men without women: Theodosius' consistory and the business of government' – Jill Harries looks closely at the workings of the *consistorium* through the prism of the *Theodosian Code*. The *Code* (commissioned in 429 and delivered in its first and only edition in 437) collected 2,700 rulings issued by emperors from Constantine to Theodosius II; heavily edited, these imperial pronouncements were arranged in chronological order by topic across sixteen books.[26] For Harries, this act of codification – previously unmatched in scope and scale – is emblematic of the routine of law-making in the *consistorium*. 'If the contents of the *Theodosian Code* are representative, then members of the consistory, or at least the minute-takers, had a culture of their own, which distanced them from the vicissitudes of day-to-day controversies' (p. 74). The *Code* reveals a 'focus on generality' (p. 78), 'an ambition for comprehensiveness' (p. 78), a 'drive for simplicity and clarity' (p. 84). For Harries, the push towards codification is itself an indication of the lack of engagement by Theodosius and 'the absence of a personal imperial agenda' (p. 83). 'Instead, we have a consistory of consolidators, well versed in the legal tradition, which they sought to systematise and perpetuate through both individual constitutions and the promulgation of the *Theodosian Code* itself' (p. 86). The *consistorium* (Harries suggests), with its emphasis on 'consultation and consensus' (p. 79) was one of the chief guarantors of the stability of Theodosian government.[27] Across four decades,

---

[25] Millar 2006: 152; delight in 'the uniquely detailed documentary evidence' (at 130) is Millar's leitmotiv: xiii–xiv, xv, 131, 149, 157, 161, 168, 197, 225, 226, 228; and note too (at 235–47) the invaluable 'The *Acta* of the fifth-century councils: a brief guide for historians'.

[26] Sirks 1993: 64–6, 2007: 83–5, 138–41; see too Matthews 2000: 75 n. 49.

[27] Note also Millar 2006: 203 'the broad principle that decisions at the Imperial court were the work of a collectivity is amply borne out in the evidence'; see also 201, 215, 227.

the emperor, despite an 'apparent disinclination for active leadership' (p. 87), was never seriously challenged – 'a tribute to the resilience of the court administration as a self-sustaining bureaucracy, in which the ambitions of individuals, sometimes over several generations, could be realised through decades of service and proximity to the imperial presence' (pp. 87–8).

The Theodosian regime was remarkably durable. In stark contrast to the West, court politics in Constantinople were not dominated by military men. Doug Lee's chapter – 'Theodosius and his generals' – focuses on the successful political containment of the highest-ranked commanders in the East. Theodosius never faced a major revolt or civil war. 'Despite the emperor's lack of military experience or ability, there appear to have been few, if any, attempts at armed usurpation during his lengthy reign' (p. 92). Certainly, like other individuals and groups within the *consistorium*, current and former holders of senior army posts (*magistri militum*) were perceived as influential and effective intermediaries. These were men of wealth, clout and connections. That no commander ever thought himself well enough placed to overshadow the emperor is, in part, the result of an organisational structure that divided the available assets: at any one time, three *magistri militum* held regional commissions (in Illyricum, the East and Thrace) and two *magistri militum praesentales* were at or near the imperial capital (p. 93). The provisioning of the army, the manufacture of weapons and the oversight of frontier troops were split between two powerful civilian officials (the praetorian prefect and the *magister officiorum*) (pp. 102–3). In part, the absence of revolt should be connected with the failure to win any decisive victory which might earn a successful general the personal loyalty of his troops: the war against the Persians in the 420s ended in a stalemate (which Theodosius claimed as a triumph);[28] the repeated attempts to deal with the destructive raids of Attila and the Huns in the Balkans were, at best, costly exercises in containment; the campaign in 441 to dislodge the Vandals from North Africa was a failure; the defeat of the western usurper John in 425 was firmly part of a Theodosian dynastic strategy.

[28] Blockley 1992: 56–8.

Despite their overall lack of achievement, senior commanders were publicly celebrated as full participants in government, and deserving of its most prestigious honours. As Lee notes, from 408 to 450 *magistri militum* held close to 40 per cent of the available (non-imperial) ordinary consulates (p. 105). Counterbalancing this policy of inclusion, the regime's presentation of legitimate imperial authority as emphatically invested in the promotion of right religion muted the traditional emphasis on military virtue; or at least transmuted it in the claim that it was Theodosius' prayers that guaranteed the empire's security.[29] Any setbacks on campaign were the responsibility of generals, not the emperor.[30] The stress on imperial piety also distanced many high-ranking commanders who – as committed Arians – were religious outsiders: 'in the midst of the emphasis on religious conformity during Theodosius' reign, the willingness to allow senior military posts to be held by religious non-conformists was a strategy for reducing the threat they might otherwise pose' (p. 108). In the competition for influence and patronage, this apparent permissiveness was a key element in the policing of military ambition by a sedentary and civilian court.

The management of these tense and shifting relationships between various interest-groups jostling to secure their place is also analysed in Thomas Graumann's chapter (the third in Part II) – 'Theodosius II and the politics of the first Council of Ephesus'. Graumann looks in detail at two official communications (*sacrae*) from the emperor: the first, issued in November 430, instructed bishops to come together in Ephesus at Pentecost the following year and thrash out their differences; the second was read by Candidianus, the imperial representative in Ephesus, on 22 June 431 (a reading interpreted by Cyril, bishop of Alexandria, and his supporters as constituting the formal opening of proceedings). Particularly striking in both these documents – and especially in the light of Jill Harries' emphasis 'on consultation and consensus' (p. 79) as key to decision-making in the *consistorium* – is their deliberate restraint. The acrimonious theological fallout from the Council of Ephesus can all too easily obscure the significant lack

[29] Below p. 53.   [30] Lee 2000: 36.

of specific reference to doctrinal controversy in these imperial communications. The emperor's concern is neither with a particular definition of orthodoxy nor the regulation of clergy (there are no explicit instructions on the expected outcomes of the Council), but with ensuring a well-attended and procedurally correct conference of bishops. Above all, what mattered was a public demonstration of consensus: 'From an imperial perspective, the first Council of Ephesus was to function as a means of demonstrating that the Church had retained (or regained) its unity and cohesion. It was not principally conceived as a deliberative assembly charged with deciding the terms on which that unity rested – that is, to define orthodoxy' (p. 123).

The *sacrae* exhibit all 'the style and character of a bureaucratic, and somewhat formulaic, government communication' (p. 115). By contrast, a much more strongly worded imperial letter sent to Cyril (in November 430, the same time as the first *sacra* was issued) brusquely objected to his insolent intransigence in failing to recognise the importance of church unity and a disciplined clergy. The emperor also pre-emptively forgave Cyril his unco-operative attitude 'lest you have an excuse or are able to claim that you were censured in defence of piety'.[31] This carefully balanced text worked hard to deprive Cyril of any grounds on which he could plausibly present himself – like Athanasius or John Chrysostom – as a martyr to misconceived imperial interference. That Cyril in his subsequent conduct at Ephesus strongly resisted any move towards reconciliation (while repeating the emperor's concerns for unity and the proper behaviour of clergy) is not a straightforward index of imperial weakness or misunderstanding of the issues at stake: that is a rush to judgement which too hurriedly withholds credit from Theodosius and his advisers for seeking to maintain a 'workable balance between imperial and ecclesiastical concerns and claims to authority' (p. 128). As Graumann points out, 'between the need to establish peace and the calls to stamp out heresy, most late-antique emperors found themselves in a no-win situation' (p. 128). Had Theodosius moved forward 'with the same unflinching determination he later displayed in empowering

[31] *Coll. Vat.* 8.4 (*ACO* I 1.1, p. 74.5–7).

Dioscorus to drive through his agenda at the second Council of Ephesus (in 449), the outcries (from both contemporaries and modern scholars) might easily be imagined' (p. 128). What failed at the first Council of Ephesus was an attempt to leverage unity, and it may be that Theodosius and his advisers deserve some criticism for believing that they could compel consensus in the face of fractious ecclesial disputes; but, equally, it would be a misstep to think that it is always more advantageous for even the severest autocracy to impose its own favoured resolution by force.

Taken together, these three chapters contribute to a more complex understanding of the process of imperial decision-making under Theodosius II. The surviving documentation (particularly the *Theodosian Code* and the conciliar *acta*) preserves – like a fossil record – the imprint of attempts to win over, cajole or pressure the emperor and his advisers. What emerges is not the comfortable dominance of any particular faction; rather what survives in the paperwork is a number of (to quote Fergus Millar) 'competing streams of rhetorical persuasion'[32] – persuasion which, as the emperor's letter to Cyril of Alexandria illustrates, could also flow in the opposite direction. This more diffuse (again to borrow from Millar[33]) view of power, influence and responsibility, stands in contrast to the approach of Kenneth Holum whose *Theodosian empresses: women and imperial dominion in late antiquity* (1982) – although in many ways still the most intelligent political history of the reign – is marked by its repeated insistence on the central importance of Theodosius' pious sister, Pulcheria, and her promotion of Marian Christianity: 'In Pulcheria's version the sacral *basileía* of empresses approached perilously near to the fullness of sovereignty.'[34] But that is to overstate a good case. Too great a stress on the suffocating pre-eminence of imperial women at Theodosius' court risks retrojecting much later Byzantine sensibilities: both admonitory tales of domineering empresses and claims for an already well-developed (and imperially sponsored) cult of the Virgin Mary in the first half of the fifth century.[35]

---

[32] Millar 2006: 231; see too 228.   [33] Millar 2006: 173, 227.
[34] Holum 1982: 111.
[35] Averil Cameron 1994: 8–13; Price 1994; see too the more cautious discussion in Cooper 1998, 2004.

Although at times undoubtedly a key figure at court, there were real limits to Pulcheria's patronage. Crucially, as Jill Harries emphasises, she had no direct say in the deliberations of the *consistorium* (pp. 72–3) nor could women hold any official positions in the imperial government.[36] 'To focus on Pulcheria to the exclusion of other informal factions and institutions of government is to exaggerate the extent of her power and influence in a multi-polar court' (p. 72). Pulcheria should be placed firmly in her dynastic context. As Harries suggests, she is the recognisable descendant of those wealthy women in the Greek East who had advantaged their communities, and were honoured in return, 'as members of a collective family enterprise, from which all members would expect to benefit' (p. 69). Pulcheria's position was fundamentally dependent on her 'opposing marriage plus maternity with voluntary celibacy, rendering female virginity a viable alternative to becoming a childbearing empress'.[37] The steadfast refusal of the emperor's sisters to marry excluded any potential rivals from exploiting the prestige of the imperial house. Theodosius' own marriage plans also passed over the established Constantinopolitan elite; his wife Athenais (renamed Eudocia) was the daughter of a professor of rhetoric in Athens.[38]

A strong emphasis on dynastic solidarity is central to the positive portrayal of the ruling family by the contemporary historian, Olympiodorus. Peter Van Nuffelen, in the final chapter in Part II – 'Olympiodorus of Thebes and eastern triumphalism' – offers a revisionist reading of Olympiodorus', now fragmentary, history (probably published before 427 and focusing almost exclusively on events in the West from 407 to 425). Van Nuffelen argues that Olympiodorus' history should be situated in the context of the jubilant self-congratulation in Constantinople which followed the defeat of the usurper John by an eastern expeditionary force in 425 and the installation of Valentinian III (Theodosius' six-year-old cousin) as western emperor. 'Rather than offering a disengaged account to serve imperial policy in relation to the West, Olympiodorus depicts the triumphant reassertion of control over the West by the eastern

---

[36] Harries 1994: 35–6.
[37] Sivan 2011: 111; see too Holum 1982: 92–3; Burgess 1993–4: 68.
[38] *PLRE* II 408–9 (Eudocia 2).

court' (p. 134). The success of the Theodosian regime in the East – or at least its affirmative self-presentation – sets a benchmark for a history of a failing West. Olympiodorus' emphasis is on a web of marriage alliances: the childless emperor Honorius (the son of Theodosius I) and his second wife Thermantia, the daughter of Stilicho, the most powerful general in the West; the arranged marriages of Honorius' half-sister, Galla Placidia, with the Gothic leader Athaulf and then Constantius, another high-ranking commander. These are connections that weaken Honorius' position: it is Galla Placidia who has a son (Valentinian); it is Honorius who is forced to share imperial power with Valentinian's father, Constantius (who died unexpectedly in 421). This is a tangled tale of family feuds, moral laxity, sexual scandal and political collapse. Olympiodorus 'highlights episodes that show how the western court systematically made the opposite choices to its eastern counterpart' (p. 141). It is the dark mirror image of a Theodosian dynasty gone awry; 'a confirmation of the wisdom of the eastern ruling family in closing itself off' (p. 140).

This implicit East/West contrast (which, for Van Nuffelen, shapes Olympiodorus' narrative), also underscores the importance of consensus and collective decision-making as vital factors in ensuring the stability of the eastern court. In organising his history around Stilicho and Constantius, Olympiodorus drew his readers' attention to a set of critical parallels. Both Stilicho and Constantius were connected by marriage to the imperial house; both were ambitious and self-interested; both were beyond Honorius' control; and both planned to use military force to impose their authority on the East. It ought also to be stressed, particularly in the light of Doug Lee's chapter discussed above, that both were also experienced and high-ranking generals. Olympiodorus' key theme is the inability of the leading figures at Honorius' court to work together in the first two decades of the fifth century. 'It is the plotting, infighting and disloyalty towards the emperor by Stilicho and his successors that caused a systemic failure in the West' (p. 143). By contrast, whatever difficulties or uncertainties might have threatened the East in the same period, by the mid 420s these could be smoothed over in a seamless story of success: 'in comparison with the West, the East had performed remarkably well.

Although run by an emperor in his minority, it had not succumbed either to infighting or to external enemies' (pp. 145–6).

Olympiodorus' presentation of successful imperial rule as a collective enterprise underscores one of the persistently difficult problems in understanding the workings of Theodosian government: in a complex decision-making process what weight or importance should be given to the emperor himself? Or (in an alternative formulation) how plausibly to explain the apparent paradox of a 'weak' emperor and a long, stable and usurpation-free reign?[39] For Jill Harries (as noted above), Theodosius' legal rulings, and indeed the whole *Theodosian Code* project, reveal a lack of imperial direction – 'no strong consistent leadership or personal legislative programme' (p. 76) – beyond a broad preference for moderation and restraint. In Harries' view, it is this very lack of imperial interference or initiative that permits a largely self-sustaining bureaucracy to curb the disruptive ambitions of powerful individuals while both allowing them (within strict limits) to promote their own policies and ensuring that they were amply honoured for their support of the regime. 'In the Constantinople of Arcadius and Theodosius II, the vagaries of the emperor were no longer important in the formulation of law; he was not a personality, he was an institution.'[40] Fergus Millar – centrally concerned with the rhythm of petition and response at the Theodosian court – recognises the possibility of a more interventionist emperor: 'no matter how many, or how forceful, the competing streams of rhetorical persuasion ... in the end the Imperial system was a monarchy, and the Emperor, at least when once arrived at adulthood, could decide.'[41] (Indeed, as Harries notes, the emperor could simply chose not to convene the *consistorium* [p. 87].) Thomas Graumann edges cautiously further. 'Yet at the age of twenty-nine, and after over two decades on the throne, Theodosius hardly remained the figurehead he had once been in his youth, and it seems ill-advised to write him out of the planning of the Council of Ephesus altogether' (p. 110). But it is difficult to tease out the golden thread of imperial opinion, even

---

[39] Lee 2000: 33–4, 2002: 185; Meier 2007: 139–42; Mitchell 2007: 104.
[40] Harries 1999: 47; see too Honoré 1998: 123; Sirks 2007: 48.
[41] Millar 2006: 231; see too 206, 227–8.

in Theodosius' seemingly more personal letter rebuking Cyril and offering him forgiveness. 'Only in the limited success of the emperor's willingness to take advice and to issue instructions for a council in his name and backed by his own authority is it possible to think of an "imperial agenda"' (p. 110).[42]

What is notable in all these approaches is a clear unwillingness to return to explanations of the dynamics of Theodosian government dependent on the dominance of one faction at court or as a series of bitter battles for influence between empresses and eunuchs. Indeed, that traditional characterisation of the regime has recently been swept firmly to once side. Passing through Constantinople on his masterly tour of the Mediterranean world in a single year – *428 dopo Cristo. Storia di un anno* (2007) – Giusto Traina rejects any sense of the emperor as timid, gentle or weak. 'L'Augusto appare soprattutto come un autocrate autoritario e carismatico ... Sapeva agire al momento opportuno e gestire non soltanto la corte e il clero, ma anche l'esercito e la popolazione urbana di Costantinopoli.'[43] Despite Traina's breezy dismissal, there is a marked reluctance to abandon an image of Theodosius II as, at least to some degree, ineffective or indecisive. The memorable and oft-repeated stories (the most exaggerated, as noted above, deep-rooted in later, Byzantine fabrications of the fifth century) continue to colour even the revisionist understandings of the workings of imperial government explored in this volume. Of course, it may be possible to find in the dramatic accounts of the clashes between the powers behind the throne some – distorted – reflection of the complex process of decision-making at Theodosius' court. Along with the competitive advocacy of 'differing perspectives and multiple interests',[44] there may be ample room for the exercise of imperial prerogative. To quote the conclusion of a brief and incisive reassessment of Theodosian court politics by Hugh Elton:

---

[42] Contrast the confidence of Luibhéid 1965: 14–15; Wessel 2001: 286–90, 2004: 99–100 and Ilski 2005: 20–1 for whom Theodosius' letter to Cyril is a transparent indication of imperial opinion, and similarly Thompson 1950: 61–6 on the formulation of foreign policy. Luibhéid and Thompson are both criticised by Holum 1982: 130 n. 81 for attributing 'too much of Theodosian policy to Theodosius himself'.
[43] Traina 2007: 53.   [44] Elton 2009: 141.

The narrative sources present the story in terms of individuals because it is easier – and in many ways more exciting – to tell stories about evil eunuchs with shining pates, glamorous princesses with clandestine love affairs, and skin-clad barbarian generals. But if this version of history is privileged, it means overlooking the fact that it was Theodosius II, the longest reigning Roman emperor, who managed relationships between these individuals.[45]

How imperial management might play out in particular cases is always a matter for debate. To return to the Rufinianae palace in September 431 and the efforts of Nestorius' supporters after the Council of Ephesus to persuade Theodosius and the *consistorium* to support their cause; and to the direct exchange between Theodoret and the emperor:

> [The emperor] said, 'And what am I to do?' So I responded to him. 'What [your officials] did in Ephesus … it was right that you gave orders to the bishop there not to allow either them or us to gather until we reached an accord.' … And to these things he said, 'I cannot give orders to a bishop.' So I replied, 'Do not then give an order to us.'

Many modern observers have been unimpressed by Theodosius' failure to take a firm or consistent line after the Council. Fergus Millar (like Theodoret himself) suspected that a campaign of bribery by Cyril's agents in Constantinople had caused opinion to shift in the *consistorium*; Kenneth Holum detected 'befuddlement' in 'a man of principle but little will'; for Adam Schor, Theodoret's report of his exchange with Theodosius 'suggests that the emperor was barely listening'.[46] Of course, it is difficult to know what weight to put on one encounter in a lengthy series of discussions. Or how correctly to read a version of events which for all its apparent emphasis on verbatim authenticity is also part of a self-conscious public presentation by those who sought to explain to their episcopal colleagues their own failure to persuade the emperor and his advisers. Certainly any view of Theodosius as indecisive or inattentive must also take into account the tactical importance in any decision-making process of delay, deferral, deadlock and derailment. There is also an uncomfortable irony

---

[45] Elton 2009: 142.
[46] Luibhéid 1965: 22 'The emperor, for whose benefit the meeting had taken place, apparently made no effort to impose order upon the debates'; Holum 1982: 173; Millar 2006: 207 (and above n. 20 on Cyril's bribery); Schor 2011: 90.

here. In such moments as these, Theodosius may appear more irresolute precisely because the fine-grained detail of the formation of imperial policy (the shifts, the negotiations, the compromises, the coalition-building) is more fully discoverable. Or put more starkly: Theodosius might perhaps be judged more favourably if the protracted process of decision-making were irrecoverable and all that was known was the comparatively clear-cut outcome.

The problem runs deeper. It seems reasonable to suggest that the confinement of the imperial court to Constantinople for the four decades of Theodosius' rule (successfully from childhood to adulthood) provided a favourable environment for the exercise of considerable influence by high-ranking officials, members of the royal household and imperial women. One of the pleasures of Theodosian court politics – at least from the historian's point of view – is that some of these powerplays can be traced in remarkable detail. It is possible to illustrate (again to quote Millar) 'the perception on the part of interested individuals and groups that power and influence were diffused, and that if success were to be achieved at the center of power, a variety of channels needed to be explored'.[47] What is less clear is the extent to which this represents a radically new set of political expectations or whether it exposes (perhaps, in some cases, for the first time) previously much less well-known aspects of imperial decision-making. It is all too easy to slip into the trap of assuming that the earliest attestation of a particular practice is always or necessarily closely coincident with its first appearance.

Similar difficulties dog judgements of Theodosius: not just (and the point is worth repeating) in deciding on the emperor's willingness or capacity to direct policy or to manage relationships between a wide range of competing powerbrokers, but also in determining to what degree a collectivist ideal of decision-making (Harries p. 76) or 'the responsiveness and preparedness to adapt'[48] made the political process under Theodosius different from that of his imperial predecessors. If a papertrail – and not even as detailed as that for the first Council of Ephesus – could be imagined surviving for Constantine (before the Battle of the

[47] Millar 2006: 173.   [48] Millar 2006: 191.

Milvian Bridge or the campaign against Licinius or the Council of Nicaea) or for Theodosius I (before his two civil wars in the West), then these moments might not seem so forcefully dominated by a single imperial personality. There might perhaps be more room for doubt, discussion, negotiation, changes of mind, compromise, collective decision-making or consensus. This is not – and it should be underlined clearly – an argument against significant political or institutional change from Constantine to Theodosius II, but rather a concern that the gradient has sometimes been set too steeply in the first half of the fifth century. Perhaps the danger chiefly lies in a distracting sense of novelty. Court politics under Theodosius II should not be assumed to be substantially or suddenly different simply because they can be more closely observed. Perhaps the problem is a too sharply contrasting (and too quickly moralising) evaluation of emperors. Praise of imperial decisiveness – like criticism of imperial irresolution – may be a misleading simplification of the complexities of politics in an autocratic society. 'Ruling' and 'reigning' may not be so easily distinguishable.

Past and present

Emperors of emperors, the greatest of emperors (repeated eight times).
May it please our emperors to live forever (repeated twenty-two times).
We give thanks for your good ordering of things (repeated twenty-three times).
You have removed ambiguity from the imperial laws (repeated twenty-three times).
Let many copies of the *Code* be made and kept in government offices (repeated ten times).[49]

These carefully scripted enthusiasms are a small selection from the forty-one acclamations – and a total of 748 repetitions, lasting over an hour – recorded in the minutes of a meeting of the Senate held in Rome in May 438.[50] The senators assembled in the house of the consul and praetorian prefect of Italy, Anicius Acilius

---

[49] *CTh Gesta Senatus* 5.
[50] On this meeting, see especially the discussions in Matthews 2000: 31–54 (46–7 for the statistics); Atzeri 2008: 119–70 (129–32 for the date), 171–211 (on the legal formalities).

Glabrio Faustus, for the formal presentation of the *Theodosian Code*. Faustus explained to his assembled colleagues that just over six months earlier he had personally received a copy of the *Code* while at court in Constantinople

> The most sacred emperor, our lord Theodosius, wishing to add this distinction to his world, ordered the preparation – after the precepts of the laws had been collected together – of a compendium (in sixteen books) of what is to be followed throughout the world, and he wished to bless these books with his own most sacred name. Our everlasting emperor Valentinian – with the constancy of a colleague and the affection of a son – approved this decision.[51]

The *Theodosian Code* (as noted above) collected 2,700 rulings issued by emperors from Constantine to Theodosius II. Heavily edited to remove any extraneous matter (such as a description of the circumstances behind a particular case[52]), these imperial decisions were arranged in chronological order by topic across sixteen books. 'We have completed a veritable undertaking of our time; darkness has been dissipated and with this compendium we have given the light of brevity to the laws … To that end, we have dispersed the cloud of volumes on which the lives of many persons – who explain nothing – have been frittered away.'[53] A decade earlier, in the project's first formulation by the emperor and his legal team (however that balance of initiative should be understood), the *Theodosian Code* had been envisaged as the final stage of a much grander (and never realised) design. Extracts from the jurists would be added to the collection of imperial rulings to result in a definitive summary of Roman law. 'This code shall permit no error, no ambiguities; it shall be called by our name and demonstrate what must be followed and what must be avoided by all.'[54]

The *Code* (as issued in 437) was a strong statement of a 'determination to assert the continuing formal unity of the Roman

---

[51] *CTh Gesta Senatus* 2 with Atzeri 2008: 119–28, preferred here to Sirks 2007: 203–6.
[52] See below pp. 37–8.
[53] *NTh* 1.1 and 3 (February 438) with (more generally on the force of this law) Honoré 1998: 132; Atzeri 2008: 172–8, 185–93.
[54] *CTh* 1.1.5 (March 429); on the complexities of the *Theodosian Code* project and its execution, see helpfully Archi 1976: 3–42; Harries 1994: 40–3, 1999: 59–64; Honoré 1998: 123–7; Matthews 2000: 55–71; Sirks 2007: 54–78, 109–47, 178–87.

Empire'.⁵⁵ Not, of course, politically: the installation of Valentinian III as western emperor in 425 was an affirmation of the dynastic partition of empire envisaged by Theodosius I thirty years earlier; equally, the enabling legislation for the *Theodosian Code* (which was, after all, an enterprise conceived and completed in Constantinople) stopped some way short of automatically applying subsequent imperial rulings issued either (by Theodosius) in the East or (by Valentinian III) in the West to the empire as a whole.⁵⁶ Rather, the *Code*'s claim to unity was implicit in the act of codification itself. To quote Jill Harries: 'The *Theodosian Code* can be read as the largest-scale attempt, thus far, to encompass everything about imperial law in one great volume' (p. 78). Imperial authority was at the core of this project. The *Code* represented a forceful assertion by one emperor over more than a century of imperial rulings.

> We confirm this concise guide to knowledge of the divine imperial laws from the time of Constantine of blessed memory ... However none of these emperors' immortality has been diminished in retrospect, the name of no lawgiver has been edited out; rather, altered with clarity in mind, the splendour of their decisions has been joined with us in an imperial fellowship.⁵⁷

The *Theodosian Code* was a showcase, topic by topic, of the development of legal thinking since Constantine. It matters too that the *Code* was issued in Latin: both another assertion of continuity with a long imperial past and a forcible reminder that the Roman empire – whatever its political divisions – was still united by a single language of government.⁵⁸ To quote John Matthews: 'The Theodosian Code, the first fully official attempt since the publication of the Twelve Tables by a Roman government to collect its own legislation, is one of the last expressions, as well as one of the last symbols, of Roman imperial unity.'⁵⁹

The confident expression by the Theodosian regime of the continued importance of the idea of the Roman empire as a unitary structure is the focus of the first chapter in Part III by Giusto Traina,

---

⁵⁵ Millar 2006: 5; see too Archi 1976: 38; Honoré 1998: 129.
⁵⁶ *NTh* 1.1.5; and see below p. 25 n. 70.
⁵⁷ *NTh* 1.1.3 with Sirks 2007: 75–7.
⁵⁸ Matthews 2000: 28–9; Millar 2006: 1–7, 84–93; Sirks 2007: 93–8.
⁵⁹ Matthews 1993: 44; see too 2000: 19, 29–30.

'Mapping the world under Theodosius II'. For Traina, that 'clear concern for imperial unity' (p. 162), so important to the *Theodosian Code*, is already evident in an earlier text, the *Notitia Dignitatum*. The *Notitia* is an illustrated catalogue of the administrative hierarchy, civil and military, in both East and West. The version for the whole empire was most probably produced in Constantinople around 401 under the Emperor Arcadius (Theodosius' father) and presented to his brother Honorius in the West.[60] While it may be possible to extract valuable data on late Roman government and the deployment of military assets from the information in the *Notitia*, it is also important (as Traina stresses) to recognise that this is no straightforward checklist. 'Both the western and eastern *Notitiae* are more readily understandable as texts framed by a strong ideological expression of concern for the unity of the empire, rather than as official documents primarily intended for administrative purposes' (p. 159). Certainly, the *Notitia Dignitatum* presents a very particular anatomy of empire. Its clear division of the business of government into administrative departments and military dispositions, its listing of officials in strict rank order, its illustration of the insignia of the most senior posts, and its use of Latin throughout, create the strong and deliberate impression of consistent imperial control across the Mediterranean world: a 'reformulation of the oikoumene in bureaucratic terms'.[61] The structural uniformity in the *Notitia*'s treatment of the East and West is itself an affirmation of the unity of empire.[62]

It is precisely this push towards 'l'unité virtuelle de l'Empire' (in Constantin Zuckerman's pleasing phrase[63]) that is also visible in the 'systematisation of geographical knowledge under Theodosius II and its connection with an ideological programme that embraced a long-standing Roman tradition linking imperial power firmly with geography' (p. 169). The public cartography of the Theodosian regime continued to insist on representing the Roman empire as a single entity dominating the known world. One

---

[60] Zuckerman 1998: 143–7; on the production of the *Notitia* in Constantinople as a single document, see Zuckerman 1998:146–7; Kulikowski 2000b: 359–60.
[61] Brennan 1996: 148.
[62] Clemente 2010: especially 123–4, 131–2.
[63] Zuckerman 1998: 147.

annotated map, commissioned by Theodosius in 435, is described in a short dedicatory poem by the calligrapher who worked on the project (pp. 164–6). The achievement is applauded in terms closely reminiscent of the emperor's own official praise of the *Theodosian Code* – a model of brevity, compression and the culmination of a long tradition.

> We servants of the emperors (as one wrote,
> the other painted) following the work
> of ancient mappers, in not many months
> revised and bettered theirs, within short space
> embracing the entire world. Your wisdom, sire,
> it was which taught us to achieve that task.[64]

The map (which does not survive) was perhaps displayed, as has been argued for the Peutinger Map,[65] in the imperial palace or a public portico. The selection of topographical features – again to quote the poem: 'seas, mountains, rivers, harbours, straits and towns'[66] – projected an image 'both celebratory and reassuring'[67] of peace and civil prosperity in a world unified by Roman rule.[68]

Of course, is not difficult to point out the fragility of the Theodosian *inventaire du monde*. In retrospect, these assertions of unity seem (to follow John Matthews' assessment) 'supremely optimistic'.[69] The completion of the *Theodosian Code* did not secure any lasting legal standardisation: Theodosius did not send copies of his post-*Code* rulings to the West until October 447 (they were published by Valentinian, but he may not have sent any of his own rulings to Constantinople).[70] The *Notitia Dignitatum* offers a misleading image of the uniformity of the empire's civil and military administration: the eastern part of the text is almost entirely frozen at the beginning of the fifth century, the western part haphazardly updated until the early 420s.[71] The map commissioned

---

[64] *Anth. Lat. Suppl.* 724.8–12.   [65] Talbert 2010: 142–57.
[66] *Anth. Lat. Suppl.* 724.2.   [67] Talbert 2010: 157.
[68] So Talbert 2010: 152 for the Peutinger Map; see too Clarke 2008: 200–2.
[69] Matthews 1993: 44.
[70] *NTh* 1.2 and *NVal* 26.1 (June 448) with Harries 1999: 61; Millar 2006: 1–2; Sirks 2007: 227–35.
[71] Zuckerman 1998: 146; Kulikowski 2000b: 374–7.

by Theodosius in 435 refused to recognise the partition of empire or the loss of Roman territory: the Goths were finally settled in southern France in 418; the Vandals invaded North Africa in 429; Roman protection of Armenia was withdrawn in 428.[72]

Yet to concentrate on the division of empire (in the full knowledge of how things turned out) – and to claim the origins of these fractures (political, theological, legal, economic, linguistic, military) as significant factors in the late fourth and early fifth centuries – is to risk losing some of the confidence of the Theodosian regime in the possibility of unity. Imperial unity based on eastern initiative was a key policy in the 420s and 430s.[73] It was a political asymmetry cheered on by Olympiodorus whose history – which climaxed with the defeat of the usurper John and the installation in Rome of Valentinian as western emperor – was (on Peter Van Nuffelen's reading) 'clearly triumphalist, justifying the newly established eastern dominance over the West and advertising the stability it promised' (p. 150). So too the *Theodosian Code*: as made clear to the Roman senators assembled at Faustus' house in May 438 this project had been entirely an eastern undertaking. Even so, the presentation of the completed *Code* to Faustus in Constantinople in early November 437 had been timed to coincide with the celebration of the dynastic marriage of Valentinian to Theodosius' daughter, Licinia Eudoxia.[74] A few days after the wedding, Faustus (newly appointed praetorian prefect of Italy) and his eastern counterpart each received a copy of the *Code* at an imperial audience held jointly by Theodosius and his new son-in-law.[75] Given the expectations surrounding the royal wedding, Valentinian (whose *consistorium* was never consulted on the *Code*) had little option but to respond favourably, as Faustus reported, 'with the constancy of a colleague and the affection of a son'. This was the theme that was echoed by the senators in Rome.

---

[72] On Armenia, see Blockley 1992: 60–1; Traina 2007: 3–13.
[73] Matthews 1975: 381, 2000: 4; Gillett 1993: 20–4.
[74] Matthews 1993: 43, 2000: 4–6; Honoré 1998: 129–30; Harries 1999: 64; Atzeri 2008: 120–1.
[75] *CTh Gesta Senatus* 3 with Matthews 2000: 6–9; Atzeri 2008: 121–7; on Valentinian's presence at court in Constantinople for the presentation of the *Code*, Archi 1976: 10; Matthews 2000: 6 n. 19; Atzeri 2008 122 n. 10, 125–6, but see Sirks 2007: 205–6.

Certainly, there could be no doubting their official expression of reiterated enthusiasm for the unity of empire.

> Roman emperors, pious and fortunate, may you rule for many years (repeated twenty-two times).
> For the good of the human race, for the good of the Senate, for the good of the state, for the good of all (repeated twenty-four times).
> We place our hopes in you, you are our salvation (repeated twenty-six times).
> Thus pious emperors wisely plan (repeated twenty-six times).[76]

The *Theodosian Code* imposed a unity on the Roman empire by imposing an order on its past. As noted above, the *Code* presented 2,700 imperial rulings issued since Constantine arranged chronologically, topic by topic, across sixteen books. It carefully classified, grouped and organised previously unrelated items of information. It encapsulated a complete body of knowledge in one volume: 'the encyclopedia objectifies knowledge by removing it from the uncertain sphere of play and speculation, and rendering it stable and quantified'.[77] It is this technical process of consolidation and classification which is scrutinised in Richard Flower's chapter (the second in Part III), '"The insanity of heretics must be restrained": heresiology in the *Theodosian Code*'. Of central concern is the law issued by Theodosius II at Constantinople in May 428 and included in the *Code* at 16.5.65. This law divided twenty-one named sects into four groups, each group subject to a different punishment: firstly, Arians, Macedonians and Apollinarians; secondly, Novatians and Sabbatians; thirdly, Eunomians, Valentinians, Montanists or Priscillianists, Phrygians, Marcianists, Borboriani and nine other sects; and fourthly, Manichaeans. Flower's purpose in this chapter is to trace the intellectual history of this law. He suggests that its careful quadripartite classification knowingly engages with the more elaborate taxonomies of late-antique heresiologies. Flower considers two prominent examples: the *Panarion* (or *Medicine Chest*) of Epiphanius of Salamis, written in the 370s, and the *De haeresibus* of Augustine of Hippo, closely contemporary with the law of 428 (pp. 176–84). What marks out these projects is a concern to demonstrate the

---

[76] *CTh Gesta Senatus* 5.
[77] Murphy 2004: 13–14; 1 and 11 for this definition of an encyclopaedia; see too König and Whitmarsh 2007b: 38.

authority and orthodoxy of the author both by emphasising the breadth of reading and research in gathering the raw data, and by the systematic presentation of individual heresies which, once correctly positioned in chronological order, could then be linked in a complete and coherent genealogy of connected unbelief.

The parallels with *CTh* 16.5.65 are illuminating. Of course, the law is less extensive in its listing of twenty-one heresies (Epiphanius catalogued eighty and Augustine, with self-congratulatory comprehensiveness, eighty-eight) and differs somewhat in its arrangement which, though not chronological, was clearly analytical. 'The reader was presented with a guiding rationale for this thematic division, based on the natures of the individual heresies, which could be identified, classified and pigeon-holed' (p. 190). *CTh* 16.5.65 is the first surviving example of what Flower neatly terms a 'legislative heresiology' (p. 189): no earlier law had dealt with heretics 'in a manner that was both comprehensive and differentiating' (p. 190); no earlier law had so explicitly sought to exploit the kind of taxonomies key to the technical enterprise of the heresiologist. 'As such, the law's claim to be an authoritative explication of orthodoxy and heresy was staked on its detailed religious knowledge as well as its status as an imperial command' (pp. 184–5).

Strikingly too, as Flower observes, within the *Code*, 16.5.65 was summative: with only a handful of exceptions (arguably, save for one case, no more than alternative designations), all the sects named in the first sixty-four rulings collected at 16.5 under the title *De haereticis* are mentioned – and classified – in the sixty-fifth (pp. 186–7). 'This was a law that spoke to earlier laws, drawing them together into a clearly defined attempt to name and catalogue heretical beliefs' (p. 186). *CTh* 16.5.65 reproduces the organisational logic of the *Theodosian Code* in miniature: it offers a concise guide to the punishment of heretical sects without replacing or diminishing previous imperial rulings 'dealing with the various penalties against different heretics'.[78] Whatever the original intention, that caveat (allowing previous laws to have full force)

---

[78] *CTh* 16.6.65.3.

and the careful fourfold classification of sects inescapably take on new meanings within the structure of the *Code*. It is the relationship of 16.5.65 with previous rulings (rather than simply its chronological position) which gives this text its particular force: with *CTh* 16.5.65, Theodosius II and his legal advisers appear to consolidate, clarify and cap a long series of imperial rulings since Constantine (16.5.1 was issued in September 326). Or almost: the final decision included under the title *De haereticis* (16.5.66 issued at Constantinople in August 435) vehemently damns Nestorius as 'the originator of a perverse superstition' [*damnato portentuosae superstitionis auctore Nestorio*]. That a codification of imperial decisions completed in 437 should end with Nestorius' recent condemnation is unsurprising. More sharply, the juxtaposition of 16.5.65 and 16.5.66 can be read as a counter to the claim, endorsed by Nestorius himself, that as bishop of Constantinople, and then favoured by the emperor, he was directly responsible for the law of 428 (that is, 16.5.65 as edited in the *Code*). Whatever the truth of Nestorius' contention, it was, as Flower points out, a bold attempt as bishop to arrogate the expert authority of a heresiologist. Once disgraced, Nestorius 'argued that his orthodoxy was not in doubt precisely because he had been an enemy of heretics, rooting them out through the medium of an imperial ruling' (pp. 193–4). But within the *Code*, there can be no doubt of the falsity of Nestorius' assertion. It is simply not supportable that the Nestorius denounced in 16.5.66 could have been the inspiration for 16.5.65. Indeed 16.5.66 (the final Theodosian word *De haereticis*) is clear – Nestorius' only credible claim as *auctor* was to have originated a heresy.

The drive towards the systematisation, classification and codification – so neatly exemplified by the *Theodosian Code*, the *Notitia Dignitatum*, cartography or heresiology – was not confined to technical literature. In institutional terms, it found expression in the restructuring of higher education in Constantinople. An imperial decision issued in February 425 forced a clear division between private and public teaching. Only those in receipt of state funds were permitted to offer public instruction; they were specifically prohibited from holding classes in private houses;

the number of state-supported positions was specified (thirteen in Latin language/literature and rhetoric, fifteen in Greek, two in law and one in philosophy); those in post for twenty years were to receive the privileges and immunities of high honorary rank; six named teachers were elevated with immediate effect (Harries p. 81); teaching was to take place in designated classrooms and so organised that 'the confusing mix of languages and voices should not distract anyone's ears or minds from the study of their texts'.[79] These reforms were not (as Alan Cameron has wryly observed) primarily directed at raising academic standards or retaining the best teachers; rather 'their most obvious and significant consequence was to tighten state control of education'[80] by the assertion of detailed imperial authority over the personnel and logistics of the public transmission of knowledge in the capital.

A preoccupation with the 'knowledge economy' – the institutional and textual organisation of information (often with the express aim of consolidating and improving on a disparate and diffuse past) – is a persistent political and intellectual priority of the first half of the fifth century. This was, as suggested by Richard Lim,

> a time of consolidation and the self-conscious formation of tradition. This was an age of compendia and epitomes. Authority ... began to be gathered, hierarchized, and centralized by those who favored a visibly stable order. The preeminent task of the fifth century was to summarize and define the accomplishments of previous ages.[81]

To be sure, not all fifth-century texts can be so neatly pigeon holed; as Mary Whitby argues in the final chapter in Part III ('Writing in Greek: classicism and compilation, interaction and transformation'), a broad and convincing claim can be made for the 'immense fertility and continuing innovativeness' (p. 196) of Greek literature. But one significant focus of this 'imaginative flexibility' (p. 218) is a marked interest in – to quote two of

---

[79] *CTh* 14.9.3 (quoting §1); see too 15.1.53 (issued on the same day and perhaps part of the same instructions to the urban prefect; *PLRE* II 318 [Constantius 4]), 6.21.1 (March 425) for the honouring of six named individuals; for discussion of the reforms, see Lemerle 1971: 63–4; Lippold 1973: 974; Alan Cameron 1982: 285–7; Matthews 2000: 26–8; C. M. Kelly 2004: 85; Traina 2007: 55–6.
[80] Alan Cameron 1982: 287; see too Matthews 2000: 26.
[81] Lim 1995: 228.

Whitby's section headings – 'manipulating knowledge: florilegia, dialogue, encyclopaedism' (p. 202) and '(re)casting text' (p. 205). Whitby tracks these themes in the adaption of the classical funeral oration, Platonic dialogue and the traditional tactics of forensic rhetoric in works intended to restore the reputation of the preacher and controversialist John Chrysostom (bishop of Constantinople, 398–403/404) following his death in exile in 407 (pp. 197–200); in the compilation of florilegia of patristic and classical proof texts for use in both teaching and theological dispute (pp. 202–4); in the verse and prose paraphrases of Scripture and saints' lives (pp. 206–12); and in the sophisticated occasional verse of the powerful courtier Cyrus of Panopolis (urban prefect of Constantinople and praetorian prefect of the East in 439) (pp. 214–15). It is important to emphasise that each of these literary forms has a long history reaching well back before late antiquity. The case for the distinctiveness of the late fourth and fifth centuries – echoing Richard Lim – rests on a conjunction of concern across a range of quite disparate enterprises which taken together (to adapt David Scourfield's neat encapsulation) derive their 'special character from the multiplicity of ways in which attempts are made to integrate the past, particularly as represented by texts which possessed special authority, into the present'.[82]

One of the most remarkable literary enterprises discussed by Whitby (p. 209) is the cento: a cento is made up of unconnected verse units taken from another work (the underlying text) and – completely out of context – recombined to create entirely new narratives. Sometime in the mid fifth century, Theodosius' wife, the Empress Eudocia, reworked centos begun by the (otherwise unknown) Bishop Patricius. These so-called *Homerocentones* reassembled lines and half-lines from Homer's *Iliad* and *Odyssey* to tell a set of stories from the Old and New Testaments.[83] (A poetic programme, as Whitby points out [p. 209], remarkably

---

[82] Scourfield 2007b: 4.
[83] On the complexities of authorship and revision (much simplified here), see Usher 1997: 310–19; Schembra 2007a: cxxxiii–clxxxi; Sandnes 2011: 186–9; and the clear and helpful discussions in Mary Whitby 2007: 218–19, 2009: 813–14, p. 209 n. 70. On the date of Eudocia's editorial intervention, see the possibilities canvassed in Alan Cameron 1982: 281–5; Agosti 2001: 85; Mary Whitby 2007: 207–9.

similar to the Virgilian centos on biblical themes composed by the aristocratic Proba in late fourth-century Rome.⁸⁴)

Χαῖρε μοι, ὦ βασίλεια, διαμπερές, εἰς ὅ κεν ἔλθοι	*Odyssey* 13.59 + *Iliad* 10.62
ἀνδράσιν ἠδὲ γυναιξὶν ἐπὶ χθόνα πουλυβότειραν	*Odyssey* 19.408 + *Iliad* 3.265
γῆρας καὶ θάνατος, τά τ' ἐπ' ἀωθπώποισι πέλονται,	*Odyssey* 13.60
σὸν δ' ἤτοι κλέος ἔσται ὅσον τ' ἐπικίδναται ἠώς	*Iliad* 7.458
τοῖς οἳ νῦν γεγάασι καὶ οἳ μετόπισθεν ἔσονται.	*Odyssey* 24.84

> Hail to you, queen, forever, until there comes
> upon men and women of the bountiful earth
> old age and death, which are the lot of mortals.
> Now surely your fame will spread as far as the light of the dawn
> both on men living now and those who shall be born hereafter.⁸⁵

As is evident – even from these few lines taken from the Annunciation – the cento confronts its reader with two overlapping texts. Aside from admiration at its technical virtuosity, any appreciation of the cento's poetic achievement is unavoidably (and self-consciously) linked to its readers' knowledge of Homer. Meaning shifts – steadily 'oscillates' (in Jeffrey Schnapp's attractive term⁸⁶) – in a continuous competitive reading between the cento and its underlying text. There seems, for example, a productive 'consonance' (to stay with Schnapp's terms) between the opening lines of the Archangel Gabriel's speech and its original Homeric context (Odysseus' blessing on Arete, the wife of Alcinous, in *Odyssey* 13); and an ironic 'dissonance' between Gabriel's promise of everlasting fame to the Virgin Mary which outstrips Zeus' boast to Poseidon (*Iliad* 7) and Odysseus' confidence on the permanence of Achilles' tomb at Troy (*Odyssey* 24).

These patterns of consonance and dissonance also allow the centoist – even within the tight technical strictures of the form – to offer an interpretation of the scriptural narrative as it is pieced

---

⁸⁴ Mary Whitby 2007: 216–17; on Proba's identity, see the useful summary of the debate in Curran 2012: 328 (adding Mastandrea 2001) and, in particular, the strong case argued in Alan Cameron 2011: 327–37.
⁸⁵ *Conscriptio Prima*, lines 235–9 (ed. Schembra 2007a: 19–20).
⁸⁶ Schnapp 1992: 112 with the prudent observations of Scourfield 2007b: 17–18; Mary Whitby 2007: 211 (part of a model close reading of the Doubting Thomas episode at 209–16).

together from the atomised Homeric text. In the brief passage quoted above, for example, Mary is addressed as βασίλεια (and again at lines 265 and 272; δέσποινα at lines 209 and 226) – a regal representation of the Virgin particularly appropriate given the investment of Theodosian imperial women in celibacy.[87] More broadly, there is no attempt by the centoist to distinguish between the Gospel narratives, rather (as Rocco Schembra has noted) the poem fuses the four together in one unified version.[88] In this sense, the cento can usefully be thought of as a reading both of its underlying text, which it disassembles, and of the narrative, which it reconstructs; but asymmetrically: Homer does not tell the Bible story and (more importantly) it is the scriptural narrative that gives the cento its coherence.[89] This is a tension that the cento is unable to resolve. It cannot break out of the cycle of disintegration and reassembly by which – paradoxically – it is itself constituted. The oscillation between text and underlying text is both enriching (as Schnapp suggests) and imperilling. After all, the most knowledgeable reader, well versed in Homer, is best placed both to applaud the bravura accomplishment of the cento and to work against it by moving to restore the fragments to their original context. As Margaret Malamud has nicely observed, 'Without the reader's collaboration, the cento, as an art form, is pointless.'[90] The better the reader knows Homer, the deeper the appreciation of the cento, the greater the risk that the poem will (quite literally) decompose.

The cento is a brittle poetic form. It is the (inescapable) combination of its tight technical strictures and the – somewhat ironic – canonical status of the familiar underlying Homeric text

---

[87] Schembra 2007a: 146–7; see too Pigani 1985: 37–9; Usher 1998: 93–4; and, more generally, Sandnes 2011: 189–228; for a useful survey of the interpretative patterns in Proba's Virgilian cento, see Sandnes 2011: 141–79; Curran 2012: 335–9.

[88] Schembra 2007a: 130.

[89] The reader of the cento might conclude that it demonstrates that Homer was a Christian *avant la lettre* (*sine Christo ... Christianum*); and that the *Iliad* and *Odyssey* had a hidden meaning waiting to be released by the centoist. It is precisely this misreading of the poetic enterprise which attracts Jerome's undiluted scorn in *Ep.* 53.7 (quoted in the previous sentence); see the elegant discussion in McGill 2007: 177–81, although whether this was Proba's view of her project is less certain; see 175–6 with Green 1997: 556 and below n. 95. Of course, a cento also inescapably changes the reader's understanding of the underlying text, see Malamud 1989: 37; Green 2006: 249.

[90] Malamud 1989: 41; see too Pollmann 2004: 87–8; McGill 2005: 9; Sandnes 2011: 113–18.

that makes it always liable to fracture. The immediacy of that risk is significantly reduced in biblical paraphrase (like the cento, a literary form, at least to judge by extant manuscripts, with a particular concentration of fifth-century examples).[91] A paraphrase is (to quote Whitby) 'the rewriting of a core text in a higher literary register ... rewriting often involves expansion, not of an arbitrary or redundant nature, but to incorporate exegesis or to change the orientation of the text' (pp. 206–7). The literary upgrade typically involves a close engagement with the style of Homer or Virgil, but not the literal reassembly of an underlying text.[92] The Empress Eudocia's paraphrase in Homeric verse of the life of the third-century martyr Cyprian of Antioch, for example, closely followed its prose models but also involved 'a sophisticated resemanticisation of Homer, and linguistic affiliation with a wide range of classical, Hellenistic and late-antique authors, as well as extensive neologism' (pp. 208–9).

The most prominent feature of paraphrase (and shared with the cento) is a blurring of the boundaries between narrative and interpretation. The paraphrase does not aim to mark off (on the page or by quotation or shift in grammar, register or style) its commentary, supplements, summaries or excisions. The text is presented as a coherent whole; biblical paraphrase (to quote Scott Johnson) 'becomes Scripture explaining itself, defending itself, and claiming itself'.[93] But this is not a process (at least in intention) of erasure or over-writing; the recomposition of an underlying text, as David Scourfield emphasises, is not 'a transfer of authority but an entrenchment and expansion of it ... the acquisition of authority rests very clearly on a relationship with existing authoritative texts'.[94] In the anonymous fifteen-line verse epistle prefaced to a

---

[91] Johnson 2006c: 99–100; and 75 on the rough equivalence of the terms *paraphrasis* and *metaphrasis*, see too Vinel 1987: 194–7; Gonnelli 1989: 51 n. 1; Whitby p. 206 n. 58, this volume; for a thoughtful and subtle discussion of late-antique paraphrase and its antecedents, see Johnson 2006c: especially 67–112 with Roberts 1985: especially 37–74 and Miguélez Cavero 2008: 309–15 on its technical foundations; note too Vessey 2002: 31–2 stressing the particular demands (on reader and paraphrast) of biblical paraphrase.

[92] Johnson 2006c: 98–9; from a stylistic point of view, there is an obvious overlap between the risks (and rewards) of the cento and the paraphrase; see, for example, on dissonance in Sedulius' Virgilian *Paschale Carmen*, Green 2006: 170–1, 195, 248–9.

[93] Johnson 2006c: 69.   [94] Scourfield 2007b: 22.

copy of Proba's Virgilian cento presented to Theodosius' father, Arcadius, the calligrapher hopes that the emperor will recognise *Maronem mutatum in melius*: Virgil changed for the better.[95] The preface to the *Metaphrasis Psalmorum* – a line-by-line recomposition of the Psalms in Homeric hexameter written in the 450s or 460s – asserts that the prose of the Septuagint 'was achieved at the expense of the grace (χάρις) of poetry which this new version aims to restore, relying on divine inspiration' (Whitby p. 210) and sure in the knowledge that Homeric verse was fashioned by God in ancient times (καὶ γλῶσσαν Ἰηόνα – καὶ γὰρ ἐτύχθη ἐκ παλαχῆς θεότευκτος).[96] Cento and paraphrase are fundamentally backward-looking projects: 'authors often sought, or felt compelled, to reclassify, reorient, and purify the textual past for the sake of their audiences and readers-to-come.'[97] These are acts of restoration and consolidation. It is in this sense that the claim made for Eudocia in an epigram accompanying the *Homerocentones* should be understood: that it was by restoring the harmony and order of Patricius' Homeric verses – a double editorial intervention – that she supplied the bishop's want of truth ('he did not set forth everything wholly truthfully': οὐ πάγχυ ἐτήτυμα πάντ' ἀγόρευεν) and fashioned a work pleasing to God.[98]

The push towards the restoration of the past was also key to a set of texts which pursued what Whitby neatly calls 'the instinct for encyclopaedism' (p. 205) through the compilation of lists and quotations. Florilegia – collections of proof-texts – were

[95] Lines 3–4 (ed. K. Schenkl, *CSEL* 16, Vienna, 1888) with the important discussion in McGill 2007: 174–5. On the disputed date and authorship of these verses, see Sivan 1993: 144–6; Green 1997: 548–9; Mastandrea 2001; McGill 2007: 174, 186–7 nn. 9–11. The solid consensus of recent scholarship is in favour of the presentation to Arcadius, rather than Theodosius II, understanding the reference to *minori Arcadio* (lines 13–14) as a straightforward diplomatic reference to any children Arcadius might yet have: see (for example) Sivan 1993: 144–5; Green 1995: 561–2, 1997: 548; Agosti 2001: 74; Mastandrea 2001: 566–9; Barnes 2007: 109–10; McGill 2007: 174, 186 n. 6; Curran 2012: 328–9; for a dissenting view (with a correspondingly different proposal for authorship), Alan Cameron 1982: 266–7, 2002: 126.

[96] *Pr.* 19 and 105–6 (ed. Golega 1960: 25–44) with the useful discussion in Agosti and Gonnelli 1995: 360–2; Agosti 2001: 87–92.

[97] Johnson 2006c: 106; see too 15.

[98] Lines 1–8 quoting 5 (ed. A.-L. Rey, *SC* 437, Paris, 1998, 518–21) with the thoughtful discussion in Agosti 2001: 76–83; the best, brief introduction to the epigram is Mary Whitby 2007: 208–9. Note too the careful accumulation of authority – both Homer's and Patricius', see Agosti 2001: 83.

central to Cyril of Alexandria's presentation of his theology at the Council of Ephesus 'establishing the principle of citing the "fathers" (eminent deceased bishops) in defence of Nicene orthodoxy' (p. 202). As Thomas Graumann has persuasively argued, it was Cyril's eventual success in these dogmatic disputes that cemented the authority of these excerpted texts as sure guides to orthodoxy. Through his argumentation at Ephesus, and his concern with the compilation of the Council's *acta*, Cyril firmly founded the 'Church of the Fathers' in textual form.[99] This broader project of quotation and collection most clearly crystallises in the work of grammarians who regularly demonstrated their propositions by offering an extensive series of exemplary proof-texts. Grammatical 'rules' were authenticated by a careful assemblage of quotations here repurposed as points of reference in a radically new context. (After all, it had scarcely been the original intention of these now excerpted authors to offer pithy illustrations of correct, or incorrect, linguistic usage.) It is precisely this process of fragmentation and reconstruction – to follow Catherine Chin's insightful reading – that establishes the authority of the grammarian's text: both in its successful subordination of previously unrelated excerpts in order to substantiate an argument, and in its steady cumulation of authority. Like any academic essay, both grammar books and florilegia underwrote their own claims to authority by arrogating the authority of others and by making that appeal visible through quotation. To fragment Catherine Chin:

> The idea of using multiple, nonlinear quotations in forming the basis for *auctoritas* both unifies the field of literary knowledge (many different authors become symbols of *auctoritas*) and expands it (*auctoritas* is derived from the reading of many *auctores*). *Auctoritas* represents more than a symbol of potency; it is the conceptual unification of a field of diverse textual elements.[100]

It is in this context – and in the broader context of the three chapters in Part III (Giusto Traina on cartography and administrative

---

[99] Graumann 2002: 255–435, especially 323–42, an analysis of Cyril's *Oratio ad Dominas* (late 430) and *Apologia aduersus Orientales* (mid 431). Both texts supported their arguments with florilegia, both are included in the *acta* of Ephesus.
[100] Chin 2008: 19 and generally 11–38.

documents, Richard Flower on heresiology, Mary Whitby on Greek literature) – that the *Theodosian Code* project can comfortably be situated. Thomas Graumann has called attention to the similar concerns of Cyril of Alexandria (at Ephesus in 431 and afterwards) and the editors of the *Theodosian Code* (in the same decade) to establish a stable set of authorised texts as a reliable basis for deciding theological or legal disputes: 'insgesamt nämlich zeigen die Kodifikationsbemühungen, die im *Codex Theodosianus* ihren Abschluß finden, ein unzweideutiges Interesse an einer sammelnden und sichernden Aufbereitung eines traditionellen Bestandes verbindlicher Texte.'[101] Graumann's important observation can be taken further. Like many of the texts discussed in Part III of this volume, the *Code* had as one of its chief declared aims the clarification of (what was presented as) a diffuse and obscure past: 'darkness has been dissipated and with this compendium we have given the light of brevity to the laws … To that end, we have dispersed the cloud of volumes on which the lives of many persons – who explain nothing – have been frittered away.'[102] The *Theodosian Code* deployed textual strategies closely allied to the cento, the paraphrase, the florilegium and the encyclopaedia to summarise and define the empire's legal history. Its editors established (to follow Richard Flower on heresiology) 'both the contours and contents of knowledge through the selection and organisation of material' (p. 176).

Fergus Millar has emphasised that the overwhelming majority of 'laws' included in the *Theodosian Code* are letters addressed to individual officeholders in response to memoranda (*suggestiones*) providing information, presenting proposals or requesting clarification. 'What it means is that the entire body of "legal" material, on which in all essentials the history of the Late Roman State has been based, consists of internal communications within the administration.'[103] That aspect of imperial decision-making is most clearly on view in the collection of post-*Code* rulings, the *Novellae*. Of the thirty-five *Novellae* of Theodosius II,

---

[101] Graumann 2002: 343–9 quoting 346; see too 426–7.
[102] Above p. 22 with Harries 1999: 59–60 on the imagery.
[103] Millar 2006: 7.

twenty-three explicitly refer to a *suggestio*; each quite lengthy text (after a personal greeting to its addressee) typically sets out something of the circumstances motivating the ruling, explains the salutary need for imperial intervention in an 'elaborate rhetoric of moralizing self-justification' and provides for the promulgation of the decision.[104] It is this material which has been stripped out by the *Code*'s editors instructed to remove 'pointless verbiage' [*inanem uerborum copiam*].[105] The resulting extracts – or perhaps better, quotations – were systematically disengaged from their original context. Certainly, these more uniform versions of imperial decisions do nothing either to prevent or forestall the 'misreading' which Millar cautions against. That is not, for a moment, to soften the impact of Millar's argument for understanding the relationship between emperor and officeholders, but rather to turn it to emphasise one of the central aspects of the *Code*'s presentation of imperial authority. As edited, these sometimes drastically abbreviated laws[106] offered a foreshortened view of the complex process of decision-making ('the workings of persuasion, command, reaction, and defiance'[107] explored in Part II of this volume). As displayed in the *Code* – and certainly compared to the *Novellae* – the cumulative effect of these extracts is a counterfeit impression of consistency in form and concision of expression. Above all (and, in Millar's terms, most seriously misleading), these rulings, now shorn of any reference to the *suggestiones* which activated and informed them, appear to be issued exclusively on imperial initiative.[108] Always superior

---

[104] Honoré 1998: 152–3; Millar 2006: 207–14 quoting 209; Sirks 2007: 61–2; see too the meticulous analysis of the *Sirmondian Constitutions* in Matthews 2000: 121–67 – at core, this is a collection of sixteen laws which survive independently of the *Theodosian Code*; ten are fuller versions of laws included in edited form in the *Code*; see especially 121–9, on the complex manuscript history of this collection, and 160–4 for a summary of the editorial conventions, closely consonant with the general differences noted above between the extracted texts in the *Code* and the *Novellae*.

[105] *CTh* 1.1.5 (March 429) further defined in 1.1.6.1 (December 435) with Matthews 2000: 57–8, 62–4; Sirks 2007: 61–2, 72–3; note the more substantive omission in 13.3.5 (July 362), Julian's ruling on the Christian teaching of classics, Harries 1997: 97–8.

[106] Honoré 1998: 152.

[107] Millar 2006: 131; above p. 9.

[108] *CTh* 1.8.1 (October 415) with Matthews 2000: 171 is an exception. In some cases, it is possible to reconstruct the lobbying behind an imperial decision included in the *Code*, see the examples discussed in Harries pp. 80–4, this volume.

to their officials (whose function here is to receive and carry out instructions), emperors in the *Code* are presented as conscientiously demonstrating both a proactive concern and a panoptic knowledge of the needs of the entire empire.[109]

In total, the *Theodosian Code* encompassed 2,700 extracts from imperial decisions of general application (*leges generales*), a concept which is not always easy to understand. Despite attempts at refinement in the early fifth century, the definition of 'generality' (as John Matthews has pointed out) still had to be applied retrospectively by the *Code*'s editors 'to texts that had been drafted without its provisions in mind'.[110] Perhaps more important was that legal rulings, no matter how apparently recondite their subject-matter or restrictive their circumstances, were henceforth to be understood as having general application by simple virtue of their inclusion in the *Code*. Importantly too – and, of course, a key aspect of any codification project – the meaning, relevance and scope of individual laws were, at least in part, determined by their categorisation, that is, their position under one of the chapter headings (or titles) which were, in turn, arranged thematically in sixteen books.[111] In her detailed study of the *Code*'s titles, Gisella Bassanelli Sommariva has pointed to examples which resolve or limit the meaning of the texts collected under that heading.[112] More generally, as Honoré remarks, 'the ordinary user of the Code was very much in the hands of the compilers. If they chose to put a law in an unexpected chapter, it could escape the attention of a judge, advocate, or consultant unless he had studied the whole Code thoroughly.'[113] The editors, for example, placed a determination on the disposal of the property of intestate clerics alongside other imperial rulings on succession (in Book

---

[109] Of course, emperors, even when offering explanations of their decisions, did not always indicate the sources of their information, and might on occasion issue rulings deliberately designed to convey the impression that they had acted on their own initiative; see Matthews 2000: 161–2, with examples from the *Sirmondian Constitutions*. What matters in the *Code*, is the cumulative, overwhelming impact of the edited texts.

[110] Matthews 2000: 65–71 quoting 67 with Honoré 1998: 160; see too the discussions in Honoré 1998: 128–9; Sirks 2007: 24–35, 70–1.

[111] Honoré 1998: 149–50; Sirks 2007: 59–60, 69–70; see Matthews 2000: 118–20 for a succinct summary of the structure of the *Code*.

[112] Bassanelli Sommariva 2003: especially 197–208.

[113] Honoré 1998: 149.

5) and not with laws on right religion (in Book 16); similarly, a detailed decision on wrongdoers' right of sanctuary in churches was put with other rulings on criminal law (in Book 9) (Harries pp. 74–5).

It mattered too, as emphasised above in the discussion of Richard Flower's chapter (pp. 28–9), that the legal texts included under each title were arranged in chronological order. Again to quote Tony Honoré: 'the texts in the Theodosian Code ... are to be taken historically, as part of an ongoing process of making, interpreting, and altering laws.'[114] The effect of that systematic accumulation of authority is overwhelming. Theodosius II is repeatedly seen to follow his imperial predecessors – when cited, his rulings conclude a topic – and to remedy the defects or omissions in their rulings. (To repeat David Scourfield on textual recomposition: this is not 'a transfer of authority but an entrenchment and expansion of it ... the acquisition of authority rests very clearly on a relationship with existing authoritative texts.'[115]) This is a powerful image of an emperor at the head of a long-standing legislative tradition. The strict sequencing of laws is an ever-present reminder that it is Theodosius who has brought unprecedented order to a previously confused mass of accumulated imperial rulings. In the *Theodosian Code*, Theodosius always has the last word.

In piecing together the *Code*, its editors engaged in a project which demanded (to recycle Scott Johnson on the paraphrase) that they 'reclassify, reorient, and purify the textual past for the sake of their audiences and readers-to-come'.[116] Each law was inescapably part of an interpretative pattern generated by the process of codification. In that sense, the *Code* functioned as 'an encyclopaedia of legal knowledge'.[117] It imposed a uniformity on the rulings selected for inclusion; it fixed them within a well-defined system; it carefully itemised, categorised and connected 'primary

---

[114] Honoré 1998: 153; Harries 1993: 6. Honoré's point has greater force if he is correct in his assumption that the *Code* included inconsistent and obsolete laws, 1986: 162–4, 1998: 142–9; Archi 1976: 51–4; Lee 2002: 187; Matthews 2000: 64–5, 290, but see Sirks 2007: 62–3, 147–50, 204.
[115] Above p. 34.   [116] Above p. 35.
[117] du Plessis 2009: 6, 15.

sources that had never before been brought together'.[118] (To reorient Catherine Chin on late-antique grammar: 'it is the conceptual unification of a field of diverse textual elements.'[119]) Above all, the *Code* presented a consolidated version of over a century of imperial decision-making from Constantine to Theodosius II. Inevitably, the structure of the *Code* and the organisation of material (over)emphasised the importance of both emperors in the legal history of the – now indisputably Christian – Roman empire.[120]

To be sure, as it stands, the *Code* is an imperfect document. Modern commentators (perhaps echoing ancient frustrations) have at times struggled to find clarity and consistency in the *Code*'s approach to general laws, obsolete rulings and the wider applicability of decisions issued in the East or West. But such difficulties, although important (and particularly to any understanding of the utility of the *Code*) should not devalue its achievement. Theodosius and his legal advisers succeeded in unifying, organising and authorising a hundred years of imperial law-making: *in corpus unius codicis diuorum retro principum constitutiones nostrasque redegimus*: 'we have compressed into the compass of a single code the enactments of previous emperors of blessed memory and our own'.[121] Only the laws contained in the *Code* were to have any validity: 'it is not permitted for anyone to cite an imperial law in court or in ordinary legal practice or in drafting documentation for a lawsuit, unless it is clear that it is taken from these books that have come to be designated by our name.'[122] The *Code* thus validated its own claims to comprehensiveness. It presented a purified legislative past in one completely self-contained volume. Like the perfect paraphrase, florilegium or encyclopaedia, the *Theodosian Code* was the exclusive measure of its own success.

---

[118] Matthews 2000: 12 with a caveat at n. 6.
[119] Above p. 36.
[120] Harries 1994: 43 (on Constantine); for the *Code* as fashioning a Christian empire, see the very helpful survey of widely divergent modern views in Sirks 2007: 41–9, 81–2; contrast, for example, the Christian enthusiasms of Volterra 1983: 217–18 with the muted approach of Honoré 1998: 124; Matthews 2000: 120; see too Harries p. 86, this volume.
[121] *NTh* 2.1.*pr.* (October 447).   [122] *NTh* 1.1.3. (February 438).

Pius princeps

Constantinople was a city on parade. On Saturdays, Sundays and festal days, liturgical processions – with candlelit silver crosses and the antiphonal chanting of psalms – were a conscious public affirmation of religious allegiance.[123] (This was a city without an early Christian history or biblical sites; it was unlike Jerusalem, where the development of a stational liturgy was closely linked to a grid of holy places, or Rome, where it knitted together urban *tituli*.) For Constantinople, 'the liturgy *in* the city was the liturgy *of* the city. The average worshipper did not so much "go to mass" as participate in the worship-life of the city as it unfolded.'[124] Annual processions offered thanks for the capital's preservation (commemorating, for example, the severe earthquakes of September 438 and January 447[125]). Most memorable of all were the splendid ceremonies that celebrated the arrival of holy relics. The presence of emperors – sometimes alongside other members of the imperial family – transformed these occasions. The pattern was set by Theodosius I at the end of the fourth century. In 391, a solemn procession greeted the head of John the Baptist. The emperor received the reliquary and, folding the casket carefully in his purple robe, carried it seven miles to a newly built church at the Hebdomon (the military parade-ground on the outskirts of the city).[126] 'The emperor's direct role in cradling the holy relics placed him at the center of this unifying new ceremonial, which brought together as common suppliants the court and clergy, aristocracy and general populace.'[127] In 406, the Emperor Arcadius, accompanied by the praetorian and urban prefects and the Senate, greeted the relics of the Old Testament prophet Samuel.[128]

---

[123] Soz. 8.8; Soc. 6.8 with McCormick 1986: 110; Baldovin 1987: 184.
[124] Baldovin 1987: 211; for imperial participation in liturgical processions, see McCormick 2000: 159–60 and the (much later) ceremonial descriptions discussed in Baldovin 1987: 198–202; Berger 2002: 15–17.
[125] Croke 1981.
[126] Soz. 7.21.5; *Chron. Pasch.* 391 (I 564.16–19); Theodore Lector 268.
[127] Croke 2010: 255–7 quoting 255; Brown 1981: 92–105; Diefenbach 1996: 44–5, 2002: 26–7.
[128] *Chron. Pasch.* 406 (I 569.12–18).

These ritual displays of consensus drew explicitly on the traditional ceremony of *aduentus*: the arrival of an emperor in a city.[129] An enthusiastic welcome by an orderly citizenry and its dignitaries confirmed an emperor's relationship with the community by providing 'a vocabulary for the encounter of different types of persons, and for their convergence into one group'.[130] The emperor's unifying presence was a symbolic expression of concord and communal solidarity. Inescapably too, an emperor parading through the porticoed streets of Constantinople to celebrate the acquisition of Christian 'spoils' replayed something of the pomp of an imperial triumph.[131] (Theodosius' procession to the Hebdomon made these associations with military success explicit.) The festivities surrounding the reception in 438 by Theodosius II and Pulcheria of the relics of John Chrysostom, and those marking Pulcheria's discovery of the remains of the Forty Martyrs of Sebaste, were both described by contemporaries in clearly traditional terms as πομπή.[132] They were reminders that – even in its most religious moments – Constantinople remained an imperial capital.[133]

This 'convergence of religion, ceremony and imperial ideology'[134] (to quote Michael McCormick) is the concern of the first chapter in Part IV of this volume: Christopher Kelly, 'Stooping to conquer: the power of imperial humility'. Kelly's focus is on two dramatic public displays: the Empress Eudoxia (Arcadius' wife) in 400/402 throwing aside her purple robes to dance in joy before martyr relics as they were transferred at night to a shrine on the shores of the Propontis (Sea of Marmara) south-west of Constantinople; and the Emperor Theodosius, following a destructive earthquake in late January 447, walking barefoot the seven miles from the Great Palace to the Hebdomon. These were impressive moments which – like the *aduentus* procession welcoming relics into the

---

[129] MacCormack 1972: 748, 1981: 64–5; Brown 1981: 98–100; Diefenbach 1996: 43–52, 2002: 25–31.
[130] MacCormack 1981: 17–45 quoting 43.
[131] Diefenbach 1996: 47; for the progress of a triumph in Constantinople, punctuated by ritual encounters with Senate, clergy and people, see McCormick 1986: 210–20.
[132] Baldovin 1987: 208, 234–5; Diefenbach 1996: 48, 57, 2002: 26; see too Soc. 7.45.3, Theophanes 5930 (92.37–93.5) with Holum 1982: 184–5 (Chrysostom); Soz. 9.2.17, *Chron. Pasch.* 451 (I 590.16–20) with Holum 1982: 137 (Forty Martyrs).
[133] Diefenbach 2002: 29–30.   [134] McCormick 2000: 160.

city – were shaped by a long history of imperial ceremonial and political thinking about autocracy. The paradox of the powerful publicly rejecting their position was brilliantly explored by Pliny the Younger in his panegyric on the Emperor Trajan (delivered in Rome in September 100). 'Central to Pliny's version of Trajan is the idea that humility – the public refusal of an emperor to behave like a ruler – might underline the power of a monarch, rather than indicate an absence of authority. By offering to act like a citizen, to bridge the gap between himself and his subjects, Trajan emphasised the distance that lay between them' (p. 227). Kelly suggests that this productive tension between the appearance of autocratic magnificence and its (no less spectacular) rejection continued to inform the public display of Christian piety by late-antique emperors: 'what connects them is that both these dramatic and highly ritualised expressions of imperial condescension turn on the same paradox: the assertion of superior position through its abdication' (p. 228). Importantly too – and key to the positive presentation of these parades of imperial humility – was the certainty that at the moment of stepping down, the emperor or empress would return to the apex of court society, completing the 'U-curve of imperial condescension: from the repudiation to the resumption of authority' (pp. 228–9). It mattered, for example, that Eudoxia's night-time dance by the seashore was followed by her morning return to the Great Palace at Arcadius' side. 'Eudoxia's presence alongside her husband, surrounded by their courtly retinue in all its splendour, only served to emphasise that her exhibition of humility was to be set firmly in the context of her (equally ceremonial) demonstration of imperial authority' (p. 232).

These 'zeremonielle Gesten der Herabneigens'[135] (in Steffen Diefenbach's phrase) were part of a much larger portfolio of imperial piety. The contemporary church historian, Sozomen, carefully catalogued examples of Pulcheria and her two sisters' steadfast faith: their benefactions and charitable works, their respect for the clergy, their serious conversation, their prayer vigils, their constitutionals in the palace grounds and their weaving.[136] (This image

---

[135] Diefenbach 2002: 33.   [136] Soz. 9.3.1–2.

of the three sisters at the loom is deliberately expansive; it was not only a Christian exemplar but one, as Jill Harries points out, that 'reverts to an older female stereotype' [p. 69].) Aside from these largely private devotions, what is most striking is Pulcheria's public piety. Sozomen had been part of the psalm-chanting πομπή that accompanied the relics of the Forty Martyrs of Sebaste through the streets of Constantinople.[137] He also noted the remarkable permanent reminder – 'visible to all' – of the sisters' vow never to marry. In 413, the fourteen-year-old Pulcheria had dedicated a glittering altar in Hagia Sophia inscribed with the pregnant phrase: ὑπὲρ τῆς ἰδίας παρθενίας καὶ τῆς τοῦ ἀδελφοῦ ἡγεμονίας: 'for her own virginity and her brother's sovereignty'.[138] This 'well-promoted dynastic preoccupation with the power of holiness' (Harries p. 70) also encompassed Theodosius' wife, the Empress Eudocia. In early 438 – just a few months after the marriage of their daughter, Licinia Eudoxia, to Valentinian III (and the presentation of the *Theodosian Code*) – Eudocia left for the Holy Land. This was a pious imperial progress; the empress' tour included the great biblical sites, encounters with ascetics and the acquisition of relics.[139] In Jerusalem, she discussed the efficacy of almsgiving with the hairy holy man, Barsauma, whose matted locks trailed on the ground. (Barsauma's uncompromising religious zeal was violently expressed in a campaign of terror against Jews, Samaritans and pagans.) Eudocia offered him her veil as an altarcloth and demanded his cloak as a souvenir.[140] Most likely it was with her when she returned to Constantinople in 439.

Such tokens of holiness fascinated her husband. Theodosius could sometimes be seen sitting with the stinking cassock of a deceased saint draped across his shoulders.[141] Perhaps he wore it when discussing theology with bishops, or when reviewing his substantial library of sacred texts or when reciting Scripture, which he had learnt by heart.[142] Like Pulcheria's continence and

---

[137] Soz. 9.2.17.   [138] Soz. 9.1.4 with Holum 1982: 93.
[139] Soc. 7.47; Holum 1982: 184–9; Hunt 1982: 229–34.
[140] *Life of Barsauma* 29 (ed. Nau 1914: 115–17) with Holum 1982: 186–7; on Barsauma and his holy terrorism, see Gaddis 2005: 156, 188–9, 246–7.
[141] Soc. 7.22.14.   [142] Soc. 7.22.5.

Eudocia's pilgrimage, Theodosius' piety (as his barefoot procession to the Hebdomon illustrates) was also a public matter. The emperor's prayers were presented as guarantors of the empire's security (below p. 53) and the city's safety. Once in the face of severe weather, Theodosius halted chariot races in the Hippodrome and led the crowd in prayers and hymn-singing: 'communicating with the people through heralds he said, "It is much better to spurn the show and for all to offer prayers together to God that we may be shielded, secure from the impending storm"'[143] (Kelly pp. 230–1). In 425, after the defeat of the western usurper John at Ravenna, the emperor exhorted the spectators: '"Please then let us set our enjoyment aside, make our way to church and offer up prayers of thanks to God whose hand has cast down the tyrant."'[144] It was Theodosius' prayers (so the church historian Socrates reported) that were said to have been directly responsible for the capture of Ravenna: an angel had shown the troops a way through the marshes that surrounded the city. The parting of the muddy waters was, so Socrates observed, 'just as it came to pass for the Hebrews crossing the Red Sea'.[145] Theodosius was a modern Moses (albeit *in absentia*).

It is important that these expressions of imperial piety not be viewed in isolation. They should be set against a wider horizon of holiness – and most particularly in Constantinople. Relations between the Great Church (Hagia Sophia) and the adjacent Great Palace were sometimes tense. Given the imperial family's emphasis on its own displays of devotion, it is perhaps not surprising that in the first four decades of the fifth century two bishops of Constantinople (John Chrysostom and Nestorius) were deposed and exiled by the same emperors (Arcadius and Theodosius) who had supported their appointment.[146] Constantinople was a city of religious rivalries. Its candlelit liturgies had been introduced by John Chrysostom (at the time with imperial encouragement) to counter the nocturnal processions of heretical Arians, banned from

---

[143] Soc. 7.22.16.
[144] Soc. 7.23.11 with Brown 2002: 99; Meier 2007: 146–7; Van Nuffelen 2012: 190–1.
[145] Soc. 7.22.21.
[146] For these depositions as political failures (by bishops and their supporters), see Schor 2011: 82–109; Van Nuffelen 2012: 193–200.

worshipping within the walls.[147] Nor in offering spiritual leadership could bishops always rely on the city's monastic communities for support. Not all holy men were welcome in the capital. In the late 420s, the charismatic monk, Alexander, was expelled along with his followers, 'the Sleepless Ones' (from their ceaseless genuflection and hymn-singing, organised in round-the-clock liturgical shifts). In dispute was Alexander's claim to apostolic authority based on his severe asceticism and solidarity with the urban poor; in his view, this warranted his insistent demand for charity which (he argued) was clearly superior to the needs and merits of the city's clergy.[148]

These were long-standing tensions. Thirty years earlier, John Chrysostom had challenged the city's monks, openly criticising (to quote Daniel Caner) 'the way they sought material support by demanding alms from others and the way they justified this support through their ascetic practices'.[149] But for others, that connection was not lightly surrendered. Constantinople had the most organised and influential concentration of monks of any city in the empire.[150] (Pulcheria was even claimed as a supporter of Alexander the Sleepless.[151]) Monks too continued to assert their independence (not least retrospectively in their heroic hagiographies): after all, it was precisely their apparent spiritual self-sufficiency that made them so attractive to those enmeshed in the great institutions of the capital.[152] In an extraordinary incident, in late June 431, Dalmatius, the most influential monk in Constantinople, led a delegation to the Great Palace to press the claims of Cyril of Alexandria and his supporters to have acted properly some days earlier at the opening session of the Council of Ephesus (Kelly pp. 234–6). Standing in the imperial audience hall, Dalmatius openly criticised Theodosius' continued support of Nestorius: 'in front of all who were present, I said to the emperor, "To whom would you rather listen, six hundred bishops

---

[147] Baldovin 1987: 183–4. [148] Caner 2002: 126–57.
[149] Caner 2002: 190–9 quoting 196. [150] Dagron 1970: 253–7.
[151] *Vita Hypatii* 41.13–14 (ed. G. J. M. Bartelink, *SC* 177, Paris, 1971) with Holum 1982: 136; Caner 2002: 140.
[152] Brown 1971: 92–3; Rapp 2005: 3–6 (on the *Life of Daniel the Stylite*).

or one impious man?'" Theodosius – astonished – apparently conceded the point.¹⁵³

Admiring biographers of holy men delighted in such tales of imperial discomfort. They were precious paradigms of the pious speaking truth to power. 'Whatever the political or theological complexities, these were moments, rather than the endless back-and-forth of debate, when the protracted process of imperial decision-making could be seen to crystallise' (Kelly p. 237). Dalmatius' tense encounter with Theodosius traced a familiar pattern. In the 370s in Trier (on the other side of the empire), Martin of Tours sought access to the Emperor Valentinian I. After seven days and nights of prayer, finally with the help of an angel he entered the palace unopposed. A ceremonial stand-off ensued: the holy man refused obeisance before the emperor, the emperor refused to rise to recognise the holy man. The deadlock was only broken when Valentinian's throne miraculously caught fire, forcing the scorched emperor suddenly to his feet. Chastened, Valentinian embraced the holy man and 'without waiting for Martin's requests, he granted everything before it was asked'.¹⁵⁴ Twenty years or so later, the holy hermit John of Lycopolis (Siut in the Nile Delta) prevented Theodosius I from levelling the city as a punishment for a riot in the circus. John convinced the imperial official (sent with troops to carry out the emperor's instructions) that he should spare the city. To ensure that Theodosius was also persuaded, John himself set off to Constantinople – in a cloud of light. He presented his own petition to the emperor (securing the destruction of the circus, but the safety of the city). In response to Theodosius' wish that his reply should be delivered to Lycopolis as quickly as possible, John extended his hand from the cloud, received the signed document and returned instantly to Egypt.¹⁵⁵ Lastly the great Syrian holy man, Simeon Stylites, who wrote to Theodosius II to protest the emperor's decision that synagogues seized by Christians should be returned to Jews:

---

[153] *Coll. Vat.* 67 (*ACO* 1 1.2, p. 69.2–4).
[154] Sulpicius Severus, *Dialogus* 2.5.5–10 quoting 9 (ed. K. Halm, *CSEL* 1, Vienna, 1866) with Matthews 1989: 269; Pazdernik 2009: 78–9.
[155] *Le synaxaire arabe jacobite* (17 novembre) (ed. R. Basset, *PO* 3.3, Paris, 1911, 323–7) with Brown 1992: 157–8.

He boldly wrote strong words filled with threats. He did not name Theodosius Emperor in his letters but wrote thus to him: 'Now that your heart is exalted and you have disregarded the Lord your God who gave you the glorious diadem and royal throne, now that you have become a friend and companion and protector to unbelieving Jews, behold suddenly the righteous judgement of God will overtake you.'

At once, the emperor reversed his policy and sacked the praetorian prefect responsible. 'Truth conquered, and God was glorified through his believer.'[156]

Such stories are not as one sided as perhaps they might at first seem. One notable aspect is the detailed knowledge that holy men (and their angelic helpers) have of court protocol – Dalmatius, Martin and John all directly intrude into the *consistorium*; John waits patiently in his cloud of light for his petition to be read to Theodosius I and for the emperor to dictate and sign the response; John's request is diplomatically finessed, conceding the destruction of the circus; Simeon Stylites' letter to Theodosius II follows the established pattern of a *suggestio* from a senior official. 'One should not be too beguiled by stories of imperial ambush ... Staged – or, perhaps better, ceremonial – capitulations in the face of manifest holiness allowed emperors to combine opportunities both to alter existing policy and to offer a justification that reached beyond factional court politics, cutting through the complex networks of persuasion and influence that sought to channel or constrain imperial action' (Kelly pp. 236 and 237). What mattered most was mutual recognition: of emperors by holy men (hence the careful respect for court ceremonial) and – as Claudia Rapp has pointed out – of holy men by emperors 'as exemplars of holiness'.[157] (It is that initial failure in the meeting between heretic emperor and saint that pushes the encounter between Valentinian and Martin towards inflammatory conflict.) 'In accepting the holy man's admonition, an emperor yielded in a momentary suspension of superiority which confirmed his own religious credentials and his willingness to accept advice and demonstrated his fitness to rule' (p. 237).

---

[156] *Life of Simeon Stylites* 121–3 (trans. Doran 1992: 189–91) with Millar 2006: 128 doubtful of the dating to the 420s proposed in *PLRE* II 160 (Asclepiodotus 1).

[157] Rapp 2005: 269.

This is by no means to imply – and the stories of holy men spectacularly intruding on the *consistorium* argue against it – that emperors were always shielded by court ceremonial. Like any complex political game, ceremony carried its own risks. Barefoot emperors processing through the streets of Constantinople were not always cheered. In 602, the Emperor Maurice was stoned by an angry crowd, and a few months later compelled to flee the capital (pp. 241–2). Bishop Porphyry (in the carefully staged incident with which this introduction began) forced the Emperor Arcadius to change his mind and confirm the destruction of pagan temples in Gaza as approved by the infant prince, Theodosius. 'This is a tough request, but much tougher to refuse, since it is our son's first ruling.'[158] Perhaps the emperor should have been more alert? Peter Van Nuffelen observes that, 'if Arcadius had been quick-witted, he might have been able to brush aside Porphyry's petition ... on the public stage one did not reflect, waver, or bargain, but showed decisive action that caught the eye and the imagination.'[159] But for Arcadius suddenly to have intervened would also have been to deny himself the advantages of court ceremonial as a means of moderating or resolving a dispute, or negotiating a shift in imperial policy. This too was a matter of calculation. As Charles Pazdernik has pointed out, the complexity and sheer artificiality of court ceremonial worked against outbursts of imperial anger (however prompted).

> The instrumentality of courtly etiquette in domesticating emperors was ... double-edged. Against the not inconsequential successes afforded to sensible men at pushing back against imperial arbitrariness and absolutism had to be set the dangers of empowering the unscrupulous, whose ability to manipulate the means by which influence was exercised at court need not reliably justify their ends.[160]

Court ceremonial might even muffle the harsh words of a holy man. In 530, the famous Palestinian monk, Sabas, journeyed to Constantinople; his holiness was immediately recognised by the Emperor Justinian who 'saw divine favour brilliantly blazing forth

---

[158] Above p. 4 n. 5.
[159] Van Nuffelen 2012: 193; see too 2010: 237–8.
[160] Pazdernik 2012: 111.

and taking the shape of a crown sending out rays like the sun around the old man's head'. Sabas' requests were immediately granted, but the monk (here rejecting a tactic so profitably employed by Porphyry of Gaza) declined to pray that the empress would have a child. In response to Theodora's direct request – '"Pray, father, that God may give me a child."' – Sabas responded obliquely (to the emperor): '"The God of glory will preserve your empire in piety and victory."'[161] As with Arcadius and Porphyry at Theodosius' baptism, it is the lack of immediate imperial objection that matters. Sabas' refusal to bless the empress was met by Justinian with even greater humility and (after Sabas had rejected any financial aid for monasteries) a generous response to the holy man's request for imperial funds to build churches, a fort and a hospital in Jerusalem.[162] To quote Harmut Leppin: 'here self-humiliation came into play, because in a Christian context humble behaviour could always lend authority and could lend even more authority to high-ranking Christians who were not normally expected to humble themselves in this way.'[163] In this courtly exercise of competitive humility, a holy man was in danger of being outdistanced by an emperor.

These patterns of co-operation, conflict and competition underscore the importance of ceremony in any full account of imperial power. For the successful, an ability to play the ritual game was inseparable from an understanding of (again to quote Fergus Millar) 'the workings of persuasion, command, reaction, and defiance'.[164] A focus on ceremonial (particularly the difficult paradox of displays of imperial humility on parade in the streets of the capital and before holy men in the *consistorium*) also exposes the importance of the close coalition between piety and power. This was by no means an innovation of Theodosius II. It runs back, at the very least, to his grandfather, Theodosius I, whose relic processions exploited the ceremonial possibilities of Constantinople.[165] It is deep-rooted in the adoption of Christianity by Constantine

---

[161] Cyr. Scyth. *V. Sabae* 71 (173–4 quoting 173.21–4 and 174.3–5) with Leppin 2009: 156–8.
[162] *V. Sabae* 72 (174.23–175.19).
[163] Leppin 2009: 164.   [164] Millar 2006: 131.
[165] Bauer 1996: 261–4; Croke 2010: especially 263–4.

at the beginning of the fourth century. (And, as suggested above, key expressions of imperial piety, such as the public demonstration of humility, drew on a long-standing set of expectations about the proper exercise of kingly power.) Certainly, Theodosius II's engagement with Christianity was no less aggressive than his predecessors' (and should not be judged by his avoidance of any direct involvement in military campaigns or – as Harries suggests [pp. 83–4] – his apparent lack of legislative initiative). It is all too easy to collude in the image of a passive, book-bound emperor (dangerously close to the literary stereotype of the nineteenth-century English country parson) whose genuine religious commitment leads him to earnest Bible-study and to convert the palace, in Socrates' much quoted phrase, 'into something resembling a monastery'.[166] But that would be too swift to dull the edge of Theodosius' piety. Against a background of intense religious competition in Constantinople, this emperor's Christianity deserves to be seen as more assertive: his wearing of a hair-shirt and a saint's tattered cassock is a strong claim to the holiness of the ascetic (an apparent paradox repeated in expressions of imperial humility or the tales of holy men at court); his serious scholarship is a forceful counter to any presumption that theological discussion should be the exclusive preserve of bishops; and his transformation of the palace into a monastery is an open challenge to the most influential religious group in the city.

This is the sharper context for the invocation of Constantine 'as a point of reference for Theodosius in the most positive achievements of his reign'.[167] Jill Harries has pointed to a pattern of comparison implicit in both Socrates' and Sozomen's accounts of the emperor's personal piety. Theodosius' night-time studies (using an oil lamp of his own invention[168]) recall Constantine who, according to his biographer Eusebius of Caesarea, 'in order to increase his understanding by thinking on the divinely inspired, would stay awake throughout the night'; both emperors had a firm grasp on theology; both prayed daily in their palaces.[169] In their

---

[166] Soc. 7.22.4.   [167] Harries 1994: 37.   [168] Soz. Pr. 8.
[169] Eus. V. Const. 4.22, 4.29–30 quoting 4.29.1 with Harries 1994: 37–40; Urbainczyk 1997: 38–9; Zecchini 2002: 538.

defeat of usurpers, both replayed the victory of the Israelites over Pharaoh at the Red Sea. Outside Rome at the Battle of the Milvian Bridge, Constantine's rival Maxentius drowned in the Tiber. To quote Eusebius, 'just like those who accompanied the great servant Moses, those who won this victory with the help of God might have chanted the same hymn as was once raised against the ancient, impious tyrant'.[170] Theodosius' troops at Ravenna (as noted above) found a path through the marshes thanks to the emperor's prayers and defeated the usurper John (to quote Socrates), 'just as it came to pass for the Hebrews crossing the Red Sea in the time of Moses'.[171]

Perhaps most striking of all is the dynastic context of Theodosius' Christianity. It cannot easily be divorced from his sisters' or his wife's piety. Certainly (as Kenneth Holum has emphasised) some of the inevitable tensions in the royal household were focused on religion, but – as the chapters in Part II of this volume suggest – aggressive expressions of imperial piety are perhaps more profitably seen as broadly characterising the Theodosian regime, rather than defining its internal divisions. Again, this is a pattern not entirely without precedent. Eudocia's journey to the Holy Land (as Harries notes [p. 71]) recalled the pilgrimage of Constantine's mother, Helena, in the 320s, as did her encounters with holy men, her concern with biblical sites and her relic-hunting.[172] (There may too be echoes of the tradition of Helena's unearthing of the True Cross in Jerusalem with Pulcheria's discovery of the relics of the Forty Martyrs of Sebaste in Constantinople.[173]) Most importantly, Pulcheria's public devotion was not aimed at undercutting her brother's authority; rather it was a radical strategy to confirm the legitimacy of an unmilitary regime: 'an experiment in the conceptualising of the imperial family as legitimised, not primarily by military victory (although that also helped), but by piety' (Harries p. 70). As argued by both Jill Harries and Peter Van Nuffelen,

---

[170] Eus. *V. Const.* 1.38.5 with ample quotation from Exodus 15; on these parallels see, Cameron and Hall 1999: 35–9; Rapp 2005: 129–31; M. S. Williams 2008: 36–42.
[171] Soc. 7.22.21; above p. 46.
[172] Holum 1982: 188; Hunt 1982: 229; Drijvers 1993: 86–7; Urbainczyk 1997: 38; Brubaker 1997: 62.
[173] Brubaker 1997: 62.

Pulcheria and her sisters' vow of virginity helped to secure their brother's position by preventing potentially threatening marriage ties with the imperial family. Pulcheria's pledge emblazoned on an altar in Hagia Sophia should be taken seriously: 'for her own virginity and her brother's sovereignty'.[174] Perhaps too, more attention should be paid to later stories of Pulcheria actively recommending Eudocia to her brother (and thus forestalling any alliance with an already powerful family at court).[175] Certainly, these complementary marriage strategies should be seen as another important element in any explanation for the length and stability of the reign. Pulcheria and Theodosius were part of a family firm. 'Pulcheria's power depended on the public face of the Theodosian regime as ostentatiously pious' (Harries p. 73). But the pious paradox of the dynastic virgin could only be pushed so far, especially as her brother seemed increasingly unlikely to father a male heir.[176] (And as Theodosius approached his fifties, the best that could reasonably be hoped for was another child-emperor.) It is perhaps then unsurprising that following Theodosius' sudden and unexpected death in July 450, Pulcheria was prepared to marry his successor – an undistinguished military officer with no imperial connections.[177] 'In the end neither piety nor propaganda could compensate where fertility failed.'[178] From a political point of view, the problem with virginity is that it has no long-term future. Celibacy is only good for a generation.

Imperial power and Christian piety (as Pulcheria's marriage to Marcian exemplifies) did not always fit easily together. In the second chapter in Part IV – 'The imperial subject: Theodosius II

[174] Soz. 9.1.4; above p. 45.
[175] The stories are usefully catalogued in *PLRE* II 408; see, for example, *Chron. Pasch.* 420 (1 575.4–578.8); Malalas 14.4. Holum 1982: 111–21 is perhaps too quick to dismiss these accounts; see the important discussion in Alan Cameron 1982: 270–9, although it is fair to point out that some of the basic elements in these prince-marries-outsider stories form part of a repeated dynastic romance, see Hans 1988.
[176] Theodosius and Eudocia had two daughters: Licinia Eudoxia (born in 422 and married to Valentinian III in 437; *PLRE* II 410–12 [Eudoxia 2]) and Flaccilla (who died in 431, still a child; *PLRE* II 473 [Flaccilla 2]); Theodosius' son Arcadius (*PLRE* II 130 [Arcadius 1]) is most likely a phantom; see Holum 1982: 178 n. 14; Sivan 2011: 164–5; for dissenting views, Scharf 1990: 445–50; Barnes 2006, 2007; and see above p. 35 n. 95 on the presentation copy of Proba's Virgilian cento, dispatched to the Emperor Arcadius (Theodosius' father) at court in Constantinople.
[177] *PLRE* II 714–15 (Marcianus 8). [178] Cooper 2004: 51.

and panegyric in Socrates' *Church History*' – Luke Gardiner considers the problems faced by one contemporary historian in writing about the Theodosian regime, particularly in terms of its public claims to piety. Socrates' decision to conclude his work with Theodosius II was itself an open rejection of the warning (most forcibly expressed at the end of the fourth century by Ammianus Marcellinus) that to write contemporary history was, in truth, unavoidably to write panegyric (p. 244). Socrates' decision to continue to the late 430s was motivated by his close engagement with Eusebius – part model, part rival – who had concluded his history of the Church midway through the reign of Constantine, and whose *Life of Constantine* was (in Socrates' critical view) 'more intent, as is the case in works of praise, on eulogising the emperor and on the panegyrical scale of its grandiloquence than on accurately capturing what happened'.[179] Socrates explicitly offered his own *Church History* as a continuation of Eusebius, but he also aimed to expose some of the underlying problems with his predecessor's project.[180] 'Socrates was as much Eusebius' corrector as his continuator' (p. 255).

The core of Socrates' account of Theodosius' character (in the seventh and final book of the *Church History*) concentrates on the emperor's piety, clemency and gentleness (7.22 and 7.42). A good deal of the material in 7.22 has already been noted in discussion so far: the emperor's daily prayer, his twice weekly fasts, his theological discussions, his collection of sacred texts, his transformation of the palace into something like a monastery, his cloak made from a deceased saint's tattered cassock, his suspension of races in the Hippodrome during a snowstorm to unite the people in hymn-singing and his successful prayers on behalf of the army at Ravenna. These items (to call them 'facts' would be wilfully to miss Socrates' point) are presented as part of an assessment of Theodosius quite clearly marked out as panegyrical: not least, by the introductory claim to accuracy and plain-speaking: 'not wishing to make a display of my language, I have elected

---

[179] Soc. 1.1.2 with Van Nuffelen 2004a: 103; Urbainczyk 1997: 41–7.
[180] The most important discussion of the relationship between Socrates and Eusebius is Van Nuffelen 2004a: 105–24.

to recount the good qualities of the emperor truthfully and without embellishment.'[181] This (Gardiner wryly notes) echoes the standard claim to sincerity with which any orator might preface a panegyric (pp. 254–6). In addition, as Giuseppe Zecchini has pointed out, Socrates' arrangement of material dealing in turn with the emperor's physical prowess, his intellectual superiority and his moral virtues follows a very familiar pattern: 'l'insieme di tali qualità contribuiva a renderlo un principe ideale anche alla luce degli *specula principis* e dei trattati sulla regalità di tradizione ellenistica.'[182]

In framing his account of Theodosius' reign with explicitly panegyrical assessments of the emperor's virtues, Socrates indicates to his readers his awareness of the problems of writing about contemporary events under an autocracy. Panegyric works against history, but (more importantly), as Gardiner argues, Socrates' history works permanently to forestall the very promise of panegyric – the possibility of closure and of a past resolved. 'Panegyric is too crude a tool for making nuanced judgements about the complex decisions of imperial governance. It offers a timeless framework ill-fitted to aid comprehension of a world inextricably embedded in the onward flow of history and human imperfection' (p. 268). Crucial to Socrates' purpose (as Gardiner argues), is a deliberate failure to disguise (or attempt to reconcile) the incongruities in his own account of Theodosius' reign. Moments in which the emperor inspired unity amongst his people (hymn-singing in the Hippodrome or leading the crowd to church to give thanks for the defeat of the usurper John) are set against his divisive support of Nestorius (pp. 262–6). Theodosius' open joy at John's execution is juxtaposed with his concerns for the *bestiarii* in the Amphitheatre (pp. 251–2). The exaggerated panegyrical claim that 'in clemency and humanity he far surpassed all others'[183] is revealed as an impossibility, which, if realised, risks impeding the good government of empire. 'Socrates exposes the unreality (and undesirability) of such claims to consistent clemency and the larger

---

[181] Soc. 7.22.1 with Urbainczyk 1997: 143; Wallraff 1997: 105–7; Leppin 2003b: 234.
[182] Zecchini 2002: 534 (but note Urbainczyk 1997: 144–5); see especially Zecchini 2002: 537–8 on Soc. 7.42 with its similar claim (at 7.42.5) to straight-talking truthfulness.
[183] Soc. 7.22.6.

inability – of which these claims are symptomatic – of panegyric, with its tendency towards the extreme, to facilitate credible, useful assessments of the necessities of imperial rule' (p. 251).

Socrates' aim, as Gardiner stresses, is not to deny the possibility of a positive assessment of Theodosius' reign – indeed the inclusion of a pair of exemplary panegyrics shows precisely how that might be (over)achieved – rather it is to insist on the complexity of any such appraisal.[184] In part, this acts as a counter to the strident triumphalism of Eusebius; it is a 'post-Eusebian' (to adopt Van Nuffelen's term) sensibility which embraces the possibility of a peaceful Christian empire, but recognises 'la perturbation continuelle de la paix universelle par un manque de moralité'.[185] Such a view is neither optimistic nor pessimistic: 'l'histoire chez Socrate n'est pas une seule ligne ascendante ou descendante.'[186] In that sense, in its demand for complexity and its suspicion of any easy resolution, Socrates' approach is closely complementary to some of the key themes explored in this introduction: the instabilities surrounding the exercise of power, influence or persuasion in a multi-polar court; the oscillation in meaning fundamental to such literary exercises as the cento or the paraphrase; and the uncertainties (for all involved) in the conduct of imperial ceremony. For Socrates, this is the context in which claims to piety should be understood. Most importantly, piety as an imperial virtue has no special status; like clemency or humanity, it is subject to the exaggeration, simplification and over-generalisation of panegyric; and (like clemency or humanity) it is open to a more nuanced interrogation by the historian. But Socrates makes no attempt to reconcile these approaches: 'Socrates, having exposed this problem, remains silent ... contradiction is starkly, and mutely, exposed. That it cannot always be resolved, or explained away, is precisely the point' (pp. 252 and 253). In the end, the reader is left wondering (for example) how Socrates' description of Theodosius' private life in the palace should be understood: a straightforward portrait

---

[184] See too the important discussions in Leppin 1996: 132–8, 215–16; Van Nuffelen 2004a: 407–25.
[185] Van Nuffelen 2004a: 117.
[186] Van Nuffelen 2004a: 117; and see too 110–12.

of a properly pious and genuinely scholarly ruler, or perhaps as a series of exemplary illustrations of how imperial piety might be defined or presented (to quote Sabine MacCormack 'thus a particular event becomes an expression of an imperial characteristic to which general validity is attributed'[187]), or perhaps the accounts of Theodosius' all-night studies, his debates with bishops and his tattered cassock are brilliant exaggerations which should be handled with all the care that panegyric demands?

The problems of such self-conscious complexity are delightfully absent from the final chapter in this volume. Edward Watts' 'Theodosius II and his legacy in anti-Chalcedonian communal memory' focuses on four Egyptian texts. First, the *Plerophories* (or *Fulfilments*) of John Rufus, a record of eighty-nine visions and the divine experiences of Egyptian and Palestinian holy men. These accounts were most likely written down in Antioch at the beginning of the sixth century, but preserved the earlier oral witness of Peter the Iberian (pp. 271–4). (Sent in 429, then a twelve-year-old, as a royal hostage to Constantinople, Peter never returned to Georgia to take up the throne. After spending his teenage years with Theodosius and Eudocia in the Great Palace, he followed an ascetic life in monasteries in Jerusalem and Gaza.[188]) Second, Pseudo-Theopistus' *History of Dioscorus*, a late sixth-century text with a focus on the church in Egypt (pp. 274–6); third, the late seventh-century *Chronicle* of John of Nikiu (in the Nile Delta) which covered the history of the world from Adam and Eve to the Arab conquest of Egypt (pp. 276–9); and fourth, the Coptic *Synaxary* (a listing of saints and their achievements to be celebrated in church liturgy), a multiplex document at whose core is a fifteenth-century Arabic translation of an earlier Coptic original (pp. 279–83). Of central concern to the authors of these four texts are the institutional and theological positions agreed at the Council of Chalcedon held in 451 – the year after Theodosius' death – under the tight control of his successor, Marcian. Confronted with over-zealous monks and a handful of excessively powerful bishops, a coalition of ecclesiastical and imperial authority looked for

---

[187] MacCormack 1972: 722.
[188] For the details, Steppa 2002: 61–70; Horn 2006: 50–106.

a workable compromise. To quote Michael Gaddis: 'Their answer, consistent with long-standing imperial tradition, was to seek a middle way between two extremes, a centrist strategy that emphasized order and stability.'[189] But the attempt to impose 'doctrinal closure'[190] by coercing consensus was not completely successful. In the view of its opponents, the Council introduced a credal formula which could be condemned as a variation on Nestorius' heretical Christology.

For supporters of Chalcedon, Marcian was to be remembered as a hero. Looking back from the end of the sixth century, the church historian Evagrius praised an emperor 'pious in divine matters and just in matters relating to his subjects ... accordingly he held the realm as a prize of virtue, not an inheritance'.[191] But for the authors of the four anti-Chalcedonian texts discussed by Watts, Marcian's reign was nothing less than a disaster on a cosmic scale. If Theodosius had been a modern Moses, then Marcian replayed Pharaoh. To quote John of Nikiu: 'on the day of Marcian's accession, there was darkness all over the earth from the first hour of the day till the evening. And that darkness was like that which had been in the land of Egypt in the days of Moses,' and the people of Constantinople 'cried aloud, saying: "We have never heard nor seen in all the previous reigns of the Roman empire such an event as this"' (p. 278). Marcian was acceptable to neither the living nor the dead. When (according to the Coptic *Synaxary*) imperial messengers brought news of the decisions reached at the Council of Chalcedon to a monastery outside Alexandria, its superior advised: 'I can do nothing without the advice of my fathers, so come with me that we may confer with them.' The messengers were led down into a crypt and the superior consulted the desiccated bodies of his deceased predecessors. In unison, they advised: 'Reject Chalcedon.'[192]

Compared to his impious successor, Theodosius' righteousness shone out. 'He belongs to an age when a man of true faith governed

---

[189] Gaddis 2005: 310, with an excellent account of the Council at 309–22; see too Price and Gaddis 2005: I 37–51.
[190] Gaddis 2005: 315.
[191] Evagrius 2.1 (trans. Michael Whitby 2000: 59–60).
[192] Amshir 2 (ed. R. Basset *PO* I 1.5, Paris, 1915, 766–7); see too Gaddis 2005: 325.

the empire, orthodox bishops presided over its most important sees and the twin pillars of political and church power responded to the commands of God communicated through pious ascetics' (pp. 273–4). Eudocia's conduct and even Theodosius' failure to father an heir were particularly to be celebrated. The latter was not presented as a dynastic crisis: rather it was part of a divine plan. The Coptic *Synaxary* remembered the forty-nine elders of Scetis, a monastery in Egypt, to whom Theodosius sent a delegation to ask about his lack of a son (pp. 281–2). The reply was clear: 'God does not wish to give you a son because after your death he would consort with heretics.'[193] Eudocia's marriage to Theodosius was loudly praised as a model relationship (pp. 277 and 279); by contrast, the final breaking of Pulcheria's virgin resolve was roundly denounced. For Pseudo-Theopistus, Pulcheria's support of her brother's imperial successor was the inevitable uncoiling of a long pent up lust: 'so Satan, that cursed serpent, began again his struggle with womankind.'[194] Pulcheria is a second Eve who in finally yielding to temptation and marrying Marcian brought heresy into the world. 'The text then marks out the reign of Theodosius as a sort of Christian paradise from which the empire was expelled when Pulcheria married Marcian' (p. 275).

These bracingly uncompromising views lend a striking clarity to fifth-century history (for some, this may be a refreshing antidote to the literary complexities explored elsewhere in this introduction). Indeed, for holy men even the future was all too predictable. When Nestorius preached in Constantinople, Peter the Iberian (as recounted in the first of John Rufus' *Fulfilments*) had no doubt of the destructive theological wrangling that was to follow. Nestorius had 'a clear and effeminate voice' and as he spoke 'his face became contorted and his right hand twisted back on itself' until, completely doubled-up, he was carried by his attendants out of sight of the congregation.[195] Peter saw Nestorius' heretical disposition earlier and more clearly than Theodosius who, according to

---

[193] Tubah 26 (*PO* 11.5: 699).
[194] *Hist.* 3 (ed. Nau 1903; trans. at 245) with Burgess 1993–4: especially 51–4, 59–61.
[195] John Rufus, *Pler.* 1 (*PO* 8.1: 12); for predictive visions in *Pler.*, see usefully Steppa 2002: 122–7, and on John's treatment of Nestorius, 147–9.

another of John's *Fulfilments*, had to be hit hard on the head with a brick before he came to his senses (pp. 271–2; Kelly p. 233). Perhaps this difference between an emperor and a king who had relinquished his throne to remain a monk was only to be expected. In his *Life of Peter the Iberian*, John Rufus was clear that, as a teenager in Constantinople, Peter (who like Theodosius wore a hair-shirt under his court dress) was even more successful than the emperor in turning his quarters in the Great Palace into a monastery: sleeping on the ground in front of martyr-relics and conducting the 'divine services with lights, incense, hymns of praise and intercessions'.[196]

Of course, even with Peter's holy perspicacity, foreseeing the future (like understanding the past) was always a competitive matter. Evagrius assured his readers that Marcian's accession had also been correctly prophesied. On enlistment in the army, the future emperor was given the position and seniority of a recently deceased soldier called Augustus, and his name entered formally as 'Marcian who is also Augustus' – 'Hence the name anticipated the appellation of our emperors, in that they are called Augusti on being invested with the purple.'[197] Auguries of Marcian's legitimacy were easily swept aside by anti-Chalcedonian writers who simply pointed to the destructive consequences of his reign. For John Rufus, Chalcedon marked the end of antiquity: 'The city which has been mistress and sovereign over all shall be captured and made subject to barbarians.' Indeed, the end of the world was not far off: the Council was 'a harbinger of the Antichrist'.[198] These were lasting scars on the memory of the Christian churches in the eastern Mediterranean. 'Compared with Marcian, the reign of Theodosius became a sort of pre-Chalcedonian utopia' whose idealised image (as the Coptic *Synaxary* demonstrates) 'remained important in Egypt long after specific memories of the emperor and the empire he ruled had faded' (Watts p. 284). For those closer to events, the death of Theodosius II and the accession of Marcian

---

[196] *V. Petri Ib.* 25 (ed. and trans. Horn and Phenix 2008: 34–5) with Hunt 1982: 227; Horn 2006: 65–7, 124–34.
[197] Evagrius 2.1 (trans. Michael Whitby 2000: 58).
[198] John Rufus, *Pler.* 89 (*PO* 8.1: 150, 154); further examples collected in Steppa 2002: 127–8; and generally 155–62; Watts 2010: 135–6.

represented a permanent fissure in the history of the fifth century. In the twenty-seventh of his *Fulfilments*, John Rufus allowed his readers to look with Peter the Iberian beyond a vision of the future and, for a moment, to glimpse eternity (p. 273).

> Come now and I will show you where you can find the Emperor Theodosius in one place and Marcian in another. And he took me to see, in one place filled with a great and inaccessible light, the venerable Theodosius in an ineffable glory and more brilliant than the sun. Then he guided me to another place full of smoke and obscurity and shadows and he said to me, 'Do you see Marcian in the torments of this place?' I said, 'I can't see anyone.' And he looked towards heaven and said, 'Lord, dispel this darkness a little, so that he may at last see and believe.' – And I saw Marcian surrounded by suffering suspended by iron hooks in the midst of flames.[199]

For the historian (if not for the visionary), the reign of Theodosius II presents something of a paradox. The devil is in the detail. The sheer volume of material surviving from the first half of the fifth century offers an extraordinarily wide range of sharply conflicting views; it allows the micro-mapping of particular controversies; it exposes in detail the networks and tactics of those who succeeded and (more strikingly) those who failed. Imperial court society is more clearly revealed than at any time in the previous 400 years. What is less certain is the degree to which this represents a significant shift from the fourth century as a result of (for sake of argument) the successful accession of a child-emperor, a long reign undisturbed by rebellion, the permanence of the court and palatine administration in Constantinople, the effective political separation of the western half of the empire or the growing strength of the Church. Despite the surviving documentation, there is (as should now be all too clear) a significant and recurrent difficulty in establishing any unobstructed view of the emperor. Certainly, Edward Gibbon parted from the fourth century and Ammianus Marcellinus, its principal political historian, with misgivings. 'It is not without the most sincere regret, that I must now take leave of an accurate and faithful guide, who has composed the history of his own times, without indulging the prejudices and passions,

---

[199] John Rufus, *Pler.* 27 (*PO* 8.1: 68–9).

which usually affect the mind of a contemporary.'[200] It is possible to share something of Gibbon's sense of change (if not his faith in Ammianus). The shift in the nature of the surviving accounts and their concerns means that the fifth century has a distinct (and for Gibbon, distasteful) texture. The risk is in exaggerating the contrast with the more focused imperial histories of the fourth century or in the case (perhaps somewhat ironically) of Theodosius I with a much narrower range of material. Understanding the first half of the fifth century – as the chapters in this volume make clear – demands a rather different approach. And, inevitably, in the absence of either a biography or a coherent and wide-ranging political history, Theodosius II remains a frustratingly indistinct figure always glimpsed in the mirror of someone else's tale.

One key theme to emerge from this volume is the difficulty of calibrating change. That the regime of Theodosius II represented a significant shift in the pattern of imperial rule established by Constantine seems undoubted. But, equally, the material discussed in the ten chapters which follow make a good case for thinking about the transition from Theodosius I to Theodosius II in less dramatic – and certainly less negative – terms. The first half of the fifth century neither cut loose from its heritage (classical, imperial or Christian), nor was it burdened by the dead weight of tradition. Such judgements are too rough-hewn. It is (regrettably) too easy to think that the reign of Theodosius can be more fully explained by a careful balancing of continuities and changes. That does not adequately capture the complexities of a society deeply committed to understanding the present by reforming – refashioning, reinventing, re-editing – the past. To repeat Richard Lim: 'The preeminent task of the fifth century was to summarize and define the accomplishments of previous ages.'[201] (Indeed, perhaps one of the first steps towards an appreciation of these creative engagements is to pause to wonder why Eudocia's centos might have been thought an improvement on Homer.) It is also a warning that any attempt to trace the relationship between the fourth and fifth centuries must also be aware of extent to which the

---

[200] Gibbon 1781a: 627. [201] Above p. 30 n. 81.

fourth century was deliberately shaped as a prolegomenon to the fifth – a project perhaps most clearly on view in the *Theodosian Code* or in the continuators of Eusebius or in the public embrace of imperial piety. Above all, the unifying aim of this volume is to demonstrate that the reign of Theodosius II should not be too quickly dismissed, simplified or partitioned. Taken together, the ten chapters which follow share a common concern to reveal a rich imperial world whose sophistication and vitality directly challenge any broad assumptions of its tiredness or inadequacy. And, in turn, these positive assessments render more fragile those traditional narratives of the passage from the fourth to the fifth centuries which suggest a sharply descendent Theodosian trajectory: from grandfather to grandson; from Theodosius I to Theodosius II; from Theodosius the Great to Theodosius the Less (*iunior*, ὁ νέος, ὁ μικρός). The danger is too dissonant a contrast. This transition from major to minor demands a careful modulation.

PART II
ARCANA IMPERII

CHAPTER 2

MEN WITHOUT WOMEN: THEODOSIUS' CONSISTORY AND THE BUSINESS OF GOVERNMENT

Jill Harries

Public power: Pulcheria Augusta

In 445 and 446, Theodoret, bishop of Cyrrhus, in the province of (Syria) Euphratensis, despatched successive dossiers of letters to high officials in Constantinople. His purpose was to gain favourable tax treatment of his (allegedly) impoverished fellow-citizens and to refute the slanders perpetrated against members of the local elite by an anonymous bishop. The officials approached were an illustrious group: Flavius Claudius Constantinus, praetorian prefect of the East;[1] the *patricius* and ex-consul, Flavius Senator;[2] and the former *magister utriusque militiae* in the East, ex-consul and *patricius*, Flavius Anatolius.[3] All these had, by virtue of their present or previous posts, official involvement with decisions on tax assessments and appeals.[4]

However, a further recipient of a plea (*Letter* 43) on similar lines, Pulcheria Augusta, the emperor's sister, had no formal connection with decisions on taxation.[5] Nonetheless, Theodoret thought it worthwhile to approach her, despite having never written to her before. He had two reasons for his confidence. One was that she had respect for bishops, a consistent feature of her interpretation of *basileia*.[6] Considerable space, therefore, is devoted to

---

[1] Theod. *Ep.* 42; *PLRE* II 317–18 (Constantinus 22); on the dating of these letters, see Schor 2011: 263 n. 83 following (with some slight modification) Tompkins 1995.
[2] Theod. *Ep.* 44; *PLRE* II 990–1 (Senator 4).
[3] Theod. *Ep.* 45; *PLRE* II 84–6 (Anatolius 10).
[4] For the wider context of Theodoret's virtual community, see Schor 2011: 156–79, especially 167–9 on this particular dispute over taxation.
[5] Theod. *Ep.* 43.
[6] On Pulcheria and *basileia*, see Holum 1982: 79–111.

undermining the credibility of his principal (but unnamed) bugbear, usually identified as Athanasius of Perrha, who had been forbidden communion by the Council of Antioch and its bishop, Domnus, in 444.[7] But Theodoret did not stop with the empress's well-attested concern with religion. He also paints a word-picture of his suffering city; of estates abandoned by their tenant-cultivators and owners; and of decurions unable to bear the tax burden and forced into bankruptcy or flight. Her 'Serenity', Pulcheria, would, he trusted, bring 'healing' to his city.

Theodoret's letter credits Pulcheria with the power to grant tax remissions independently of her brother and his advisers and is thus remarkable testimony to the perceived influence of Pulcheria in departments of government traditionally the preserve of men. This does not mean that she independently granted tax reliefs. What mattered was Theodoret's belief that she could, somehow, influence the decision in his favour. Theodoret's perception of the Augusta's authority conferred power on Pulcheria in actuality, assisting the diffusion of patronage, which was a feature of the Theodosian government.[8] The confidence expressed by the bishop that Pulcheria could act effectively (despite the unacknowledged threat from opposing factions at court, not least the favoured eunuch Chrysaphius) allowed her to maintain a patronage network and an influence which would be reasserted decisively in the aftermath of Theodosius' death in 450, with her conferment of the succession on Marcian and her marriage to him.[9]

Accounts written long after Pulcheria's death, and therefore distorted by the yet more high-profile examples of empresses like Theodora in the sixth century,[10] credited her with the arrangement of Theodosius' marriage to the professor's daughter, Athenais, renamed Aelia Eudocia, with direction of Theodosius' foreign policy, especially against Persia in the early 420s, and with an outspoken intervention in the Senate, where she openly castigated

---

[7] Schor 2011: 123, 158.   [8] Millar 2006: 192–234.
[9] *Chron. Pasch.* 450 (1 590.8–12); Evagrius 2.1; Malalas 367. On the events of 450, see Burgess 1993–4 and, with reservations, Chew 2006.
[10] Herrin 2001: 4–5.

Theodosius for his failure to assert himself in government.[11] These later interpretations echoed perceptions of her status also advertised by contemporaries, such as the church historian Sozomen, writing in the early 440s. According to Sozomen, Pulcheria celebrated her public consecration to virginity in her fourteenth year with the presentation to the Great Church in Constantinople of a sacred table, adorned with an explanatory inscription, gold and jewels.[12] Soon after, in July 414, she was proclaimed Augusta and, a few months later, a portrait bust of her was dedicated in the senate-house at the Augusteum in Constantinople.[13] As a young girl, Sozomen claimed, Pulcheria, already fluent in both Latin and Greek, had 'directed the state' and, while educating her young brother in horsemanship, literary culture, deportment and piety, she 'caused all business to be transacted in his name'.[14] For Sozomen, naturally, Pulcheria was most to be praised for her love of orthodoxy, her building of churches and the favour shown her by God. But, as an adult woman, Sozomen's Pulcheria reverts to an older female stereotype, albeit in Christian guise; she and her sisters live together, engaging in godly works and conversation – and weaving wool.[15]

This composite portrait of Pulcheria is both traditional – she stays at home and sews – and revolutionary – she exercises powers of government traditionally reserved for men. But a focus on Pulcheria's individual influence can mislead. Women, especially in the Greek East, had long acted as patrons of their communities, receiving public honours and recognition, but they did so as members of a collective family enterprise, from which all members would expect to benefit; such women would have seen themselves as empowered rather than inhibited by their dynastic context.[16] Moreover, in Rome too, imperial women had received statues and monuments, erected in settings which advertised the

---

[11] Holum 1982: 120–1 rejects later tales of Pulcheria's role in finding Theodosius' bride, but argues for her influence in the war against Persia (1977 and 1982: 101–11; see too Blockley 1992: 55–8); for Pulcheria's criticism of her brother, see John of Nikiu, *Chronicle* 87.29–31 (trans. Charles 1916: 107).
[12] Soz. 9.1.4.
[13] Marcell. com. 414; *Chron. Pasch.* 414 (I 571.17–20).
[14] Soz. 9.1.5–6.   [15] Soz. 9.3.2.
[16] See the classic study by van Bremen 1996: especially 82–113.

dynastic strength of the imperial house.[17] The failure of Diocletian's Tetrarchy to do so – partly because of Diocletian's and Galerius' unfortunate lack of male heirs – was one notable exception.

Pulcheria's public piety, therefore, was exercised in the context of a well-promoted dynastic preoccupation with the power of holiness, peculiar to this, the third and last male generation of the house of Theodosius I. A century before, Constantine had been no less 'god-beloved', but the character of his administration and his household reflected his military background. His women, although occasionally granted coins or inscriptions in their honour, were seldom seen and never heard; they therefore lacked the dynastic context which would have granted them the space to develop significant patronage networks.[18] By contrast, from their early youth, Pulcheria and her sisters, who functioned in a more benign, civilian environment, were essential to the ostentatiously pious ethos and image of the Theodosian *familia*. The emperor's learning and piety, and his sisters' dedication to holy virginity, guaranteed the favour of God and provided essential support for the legitimacy of the dynasty. Theirs, therefore, was an experiment in the conceptualising of the imperial family as legitimised, not primarily by military victory (although that also helped), but by piety.[19] To that end, the production of heirs came second to the renunciation of sex held to be essential for the holy life, with the additional advantage that would-be emperors, hoping to exploit a marriage connection with the imperial house, were kept at a safe distance.[20]

In their stress on the peaceful virtues of scholarship and piety, Theodosius and his propagandists reshaped the rhetoric of empire. The nature of 'power' itself was revisited – to the benefit of Pulcheria, her sisters and Aelia Eudocia. The last, although lacking powerful connections outside her immediate family circle, who may have profited from her elevation, was, as the mother of the emperor's children, a more conventional 'empress' figure, performing the duties expected of an imperial consort. But, like her sisters-in-law,

---

[17] For late second- and early third-century Rome, see Boatwright 2011: 130–5.
[18] Note the relatively obscure status of the senatorial dedicators of inscriptions to Helena at Rome and in Italy; for details, Drijvers 1992: 45–52.
[19] Cf. Soz. 9.1.2: 'without piety, armies, a powerful empire and every other asset count for nothing'.
[20] Soz. 9.1.3.

she understood and exploited the potential for self-assertion inherent in Christian queenship. In the 440s – sidelined in the factional struggles at court – she would reinvent herself as another Helena, as patron of, and pilgrim to, the holy sites at Jerusalem. Still, if real power rested in the hands of the meek and lowly of heart (as the emperor represented himself on some public occasions[21]), then it could also properly be exercised by divinely favoured imperial women. The big losers in this privileging of 'soft power' were those (men) who had exercised military commands in past, less happy, times. In this rhetorically constructed world, officials could be represented by others as brave, just and wise, but not as 'powerful': 'your disposition is not one associated with raw power', wrote Theodoret, 'but with a man wise, understanding and thoughtful'.[22]

The soldierly dynasty of the two Ardaburii and Aspar was thus discreetly distanced from influence in the Theodosian corridors of power. The strategy was surprisingly successful but stored up problems for the future; in the reign of Leo, the pressure from Aspar and his family on imperial security became all but intolerable. Under Theodosius II, they had some short-term but limited success. The elder Ardaburius' laurels gained in the war against Persia in 421–422 started to fade when he was imprisoned by the western usurper John in 424, although he held the consulship in 427.[23] His son Aspar, the most famous of the line, had greater success against John, whom he overthrew in 425, and won victories against the Vandals in Africa in 431; despite this and the consulship in 434, the kudos that would have been his in more warlike times eluded him.[24] The same was true of his relative by marriage, Flavius Plinta, *magister utriusque militiae* for nearly twenty years (419–438); his career shows little evidence of military engagement, let alone success.[25] Too often there were failures, notably the missed opportunities against the Vandals in 441 and the defeat of Aspar, Ariobindus and Arnegisclus by Attila in 447.[26] These

---

[21] See Kelly pp. 221–33 and Gardiner pp. 262–4, this volume.
[22] Theod. *Ep.* XLVI to Helladius, *curator* (*PLRE* II 535 [Helladius 4]): οὐ σύμμετρον τῇ δυνάμει ... ὑμῖν εἶναι τὸ φρόνημα, ἀλλ' ἀνδρὶ σοφῷ τε καὶ συνετῷ καὶ τὴν φύσιν ἐπεσκεμμένῳ συμβαῖνον.
[23] *PLRE* II 137–8 (Ardabur 3).   [24] *PLRE* II 164–9.   [25] *PLRE* II 892–3.
[26] For the date of Attila's victory, see Zuckerman 1994: 164–8.

reverses, which did not affect the security of the eastern empire as a whole, may not have been entirely unwelcome to the civilian coterie around Theodosius. The targeting of Arianism, the doctrine of the generals, by the law-makers at Constantinople and the release in 438 of a poem (now lost) celebrating the failure of the coup of Gainas in 400 were two elements in the systematic distancing of the 'barbarian' military leadership from the sources of power in the capital.[27] Little wonder that there was embarrassment at the allegation made in the presence of Attila in 449 that the generals Aspar and Ariobindus had 'no influence' with the emperor.[28]

'Law and tradition mattered little,' writes Kenneth Holum, 'because in a pious court Pulcheria exerted influence that could hardly be resisted.'[29] It is true that the Augusta enhanced the pious image of Theodosius' court, creating an ambience, which gave maximum authority to her Christian vocation, the source of power she was best placed to exploit. But to focus on Pulcheria to the exclusion of other informal factions and institutions of government is to overstate the extent of her power and influence in a multi-polar court. For example, it is not necessary to follow Holum and see Pulcheria's hand behind the ending of the dominance of the Praetorian Prefect Anthemius, *comes sacrarum largitionum* in 400, *magister officiorum* in 404 and praetorian prefect of the East from mid 405.[30] He probably died of natural causes, his son Flavius Anthemius Isidorus and his son-in-law Procopius continued their careers, apparently unaffected by Anthemius senior's demise, and his grandson, another Anthemius, would become Augustus of the West for five troubled years (467–472).[31]

---

[27] See Alan Cameron 1982: 255 on the significance of the *Gainea*. The end of Plinta's tenure as *magister utriusque militiae* coincides with the poem's release – perhaps not a coincidence? Soc. 6.6.37 reports that the poem was read out by Ammonius to the emperor and his courtiers.
[28] Priscus 14.87–91.   [29] Holum 1982: 111.
[30] Holum 1982: 94–6; *PLRE* II 93–5 (Anthemius 1).
[31] *PLRE* II 631–3 (Isidorus 9), 920 (Procopius 2), 96–8 (Anthemius 3). Isidorus was urban prefect of Constantinople in 410, returned as praetorian prefect of Illyricum in 424 and was praetorian prefect of the East in 435–436, holding the consulship in 436. Procopius, a probable descendant of the Procopius related by marriage to the house of Constantine and would-be emperor in 365, was *magister utriusque militiae* (422–424) and *patricius*; see Alan Cameron 1982: 271–2.

Moreover, it is from the period when Pulcheria's ability to shape the administration to her liking should have been at its height that a small but significant detail emerges, showing the limits to Pulcheria's self-assertion: in 418, employees on the urban estates of the Augusta were specifically singled out as *not* being exempt from the *collectio lustralis* (the periodic tax on the capital assets of merchants and tradesmen).[32] Clearly Pulcheria had lodged a request for exemption but the emperor's advisers thought otherwise. Her influence, on this occasion, stopped at the consistory door.

Secret power: the imperial consistory

Pulcheria's power depended on the public face of the Theodosian regime as ostentatiously pious, an image systematically projected by imperial spectacles for the benefit of the people of Constantinople and, very occasionally, further afield. By contrast, much of the deliberative work of the consistory was done in secret, within the council chambers of the palace complex. Through the access of its membership to the imperial 'oracle',[33] the consistory controlled the levers of power in the routine tasks of government. Only after decisions were made were they published abroad through imperial letters and the edicts of officials. Within the bounds of the consistory, where the laws were given agreed written form, the voices which we hear so clearly from the church councils or the ecclesiastical historians, who observed the outward symbols of court ceremonial and policy, are muted. This is not to deny that ecclesiastical controversies impinged and, for short periods of time, even dominated consistory business, but, statistically, these are the exception and far less significant than the emperor's councillors' overall concern with running the empire, its taxes, administration, military establishment and civil law.

If Pulcheria, and, from the early 420s, the emperor's wife, Aelia Eudocia, could consistently affect the decisions of the consistory

[32] *CTh* 13.1.21 (August 418); Holum 1982: 134.
[33] *CTh* 6.22.8.1 (September 425).

by personal pressures on 'their' officials, then their influence should clearly be visible in Theodosius II's laws, as preserved in truncated form in the *Theodosian Code* down to 437, and thereafter in the *Code* of Justinian and, unexpurgated, as the *Novellae* of Theodosius II. Theodosius' sisters and wife had access to his presence at will, and, unlike officials, who held office for only a few years, they were a permanent part of his life. Moreover, Eudocia was related to key male players, who would have been present at the meetings: Asclepiodotus – praetorian prefect of the East (423–425), consul in 423 and recipient inter alia of a law remarkably tolerant of Jews and pagans – was her maternal uncle[34] and the *magister officiorum* Valerius probably her brother.[35] The empresses were thus well placed to lobby individual courtiers and doubtless did so, but they were one of several 'competing streams of rhetorical persuasion'.[36]

If the contents of the *Theodosian Code* are representative, then members of the consistory, or at least the minute-takers, had a culture of their own, which distanced them from the vicissitudes of day-to-day controversies. Even on matters Christian, consistory decisions were reached in line with precedent. For example, late in 434, the emperor, that is his consistory, issued a law about what happened to the estates of clerics (whatever their rank) and monks if they died intestate.[37] The property would pass to the church or monastery, to which he or she was attached, but only if there were no close relatives living, including cognates and wives, and only if there were no other charges upon the estate, such as unpaid taxes or burdens incurred by the deceased's membership of the curial order. In other words, the position of the Church in the line of intestate succession was very far from privileged; the claims of the family, widely interpreted, came first and the Church was made equivalent to the *fiscus* in non-clerical cases. In due course, the compilers of the *Theodosian Code* filed it under the succession regulations included in Book 5 (the last of the books on the civil

---

[34] *PLRE* II 160 (Asclepiodotus 1); Holum 1982: 123–6.
[35] *PLRE* II 1145 (Valerius 6).
[36] Millar 2006: 37–8, 230–1 quoting 231; and generally 204–7 on the role of the consistory.
[37] *CTh* 5.3.1 (December 434).

law as set out in the Praetorian Edict); it was categorised as part of the law of succession, not of right religion, a topic reserved for Book 16.

The same principle was applied to reform of the law of asylum, or sanctuary. Because it regulated the rights of (alleged) criminals seeking a safe haven, the Theodosian lawyers who compiled the *Code* would categorise it as an element in the criminal law, as set out in Book 9. The constitution was issued in 431 and addressed to Antiochus Chuzon, son of the praetorian prefect of the same name. *Quaestor sacri palatii* in 429, main mover of the *Theodosian Code* project and now himself praetorian prefect, he would also be closely involved with the Council of Ephesus.[38] Given his known interest in both Christianity and law, it is likely that Antiochus was not only the recipient but also in effect the author of the constitution. The right of sanctuary was to be extended to a fixed limit outside church buildings, suppliants were to be debarred from the building itself for purposes of eating or sleeping, and overnight, and they were not to bear arms. The bishop and clergy were granted full authority to explain the conditions and reassure the doubtful about their safety (although in a rider it was stated that slaves were allowed only a single day before being returned to their masters, who were expected to forgive them).[39] However, if the conditions were breached, 'reverence for religion was to be preferred to humanity',[40] the right of asylum no longer obtained and, with the consent of the bishop and local governor, armed servants of the state were permitted to enter and remove the suppliant. The aim, clearly, was not to undermine the right of sanctuary, which was safeguarded by the bishop's involvement at every stage, but to ensure that those seeking refuge behaved in accordance with the clergy's expectations.

Though Christian, therefore, the consistory made of government – or at least of law-making – a science that drew on a discourse that was, in general and with the obvious exception

---

[38] *PLRE* II 103–4 (Antiochus 7); Honoré 1998: 115–18; *CTh* 9.45.4 (23 March 431, posted at Alexandria on 7 April). For restrictions on the rights of asylum by Arcadius, see *CTh* 9.45.2 (June 397) and 3 (June 398) with Liebeschuetz 1990: 151.
[39] *CTh* 9.45.5 (March 432).   [40] *CTh* 9.45.4.2 (March 431).

of legislation on ecclesiastical controversies, religiously neutral.⁴¹ It may also hold one key to the longevity of Theodosius as the longest serving Augustus in Roman history. Its decision-making process worked to contain the ambitions of individuals (including external lobbyists and empresses) by obliging them to conform to the will of the collective. At the same time, judicious selection of its membership enabled families of officials to accumulate experience and contacts, and thus hold power over several generations. Both the Anthemii and other great dynasties of officials could trace their genealogy back to high administrators in the time of Constantius II; it was a source of pride that an administrator could boast descent from other administrators. Lacking the clout to become emperors themselves, the Theodosian descendants of the would-be emperor Procopius, or of Flavius Taurus, praetorian prefect to Constantius (355–361), contented themselves with a share in what the emperor did, while systematically keeping rival powers, such as those of the military establishment, largely at arm's length.⁴² The powers of the ruling group were enhanced by the fact that, unlike, say, Constantine I, Theodosius provided no strong consistent leadership or personal legislative programme, leaving it to his officials to promote their own agendas.⁴³ As an institution, therefore, the consistory lent strength to Theodosius' position, by keeping internal threats to his (and their) power at a distance, while also controlling his freedom of manoeuvre.

What marks out the achievement of Theodosius' consistory over nearly half a century is its preference for consistency in the application of rules and a corresponding dislike for special concessions; its generosity in the distribution of honours, which

---

⁴¹ For name-calling within a law, see the designation of Nestorian as 'Simonian' in *CTh* 16.5.66 (August 435), which refers back to Constantine's practice of applying pejorative labels to enemies of the Church.

⁴² On the Anthemii as descendants of Procopius, related to the Emperor Julian on his mother's side, above n. 31; see *PLRE* II 1056–7 (Taurus 4) for Flavius Taurus, consul in 428 and praetorian prefect of the East (433–434 and 445); his grandfather, Flavius Taurus (*PLRE* I 879–80 [Taurus 3]) was also *quaestor* to Constantius II in 354; his father was the Aurelianus (*PLRE* I 128–9 [Aurelianus 3]) who succeeded Anthemius in 414 (see above p. 72). For dynasties of officials in the time of Arcadius (inherited by Theodosius II), see Liebeschuetz 1990: 132–5.

⁴³ But note the contrary view of Traina 2007: 48–59 that Theodosius, a 'un autocrate autoritario e carismatico' (at 53), provided more direction than is usually credited.

would also serve to consolidate support among the palace bureaucrats; and its collective interest in system and simplification. The concern of the consistory members, understandably, was that government was too complicated, anomalies too frequent and the laws too obscure (the last a complaint made throughout the ages). But although their concerns were primarily practical, in that they wanted government to work better, they could not legislate for the complexities of human life.

Agenda for government

The volume of legislation on right religion preserved in the *Code* and *Novellae* is small, in comparison with the public focus on Christian piety presented to the world by the Theodosian regime and its sympathisers. Religious controversies were public and passionate. What happened in consistory business meetings was, as a rule, neither. Instead, the emperor's council was where an agenda for government evolved, which concentrated on consolidation. From the consistory lawyers came the concept of the general law, which would be fundamental to the Theodosian codification, a change which reflects the lawyers' preoccupation with form and validity, rather than content. The accepted operational combination of legislative responses to promptings from outside with measures originating with an imperial initiative, *spontaneus motus*, was also explained in an *oratio* to the Roman Senate in November 426, along with a reminder that the emperors too were subject to the laws.[44] The use, or misuse, of rescripts as 'general', rather than as rulings with reference only to the case to which they applied, had been restricted by Arcadius with reference to rescripts issued in response to referrals by judges (*consultationes*);[45] and all rescripts were, in theory, excluded from the *Theodosian Code*. Along with

---

[44] *CJ* 1.14.3 defining the *lex generalis* as a constitution designated as an edict or of general application, whether issued on the emperor's initiative or in response to proposals, petitions or reports. In 426, the young Valentinian III had been recently restored by his cousin Theodosius II, many of whose courtiers, such as the *magister officiorum* Helion (*PLRE* II 533 [Helion 1]), could have been still in the West and influenced, if not dictated, the content of the law. On the *Code*, see Matthews 1993: 25–9; Sirks 2007: 20–35, 196–7.

[45] *CTh* 1.2.11 (December 398).

the focus on generality came an ambition for comprehensiveness, unlikely ever to be achieved in practice. Laws elicited on a particular point raised by an official or petitioners were expanded to provide additional general guidance on related points. The *Theodosian Code* can be read as the largest-scale attempt, thus far, to encompass everything about imperial law in one great volume; predictably, as the deluge of constitutions issued in 439 shows, it was, in this respect, a failure.

The 440s saw two significant innovations in the powers of high officials and the consistory in which they served. One was Theodosius' delegation of his powers as supreme judge to a panel consisting of the *quaestor* and the praetorian prefect of the East.[46] It was true that the hearing of appeals was an onerous part of the emperor's job and that the emperor's chief law officer might be better qualified to adjudicate on the abstruse legal points likely to be raised before the new court. Moreover, praetorian prefects, like urban prefects (of Rome and of Constantinople), already had the right to 'judge as deputies of the emperor' (*uice sacra iudicans*). However, as the official correspondence of Q. Aurelius Symmachus as urban prefect of Rome in 384 demonstrates, referrals to the emperor were often made when there were political issues involved or a case for clemency to be made.[47] This was not, therefore, a role that the emperor could, or should, have surrendered to others.

That this system worked overall, despite the emperor's increasingly detached attitude from his responsibilities, was due to the consistory's political astuteness, which was to be demonstrated in the second reform of the decade, the formalising of the involvement of the Senate of Constantinople in the process of law-making.[48] In 446, the process by which a law was created was set out in a constitution addressed to the Senate. Senators participated alongside the consistory in the preliminary discussion about the need for,

[46] *CJ* 7.62.32.*pr.* and 7.62.32.1 (May 440), see Honoré 1998: 161.
[47] See for example Symm. *Rel.* 49 on a procedurally incorrect *agens in rebus*, and usefully C. M. Kelly 2004: 216–19; Sogno 2006: 34–40.
[48] *CJ* 1.14.8 (October 446); discussed by Honoré 1986: 136–7; Harries 1988: 165–6; Matthews 2000: 171–2; Millar 2006: 201–3. Although I read this as a reform, it is possible that the law merely formalised existing practice; for earlier examples of Senate and consistory working together, see Millar 2006: 203–7.

and contents of, a new law. Once agreement had been reached, the *quaestor* was ordered to make a draft, which was then to be submitted to both Senate and consistory for further discussion and amendment. Finally, the agreed law was to be read out and the imperial signature affixed. Much is made of consultation and consensus at every stage, and, while emphasis on unanimity is a standard part of imperial rhetoric, in this context, it has a particular resonance. Procedures had been set out which brought the Senate into the heart of governance. While this would also make the process more cumbersome, the Theodosian regime, confronted by the threat of Attila in the Balkans and perhaps undermined by a perceived lack of direction at home, was reinforced by the recruitment of the Constantinople senators as stakeholders in the existing imperial order.

Honours, status, patronage

Although the consistory was a low-key institution, for its individual members it mattered that their contribution be visibly and permanently acknowledged. While the membership fluctuated, the system over which the consistory presided enabled a powerful official, on leaving office, to perpetuate his standing through continuing access to the imperial presence, the right to attend the emperor's feasts and to participate in other festivities, in his own allocated place of honour.[49] The institutionalising of precedence in public social and ceremonial contexts by consistory fiat and the consistory control over allocation of privileges, when requested, bound the court to the emperor and the emperor himself to his advisers. Those honoured by direct communication from the inner sanctum were more restricted in number, as the hierarchy became more entrenched. Praetorian prefects and urban prefects of Constantinople predominate, although we occasionally glimpse the other dignitaries copied in for information.[50]

---

[49] *CTh* 6.8.1 (November 422), 6.13.1 (March 413) and 6.22.8.1 (September 425) (right of *consistoriani* to approach 'our oracle').

[50] *CTh* 8.7.21 (22 June 426), 22 and 23 (both 1 July 426), the same law modified to three addressees; 6.28.8 (January 435) to the *magister officiorum* Valerius, with copies to the praetorian prefects of the East and Illyricum, the urban prefect of Constantinople, the

The consistory was a group of power players in their own right. Membership allowed them regulation of an administrative system, which they knew well already, from within. Thus power struggles could be almost literally papered over. Take registers (*laterculi*), for example. The *quaestor sacri palatii* Sallustius, who, as *quaestor*, had no dedicated departmental staff, is assured, in 424, of his complete control of the Lesser Register, *Laterculum Minus*, of which a half had to be reclaimed from the *magistri militum*; the *magister officiorum* Helion was copied in to ensure enforcement.[51] Later in the same year, a lesser official is given oversight of another register, ensuring that vacancies were filled in accordance with the order of the names on the register and not by queue-jumpers benefiting from 'corrupt solicitation'.[52] In 430, the *magister officiorum* Paulinus submitted to the consistory a full report on the persistently troublesome imperial messenger service (*agentes in rebus*) – whose duties had always and inevitably involved some degree of surveillance – along with a proposal for a register of 1,174 names. The consistory agreed that even those excluded should be allowed to retain some privileges.[53] Registers mattered because their contents provided scope for patronage; their contents had to be protected from rival, unauthorised patrons bent on tampering with them. It would be up to the controller of the register to decide on who was included and on the order of names; this form of patronage was accepted as in line with the rules.

Honours were, in theory, solely in the emperor's gift. *Beneficia*, one-off favours to individuals, were, however, frowned upon by a consistory determined to prioritise rules at the expense of discretion and *beneficia* were repeatedly disallowed if they were incompatible with the content of consistory law.[54] Here, the two cultures

---

comes Aegypti and *comes Orientis*, the *praefectus Augustalis* (in Egypt), the proconsul of Achaea, and the *uicarii* of Asia and Pontus. For the role of the praetorian prefect in proposing and promoting *suggestiones*, see Millar 2006: 207–14; for lack of sources for private law initiatives, Honoré 1998: 158–9.

[51] *CTh* 1.8.2 and 3 (both April 424); Jones 1964: II 641.
[52] *CTh* 1.6.12 (December 424).   [53] *CTh* 6.27.23 (April 430).
[54] For example, *CTh* 4.14.1 (November 424) to Asclepiodotus; 6.2.26 (21) (January 428) to Proculus, urban prefect of Constantinople; 8.4.29 (July 428) to Florentius, praetorian prefect of the East. Contrast the flexibility of the consistory with regard to numbers of *parabalani* (health workers) in Alexandria, *CTh* 16.2.42 (September/October 416) and 16.2.43 (February 418).

attendant on the operation of patronage and of rule-making were directly in conflict and the implication of the *consistoriani* in networks of patronage undermined their resolve to limit its abuse. Instead, the conferment of *beneficia* on individuals was elevated to a general principle; a privilege granted to a favoured, sometimes named, individual was extended to all. As part of the reform of teaching, for example, which, in 425, set out how education in the capital was to work, Theodosius informed the urban prefect of Constantinople that five named teachers of Latin and Greek grammar and rhetoric, along with one legal expert (*iurisperitus*), Leontius, were to receive the status of count of the first rank (*comes primi ordinis*) and a place in the official hierarchy equivalent to that of a *uicarius*;[55] thereafter those who combined good morals with effective teaching for twenty years in the imperial capital would receive the same recognition.[56] Privileges could also be extended to reinforce policy. In education, the one area that Theodosius made his own,[57] extensive and anomalous exemptions were allowed to educators, who were granted the rank of *comes primi ordinis*, exempted from the general requirement to provide lodgings for soldiers[58] and freed from payment of the *collatio glebalis*, one of many exceptions from the general regulation making those promoted to senatorial rank liable to senatorial taxes and *munera*.[59]

Theodosius' generosity – or his inability to say no – both extended honours and cheapened them. In a series of laws from 416, leading members of the emperor's elite military entourage (*domestici*), followed a few weeks later by their sister corps (*protectores*), achieved senatorial status and exemption from senatorial burdens.[60] After this was extended further down the ranks in 427,[61] the Senate of Constantinople also became involved, as loose

---

[55] *CTh* 6.21.1 (March 425).
[56] For the restrictions on the numbers of the official teachers at Constantinople, see *CTh* 14.9.3 and 15.1.53 (both February 425).
[57] Lemerle 1971: 63–4; Alan Cameron 1982: 285–7.
[58] *CTh* 13.3.18 (August 427).
[59] *CTh* 13.3.19 (July 428) to be read with 6.2.26 (January 428), to Proculus; see also Jones 1964: II 707–8.
[60] *CTh* 6.24.8 (November 416), 6.24.9 (December 416) with Jones 1964: II 639–40.
[61] *CTh* 6.24.10 (March 427).

ends were tidied up and it was agreed that the privileges should be extended to the end of the year in which the beneficiary died, so that his family would be less upset by his loss.[62] Also in 416, a generous year it seems, three deputy heads of the secretariats (*scrinia*), named as Benagius, Hypatius and Theodorus, petitioned for recognition as *comites secundi ordinis*, again with equivalent rank to a *uicarius*; this was granted and extended to all deputies in the future. Like generosity was shown in the 420s, when the Praetorian Prefect Florentius received a constitution ordering a grant of the same privileges to the palace administrators (*palatini*) of the imperial estates (*res priuata*) as those already enjoyed by the office of the *sacrae largitiones*; clearly the *comes rei priuatae* had been quick to spot, and complain about, the anomaly.[63] Given their open-handedness with honours, it may have been a relief to many that the consistory counts (*comites consistoriani*) contented themselves with the privileges already sanctioned by Theodosius I, insisting only that those who had performed actual service should always outrank absentees who had received letters of support, regardless of the dates on the testimonials.[64]

Most remarkable was the elevation in status of the *praepositus sacri cubiculi* (head of the imperial bedchamber), an official, sometimes a eunuch, whose privileged access to emperors over the years had made him both envied and suspect in the eyes of contemporaries; previous holders of the position had included the controversial Eutropius, chief minister of the emperor Arcadius.[65] In 422, Florentius, as urban prefect of Constantinople, received instructions that the *praepositi* were, from the date of the law, to rank alongside former praetorian and urban prefects and *magistri militum* as *illustres*.[66] Within the grade, precedence was to be determined by date of promotion although, by post-dating the elevation of all former *praepositi* to the date of the law, the ruling avoided offence to past prefects and generals, who might have found themselves unexpectedly outranked. The constitution may

---

[62] *CTh* 6.24.11 (June 432).
[63] *CJ* 12.23.14.
[64] *CTh* 6.22.8 (September 425).
[65] See Jones 1964: II 566–70; also, in a more literary vein, Long 1996b.
[66] *CTh* 6.8.1 (November 422).

have caused some disquiet. An official, of suspect antecedents, who was a personal servant of the emperor, rather than holder of a public post, had been intruded into the political and social elite of the capital. Moreover, and in line with the practice noted above, the constitution was framed in terms of a *beneficium* to an individual, Macrobius, whose outstanding services as *praepositus* had prompted the upgrading of his job for all past and future holders.[67]

Codification and innovation

The absence of a personal imperial agenda affects the quality of the Theodosian legislative programme as a whole. It is possible to identify the interests of some individual officials, such as the pushy Florentius, with his earnest but ill-fated concern to reform the morals of the capital by banning prostitution, an aspiration frustrated by the heads of the taxation bureaux, concerned for their revenues.[68] Florentius must also have acquired a reputation as a scourge of delinquents. His report in 428 on decurions who had entered the imperial service illegally was rewarded with a law reiterating previous policy banning the recruitment of decurions and invalidating past and future imperial rescripts to the contrary.[69] A decade later, as praetorian prefect for the second time, his powers over the appointment of governors were reinforced with repetition of the rules governing their expense claims, which derived ultimately from the Augustan law on extortion, and which stipulated a penalty

---

[67] He is not to be confused with the author of the *Saturnalia*, Macrobius Ambrosius Theodorus, praetorian prefect of Italy in 430; see Alan Cameron 1966 and 2011: 231–9.
[68] *CTh* 15.8.2 (April 428) to Florentius, and *NTh* 18.1 to Cyrus of Panopolis; on Florentius and prostitutes in 428, see Traina 2007: 57. More generally, *PLRE* II 478–80 (Florentius 7); not all of his prefectures can be identified. His extensive concern for church politics is not discussed here: see, for example, the law addressed to Florentius requiring clerical visitors to carry references from their bishop, *CJ* 1.3.22.2 dated in the mss to 445, but perhaps earlier (430?). For a comprehensive law on different manifestations of heretical belief, see *CTh* 16.5.65 (May 428) and the fines to be imposed, which provincial judges have no power to mitigate; the prime mover may be Florentius or Nestorius (or both). For a full discussion of these laws and Theodosian policy on heresy, see Flower pp. 184–94, this volume.
[69] *CTh* 8.4.29 (July 428).

of fourfold restitution of money improperly acquired.[70] A second prominent individual, Cyrus of Panopolis, praetorian and urban prefect in the early 440s, was credited with legislation allowing the issue of judicial decisions by the ruling power and the framing of wills in Greek;[71] as urban prefect he is said to have introduced street lighting in the capital.[72] But, although Florentius and others could sustain their influence over decades, whether or not they were in office, their power to affect matters directly was limited by the restrictions placed on their terms of office. All officials therefore, when they left office, ran the risk that others might reverse their decisions, unless the emperor could be relied upon to uphold them. However, there is no sense, as there is with, say, the laws of Constantine or Theodosius I, that Theodosius II had a vision of what he wanted his Greek-Roman imperial society to be.[73]

In the absence of a reformist steer from the top, the consistory lawyers sought to impose a system on the vast body of law already available to them. The lengthy *oratio* to the Senate at Rome, issued in November, 426, set out how the law and the judicial system were to work, including which jurists were to be cited in law courts. It also provided an extraordinary brief guide to the law of succession. Whether this was the work of the lawyers of Valentinian III or of Theodosius II, it reflects a legal culture shared, still, by the lawyers of Rome and Constantinople – perhaps one of the last vestiges of imperial unity. The aim of the *oratio* was to reduce the complexities of legal procedure and the rules of inheritance to a manageable statement, which could act as a point of reference thereafter – as the *Theodosian Code* would also do.[74]

This drive for simplicity and clarity is evidenced also in Theodosius' social legislation. In February 428, the emperor issued to Hierius, praetorian prefect of the East, a set of regulations on

---

[70] *CJ* 9.27.6 (November 439).
[71] Joh. Lydus, *Mag.* 2.12 = 3.42 with Jones 1964: II 601–2; C. M. Kelly 2004: 32, 253 n. 32. *NTh* 16.1.8 (September 439), addressed to Florentius, extends the use of Greek to legacies, manumissions and the appointment of tutors. On Cyrus' career, see *PLRE* II 336–9 (Cyrus 7) and Alan Cameron 1982: 221–70; for a different reading, Holum 1982: 189–93.
[72] *Chron. Pasch.* 450 (I 588.11–12).
[73] Honoré 1998: 159, 'it is difficult to point to any personal imprint of the emperor on the laws, apart from an emphasis on moderation and restraint'.
[74] Above n. 44.

marriage and the law of succession. Repeatedly, peripheral formalities are set aside. No formal record was required at all for gifts worth less than 200 *solidi*; or for gifts received by under-age girls without a father to take care of their interests.[75] Wives or their heirs defrauded by their husbands (or their heirs) were to receive their rights, regardless of legal technicalities, *scrupulositas iuris*.[76] Any form of words would suffice to ratify a dowry agreement, even if a formal *stipulatio* failed to materialise.[77] And Romans of Cicero's day and earlier would have recognised the Theodosian definition of marriage, which depended, the emperor wrote, not on the presence of a dotal or prenuptial agreement, or on a wedding procession (*pompa*) or other form of ceremonial but on a number of simple conditions: that the parties were equal in status, that no law prevented them and that there existed the consent of the parties themselves and the *fides* of their friends.[78] The centrality to what marriage was of the *affectio maritalis*, the agreement to be married, had survived the Christian revolution intact, although policy on divorce would prove more controversial.[79]

The consistory therefore came to the codification project in March 429 with a set of traditionalist assumptions already put into practice about how system could be imposed on heterogeneous collections of legal material. The initial idea was a bold one: to collect and excerpt not only imperial constitutions from the time of Constantine onwards, but also the writings of the jurists, which would be combined, finally, in a comprehensive statement of the law to be remembered forever under the name of Theodosius II.[80] After eight years of work, collecting and then editing their

---

[75] *CTh* 3.5.13 = *CJ* 5.3.17 which omits the 200 *solidi* exemption.
[76] *CTh* 3.5.13 passage again omitted from *CJ*.
[77] *CTh* 3.13.4 = *CJ* 5.11.6.
[78] *CTh* 3.7.3 = *CJ* 5.4.22.
[79] *NTh* 12.1 (July 439) removes penalties for unilateral divorce, largely nullifying *CTh* 3.16.2 (March 421); but some penalties were reimposed in 449/450 (*CJ* 5.17.8.4, with *PLRE* II 571 on the date) – divorce was clearly controversial within the consistory; see usefully Evans Grubbs 1995: 235–7.
[80] *CTh* 1.1.5 (26 March 429); for rules on editing collected material, see *CTh* 1.1.6 (December 435). Note also the law of the same date in March 429, addressed to Florentius, that copies of supporting documentation should not be attached to petitions unless necessary for the elucidation of the content (*CJ* 1.19.8). The *Theodosian Code* was not the only item of business.

material, the compilers produced, in late 437, the first, and only, result of their efforts, the first stage of the project, which was duly adorned by the emperor's name, although the larger enterprise was never formally abandoned.[81] The arrangement of the *Code* was in line with legal tradition, beginning with five books effectively commenting on the Perpetual Edict, and ending with material on right (and wrong) religion. The compilers did not see legislation relating to Christianity per se as a separate category; the asylum law referred to above is included in the 'crime book', Book 9, which also contained earlier Christian emperors' laws on the abuse of magic and unlawful divination.[82] On the same principle, regulations about episcopal jurisdiction belonged with material on courts, not on bishops, as did also regulation of manumission of slaves in churches. The ministers of the Christian emperor, though Christian themselves, were not about to sacrifice the traditions of their discipline to the new religious order.

Theodosius II reigned for half a century, for thirty years of which he was an adult and therefore in theory capable of self-assertion. His survival in difficult times over so long a period, terminated not by assassination or revolt but by an apparent accident, was itself an achievement. Yet, as I have argued, the laws issued by his consistory and included in his *Code* do not show a single driving force for any kind of reform, consistently advocated and pursued. Instead, we have a consistory of consolidators, well versed in the legal tradition, which they sought to systematise and perpetuate through both individual constitutions and the promulgation of the *Theodosian Code* itself. Some individuals, like the remarkably durable Florentius, emerge from the shadows, as do administrative dynasties, such as the families of Anthemius and Flavius Taurus. Continuity of tenure of office, however, and of influence could

---

[81] See Harries 1993; Honoré 1998: 123–53; Matthews 2000: 55–84.

[82] Perhaps due to accidents of survival, there is no evidence in the *Code* that the Theodosian jurists had any interest in criminal law. The latest constitution included was issued by Honorius to Caecilianus, praetorian prefect of Italy and Illyricum, in January 409, for which see *CTh* 9.2.6; 9.3.7; 9.16.12 (astrologers); 9.31 (children not to be given to herdsmen to rear); 9.36.2; 9.37.4.

not be guaranteed and access to consistory deliberations depended ultimately on the emperor's patronage. The fate of Cyrus of Panopolis, exiled in the early 440s, was a reminder that courtiers could fall from grace. There was therefore a lack of consistency over time at the heart of government. The Theodosian legal project, initially conceived as three codes consisting of a collection of imperial constitutions, a definitive collection of extracts from the jurists and a final code containing a complete statement of 'law', was one casualty of the lack of central direction. Had Theodosius shared the convictions of Antiochus, Justinian's *Corpus Iuris Civilis*, which consisted of the *Codex* of imperial constitutions, the *Digest* (of extracts from the jurists) and the *Institutes*, a summary statement of legal principle, might have emerged a century earlier than it did.

Formally, decisions affecting the daily lives of the peoples of the empire rested, not with the imperial sisters, or even the imperial consort, but with the secretive group of all-powerful advisers, who issued rulings on matters as diverse as the purchase of crown lands in the Thebaid by their tenants[83] or the abuse of bath privileges by *duces* on the Euphrates frontier.[84] The consistory both protected and controlled the emperor. Yet it was possible, in practice, for the emperor to dispense with the services of his advisers, simply by not convening meetings, if he so chose.[85] Certainly, in the 440s, the consistory's productivity, in terms of constitutions, abruptly declined. On Honoré's reckoning, after a rush of twenty-eight laws drafted by the *quaestor*, Martyrius, in 438–439, the rate of issue in 440 slowed to nine, and a mere fifteen laws were issued between 445 and 450, making an average of three a year.[86]

The emperor's apparent disinclination for active leadership, as evidenced in his delegation of appeals and abandoning of the full codification project, when combined with the instability created by competing foci of power at court, could have seriously destabilised the governance of the empire and threatened the survival of the Theodosian regime. That they did not is a tribute

---

[83] *CTh* 5.12.2 (August 415).
[84] *CTh* 7.11.2 (July 417).
[85] But for an alternative view see Jones 1964: I 337.
[86] Honoré 1998: 167–9 (Martyrius); 173 (number of laws post 445).

to the resilience of the court administration as a self-sustaining bureaucracy, in which the ambitions of individuals, sometimes over several generations, could be realised through decades of service and proximity to the imperial presence. The concomitant evolution of a rule-based culture from which not even the emperor was exempt enabled his officials to impose their own agenda and even, in exceptional cases, such as that of the *Theodosian Code* itself, to implement, if only in part, a project of major and lasting significance.

With all this, Pulcheria, her sisters and Eudocia had little to do. Theirs was a different kind of power, exercised in parallel with the traditional functions of government. The Theodosian women acted as the public projection of a dynastic image; the piety of the imperial house provided divine sanction for their rule. Yet, although buttressed by co-operative administrators, the Theodosian dynastic experiment also spelled potential danger, because it prevented the family from fortifying itself by intermarriage against the pretensions of rivals. There could be no sons-in-law of Arcadius and their descendants, who could identify themselves with the longer-term interests of the Theodosian dynasty. Imperial celibacy also limited the potential production of heirs, laying a heavy responsibility on the only married child of Arcadius, Theodosius himself, to produce a son and rear him to adulthood.[87] Had the hunting accident which unexpectedly ended the emperor's life happened ten or twenty years earlier, the Roman empire, though nominally reunited under the unimpressive aegis of Valentinian III, could have risked slipping into chaos and civil war.

The publicity accorded the imperial women and the relative secrecy attendant on the consistory also challenged conventional gender discourse.[88] The public world was, traditionally, that of men; the portrayal of Theodosius' education in the martial arts (by Pulcheria) and the celebration of victories (where possible) were conventional adjuncts to imperial masculinity. But ascetic Christianity had made it possible for dedicated virgins also to be

---

[87] Of Theodosius' three children by Eudocia, Flaccilla and Arcadius (if he existed) both died young and only Licinia Eudoxia, wife of Valentinian III, reached adulthood; see Alan Cameron 1982: 266–7.
[88] See Cooper 2009, although the problems raised by Pulcheria are, sadly, not addressed.

regarded as 'men'. Pulcheria's translation of (masculine) virginity into a new imperial familial, but celibate, discourse was thus a creative extension of the boundaries of what a woman could achieve in a world of men. Yet she had not substituted the family of Christ for that of Theodosius; her dual role, as virgin and dynast (but not mother or wife) was made possible by her membership of an imperial family, which supported her pretensions. Conversely, and despite its ceremonial role and public honours for individuals, consistory deliberation was the preserve of the confidential spaces of the inner imperial *domus*, traditionally the domain of women. This partial role-reversal, characteristic of a regime more addicted to diplomacy than military aggression, and to pious sexual continence more than to the dynastic imperative of reproduction, was an experiment endorsed by the acquiescence of the civilian governing classes in Constantinople and reinforced by the utterances of self-interested panegyrists. In its denial of the military and political realities beyond the city walls, it was also one that could not last.

CHAPTER 3

THEODOSIUS AND HIS GENERALS

Doug Lee

In the course of his account of the reign of Theodosius I, the church historian Sozomen describes how divisions emerged among Arian Christian groups in the 380s, and comments on their subsequent development. He notes that while the divisions persisted in most cities, the Arians in Constantinople were reunited thirty-five years later, in the reign of Theodosius II. That reunion was effected through the agency of the general Flavius Plinta, a Goth, whom Sozomen describes as being one of the most powerful men at court in the mid 420s.[1] He does not, regrettably, elaborate on any other ways in which Plinta exploited his influence, but his comment serves to draw attention to one of the paradoxes presented by the generals of Theodosius' reign. As Sozomen's account implies (and as is confirmed in the parallel version of the church historian Socrates[2]), Plinta was himself an adherent of one of the Arian groups in question, which made him a religious outsider from the perspective of the imperial establishment; yet it seems that this did not prevent him from holding high military office or exercising significant influence in state affairs.

Furthermore, Plinta was not the only prominent general during Theodosius' reign to be at odds with the regime's religious stance. Flavius Ardabur, an Alan and also a leading general during the 420s, was another Arian Christian,[3] as too was his son

---

I am grateful to participants at the original colloquium in March 2011 for questions and comments, but above all to Christopher Kelly for his meticulous editing and suggestions for improvements.

[1] Soz. 7.17.14: δυνατώτατος τότε τῶν ἐν τοῖς βασιλείοις γεγονώς; *PLRE* II 892–3.
[2] Soc. 5.23.12.
[3] Theophanes 5943 (104.19–20), not cited as evidence of his Arianism in *PLRE* II 137–8 (Ardabur 3).

Aspar, already a significant military figure (even if his period of greatest political influence came after Theodosius' death).[4] In addition, their ethnic origins are likely to mean that the Goths Flavius Ariobindus and Arnegisclus – both senior generals in the latter half of Theodosius' reign – were Arians as well, as also the Vandal Ioannes.[5] Perhaps even more surprisingly, a number of Theodosius' generals are attested as being pagan in their religious allegiance.[6] The best known of these was Flavius Zeno, an Isaurian who was prominent in the final years of Theodosius' reign,[7] to whom can be added his associate Apollonius[8] and the mysterious Lucius, known from a somewhat vague passage in the (now fragmentary) *Philosophical History* by the sixth-century Neoplatonist Damascius.[9] It is perhaps worth adding, lest the impression should be given that all of Theodosius' generals were religiously heterodox, that there were also at least some orthodox Christians holding high military office, for example, Dionysius and Anatolius.[10]

It is no doubt tempting to relate this pattern of apparent religious *laissez-faire* to Theodosius' own lack of military experience

---

[4] *PLRE* II 164–9, with references to Arianism at 168; discussion of his career in Croke 2005 (though focusing primarily on the post-Theodosian period).

[5] Ariobindus: Malalas 364; *PLRE* II 145–56 (Ariobindus 2). Arnegisclus: his son Anagastes was of Gothic origin, see John of Antioch 297; *PLRE* II 151 (Arnegisclus), 75–6 (Anagastes); Ioannes: *PLRE* II 597 (Ioannes 13).

[6] A law of December 416 (*CTh* 16.10.21) banned 'those who are defiled by the wicked delusion or indeed offence of pagan observances, that is the pagans' from admission to the *militia*, which might be taken to mean a prohibition on pagans serving in the army. However, the term *militia* was also used of the civilian bureaucracy, which seems to be its sense here, since the law continues with more specific reference to *administratores uel iudices*.

[7] Theod. *Ep.* 71; cf. Damascius, *History* 115A (ed. P. Athanassiadi, Athens, 1999), where the allusion to 'the great general of the East' is generally accepted as being a reference to Zeno: *PLRE* II 1200 (Zenon 6); Thompson 1946: 28; Demandt 1970: 743; von Haehling 1980: 87–8.

[8] Theod. *Ep.* 73; *PLRE* II 121 (Apollonius 3) argues on the basis of Theod. *Ep.* 103, that by 448 Apollonius had converted to Christianity, but this seems unlikely given that he remained a supporter of the pagan Zeno; it is more likely, as argued by Azéma 1964: 158 n. 1, that Theod. *Ep.* 103 was addressed to a different Apollonius.

[9] Damascius, *History* 115A; although this text does not specify which Theodosius was emperor at the time, it is generally accepted that Lucius held office as general during the reign of Theodosius II: *PLRE* II 692 (Lucius 2); Demandt 1970: 747; von Haehling 1980: 85–6.

[10] *V. Sym. Styl.* (Syr.) 83–4 (ed. P. Bedjan, *Acta Martyrum et Sanctorum* 4, Paris, 1894; trans. Doran 1992: 163–5); Theod. *Ep.* 79, 92 with useful discussion in Schor 2011: 49–52, 146–8, 173–6; *PLRE* II 364–6 (Dionysius 13), 84–6 (Anatolius 10).

or ability; after all, he was, as the historian Priscus observed bluntly, ἀπόλεμος – 'unwarlike'.[11] This could be taken to imply that he was in no position to stand up to generals who did not conform to imperial norms in their religious beliefs. However, before accepting this conclusion, it is worth bearing in mind another paradox presented by the generals of Theodosius' reign. Despite the emperor's lack of military experience or ability, there appear to have been few, if any, attempts at armed usurpation during his lengthy reign.[12] At one point, Damascius in his *Philosophical History* does claim that the otherwise unknown general Lucius entered the palace (date and circumstances unspecified) intent on killing the emperor until apparently prevented from doing so by some sort of apparition[13] – but given the obscurity of this episode, little can be made of it. Theodosius is also reported to have feared, in the final years of his reign, that Flavius Zeno was planning to overthrow him.[14] Theodosius' concern was such that he was said to have been contemplating the despatch of military forces against him: one army to Isauria, and another 'to the east' – presumably Antioch, where Zeno would have been based in his capacity as *magister utriusque militiae per Orientem*.[15] But if Theodosius' fears were warranted, then Zeno's plans came to nothing, although that may well have been because Theodosius' unexpected death in summer 450 removed the need for action, as Damascius' (rather confused) account implies.[16]

---

[11] Priscus 3.2; see further below p. 96.
[12] As noted by Millar 2006: 41; Elton 2009: 142; cf. Szidat 2010: 391.
[13] Damascius, *History* 115A; *PLRE* II 692 (Lucius 2); cf. Holum 1982: 82 with n. 17.
[14] Priscus 15.4.25–6, 16; cf. Damascius, *History* 115A.
[15] Priscus 16; for a reading of this passage as indicating planned military action against Zeno, rather than actual implementation (as Blockley 1983: 301 translates), see Zuckerman 1994: 173 n. 52 (endorsed by Feld 2005: 219 and, implicitly, by C. M. Kelly 2009: 233), who notes that implementation would effectively have initiated a civil war.
[16] Damascius, *History* 115A with *PLRE* II 1200. In addition to Lucius' and Zeno's attempted *coups*, Theodosius is also said to have 'banished Baudo and Daniel on the grounds that they were aiming at usurpation' (Priscus 16.7–8), but nothing further is known about either of them; *PLRE* II 221 (Baudo), 345 (Danielus 2). However, Baudo's name implies he was of Germanic origin, possibly a Frank given the similarity of his name to that of Flavius Bauto, *magister militum* in the 380s (*PLRE* I 159–60), which, in turn, makes it likely that he too was a military man.

THEODOSIUS AND HIS GENERALS

The aim of this chapter is to explore the evidence for the influence which generals exercised during Theodosius' reign, before turning to a consideration of the factors which contributed to that influence, alongside the strategies which Theodosius and his advisers used to manage and keep in check their power and ambitions. This is an appropriate point to make explicit what has so far been implicit – namely, that the focus of this chapter is on those men who held the highest rank in the army in this period, that of *magister militum*. That clarification in turn leads to another which it is important to register at the outset – namely, that the number of generals about whom any sort of detail is known from this period is rather fewer than might be expected for a span of nearly half a century and a high command which consisted of five senior posts. Those five posts comprised two *magistri militum praesentales*, who were based in the imperial 'presence' at or near Constantinople, and three regional *magistri* – of the East, Thrace and Illyricum respectively.[17] During the forty-two years of Theodosius' sole rule, therefore, there are 210 (42 x 5) years of service by *magistri* to be accounted for. However, the surviving evidence allows only about half of those years to be assigned to specific individuals.[18] Those individuals number somewhere in the low to mid twenties – there is scope for debate about the status of some – and of those, seven are no more than names, receiving only fleeting mention in imperial laws or the fragments of Priscus' history.[19]

That senior generals in this period were influential figures, and were viewed as such, is apparent from a range of evidence beyond Sozomen's comment about Plinta's position at court in the mid 420s. The correspondence of Theodoret, bishop of Cyrrhus in Syria, includes a number of letters addressed to one or other of Theodosius' generals. Some of these letters were concerned with enlisting their aid in the ecclesiastical turmoil in the two decades after the Council of Ephesus and in reversing the imperial order

---

[17] *Not. Dig. Or.* 5–9.
[18] For *fasti* (not in agreement in every detail), see Demandt 1970: 789–90 and *PLRE* II 1290–3.
[19] Those seven, as they appear in *PLRE* II, are: Agintheus, Florentius 2, Hypatius 1, Lupianus 1, Macedonius 4, Sapricius, Theodulus 2.

which in 448 confined Theodoret to Cyrrhus. It is unsurprising to find the orthodox Anatolius as the recipient of a good number of such missives,[20] but Theodoret also wrote to the Arian Aspar to thank him for his help.[21] Even those letters which were not explicitly related in some way to their assistance – a letter expressing regret on Anatolius' reposting from Syria to Constantinople, a letter of condolence to Zeno on the death of his brother, a letter of congratulations on Zeno's elevation to the consulship in 448, a letter to Apollonius combining praise for his military abilities with the hope that he might one day accept the truth of Christianity[22] – are nonetheless indicative of the assumption that these were men whose goodwill was worth cultivating.[23] The status of generals as figures of influence is also reflected in a rather different type of evidence arising from the ecclesiastical turmoil at the end of Theodosius' reign. A record of acclamations from the inhabitants of Edessa prior to the Council of Ephesus included both Anatolius and Zeno among the senior courtiers who received praise alongside the emperor.[24]

Laws later collected in the *Theodosian Code* provide some specific illustrations of the influence of generals at work. First, in a law of October 415 addressed to the *magister militum praesentalis*, Florentius, and copied to the other praesental *magister*, Sapricius, it becomes apparent that the generals had encroached on one of the areas of responsibility which had traditionally been within the remit of the *quaestor sacri palatii* (the senior imperial legal official) – namely, the issuing of commissions to tribunes, prefects and other officers in command of units in the *limitanei* (stationed in frontier provinces). It seems that the underlying issue was one of fees and the *quaestor*'s staff were not pleased at losing this source of income, while the *magistri* must have been keen to annex this role, both for its financial benefits and for the opportunities that it offered for the exercise of patronage. The result

---

[20] Theod. *Ep.* 79, 92, 111, 119, 121, 139 with Millar 2006: 222–4 for context and further detail.
[21] Theod. *Ep.* 140 with Schor 2011: 178.
[22] Theod. *Ep.* 45, 65, 71, 73.
[23] For a more general discussion of episcopal correspondence with generals in late antiquity, see Lee 2007: 153–63.
[24] Millar 2006: 200 with references.

was a compromise: the law did not attempt to reverse the situation completely, instead reassigning only a portion of the commissions (forty – out of how many?) to the *quaestor*.[25]

Second, in a law of March 441 addressed to Ariobindus, at that time one of the two *magistri militum praesentales*, the emperor agreed to grant certain legal privileges traditionally enjoyed by soldiers to some members of the administrative staff attached to *magistri militum*, doing so in response to a *suggestio* from Ariobindus himself.[26] The physical proximity of the *magistri militum praesentales* to the imperial court when not on campaign obviously facilitated such initiatives, as did their membership of the imperial consistory. Although the functioning of this advisory body during late antiquity is poorly understood due to the limited detail provided by surviving accounts – minutes were kept but have not been preserved apart from the occasional excerpt quoted in a law,[27] and there was no tradition of senior officials producing memoirs in their retirement – a couple of fourth-century examples show generals participating in, and seeking to influence, its deliberations, and it is likely that it remained a valuable forum in which generals could exert their influence in the first half of the fifth century.[28]

However, the most striking indication of the influence of Theodosius' generals may well have come in the immediate aftermath of the emperor's death. While Theodosius' sister Pulcheria no doubt had some role in the approval of Marcian as successor to the imperial throne, Marcian's close association with Aspar over many years as one of his staff officers, including service under him during the campaign against the Vandals in the early 430s, makes it inconceivable that Aspar did not have a significant hand in Marcian's elevation. At the same time, it has been argued persuasively that Zeno was the general in the strongest position at

---

[25] *CTh* 1.8.1 with Jones 1964: II 641; a subsequent law a decade later restored the rest of the commissions to the *quaestor*'s office: *CTh* 1.8.2 (April 424).
[26] *NTh* 7.4 with Jones 1964: I 352.
[27] See Jones 1964: I 103, 336, citing *CTh* 1.22.4 (383).
[28] See Jones 1964: I 333–5 for membership and fourth-century examples: the responses to the usurpation of Silvanus in 355 and to the Senate's request for the restoration of the Altar of Victory in 384. Sozomen's comment on Plinta's influence at court (above n. 1) perhaps reflects, at least in part, his role in Theodosius' consistory.

the time of Theodosius' death and must therefore also have given his agreement – perhaps in return for his promotion to the rank of *patricius*.[29]

What, then, were the bases of generals' power in the age of Theodosius? In answering this question, it is natural to focus on their control of military units and the potential leverage this gave them, particularly in relation to an emperor who had little opportunity or inclination to interact with his troops. To be sure, Theodosius was alert to opportunities to celebrate (and to capitalise on) their successes, most obviously in 425 following news of the defeat of the usurper John in Italy by eastern forces. The news reached Constantinople during races at the Hippodrome, and, having announced the news, Theodosius proceeded to lead an impromptu procession of thanksgiving through the Hippodrome to church.[30] However, the only known circumstance in which Theodosius might have had sustained contact with some of his armed forces occurred in that very context when, according to one source, he planned to accompany the expedition to place Valentinian III on the imperial throne in the West in 425, until he fell ill en route in Thessalonica and had to return to Constantinople.[31] There is never even a hint that he addressed troops at the parade-ground of the Hebdomon outside the walls of Constantinople.[32]

[29] Burgess 1993–4 argues trenchantly against Pulcheria having had any influence in the decision; Zuckerman 1994: 172–6 argues for the strength of Zeno's position in relation to Aspar in 450 and for both having a role in Marcian's elevation; Michael Whitby 2000: 60 n. 12 advances further arguments in favour of Pulcheria playing some part.

[30] Soc. 7.23.11–12; see Kelly pp. 230–1 and Gardiner pp. 251–2, this volume. An inscription commemorating the defeat of a usurper and the inauguration of a Golden Age, which has often been associated with these events, is much more likely to have been the work of Theodosius I following his defeat of Magnus Maximus in 388; see Bardill 1999.

[31] Soc. 7.24.4. There is no suggestion in Socrates' notice that Theodosius intended to participate in any actual combat; presumably the plan was analogous to Claudius' carefully orchestrated involvement in the invasion of Britain in 43, which allowed him to garner the kudos of military success, without any attendant risks to his personal safety (Suet. *Claud.* 17, Cassius Dio 60.19–22 with Levick 1990: 141–3).

[32] Had Theodosius not been only a few months short of his first birthday when he was proclaimed Augustus by his father Arcadius at the Hebdomon in January 402, he might have addressed the assembled troops as, for example, Leo (then in his late fifties) was able to do at his accession in February 457 (Const. Porph. *Cer.* 1.91). In adult life, Theodosius clearly took an interest in hunting, since it was his fall from his horse while hunting which led to his death in July 450 (*PLRE* II 1100), and it may be that his involvement

As for the troops available to the *magistri*, these did not directly include all armed forces in the eastern empire, since troops were divided into the two broad categories of field army units (*comitatenses*) under the direct command of the *magistri*, and units stationed in frontier provinces (*limitanei*) under the command of *comites* and *duces*. Nonetheless, *magistri* had by this period come to acquire a degree of authority over *limitanei*,[33] while the units classified as *comitatenses* must still have been substantial in number, even if that number is impossible to determine with any real degree of accuracy. For although the eastern section of the *Notitia Dignitatum* lists the names of the units under the command of each of the five *magistri* in the late fourth/early fifth century,[34] the size of units remains a matter for debate. On one estimate, however, each *magister* might have had something of the order of 20,000 soldiers at his disposal[35] – soldiers, moreover, who were regarded as being of superior quality to those in the *limitanei*. Furthermore, it is generally accepted that the armies of the two praesental *magistri* must have been based in close proximity to Constantinople,[36] and therefore in an ideal position to seize control of the capital and the palace, had their commanders wished to do so.[37]

However, while their control of armed forces was the most obvious factor underpinning their influence, one should not lose sight of other factors. One such aspect is the personal wealth which generals increasingly came to possess during late antiquity, glimpses of which are provided by texts and objects from the Theodosian period. Theodoret's correspondence includes two letters to the general Ariobindus, requesting that, in the context of difficult environmental conditions, he show leniency towards local peasants in the levying of, in one case, olive oil as a tax or rent, and in the other, of land rents.[38] In the first of these letters, he refers to a specific locale – that of Sergitheon, otherwise unknown

in this traditionally quasi-martial activity was at least partly an attempt to offset his non-military image; see Lee 2000: 36.
[33] Boak 1915: 145. [34] *Not. Dig. Or.* 5–9.
[35] Treadgold 1995: 63. [36] Jones 1964: II 609; Lee 2007: 166.
[37] Theodosius apparently feared Zeno as a threat requiring a military response (above n. 15), although Zeno was not a praesental *magister*, but, as *magister utriusque militiae per Orientem*, was based much further away in Antioch.
[38] Theod. *Ep.* XVIII, 23.

but presumably lying within Theodoret's diocese of Cyrrhus – where it is apparent that Ariobindus was a landowner; the second letter refers more generally to Theodoret's diocese, where again it is clear that Ariobindus possessed land. One of the Ardaburi owned a villa in the desirable suburb of Daphne near Antioch, where an inscription refers to τὸ πριβᾶτον Ἀρδαβουρίου – perhaps referring to a bath-house – while a villa near Constantinople, on the bay of Sosthenium, is described as having been that of an Ardabur.[39] According to some much later accounts, the Emperor Leo had previously been *curator* with responsibility for Aspar's estates.[40] A further intriguing item is the verse inscription from the floor of a bath-house in Isaurian Seleucia, complete with Homeric vocabulary and epithets. The inscription – here strikingly voiced in the first person – narrates the floor's sumptuous restoration by Paulina, patrician and wife of Zeno, 'dear to Ares', whom it is generally accepted must be Flavius Zeno:[41]

> Me – the floor – worn down by the passage of time, has the mistress
>   of women
> the patrician, spouse of Zeno, dear to Ares,
> Paulina, excelling in understanding and also in deeds,
> graciously adorned, and has not neglected me.
> For I lost my impressive appearance on account of old age;
> but now, thanks to a prudent and faultless woman,
> I glisten much more with marble ornaments,
> and after the burden of old age, I have embarked once more upon
>   my former youth.

[39] *IGLS* 998c; Just. *Nov.* 159.*pr.*; *PLRE* II 137 assigns both properties to the younger Ardabur, who only held the post of *magister* after Theodosius' death, while *IGLS* also assigns the villa at Daphne to him on the strength of his position as *magister militum per Orientem*. However, the repairs to the villa associated with the inscription are only dated broadly to the fifth century, and since his homonymous grandfather also held the post of *magister militum per Orientem* in the early 420s (*PLRE* II 137–8), and so was presumably based in Antioch, he could equally have been the owner. There is also no obvious reason why the villa near Constantinople could not have belonged to Ardabur senior.
[40] Theophanes 5961 (116.7–9); Zonaras 13.25 (III 250–1A) with Jones 1964: I 221 and III 41 n. 5.
[41] *SEG* 41.1408 with discussion in Şahin 1991: 155–63; Feissel 1999: 9–11; Lenski 1999: 452; Feld 2005: 221. As a number of these commentators remark, the literary qualities of the inscription are indicative of the cultural aspirations of a group whose vocation was not normally associated with gentility. Feissel further notes that a reference to a district of Constantinople named after a Paulina could well derive from her also owning property in the capital. For Seleucia's reputation for the beauty of its bath-houses in the mid fifth century, see *V. Theclae* 27 (ed. G. Dagron, Subsidia Hagiographica 62, Brussels, 1978).

To this register of property can be added items of portable wealth, including a silver reliquary which Anatolius is reported to have given to a church in Edessa in the 440s,[42] and a large decorated silver plate, 42 cm in diameter, which commemorated Aspar's consulship in 434. This latter item was used to present a clear visual image of three thoroughly Romanised generations of the Ardaburi clan: dressed in his toga and clasping sceptre and consular napkin, Aspar sits in a curule chair with his togate son Ardabur junior by his side, the two of them flanked by personifications of Rome and Constantinople, while (overhead) two roundels contain busts of Aspar's father, Ardabur senior, and of Plinta, both former consuls.[43]

These instances constitute what are surely only glimpses of a much more significant phenomenon. As for how such wealth was acquired by generals, some educated conjectures may be proposed. The regular salary of generals is not known, but, as noted by Alexander Demandt, the eagerness of barbarian leaders such as Alaric and Attila to extract the position of *magister militum* from the empire in the fifth century, while undoubtedly motivated in part by a desire for prestige and recognition, implies that the salary was substantial.[44] One might also have expected campaign booty to have been a valuable source of income, although explicit evidence to that effect from this period is limited.[45] Corrupt practices were clearly another possible means of enrichment, as implied by the praise given to Stilicho for abstaining from the sale of military office and the embezzlement of soldiers' allowances.[46] Of course, it is also possible that some of this wealth was received as gifts

---

[42] *Chron. Edess.* 61 (ed. L. Hallier, *TU* 9.1, Leipzig, 1892).
[43] Painter 1991–2 (inaccurate, however, on some details of historical context); Leader-Newby 2004: 46–7. The plate is now in the Museo Archeologico in Florence.
[44] Demandt 1980: 630–1; cf. also Zos. 5.10.1, concerning an individual given 'a military command [of an unspecified rank] which brought him a pleasing income (χρήματα ... κομψὰ)'; *PLRE* II 210–11 (Bargus).
[45] Arbazacius, who held fairly high military rank (*PLRE* II 127–8 [Arbazicius 1] suggests that of *comes rei militaris*), is said to have gained a great deal of booty from an Isaurian campaign in 404, after which he lapsed into a life of luxury; he is then said to have used some of this booty as a bribe to escape prosecution for dereliction of duty (Zos. 5.25.2–4). While this account is clearly tendentious in many respects, it presupposes the possibility of significant booty.
[46] Zos. 5.34.6.

from the emperor, for which there is explicit evidence from the fourth century and from the fifth-century West, if not directly from Theodosius' reign.[47]

The possession of such wealth was important because, among other things, it enhanced senior military commanders' ability to exercise patronage. The combination of landed estates and other income must also particularly have facilitated the building up of bodies of armed retainers in their personal employ, referred to by a range of terms including that of *bucellarii*. This phenomenon is best attested in the West in the earlier fifth century, with reference to Stilicho, Bonifatius and Aetius,[48] but there are, again, glimpses of the practice in the East during the fifth century. The clearest evidence derives from Aspar's post-Theodosian career, when his murder by the Emperor Leo in 471 led to serious public disorder in Constantinople through the activities of his large body of retainers,[49] while a few years earlier Leo had issued a law banning individuals from maintaining *bucellarii*, Isaurians or armed slaves as personal attendants – a measure perhaps directed, at least in part, at Aspar's personal retinue.[50]

> We want no one, in cities or the countryside, to have permission to have *bucellarii* or Isaurians or armed slaves [*armati serui*].
>
> 1 We ordain that if anyone, contrary to this wholesome ordinance of Our Clemency, attempts to have armed slaves [*manicipia armata*] or *bucellarii* or Isaurians on his estates or as his personal attendants [*in suis praediis aut iuxta se*], he shall, in addition to the fine of one hundred pounds of gold, be visited with very severe punishment.
> 2 The governors of the provinces must be on the watch that no one dares to violate these provisions of Our Clemency in any particular, knowing that if they disregard this order, they will be deprived of the belt of their rank and office, will be fined one hundred pounds of gold, and their safety and their life will be in danger. The chiefs of their staff will, besides the loss of their property, be visited with capital punishment.[51]

---

[47] Lee (in press) for the fourth-century evidence; for the fifth-century West, see Olymp. 23.3–9, discussed further below p. 106.
[48] Liebeschuetz 1990: 43–4; see also Schmitt 1994.
[49] *Chron. Pasch.* 467 (I 596.17–597.1).
[50] Liebeschuetz 1990: 47 n. 134.
[51] *CJ* 9.12.10 (August 468), with discussion in Feld 2005: 229–35.

Although this law post-dates Theodosius' reign by nearly two decades, *bucellarii* were certainly not a post-Theodosian phenomenon in the East. According to the *Notitia Dignitatum*, forces under the command of the *magister militum per Orientem* at the start of the fifth century included a unit of *comites catafractarii bucellarii iuniores*, although this cannot have been the *magister*'s personal retinue.[52] However, at around the same time, Alaric, who had probably recently been appointed *magister militum per Illyricum*, is said to have had ὀπαδοί, one of the other terms used of private retainers.[53] During Theodosius' reign itself, Priscus refers to individual retainers of both Plinta and Zeno,[54] while the large force of Isaurians with which Zeno defended Constantinople in 447 has likewise been interpreted as his personal retainers.[55] It also seems unlikely that Aspar only acquired his retinue during the reign of Leo. While such troops could be used for the benefit of the empire (as in Zeno's defence of Constantinople) they must also have given the political influence of *magistri* an additional edge.

A further factor worth noting briefly is the use of family connections to consolidate influence. One dimension of this is the way in which the sons of generals became senior officers themselves, most obviously the Ardaburii whose three generations held senior commands during the fifth century. To that well-known case can be added that of Plinta, whose son, Armatius, was a commander in Libya.[56] It is difficult to believe that, in these instances, the father's position did not have some part to play in the promotion of the son. Another dimension of family connections is the use of marriage by late Roman *magistri* to strengthen their position, an aspect which has been particularly emphasised by Alexander Demandt.[57] The highest profile examples of this phenomenon

---

[52] *Not. Dig. Or.* 7.25: 'one might conjecture that this unit was intended to enjoy a specially close relationship with the commander-in-chief' (Liebeschuetz 1990: 44).
[53] Syn. *De regno* 20.1 (ed. J. Lamoreux, Paris, 2008).
[54] Plinta: Priscus 2.13 (Sengilach, ἄνδρα τῶν ἐπιτηδείων); Zeno: Priscus 14.43 (Rufus, τῶν ἐπιτηδείων), 23.3.6–7 (Apollonius, τῶν ἐπιτηδείων); and see *PLRE* II 991 (Sengilachus), 958–9 (Rufus), 121 (Apollonius 3).
[55] Priscus 14.40 with Demandt 1980: 624; Jones 1964: I 203, on the other hand, considers them more likely to have been regular troops.
[56] Priscus 15.4.18–24; *PLRE* II 148.   [57] Demandt 1980: 622–8.

derive either from the West (for example, Stilicho's marriage to Theodosius I's niece and adopted daughter Serena) or from the post-Theodosian period in the East (for example, the marriage of Aspar's son Patricius to Leontia, daughter of the Emperor Leo), but during Theodosius' reign there does at least appear to have been a consolidation of ties between some military families: the presence of Plinta's name and image alongside those of Aspar and his father and son on Aspar's silver plate is generally assumed to reflect a marriage alliance between the two families.[58] It has also been suggested that, assuming Zeno's wife was indeed the Paulina of the bath-house inscription from Seleucia, then it might have been a case of his marrying a female relative of Paulinus, a high-ranking palatine bureaucrat (*magister officiorum*) in the middle years of Theodosius' reign.[59]

Before looking more closely at the ways in which the power and ambitions of generals were managed and constrained, it is worth reiterating briefly a few contextual matters. First, there is the institutional arrangement of senior commands which Theodosius inherited (that is, the five senior military commands: two *magistri militum praesentales* and three *magistri* responsible, respectively, for the East, for Thrace and for Illyricum). This was an arrangement which obviously served to reduce the chances of military power becoming concentrated in the hands of one man, as had happened, for example, with Stilicho in the West. It was an arrangement which also had the potential to encourage competition and rivalry between the generals, to the benefit of the emperor. More particularly, the existence of *two* praesental *magistri* was an important safeguard, given their proximity to the capital and the palace.

A further long-standing aspect of institutional arrangements which acted as a potential constraint on the ambitions of generals was the fact that the holders of the office of praetorian prefect, the most senior and powerful position in the civilian administration,

---

[58] *PLRE* II 892; Demandt 1980: 626; above p. 98.
[59] Croke 2005: 155 n. 32; *PLRE* II 846–7 (Paulinus 8).

continued to control the empire's fiscal arrangements and therefore the provisioning of the army.[60] Similarly, another civilian official, the *magister officiorum*, had oversight of the *fabricae*, the state arsenals responsible for the manufacture of armour and weapons.[61] Moreover, during Theodosius' reign, this same official acquired responsibility for the condition of *limitanei*, with the obligation to 'report back to us in the sacred consistory in the January of each year',[62] and although these units were not under the direct control of the *magistri*, they did fall more generally under their authority, on which this measure was therefore an encroachment.

Another contextual matter of a different sort – since it was beyond the emperor's control in any obvious sense – is the military record of generals under Theodosius. While they undoubtedly enjoyed some successes, notably in the war against Persia in the early 420s and in the campaign to overthrow the usurper John in the West in 425, they also experienced major setbacks, above all against the Vandals and against Attila in the 440s. While such setbacks will hardly have been a cause for secret rejoicing on Theodosius' part, they must nevertheless have helped to keep political ambitions in check, at least in the short to medium term. (By contrast, it was Zeno's – relative – success in the late 440s which enhanced his position and must have contributed to Theodosius' anxieties about his intentions.) The experience of defeat will also not have been conducive to the strengthening of the loyalties of soldiers towards their commander.

Alongside such contextual considerations can be placed proactive measures by the emperor and his advisers to encourage the loyalties of generals towards their 'commander'. Promotion of rising stars to senior military rank was an obvious strategy, and can be observed in a number of cases from Theodosius' reign. Plinta held the post of military *comes* in the East in 418, in which capacity he suppressed a rebellion in the province of Palaestina which was sufficiently significant to warrant an entry in the *Chronicle* of Marcellinus *comes*. Since, by the following year, Plinta was

---

[60] Jones 1964: I 448–62. [61] Lee 2007: 93–4.
[62] *NTh* 24.5 (September 443); on the *fabricae* and *limitanei*: Jones 1964: I 337, II 649–54, 834–6; Clauss 1980: 51–4, 125.

holding the post of praesental *magister militum*, it has seemed a reasonable deduction that he was promoted as a reward for his endeavours in Palaestina.[63] A few years later, a senior officer, Procopius, appears to have been advanced to the rank of *magister militum* of the East on the strength of the important role he played during the Persian War in 422.[64] While the granting of high rank in this way was partly a reward, it was presumably also expected to create a tie of obligation on the part of the recipient towards his benefactor.

Of course, promotion to a senior command could be double-edged since it might encourage an individual's ambitions to expand. And how did one continue to reward a general once he had gained one of the most senior ranks? One way was to bestow the high honour of patrician status, as attested for at least three of Theodosius' generals: Anatolius, Ariobindus and Procopius.[65] The laws of the Theodosian period also show evidence of ever more elevated epithets being applied to *magistri* – *ementissimus* ('most eminent'), *sublimis* ('lofty'), *culmen tuum* ('your highness').[66] However, the most obvious and, in some ways, more effective way of rewarding *magistri* was by granting a consulship. Because the consulate had long ceased to carry any of the powers which had once given it such pre-eminence, it is perhaps easy to underestimate its value in the emperor's armoury of strategies, but the consulship remained an honour which brought unparalleled prestige to its holders.[67] That prestige derived partly from the antiquity of the office which, by the start of Theodosius' reign, had been in existence for nearly a millennium; partly from the fact that the

---

[63] Marcell. com. 418.1; *PLRE* II 893; Sabbah 2008: 158 n. 1.
[64] *PLRE* II 920.
[65] *PLRE* II 84–6 (Anatolius 10) at 85, 145–6 (Ariobindus 2) at 146, 920 (Procopius 2). Plinta's absence from the list, despite the influence he is reported to have exercised (above n. 1), could simply be due to the limited evidence for his career; in particular, he does not appear to have been the recipient of any of the laws preserved in the *Theodosian Code*, where the record of such titulature is a particular feature. Aspar also gained patrician status, but the first attestation falls in 451 (*PLRE* II 167), raising the possibility that it was bestowed by Theodosius' successor Marcian, as seems more certain in the case of Zeno (see Zuckerman 1994: 174 n. 56).
[66] Boak 1915: 137–40.
[67] All reference to the consulate in what follows is to the so-called 'ordinary' consulate, 'whose holders entered upon office on the Kalends of January and gave their names to the year' (Jones 1964: II 532), as distinct from suffect consulships.

names of the consuls continued to provide the official dating formula for the year in which they held office, appearing on public inscriptions and imperial laws set up throughout the empire;[68] and partly from the unbroken exclusivity of the office, still restricted to only two individuals per year[69] – a particularly striking feature in the late Roman world where there was a tendency for other official posts to be multiplied with the passage of time. These features made the consulship an invaluable resource at the emperor's disposal.

From Theodosius' reign, eight generals can be identified as having held a consulship, distributed fairly evenly across the decades, and sometimes bearing a clear link with some recent military achievement – most obviously, Zeno in 448 following his successful defence of Constantinople against Attila the previous year, but probably also Plinta in 419 for his suppression of the rebellion in Palaestina and Ardabur, father of Aspar, in 427 for the defeat of the usurper John in 425.[70] Eight consulships across forty-two years might, however, seem a rather paltry return – less than 20 per cent of the total. However, it must be borne in mind that Theodosius himself held the consulate sixteen times during his sole reign, making eight consulships closer to 40 per cent of the remaining opportunities. This figure gains further significance when placed alongside the data from the reign of Theodosius' father, Arcadius, when only one out of thirteen consuls was a general (Flavius Fravitta in 401).[71]

Needless to say, granting the consulship to individuals outside the imperial family carried attendant risks, since the office gave those individuals greater prominence, while also potentially encouraging enlarged ambitions. However, the office also had certain double-edged duties, specifically the obligation to provide

---

[68] Cf. Joh. Lydus, *Mag.* 2.8, where the office of consul is superior in honour to that of praetorian prefect in part because 'it gives its name to the year'.
[69] Cf. Jones 1964: II 532–3; Bagnall *et al.* 1987: 6.
[70] The other cases comprise Varanes (410), Constans (414), Dionysius (429), Ariobindus (434) and Anatolius (440) (full details in Bagnall *et al.* 1987). Aspar also held the consulship in 434, but this honour was bestowed by the western court, perhaps at the instigation of Galla Placidia in (belated) recognition of his role in overthrowing John and ensuring the accession of her son Valentinian III (Bury 1923: 225; Oost 1968: 228).
[71] Cf. Demandt 1970: 755.

games for the urban populace in Constantinople.[72] It might be feared that the acclamation which successful games brought their provider would increase the danger to the emperor, but this is to overlook their financial implications; as one middle-ranking sixth-century bureaucrat observed, in a striking image, the consular dignity 'pours forth vast wealth to the citizens, after the manner of snowflakes, from private resources'.[73] There can be no doubt that provision of games remained a significant drain on the economic resources of the provider, as the early fifth-century historian and contemporary observer Olympiodorus testified. He reported that the sums spent by senatorial aristocrats of varying means on praetorian games in late fourth-century Rome ranged from 1,200 pounds of gold to 4,000 – figures which were close to the annual incomes of these individuals.[74] Although, as previously seen, generals could also become wealthy, it is unlikely to have been on the scale of senators, whose families had had many generations to accumulate riches, and indeed Olympiodorus again provides insight into the challenges they faced in this respect. He refers to the assumption of the consulship by two generals in 414 – Constans in the East and Constantius in the West – noting that the latter was able to fund his consular expenses only because, at his request, the Emperor Honorius gifted him the estate of the usurper Heraclianus, worth about 4,000 pounds of gold.[75] Individuals who did not receive imperial assistance in this way presumably faced a dilemma: if they endeavoured to make a significant impact through their consular games, they would consume significant personal resources, while if they tried to be more economical in their expenditure, they were likely to reduce their chances of impressing on a grand scale. A consulship was, then, an honour – but it could come at a high price.

---

[72] Jones 1964: II 537–9; Dagron 1974b: 150 n. 5.
[73] Joh. Lydus, *Mag.* 2.8.
[74] Olymp. 41.2 with Wickham 2005: 162–3. By this period, the office of praetor had become a purely honorific one held by senators in early adulthood and imposing an obligation on the individual's father to stage public games – an opportunity sometimes exploited for purposes of competitive display: Jones 1964: II 537–42; Matthews 1975: 13, 18.
[75] Olymp. 23.1–9.

Proactive measures might also have been expected to include the less subtle but obvious step of eliminating a general seen as too great a threat, in the way that the father of Theodosius I was executed in the mid 370s, and as Aspar was to be assassinated at Leo's command in 471.[76] Yet there is no clear-cut evidence for such a step during Theodosius' reign. Theophanes alleges that Theodosius' eunuch Chrysaphius was behind the death of the general Ioannes in 441,[77] and as already noted above, it is possible that the Baudo whom Theodosius exiled for plotting rebellion was, on the basis of his Germanic-sounding name, a military officer of some sort. However, neither case provides conclusive evidence.

Some of Theodosius' generals, then, undoubtedly exercised significant influence during his reign, occasionally to the point of causing the emperor to fear for his position. It remains striking, however, that such an unmilitary emperor never faced any serious military challenges. In part this was due to institutional safeguards which he inherited or were developed during his reign, and in part to the judicious dispensing of imperial largesse which enhanced an individual's wealth or prestige. In the end, however, it is tempting to wonder whether the point with which this chapter began – the fact that a surprising number of Theodosius' generals were religious outsiders – was itself another of the strategies of Theodosius and his civilian advisers for neutralising their political ambitions – and perhaps the most potent one.

Writing of Aspar's influence in the post-Theodosian period, the sixth-century historian Procopius commented that 'he was a supporter of the Arian doctrine, and since he had no intention of changing this, he was not able to assume the position of emperor, though he had the influence to advance someone else to it without difficulty'.[78] Procopius' comment does not seem to refer to any sort

---

[76] For Theodosius the Elder, see Demandt 1969; Errington 2006: 443–7; for Aspar, Croke 2005: 195–200.
[77] Theophanes 5943 (103.27–33); for discussion of the various and difficult accounts of this episode, and the possible complicity of Chrysaphius, see Croke 1995: 85; however, it is not obvious that Ioannes was eliminated because he was seen as a possible threat to Theodosius.
[78] Proc. *BV* 1.6.3.

of constitutional obstacle to an Arian becoming emperor (in the way that a Roman Catholic cannot become the British monarch) for another account reports that the Senate in Rome offered Aspar the imperial throne in 457 – an offer which he declined, however, with the cryptic observation: 'I fear that a tradition in ruling might be initiated through me.'[79] This has been interpreted as an allusion to his Arianism,[80] with the implication that an Arian ruler would have difficulty gaining wide acceptance – a readily comprehensible concern given the popular passions aroused by Christological issues during and after Theodosius' reign. Confirmation of this is provided by the reaction against the Emperor Leo's elevation of Aspar's son Patricius to the rank of Caesar in 470, with Leo having to issue assurances that Patricius had been promoted only after renouncing his Arianism for orthodoxy.[81] It is surely not inconceivable, then, that, in the midst of the emphasis on religious conformity during Theodosius' reign, the willingness to allow senior military posts to be held by religious non-conformists was a strategy for reducing the threat they might otherwise pose, since their religious allegiances – whether to Arian Christianity or to pagan traditions – must have made them much less acceptable as potential candidates for the imperial throne.

---

[79] *Timeo ne per me consuetudo in regno nascatur: Anagnosticum Regis = Acta synhodorum habitarum Romae* 5 (ed. T. Mommsen, *MGH (AA)* 12: 425.24). This incident was reported by the Gothic king Theoderic in a communication to a synod of bishops in Rome in 501 during the so-called Laurentian schism (for the background, see Moorhead 1992: 114–26). To Theoderic's annoyance, the bishops refused to come to a decision, and in his efforts to change their minds, he cited this anecdote as part of an argument against setting a bad precedent. As noted by Croke (2005: 150 n. 10), Theoderic's period as a hostage in Constantinople in the 460s means that 'there is every likelihood that he heard Aspar tell this story at first hand'.

[80] von Haehling 1988: especially 98–100; Croke 2005: 150 n. 10. The placing of the episode in 457, rather than 450, is strengthened by the arguments of Zuckerman 1994: 172–6 for the importance of Zeno in 450.

[81] *V. Marcelli* 34 (ed. G. Dagron, *AB* 86 [1968]: 271–321), Theophanes 5961 (116.20–4), with Croke 2005: 190–1.

CHAPTER 4

THEODOSIUS II AND THE POLITICS OF THE FIRST COUNCIL OF EPHESUS

Thomas Graumann

The story of the first Council of Ephesus is conventionally told as one of a contest between two main protagonists: the bishops of Alexandria and Constantinople, Cyril and Nestorius.[1] Political factors also contributed significantly to the course and eventual outcome of events.[2] Yet, in comparison, the role of Theodosius II in these ecclesiastical quarrels remains obscure, and his aims and objectives for the Council appear anything but clear.[3] Conventional

---

I should like to thank the editor, Christopher Kelly, for his invaluable suggestions and generous help in improving this chapter.

[1] For a narrative of the main events in the unfolding controversy and preparations for the Council, see Hefele and Leclerq 1908; Kidd 1922; Perrone 1993: 71–85; McGuckin 1994; Fraisse-Coué 1995.

[2] In addition to the studies cited in n. 1 above, see McGuckin 1996. In all these accounts, Pulcheria is presented as the main patron, and at the centre, of a web of dissident voices and competing interests either originating in the urban aristocracy and the monastic communities or associated directly with her own assumed personal connection with Marian piety. The latter view is advocated most strongly by Holum 1982: 147–74; see too the reservations in Cooper 2004.

[3] Millar 2006 offers a thorough discussion of official communications under Theodosius and a useful analysis of a range of influences on court politics. While making significant use of conciliar documents, Millar does not offer a sustained interpretation of the *sacrae* discussed in this chapter. On the workings of bureaucracy and the various ways to secure influence, see also C. M. Kelly 2004. Elton 2009 illustrates the complexities of imperial decision-making in the face of conflicting representations from interested individuals and groups, but warns against over-emphasising the influence of certain individuals, whether eunuchs, generals or princesses. Destephen 2008: especially 109–14 discusses the distribution by province of participants at church councils. He considers councils an important tool for Theodosian government in its attempts to influence ecclesiastical matters without, however, exploring the mechanics and theoretical underpinnings of this engagement. The most sustained treatment of Theodosius' religious policies up to 449/450 is offered by Wessel 2001 (for the most part focusing on events after the convocation of the Council). For Wessel, Theodosius 'articulated and exercised a coherent ecclesiastical policy' (at 286) – the substance of which, however, receives no precise description. Wessel 2004 adds little to the discussion of Theodosius' policies; its concern is principally with the strategies of the main ecclesiastical combatants.

109

assessments of Theodosius' character as weak have compounded the uncertainty about – and explain a certain lack of scholarly interest in – the emperor's role and stance in the conflict.[4] To be sure, the interplay of competing interests and influences at court cannot be denied, even if much has to remain conjectural as, by its very nature, it was acted out 'behind the scenes'. Yet at the age of twenty-nine, and after over two decades on the throne, Theodosius hardly remained the figurehead he had once been in his youth, and it seems ill-advised to write him out of the planning of the Council of Ephesus altogether, ascribing instead all decisions to powers behind the throne. Of course, what drove Theodosius to call a church council, and what hopes and plans he may have had for such an event, can only – and at fragile best – be inferred from the documents issued in his name. And only in the limited sense of the emperor's willingness to take advice and to issue instructions for a council in his name and backed by his own authority is it possible to think of an 'imperial agenda'. The focus of this chapter, therefore, is on the official pronouncements emanating from court in Constantinople. Its concern is to assess how Theodosius, along with his chief advisers and aides, saw and approached the conflicts involved, and how, in particular, they understood the purposes and tasks of the Council. To this end, three of Theodosius' letters from the period before the first Council of Ephesus will be analysed in detail, in each case arguing that, despite the use of conventional imperial rhetoric, they offer plausible indications of the emperor's substantive concerns and main presuppositions.

On 19 November 430, Theodosius issued a *sacra* convening a council in Ephesus at Pentecost the following year (7 June 431).[5]

---

[4] For the origins of this approach, see Ilski 2005: especially 3–6; for the influential interpretation of Eduard Schwartz, see in particular Meier 2011. Elton 2009 also rightly cautions against overly stereotypical accounts of Theodosius' dependency and 'weakness'. Ilski offers a nuanced reassessment, taking into account different phases in the reign. The specific link between judgements of Theodosius' character and piety can be traced back to the portrayal of the emperor as a pious prince in fifth-century church historians; see, generally, Leppin 1996 on the church historians' presentation of 'Christian' emperors (132–45 on Theodosius specifically), and Harries 1994 for a useful comparison with the imperial image emerging from Theodosius' project to codify the law.
[5] *Coll. Vat.* 25 = *ACO* I 1.1, pp. 114–16.

THEODOSIUS II AND THE FIRST COUNCIL OF EPHESUS

The letter opens with a straightforward preamble expressing Theodosius' self-awareness as a divinely appointed ruler charged with the task of mediating between providence and human affairs. In this role, the emperor's concern was to safeguard and work for a Church that is 'pleasing to God' and 'beneficial for our times', aiming for tranquillity, unanimity, concord and peace.[6] At the very end of this opening passage, one element is emphasised. This offers an initial indication of a centrally important perspective in the assessment of the problems faced by Theodosius' government and arguably points beyond its rather obviously conventional expression. The necessary conditions of the peaceful and beneficial state of affairs in both Church and empire, for which the emperor strives, include – and indeed culminate in – the requirement that 'those in the clergy and major priesthood [that is those holding episcopal office]' should be 'free from all censure in their mode of life'.[7]

On the evidence of this opening section alone, doctrinal controversy (to which only veiled allusions are made) does not appear as the sole – and perhaps not even the main – issue demanding imperial action. The conduct and character of individual clergy and bishops constitute an equally major concern that will resurface repeatedly in the imperial letters issued in the run up to the Council. The *sacra* also emphasises the emperor's long-standing desire to convene a council for the benefit of the Church and the empire generally; only the inconvenience that a council would cause to bishops had prevented it from being called before. However, in the emperor's view, the need to resolve current problems now outweighed these considerations and made a council unavoidable.[8] The rhetoric creates a paradoxical effect: emphasising the urgency and importance of present problems, while locating the convocation of a council

---

[6] *Coll. Vat.* 25.1 (*ACO* 11.1, pp. 114.29–115.14). For conventional expressions in imperial ideology (beginning with Constantine) of the divinely appointed emperor, see Dagron 1996: especially 141–68.

[7] *Coll. Vat.* 25.1 (*ACO* 11.1, p. 115.13–14): τοὺς εἰς τὸν κλῆρον τήν τε μεγάλην ἱερωσύνην τελοῦντας πάσης τῆς κατὰ τὸν βίον μέμψεως ἀπηλλάχθαι. Unless otherwise noted, translations are my own; they frequently make use of those prepared jointly with Richard Price for a forthcoming edition of the *acta* of the first Council of Ephesus. Distant echoes of Theodosius' rhetoric can still be heard in Just. *Nov.* 6.

[8] *Coll. Vat.* 25.2 (*ACO* 11.1, p. 115.14–19).

within a much broader set of concerns which seem to play down these problems' particular significance. Indeed, the *sacra* adumbrates the task of the Council in rather vague terms, referring only to 'a proposed investigation of such profitable matters'[9] (without, however, defining the object of the investigation), and later voices the expectation that any decision (τύπος) will be taken by a common vote.[10] It is also made clear that any delay in the investigation will result in a turn for the worse – and again without any specific illustration of either the problem or the threatened consequences of its neglect.[11] Speaking in general terms of the reasons for holding a council may well have been considered proper for a widely circulated letter of convocation, and is probably also a reflection of the standard administrative jargon employed by the court. Yet it contrasts markedly with the equivalent letter that called a second council to Ephesus eighteen years later (in 449) and perhaps, therefore, deserves to be taken rather more seriously. The later *sacra* also relies on a similar claim by the emperor to be divinely appointed; but here this provides the basis for a much more specific focus on the recent strife over orthodoxy and its detrimental effects. In turn, this underwrites a far more determined imperial instruction for the bishops: their task is to confirm orthodoxy and to eradicate heresy completely.[12]

On a first assessment of the *sacra* issued on 19 November 430, the convocation of a council serves to prevent the deterioration of an already problematic situation, which goes deliberately undescribed. It is an exercise in damage limitation and control, and as

---

[9] *Coll. Vat.* 25.2 (*ACO* I 1.1, p. 115.19–20): τῆς προκειμένης τῶν οὕτω χρησίμων ἐξετάσεως.
[10] *Coll. Vat.* 25.3 (*ACO* I 1.1, p. 115.31–2): τοῦ μέλλοντος παρ' αὐτῆς [sc. τῆς συνόδου] κοινῇ ψήφῳ ἐφ' ἅπασι δίδοσθαι τύπου. τύπος is not a technical term specifically referring to a document expressing or communicating a synod's decision (see n. 35 below). A synodical decision of any description is most often referred to as ὅρος; for the main examples and a discussion of 'genre', see Uphus 2004: especially 15–20; for the various textual representations of decisions issued by the Council of Ephesus, Graumann 2010. A doctrinal exposition or definition, in particular those discussed or issued in fourth-century synods, may be referred to as ἔκθεσις, or in appropriate cases as πίστις. A disciplinary ruling is usually called κανών, a term also used for doctrinal norms; see Ohme 1998.
[11] *Coll. Vat.* 25.2 (*ACO* I 1.1, p. 115.19–20).
[12] A Greek version of this *sacra* is preserved in *CChalc., sessio* I 24 = *ACO* II 1.1, pp. 68–9; a Latin version in the *Collectio Novariensis* = *ACO* II 2, pp. 42–3.

such is part of a wider, concerted effort by the emperor to secure a Church that benefits the public good. In so doing, it also reflects an imperial weariness about 'commotion arising from disputes'[13] – for which Theodosius had ample illustration in Constantinople both in the recent past and at the time of writing. Even though the particular problem that ultimately justified the calling of a council remains studiously unexpressed, it is also clear from the emperor's concerns that a serious conflict had been in train for some while. It is important, therefore, also to realise that this letter aims to impose a moratorium on any decisions being taken before the Council convenes.[14] It is another clear indication that Theodosius and his advisers had a strong interest in preventing any further escalation. The calling of a council was an attempt to halt a process of confrontation that could spiral out of control.[15] In contrast to its cautious, even oblique, references to the issues requiring urgent resolution, the *sacra* is decisive in its stark

[13] *Coll. Vat.* 25.3 (*ACO* I 1.1, p. 115.28–30).
[14] *Coll. Vat.* 25.3 (*ACO* I 1.1, p. 115.31–2): μηδεμιᾶς πρὸ τῆς ἁγιωτάτης συνόδου [...] καινοτομίας ἰδίᾳ παρά τινων γινομένης.
[15] As viewed from Constantinople, the decisive element in this escalation most likely would have been news about the decisions reached by a Roman synod in August 430. The synod issued a condemnation of Nestorius unless he recanted within ten days of receiving its judgement. While this decision was only formally communicated to Nestorius by Alexandrian emissaries on 30 November, and therefore after the publication of the imperial *sacra*, it seems implausible to suggest that no information had made its way to Constantinople before then. The uncertain channels by which the accusations against Nestorius had first reached Rome could also have worked in the opposite direction. Moreover, at least some of the letters on the decisions taken in Rome written by Pope Celestine to the clergy and people of Constantinople, and to selected bishops in the East, may have found their way to their addressees before the official delegation approached Nestorius. John, bishop of Antioch, was certainly aware of the Roman point of view when he urged Nestorius some time in the late autumn (November?) 430 to accept the description of Mary as *Theotokos* as not necessarily heretical; see *Coll. Vat.* 18 (*ACO* I 1.1, pp. 101–2) and Fairbairn 2007. While the flow of news cannot be reconstructed with any certainty, it is unlikely that the position taken by the Pope would have gone unnoticed in the East and especially in Constantinople, giving Theodosius further reason to contemplate an attempt – and at the very last moment – to halt the attack on Nestorius. The fairly recent recovery of the West, the installation of Valentinian III and the restoration of close political ties provide the background for real concerns over ecclesiastical friction between Rome and Constantinople. It is evident nevertheless that Theodosius remained supportive of Nestorius well into the period of the Council. Gregory's assertion that the emperor was reluctant – even in the face Nestorius' lobbying – to call a council because he preferred to defend his bishop rather than have the issue debated is untenable; see Gregory 1979: 101, with a mistaken dating of the *sacra* of convocation, and generally 95, 100.

warning that any non-compliance with the invitation would not be tolerated.[16] The importance placed on personal attendance might then be read as an expression of a confident imperial expectation that a joint meeting of all relevant ecclesiastical dignitaries would allow them to solve, or at least to contain, a conflict which so far had been conducted at a distance through epistolary propaganda and polemics.[17]

As regards more practical matters, the imperial *sacra* also permitted metropolitans to nominate participants, so as to ensure both a proper representation at the Council and the smooth running of the churches in the provinces by those bishops remaining behind.[18] The absence of more explicit instruction has a sharper edge when contrasted with the strict and specific stipulation for the later, second Council of Ephesus in 449. Then the emperor commanded the attendance of ten metropolitans and ten ordinary bishops from the diocese of Egypt and analogous arrangements were made for other provinces.[19] Apparently Theodosius had learned from the disputes at the first Council and was now no longer willing to trust the bishops to take their own decisions. The significant level

---

[16] *Coll. Vat.* 25.3 (*ACO* I 1.1, p. 116). The warning is echoed in other documents, underscoring the importance of the point.

[17] A similar goal for the Council is detected by Lim 1995: 220–4; Lim's suggestion that it was Nestorius who 'put into the mind of Theodosius II' the ideas for a procedure by which the Council might 'examine and resolve the disputed issues through dispassionate research' (quoting 220) cannot be corroborated by any extant sources, and can remain only speculative.

[18] *Coll. Vat.* 25.2 (*ACO* I 1.1, p. 115.21–6): φροντίσει ἡ σὴ θεοσέβεια … εἰς τὴν Ἐφεσίων τῆς Ἀσίας παραγενέσθαι … ὀλίγους οὓς ἂν δοκιμάσειεν, ἐκ τῆς ὑπ' αὐτὴν τεταγμένης ἐπαρχίας ἁγιωτάτους ἐπισκόπους εἰς τὴν αὐτὴν συνδραμεῖν παρασκευάσασα, ὥστε καὶ τοὺς ἀρκοῦντας ταῖς κατὰ τὴν αὐτὴν ἐπαρχίαν ἁγιωτάταις ἐκκλησίαις καὶ τοὺς τῇ συνόδῳ ἐπιτηδείους μηδαμῶς ἐλλεῖψαι ('your religiousness [the form of address in copies of this *sacra* individually sent to metropolitans; the version preserved in the *acta* is addressed to Cyril of Alexandria] shall give heed … to repair to Ephesus in Asia … while securing the attendance at the same [city] of a few most holy bishops of your choice from the provinces assigned to you, in such a way that there shall be no shortage either of bishops sufficient for the most holy churches in the same province or of those needed at the Council'). McGuckin 1994: 53 considers this 'first vague instruction' as a case in point for Theodosius' aims being 'admirable in theory but easily subverted in practice'. On the actual representation of Asia and Egypt at the Council, see McGuckin 1994: 55–6.

[19] *CChalc.*, *sessio* I 24 (*ACO* II 1.1, p. 68.18–21) The *sacra* further specifically bars Theodoret of Cyrrhus from attending unless the Council requests his presence (I 24, *ACO* II 1.1, p. 69.1–4). Conversely and departing from convention, the monk Barsaumas, a notorious firebrand, was invited to attend (I 48, *ACO* II 1.1, p. 71).

of imperial interference and 'direct management' at the second Council underlines the emperor's earlier restraint. Details of the proposed agenda and internal workings of the Council were deferred to the *sacra* composed for its formal opening (discussed below). The first imperial letter of convocation merely expresses, and again in a rather circumspect manner, the emperor's expectation that any problems will be resolved 'in accordance with ecclesiastical canons'[20] – a requirement that amounts to little more than a reminder to the bishops of the prevailing ecclesiastical convention and the need to ensure good order. Similar documents pertaining to other church councils show that letters of convocation regularly contained little detail. Even so, it is noteworthy that at this stage any recipient of the imperial *sacra* initiating a council would not yet have gained any firm understanding of the emperor's wishes as regards a specific outcome or the specific procedures to be followed. Rather, the emphasis is placed repeatedly on the communality of engagement and on an insistence that all those so instructed should be present at Ephesus.

Much of what remains deliberately general and vague in the letter of convocation is thrown into sharp relief in a letter addressed to Cyril personally. This letter refers to the *sacra* discussed above and is probably best explained as part of the same dispatch. The contrast in tone of this document with the formal *sacra* is remarkable. While the *sacra* retains the style and character of a bureaucratic, and somewhat formulaic, government communication, the letter to Cyril expresses much more immediately the sentiments of the emperor. (It is also tempting to sense in this change of tone a tension between official government policies, potentially reflective of the varying interests at court, and the personal views of the emperor himself – but, of course, any such surmise can only be hypothetical.) In the letter, a markedly different note is struck right from the start by the emperor's brusque expression of exasperation at the disreputable behaviour of some clergy.[21] The contrasting priestly ideal set before Cyril combines exact

---

[20] *Coll. Vat.* 25.3 (*ACO* I 1.1, p. 115.28–9). McGuckin 1994: 70–4 makes rather too much of the purported procedural implications of 'canons' and their supposed support for Cyril's actions.

[21] *Coll. Vat.* 8.1 (*ACO* I 1.1, p. 73.3).

orthodoxy (τῆς περὶ τὴν πίστιν ἀκριβείας) with simplicity of conduct (ἁπλότητα τοῦ βίου),[22] expressing the joining of intellectual disposition and doctrinal stance with that clear sense of correct socio-moral comportment traditional in ancient assessments of character and personality. Most of the letter is concerned with the required behaviour of a bishop rather than with the intricacies of theological discussion. In a series of contrasting pairs, Theodosius emphasises the proper disposition necessary for dealing with the issues at hand and, more generally, with questions of faith and ecclesiastical order. Investigation (ζήτησις) is required, not stubbornness (αὐθάδεια); a domineering attitude (δυναστεύειν) and imperiousness (κέλευσις) do not safeguard religion, but rather consensual approval (συναίνεσις).[23] The emperor criticises the improper approach evidenced by Cyril's activities and warns against similar activities at the Council. On this imperial view, Cyril's actions arose from an impudent impulse, they indicated insolence (θράσος) and deceptive subtlety (ποικιλία) where precision (ἀκρίβεια), harmonious grace (ἐμμελεία) and straightforwardness (ἁπλότης) should have prevailed.[24] Rather than focusing on the merits or demerits of any doctrinal position, Theodosius' angry comments repeatedly return to the attitudes revealed by Cyril's actions and to their potentially disastrous effect on both Church and state. In turn, this sharp critique of Cyril serves as mirror reflecting the emperor's expectations for the ideal resolution of conflict in the forthcoming Council.

Theodosius' criticism of Cyril is built up over the course of the letter before it is briefly tempered: 'but now our concern will be with sacred peace'.[25] This is more than an empty phrase. From the very start of the letter, indeed in its opening sentence, Theodosius had given an important indication of his aim. There,

[22] *Coll. Vat.* 8.1 (*ACO* I 1.1, p. 73.6–7).
[23] *Coll. Vat.* 8.1 (*ACO* I 1.1, p. 73.5–12): τοὺς δὲ ἱερέας χρὴ καὶ ἀπὸ τῆς τῶν ἠθῶν χρηστότητος καὶ ἀπὸ τῆς περὶ τὴν πίστιν ἀκριβείας θαυμάζεσθαι καὶ τὴν ἁπλότητα τοῦ βίου διὰ παντὸς ἐπιδεικνύναι γινώσκειν τε ὡς τὴν ἑκάστου πράγματος φύσιν καὶ τοὺς περὶ τὴν εὐσέβειαν μάλιστα λόγους μᾶλλον ἂν εὕροι ζήτησις ἤπερ αὐθάδεια. καὶ γὰρ ἐξ ἀρχῆς ἡμῖν αὐτοὺς οὐκ ἀπειλή τινος δυναστεύοντος ἢ δυναστεύειν νομίζοντος, ἀλλ' ἡ τῶν ἁγίων πατέρων καὶ τῆς ἱερᾶς συνόδου βουλὴ κατεστήσατο, καὶ παντὶ δῆλον ὡς ἡ θρησκεία τὸ βέβαιον οὐκ ἂν ἐκ κελεύσεως σχοίη μᾶλλον ἢ συναινέσεως.
[24] *Coll. Vat.* 8.2 (*ACO* I 1.1, p. 73.14–17).
[25] *Coll. Vat.* 8.3 (*ACO* I 1.1, p. 73.19–20).

announcing a *leitmotif*, he defined religion chiefly as a means for sinners to receive forgiveness (συγγνώμη).²⁶ This forgiveness will soon be offered to Cyril. Yet, having briefly softened his censure, Theodosius nevertheless goes on to rebuke Cyril for suggesting a split between members of the imperial family. Only at this peak of the emperor's angry criticism is forgiveness offered in a more direct way: 'your religiousness has been granted forgiveness.' The same sentence makes clear that this offer of peace did not have its origin in any change in the emperor's personal dislike of Cyril, but is entirely political in its motivation. In a subtle and perceptive realisation of the evasive strategies commonly employed in ecclesiastical argument, forgiveness is granted to Cyril 'lest you have an excuse or are able to claim that you were censured in defence of piety'.²⁷ Theodosius clearly recognised that his criticism of Cyril might be seen, or construed, as a pre-emption of the business to be conducted at the Council. It might allow the person thus targeted to present himself as a martyr-like figure, the innocent victim of undue imperial interference in matters of orthodoxy. This shows a keen awareness on Theodosius' part of the modes and models by which competing ecclesiastical interest groups sought to buffer the effective reach of imperial power. Whatever his personal sentiments, an emperor needed to be seen to follow proper procedure in matters of faith – to defer to the authority of the bishops in council and to do no more than facilitate and eventually enact their decisions.

This does not mean, however, that Cyril's position was completely secured by the emperor's announcement of forgiveness. Indeed, Theodosius leaves it to the Council to decide whether 'the defeated party is to receive forgiveness ... or not'.²⁸ Thus Theodosius is not interested in acquitting Cyril of any accusation or insulating him from criticism, but rather is concerned to allow the Council to make the relevant decisions on its own authority.²⁹ The emperor's

---

²⁶ *Coll. Vat.* 8.1 (*ACO* I 1.1, p. 73.2–3).
²⁷ *Coll. Vat.* 8.4 (*ACO* I 1.1, p. 74.5–7): καὶ δεδόσθαι τῇ σῇ θεοσεβείᾳ συγγνώμην, ὡς ἂν μὴ πρόφασις εἴη μηδὲ λέγειν δύναιο διὰ τοὺς ὑπὲρ τῆς εὐσεβείας ἐγκεκλῆσθαι λόγους.
²⁸ *Coll. Vat.* 8.4 (*ACO* I 1.1, p. 74.8–9): εἴτε μεταλαμβάνοιεν συγγνώμης εἴτε μὴ παρὰ τῶν πατέρων οἱ νικηθέντες.
²⁹ The protection of individuals from criminal accusation (*Coll. Vat.* 31 [*ACO* I 1.1, pp. 120–1]) therefore, was most likely not intended to remove Cyril from the firing line (as

ostentatious forgiveness of Cyril (almost despite himself) may then be understood as an attempt to ward off any suggestion of outside influence or interference. In particular, it is mindful of the dangers of any perception of imperial involvement in such affairs, and of the advantages even the slightest hint of such involvement afforded to the bishops concerned. It may be understood as a lesson learned from the ecclesiastical disputes of the fourth century when bishops such as Athanasius presented themselves as the persecuted victims of ill-intentioned imperial policy.[30] It was also an acknowledgement of the disastrous effects of more recent strong-arm tactics. The forcible removal of John Chrysostom from office had prolonged and exacerbated a schism in the church in Constantinople and beyond.[31] That had established a reputation for Chrysostom as a holy martyr before whose relics Theodosius and his family would later have to bow, seeking forgiveness for their parents now judged culpable for the bishop's death in exile.[32]

The reading suggested above for the imperial letter of convocation and the impression of political astuteness in the emperor's personal (and harsher) letter to Cyril of Alexandria both gain in plausibility from Theodosius' instructions to the *comes* Candidianus, the imperial representative at the first Council of Ephesus. The *sacra*

is conventionally inferred; see, the influential assessment by Schwartz 1928, still echoed, for example, in McGuckin 1994: 53), but rather to shield Nestorius, who also faced potential accusations from dissident clergy: see the petition by the monk and deacon Basil, *Coll. Vat.* 143 (*ACO* 1 1.5, pp. 7–10). Theodosius' assessment of Cyril's character also helps to explain why he did not doubt for a moment the reports and accusations about the bishop's wilful and authoritarian behaviour at the first meeting of the Council of Ephesus, and did not hesitate to confirm his 'deposition' as entirely justified.

[30] For the recollection of martyrdom and persecution as a counter to (imperial) authority as well as real violence, see Gaddis 2005: 68–102.

[31] See J. N. D. Kelly 1995: 272–81 and, for popular unrest during the controversy generally, Gregory 1979: 41–69. Interestingly, it is in this context – and in a manner not dissimilar from Theodosius' professions – that the western emperor Honorius admonished his brother Arcadius about the need for imperial restraint in dealing with John Chrysostom (*Coll. Avell.* 38; ed. O. Günther, *CSEL* 35: 85–8). For this letter and the related claims and position of Pope Innocent I, cf. Pietri 1976: 1310–32.

[32] Nestorius had celebrated the memory of John Chrysostom in the liturgy in Constantinople in September 428, but it was Proclus who brought back John's remains to the city in a triumphant procession on 27 January 438 (Soc. 7.45). Theodosius personally received the sarcophagus at the harbour and, bending down, offered prayers on behalf of his parents, Arcadius and Eudoxia (Theod. *HE* 5.36).

read out at the opening of the Council on 22 June (a session at which only Cyril and his supporters were present) clearly defined Candidianus' role. (And indeed it was only a result of Cyril's subterfuge that Candidianus agreed to read the *sacra*. His willingness, in response to Cyril's request for clarification of the emperor's wishes, was then construed as constituting the formal reading of the *sacra* required for the opening of the Council.) According to Theodosius' instructions, Candidianus' main responsibility was to police the city and prevent any disruption to the Council's deliberations.[33] In close conformity with the emperor's sentiments in the two earlier letters (discussed above), Candidianus was specifically prohibited from taking part in the Council's discussions. In Theodosius' view, any involvement would properly be regarded as illegal (ἀθέμιτον), as bishops were to retain their autonomy in making these kinds of decisions.[34] The limitations placed on Candidianus are also consonant with the general ideas and sentiments set out in the earlier *sacrae* on the role of emperors in relation to divine worship and the Church. It seems that Theodosius was trying hard not to appear to be effecting any autocratic imposition of his will. This, in turn, mirrors the emperor's censure of authoritarian activities within the episcopate and, in particular, his sharp criticism of Cyril. Imperial restraint from interfering with the Council's deliberations contrasts with – and is, at least implicitly,

[33] *Coll. Vat.* 31 (*ACO* I 1.1, p. 120.15–19; cf. pp. 120.25–121.8). The intended neutrality of Candidianus deserves to be taken seriously. Gregory 1979: 101, 106 places him firmly in Nestorius' camp from the outset. More cautiously, McGuckin 1994: 52 considers Candidianus' 'neutrality at least suspect' and interprets Theodosius' decision to provide 'a sympathetic military presence' as offsetting 'his concession' about the location of the Council. There is little evidence to support these judgements. Over time, and in particular in response to the events of 22 June, Candidianus increasingly identified himself with the complaints of those bishops led by John of Antioch. But a particular closeness to Nestorius is not in evidence even then.

[34] *Coll. Vat.* 31 (*ACO* I 1.1, p. 120.14–15; cf. 12–14). The instructions of the *sacra* are read as evidence for the working out of a 'division of responsibilities' between ecclesiastical and imperial powers by Dagron 1996: 305. However, for McGuckin 1994: 52–3 this position was the 'fatal flaw' in Theodosius' plans, since 'the separation of state legal prescript ... and ecclesiastical canonical precedents ... were [both] far too complicated to have been theoretically divided out in such a crude way as Theodosius does'. Yet McGuckin also detects in this instruction a realisation of the theological complexities sufficient to counsel against any involvement (at 53). For McGuckin's claims, only implied here, about the relevance of canonical procedure (which he assumes to be already well developed), see above n. 20.

suggested as a counter-model to – attempts at arrogating authority by those within the Church not entitled to it, a criticism again, it seems, aimed principally at Cyril. All of this is concerned first and foremost with the correct frame of mind and proper behaviour best suited for the work of the Council, and for the resolution of the problems faced by the Church and the empire. Much less attention is given in this *sacra* to the details of the Council's agenda and proceedings. These are not framed as imperial orders but rather as expectations about propriety, which, in turn, derive from a concern with the personal attitude and comportment of the participants. The Council's success will be guaranteed by the conformity of all present to accepted social standards. At no point is the expectation of a particular outcome enunciated, either with regard to theological positions or in terms of decisions about individuals (even though the earlier letter to Cyril imagines there might be winners and losers). As noted above, the initial *sacra* of convocation envisaged the Council as reaching a decision (τύπος) by a common vote (κοινῇ ψήφῳ). The language of τύπος and ψῆφος, and their cognates, recurs in the *sacra* opening the Council, but here the emperor also expects a 'precise investigation of the truth' (ἀκριβὴς τῆς ἀληθείας ζήτησις), also referred to as an examination of '(true) doctrine' (τοῦ δόγματος διάσκεψις – περὶ τοῦ ἀληθοῦς δόγματος ἔρευναν). It is the emperor's expectation that participants will be able freely to advocate or oppose an opinion (προστιθέναι τὸ δοκοῦν ἢ ἀντιτιθέναι), and that the debate will proceed through the exchange of questions and answers (κατὰ πρότασίν τε καὶ λύσιν).[35] The

---

[35] *Coll. Vat.* 31 (*ACO* I 1.1, p. 120.17–25): ἐπειδήπερ οὐ χρὴ τοὺς κατ᾽ οὐδὲν ἀναγκαίους ὄντας τῇ μελλούσῃ τοῦ δόγματος διασκέψει κινεῖν θορύβους καὶ διὰ τοῦτο ἐμποδίζειν τοῖς εἰρηνικῶς τυπωθῆναι παρὰ τῆς ὑμετέρας ἁγιωσύνης ὀφείλουσι, καὶ φροντίσαι τοῦ μή τινα διχόνοιαν ἐξ ἀντιπαθείας ἐπὶ πλέον παραταθῆναι, ὡς ἂν μὴ ἐκ τούτου ἡ τῆς ἁγιωτάτης ὑμῶν συνόδου παρεμποδίζοιτο διάσκεψις καὶ ἡ ἀκριβὴς τῆς ἀληθείας ζήτησις ἐκ τῆς ἐγγινομένης τυχὸν ἀτάκτου περιηχήσεως διακρούηται, ἀνεξικάκως δὲ τῶν λεγομένων ἕκαστον ἀκροώμενον προστιθέναι τὸ δοκοῦν ἢ ἀντιτιθέναι καὶ οὕτως πᾶσαν κατὰ πρότασίν τε καὶ λύσιν τὴν περὶ τοῦ ἀληθοῦς δόγματος ἔρευναν δίχα τινὸς ταραχῆς διακριθῆναι καὶ κοινῇ τῆς ὑμετέρας ἁγιότητος ψήφῳ ἀστασίαστόν τε καὶ τὸν πᾶσιν ἀρέσκοντα τύπον λαβεῖν. For question and answer as a method for solving intellectual problems across a wider range of exegetical, philosophical and doctrinal issues, see Dörrie and Dörries 1966, Papadoyannakis 2006 and – with a special focus on questions of genre – the papers in Volgers and Zamagni 2004. For a detailed analysis of the

variation in the language employed to refer to examination and decision-making indicates that some flexibility was envisaged in the conduct of the meeting. The emperor aimed to construct a framework which would preserve both the social propriety and the efficacy of the Council's debates; that is, he sought to establish a set of protocols which respected the rights of individuals and accorded due reverence to the religious subject-matter under discussion. The emphasis is firmly on the ability of all present to have their say without hindrance. But the *sacra* stops deliberately short of offering any detailed procedural instructions. Rather, the imperial directives target any disturbance that might impede the Council's ability to hold the kinds of debates envisaged in the *sacra* – thereby effectively prescribing them.

The dominant interest in procedure is confirmed by a number of imperial directives also aimed at ensuring that the discussion would run smoothly. Theodosius could foresee – and seek to forestall – some of the tactics frequently used by bishops to frustrate a council's intentions: attempting to prevent it reaching any decision or undermining a decision by contesting its validity on procedural grounds. Bishops might absent themselves altogether, finding some pretext to return to their sees and then disowning any decision reached in their absence; if sufficient numbers were absent, it might even be possible to break up a council before any decisions had been made. Bishops might also attempt to approach the imperial court, in effect seeking a different and competing route of adjudication by appealing to the emperor against the decisions of their peers. For all these reasons, the *sacra* specifically instructed Candidianus to prevent bishops from leaving Ephesus either to return home or to travel to the capital. The presence and active participation of all involved was centrally important to the emperor's strategy and to the success of the Council. Those bishops in the minority had to be seen to participate in their own marginalisation for the Council to have its desired effect of demonstrating Church unity.[36] Theodosius also moved to prevent the

---

application and accommodation of the procedural guidance contained in the *sacra* at the contested first session of the Council, see Graumann 2002: 360–2.

[36] The same might also be said, for example, of the treatment of Palladius at the Council of Aquileia in 381. There the bishops took great pains to secure his cooperation – however

Council's agenda from being overloaded by issues deliberately intended to delay discussion of the central issues. The *sacra* prohibited the bringing of a legal case, either civil or criminal, before the Council or the local courts; such cases were to be referred directly to Constantinople.[37] These spoiling tactics had all been deployed in the fourth century and in more recent ecclesiastical disputes. Again, Theodosius demonstrated an awareness of the various manoeuvres used by those seeking to undermine a church council and escape its consequences. At the same time, it is telling that, despite foreseeing these difficulties, Theodosius proved unable to block them entirely.

The impression created by the imperial *sacra* is then to some extent paradoxical. Even though there are no explicit instructions on the specific outcomes of the Council, the imperial directives are clearly aimed at the close regulation of its proceedings. Only harmony and peace are repeatedly highlighted as the expected conclusions of a consensual procedure in which all are seen to participate fully and without impediment. In marked contrast to the orders issued before the second Council of Ephesus, Theodosius does not appear to prefer any specific substantive result – save that there should be a decision (τύπος) taken jointly. Given that historians of theology have been most concerned with the question of a potential expression of 'orthodoxy' by the Council, it is noteworthy that this *sacra* (written to be read out to the assembled bishops at the opening of the Council) should avoid any direct reference to the specific points at issue in particular doctrinal disputes – indeed it required an up-to-date knowledge of current theological debates to know precisely what the problem was – let alone prescribe what kind of orthodoxy the Council should declare. The absence of any explicit instruction deserves attention, not least because traditional scholarly accounts have noticed (and

---

unwilling – with a procedure intended, as he found to his dismay, to condemn him; see Graumann 2007. The efforts of the Cyrillian part-council at Ephesus, initially to invite and then to summon Nestorius, and his refusal to attend, also illustrate the same point.

[37] *Coll. Vat.* 31 (*ACO* I 1.1, pp. 120.25–121.8); cf. Wessel 2001: 292.

sometimes criticised) the failure of the Council to agree a statement of doctrine or have, in effect, taken the formula of reunion issued in 433 as a substitute for it. And it is all too easy to assume that the emperor must originally have expected something like that formula to emerge from the Council. Yet in its careful avoidance of the technical language of conciliar decision-documents, the *sacra* is not even clear on whether the determination of 'true doctrine' requires any particular form of positive declaration (for example, a statement of orthodox beliefs, such as the formula of reunion) or negative condemnation (for example, the list of anathemas drawn up by Cyril's supporters and handed to Nestorius in December 430[38]). The *sacra* leaves it open to the Council to decide whether those found deserving of censure should receive forgiveness. In other words, Theodosius appears willing either to enforce any deposition from office determined by the bishops or to allow all concerned to retain their sees.[39] From an imperial perspective, the first Council of Ephesus was to function as a means of demonstrating that the Church had retained (or regained) its unity and cohesion. It was not principally conceived as a deliberative assembly charged with deciding the terms on which that unity rested – that is, to define orthodoxy. Put more cautiously, determining the precise doctrinal basis for unity was of lesser importance to Theodosius and his government than the actual demonstration of that unity through the convocation of bishops from across the empire and their communal willingness to participate in debate and discussion.[40] What mattered was that the holding of a church council in Ephesus should be seen as an event of dramatic and symbolic significance in itself. Such a perspective may perhaps be seen as consonant with the Theodosian regime's noticeably strong interest in ceremonial (and a certain deftness in its employment) as a strategy for securing and displaying authority as well as for

---

[38] Cyr. *Ep.* 17.12 (ed. L. Wickham, Oxford, 1983).
[39] In fact, this is precisely the initial imperial response to the competing judgements of the rival part-councils in June and July 431.
[40] See too (as a complement to the argument advanced here) the observations in Destephen 2008 on the government's interest in the full representation of regions and provinces at church councils.

balancing competing social and political interests.[41] From that point of view, procedure – in a church council too – could seem more significant than outcome.

But the contrast should not be too starkly drawn. At least in part the deliberate reticence of the *sacra* on doctrinal matters is deceptive. A series of responses to Theodosius' directives – both from the bishops assembled in Ephesus and from imperial officials – may fairly be taken as indications of the emperor's intentions (and even instructions). These responses show a certain degree of uniformity in their interpretation of what was expected. This may, in turn, suggest additional and more precise imperial direction, perhaps given orally to the Council by Candidianus. Certainly, Candidianus in his report on the opening of the Council at the session held on 22 June refers to the instructions he had received.[42] These (if ever written or recorded) are not preserved in any extant *acta*. It is also relevant here to recognise the importance of officials tasked with carrying out imperial orders on the ground, and the decisive role of messengers who not only transmitted imperial or ecclesiastical communications but who might also be expected to fill in some of the thinking behind the documents they carried. While modern analysis is for the most part (and understandably) confined to surviving documents, it is important to recognise the limitations these inevitably impose. Conversations with messengers and officials were an integral part of government communication that was initiated and framed – but by no means exhausted – by official documents.[43]

While Theodosius' statements on the need for a church council were fairly clear, the lack of specific direction on its form and content as well the desired outcome demanded interpretation – and that allowed those in Ephesus to draw a range of subtly different

---

[41] See Soc. 7.23 and the incisive sketch in Traina 2007: 48–65, especially 53–7; and, more generally, McCormick 1986, with 58–60, 118–19 on Theodosius II; Meier 2007.

[42] *Coll. Cas.* 84 (*ACO* 1 4, p. 32.37–9).

[43] In the context of the Council, the mission of the *comes* John in August 431 demonstrates the importance of imperial officers in relaying and interpreting the emperor's wishes. Theodosius writes: 'May your sacredness know that we have sent the most magnificent and most glorious John, count of the sacred largesses, so that, since he knows the aim of our divinity as regards faith [αὐτὸν εἰδότα τὸν περὶ τὴν πίστιν τῆς ἡμετέρας θειότητος σκοπόν], he may bring about whatever he perceives to be beneficial' (*Coll. Vat.* 93.4; *ACO* 1 1.3, p. 32.7–10).

THEODOSIUS II AND THE FIRST COUNCIL OF EPHESUS

conclusions. In his protests immediately following his deposition by the Council's opening session, Nestorius (who had not been present) summed up his understanding of what Theodosius had charged the bishops to do. The emperor's central demand was for a 'joint meeting of all', at which the bishops 'by a joint decree confirm the creed of the holy fathers convened at Nicaea'.[44] In stark contrast to his own compliance, the Egyptian bishops led by Cyril in forcing the opening of the Council on 22 June had (so Nestorius' claimed) directly disobeyed this instruction: 'for in the letter sent out by your piety you said that a single concordant faith should be issued by all, corresponding to the writings of the evangelists and the apostles and the doctrines of the holy fathers.'[45] None of Theodosius' surviving letters had been so specific, either about the need for a πίστις or in demanding the Council's confirmation of the Nicene Creed. Yet, on their arrival in Ephesus, the eastern bishops made the same point at the first meeting of their part council on 26 June (from which those bishops supporting Cyril were absent). After the imperial *sacra* which had opened the contested session on 22 June had been read to them, John of Antioch summarised it – with one important addition. According to his understanding of what he had just heard, the *sacra* demanded an 'exact examination and confirmation of the pious faith of the holy and blessed fathers who assembled at Nicaea in Bithynia'.[46] Nicaea was not explicitly mentioned in the *sacra* but, it appears, was readily understood by the *sacra*'s references to true doctrine.[47] That the Nicene Creed represented correct belief, and that any doctrinal decision could consist only in its confirmation, seems to have been the unquestioned assumption of all present; hence it was read into the emperor's more general statements on orthodoxy. Of course, what 'confirming Nicaea'

---

[44] *Coll. Vat.* 146.1 (*ACO* I 1.5, p. 13.31–2): οὕτως κοινὸν ἁπάντων ποιῆσαι συνέδριον καὶ κοινῇ ψήφῳ κυρῶσαι τῶν ἁγίων πατέρων τὴν πίστιν τῶν ἐν Νικαίᾳ συναθροισθέντων.

[45] *Coll. Vat.* 146.3 (ACO I 1.5, p. 14.13–15): μίαν γὰρ παρὰ πάντων σύμφωνον ἐκτεθῆναι πίστιν ἐν τοῖς ὑπὸ τῆς ὑμετέρας εὐσεβείας ἀποσταλεῖσι διηγορεύσατε γράμμασι πρόσφορον τοῖς τε εὐαγγελικοῖς καὶ ἀποστολικοῖς γράμμασι καὶ τοῖς τῶν ἁγίων πατέρων δόγμασιν.

[46] *Coll. Vat.* 151.10 (*ACO* I 1.5, p. 121.14–15).

[47] See n. 35 above.

meant in practice and which theological position could be considered a full and proper expression of such an affirmation, was the centrally disputed issue at the Council.

Candidianus' report on his unsuccessful attempts to halt the Council's opening session on 22 June also offers more specific information on Theodosius' instructions. Without mentioning Nicaea, Candidianus echoed the emperor's expectation that 'a confirmation of the faith' should be achieved.[48] The Council – in Candidianus' interpretation – had two options. The assembled bishops could declare that 'they all equally professed correctly according to the religion of the holy fathers'. Alternatively, they could identify those who held views not in conformity with orthodox belief.[49] Again, this version of the emperor's will is more specific than the general guidelines set out in the *sacra* read out at the Council's opening session. Yet even meeting Candidianus' conditions would not have necessitated the drafting of a doctrinal statement (such as the one issued by the Council of Chalcedon in 451), even less any subscription to a freshly drafted creed (on the model of Nicaea). Traditionally, church councils had used a variety of textual forms to communicate their decisions. The most common was an encyclical letter, sometimes accompanied by further documentation.[50] The alternative to the ratification of a positive statement of orthodox belief (and an option clearly also envisaged by Candidianus) was to issue anathemas or simply condemn particular individuals.

These immediate responses to the *sacra* (first read on 22 June at the Council's opening session to the bishops joining Cyril, and again four days later to the bishops in alliance with John of Antioch) all point to the possibility of further explanation and instruction by Candidianus. In addition, it seems the *sacra*'s references to true doctrine were understood on all sides to refer to the Nicene Creed. This interpretation may have been in line with

---

[48] *Coll. Cas.* 84 (*ACO* I 4, p. 32.8–9): *uelle namque eum [sc. imperatorem] dixi [sc.* at the meeting of the bishops on 22 June] *fidem nostram ... roborari.*

[49] *Coll. Cas.* 84 (*ACO* I 4, p. 32.24–6): *cunctis uobis praesentibus iudicarentur et tunc cum consensu omnium uestrum ostenderetur quis praue ac praeter regulas ecclesiasticas credere uideretur an certe recte omnes pariter confiteri, sicut sanctorum patrum religio habet.*

[50] Cf. above n. 10 with the studies cited there; and Chrysos 1983.

THEODOSIUS II AND THE FIRST COUNCIL OF EPHESUS

Theodosius' unspoken assumptions; it certainly reflects the dominant presumption in contemporary doctrinal debate. Even so, there remains a noticeable, and arguably purposeful, restraint in the imperial communications discussed above about the specific ways in which orthodoxy was to be examined and whether – and if so, in which form – it might require formal ratification. Even after the initial reports of the turmoil in Ephesus, the responses from Constantinople insisted almost exclusively on good order, a joint engagement with the issues in hand and the prevention of episcopal subterfuge and evasion. In short, the emperor relied above all on a procedural framework as a guarantee for fairness of the Council's conduct and a universally beneficial outcome.[51]

Taken together, the two imperial *sacrae* issued before the first Council of Ephesus (however they might have been glossed orally by imperial officials) offer an important insight into Theodosius' approach to the occasion. On their own, generalised statements about the divinely appointed role of an emperor or the need for peace and unity in Church and empire might seem no more than virtuous commonplaces and far from firm indications of Theodosius' aims and opinions. Yet the cumulative impact of their repeated insistence suggests that they amount to more than mere rhetorical ornament. Rather, they reveal a set of assumptions and expectations that shaped Theodosius' thinking about church councils in general and the forthcoming assembly in Ephesus in particular. These assumptions do not perhaps add up to a sharply

---

[51] Even Theodosius' instructions of 29 June (*Coll. Vat.* 83 [*ACO* I 1.3, pp. 9–10]), responding to the alarming reports of events in Ephesus on 22 June (and perhaps also to early indications of their further escalation following the arrival and separate meeting of the eastern bishops led by John of Antioch), only forcefully insisted on the requirement for matters of faith to be examined by the whole Council jointly (and therefore declared decisions taken in part-council invalid). The repeated prescription barring any bishop from leaving Ephesus – given added emphasis by the introduction of additional measures for the city's policing – served the same purpose. Importantly, the *sacra* still refrained from prescribing how the Council might formalise any decision reached after such examination, and does not demand a specific text or document setting out its findings. Theodosius' approach changed two months later with the mission of the *comes* John; see *Coll. Vat.* 93 (*ACO* I 1.3, pp. 31–2); *Coll. Ath.* 48 (*ACO* I 1.7, pp. 69–70); and n. 43 above.

conceived and successfully implemented political agenda. But (as argued above) the lack of a more determined and specific programme is not a reflection of a weak or ineffective emperor, but rather a deliberate stepping back from any immediate interference with the Council's dealings. In part, this was a recognition of how easily attempts at imperial intervention could be misrepresented and, in part, an acceptance of the limits to involvement in church affairs – a restriction bishops had been advocating for some time, and which, in varying degrees, most emperors had followed since Constantine. It was also a recognition that any resolute exercise of autocracy might risk retarding the possibility of negotiating any workable balance between imperial and ecclesiastical concerns and claims to authority.

Between the need to establish peace and the calls to stamp out heresy, most late-antique emperors found themselves in a no-win situation. What might Theodosius' options have been? Had he resolved to protect Nestorius with the same unflinching determination he later displayed in empowering Dioscorus to drive through his agenda at the second Council of Ephesus (in 449), the outcries (from both contemporaries and modern scholars) might easily be imagined. Given its lack of success, Theodosius' policy of seeking to use problem-solving mechanisms that exploited nascent conventions internal to the Church may now seem naïve – but probably stood as good a chance of working as any.[52] Theodosius' initial stance could even reflect a political wisdom and realism not in evidence in his subsequent more forceful interventions. It took the inability of the officials dispatched to Ephesus to reconcile the quarrelling parties and weeks of fruitless negotiations over the summer at Chalcedon before Theodosius decided to become personally and visibly involved, granting audiences to the delegates from both sides and discussing matters with them face to face.[53] Even this level of imperial engagement had little effect on the disputants. Theodosius dissolved the Council, leaving only unfinished business and heightened tensions. He firmly intended to enforce

---

[52] Even Constantine is criticised by modern scholars for an allegedly 'naive and dangerous ... respect for bishops as theological experts', which prevented him from more decisive interventions (Barnes 1981: 225).

[53] For this phase, see, briefly, Fraisse-Coué 1995: 538–40; Wessel 2001: 295–9.

Cyril's deposition and to keep Nestorius, now also removed from office, confined to his monastery. Yet even this resolve was overtaken by events. Cyril had already returned to Alexandria and it was left to Theodosius grudgingly to sanction the status quo. Certainly – and (as suggested here) despite the emperor's intentions – the first Council of Ephesus had not established unity in the Church. As a means of conflict resolution, it was a spectacular failure.

CHAPTER 5

OLYMPIODORUS OF THEBES AND
EASTERN TRIUMPHALISM

Peter Van Nuffelen

The history of Olympiodorus of Thebes is strangely paradoxical.[1] Published probably before 427,[2] and shortly after the last events it describes, it offers a valuable account of crucial events in the West from 407 to 425.[3] The history as a whole is lost, but it was summarised by the ninth-century Byzantine patriarch Photius and used by the fifth-century church historians Sozomen and Philostorgius, and by the (probably) early sixth-century historian Zosimus. In particular Zosimus is thought to reflect Olympiodorus relatively faithfully in his account of the years after 407.[4] Highly esteemed by modern scholars, the history nevertheless displays some peculiar characteristics. It presents itself as a history of the Roman empire from 407 to 425, yet the work only covers the history of the West. This bias cannot be blamed on Photius' summary: in their use of Olympiodorus, both Philostorgius and Sozomen as well as Zosimus all share this western focus. When Olympiodorus does include eastern material in his history, it is usually in relation to himself: his embassy to the Hun leader Donatus around 412, his success (around 415) in obtaining a chair of rhetoric for

I wish to thank the conference audience for questions and remarks, and in particular the editor, Christopher Kelly, for his numerous helpful suggestions.

[1] Olympiodorus calls his own work ὕλην συγγραφῆς and ὕλην δὲ αὐτὸς ἱστορίας ταῦτα καλῶν = Phot. *Bibl.* 80 (56b.19 and 25); this need not be anything more than a statement of modesty, along the lines of Caesar's *commentarii*, rather than a denial that the work is a history, see Haedicke 1939: 207 and, generally, Treadgold 2007: 95–6.
[2] Thompson 1944; Baldwin 1980: 218–19; later dates have been advocated (Blockley 1981: 29–30; Clover 1983: 144–50; Gillett 1993: 11–12; Baldini 2000), but fail to convince, see Treadgold 2004: 727–9; Van Nuffelen 2004b: 86 n. 40.
[3] Paschoud 1985, 1986: 192–3 argues for a start date in 408; Baldini 2000: 497–502 for 378.
[4] For full discussion, see Paschoud 1986: 191–6, 1989: 100.

Leontius, the father of the future empress Eudocia, and his dealings with the Blemyes in Egypt.[5] A striking lack of balance is also evident in Photius' summary: the latter two episodes, in particular, seem completely disconnected from the rest of the narrative with its firm focus on the West. Moreover, in Photius' summary, it is only in connection with these eastern episodes that Olympiodorus deploys a distinctly Herodotean emphasis on travel for the sake of knowledge, an emphasis intended to establish his credentials as a historian.[6] A detailed description of Rome, shortly before the end of the work, is traditionally taken to betray an eyewitness account; yet Photius fails to report any personal statements to that effect – and in marked contrast to the accounts of Egypt and Athens.[7] The impression created by the surviving fragments of Olympiodorus is thus strangely imbalanced: that this was a history of the West written by an author based in the East; and by an author who founded his claim to be a good historian on experiences that had little or no relevance for his overall narrative.

The apparent disconnect between author and narrative, as revealed by Olympiodorus himself, has rarely been discussed explicitly. It has been addressed implicitly by an emphasis on the particular historical circumstances of 425, and on Olympiodorus' personality and social position. The focus on the West has been set against the background of the triumphant installation by eastern troops of Valentinian III on the throne of the western empire, after the death of Honorius and the defeat of the usurper John.[8] Valentinian was the son of Constantius III and Galla Placidia, whose respective elevations to Augustus and Augusta in 421 had never been recognised by the eastern court. The new-found alliance between East and West, after the successive deaths of Constantius III (421), Honorius (423) and John (425), had been sealed with the betrothal of Valentinian III and the two-year-old daughter of Theodosius II, Licinia Eudoxia, in 424. Such a reversal of fortunes, it has been suggested, coming after years of tension – which

---

[5] Olymp. 19 (Donatus); 28 (Leontius); 35.2 (Blemyes).
[6] Olymp. 35.2.2: ἱστορίας ἕνεκα; for a different, but speculative, interpretation of this passage, see Treadgold 2004: 720.
[7] Olymp. 41.1; cf. Matthews 1970: 80, 88–9; Blockley 1981: 27–8.
[8] Gillett 1993: 18–26.

had started with Stilicho's alleged interest in controlling the East – cried out to be recorded by a historian. Scholars have been eager to assert Olympiodorus' unique suitability for that task, either by arguing that he was already serving the western court in the 410s[9] or by depicting him as an intrepid ambassador. Olympiodorus' travels thus allowed him to pick up the information he needed, effectively turning his history into an account of his own experiences.[10] Apart from his life-long travels, the second element routinely highlighted is Olympiodorus' social position as a bureaucrat.[11] Even though he travelled on official missions, he was (it has been asserted) disengaged and objective, thus making him the ideal historian. His work has been characterised as independent – and even as advice offered by a civil servant to the emperor.[12] Even though written by an easterner, Olympiodorus' travels and his official post have together served as a reassurance that he can reliably be read as transmitting a western perspective[13] or western sources.[14] Finally, Olympiodorus was a pagan and did not attempt to conceal the fact in his history. In line with the older view that religious oppositions marked every aspect of late-antique society, his paganism has been adduced as another argument for his objective, not to say critical, stance towards the 'monastic' court of Theodosius II.[15]

---

[9] On the basis of Olymp. 35.1, Maenchen-Helfen 1973: 74 and Blockley 1981: 27 assert that the embassy to the Huns was sent by the western court; there is no need for this, see Gillett 1993: 12; Treadgold 2004: 714.
[10] Matthews 1970: 90; Baldwin 1980: 213; Gillett 1993: 12–14.
[11] For bureaucrats (especially lawyers) as historians, see Harries 1986 and Greatrex 2001.
[12] Thompson 1944: 52: 'sturdily independent attitude of the author towards the class divisions of the empire'; Blockley 1981: 47: 'independent and a realist'; Gillett 1993: 2: 'Olympiodorus's account is a characteristic product of the highly literate class of eastern imperial civil servants, and of their genuine preoccupation with the relationship between the eastern and western halves of the Roman Empire at a time when both were threatened by the rise of the new Carthaginian power of the Vandals'; Treadgold 2004: 731: 'an official memorandum ... Olympiodorus' history would therefore have been a sort of confidential report or briefing book on his government missions, especially the one to Rome' (repeated in Treadgold 2007: 96); in a similar vein, see Maisano 1979: 23.
[13] Matthews 1970, 1975: 382–8; Zecchini 1983: 23.
[14] Paschoud 1975: 180–1, 2006a: 73–4; Baldini 1998, 2004: 225–66.
[15] Kaegi 1968: 86–91; Paschoud 1975, 1986, 1989, 2006a; Baldini 2004: 155–94; more generally, Alan Cameron 2011 de-emphasises the importance of religious differences for Latin literature.

Such a view of Olympiodorus is open to question, on several levels. First, it is not hard to detect a traditional Weberian opposition in the judgements quoted above: Olympiodorus as a bureaucrat, safely distant from the compromising influences of court life, pursued the interests of the state. Such views oppose, on the one hand, a 'rational' and 'objective' bureaucracy, focused pragmatically on carrying out decisions, and, on the other hand, a political class that makes these decisions. At best, the idea of the 'objective bureaucrat' is a projection of a modern ideal on to Antiquity: whenever we can see the late-antique bureaucracy in action – for example, in John Lydus' account of his own career – it is fiercely political.[16] Second, scholars have tended to take the image that Olympiodorus paints of himself in his digressions at face value. Yet they are principally a literary pose aimed at insinuating his suitability for the historical enterprise: most of them situate the author in the tradition of Herodotus, whilst the story about his efforts to get Leontius a chair of rhetoric in Athens flaunts his own relationship with the Empress Eudocia.

Much depends on how one understands the political context of 424/425: was it a *rapprochement* between two equal parts of the empire or the imposition of eastern authority on the West? Scholars have hesitated between both options.[17] The sources from the East, however, all play the same triumphant tune and emphasise eastern superiority. For the church historian Socrates, the defeat of the usurper John is an almost miraculous event that underlines God's providential care of the eastern empire.[18] Valentinian's betrothal to Licinia Eudoxia may seem to suggest the reintegration of the families, but was based on a clear hierarchy of status. Indeed, when reporting the marriage of Valentinian and Eudoxia thirteen years later, Socrates records two crucial details: first he notes that Valentinian had once again to ask for the hand of Eudoxia (suggesting that the deal of 424 was always subject to review by Theodosius) and, second, that although Theodosius had offered to celebrate the marriage in Thessalonica (on the grounds that it was

---

[16] C. M. Kelly 2004: 11–104.
[17] Matthews 1975: 381; Gillett 1993: 18–25; Blockley 1998: 136–7.
[18] Soc. 7.23.9–12.

halfway between Rome and Constantinople) Valentinian decided to journey to Constantinople himself.[19] As symbolised in this act of submission, the relationship between East and West was asymmetrical. Olympiodorus himself shows Theodosius II firmly in charge: he sends Galla Placidia and Valentinian back, three eastern commanders are dispatched with armies and the *magister officiorum* Helion is proxy for Theodosius, conferring the title of Augustus on Valentinian in Rome in October 425.[20] The victory over the usurper John and the crowning of Valentinian III probably generated the same triumphant atmosphere in Constantinople as is recorded by Socrates for the victory over the Persians in 422. According to the historian, the victory was celebrated with an outburst of heroic verse and prose, from the empress herself down to ambitious *literati* desirous of attention.[21] The events of 425 were at least as glorious and, crucially, the actors were largely the same (Helion, Ardabur and Aspar, the leading generals of 425, had all played a role in the campaign of 422).

I wish to suggest that Olympiodorus' history should be situated in this context of patriotic fervour. Rather than offering a disengaged account to serve imperial policy in relation to the West, Olympiodorus depicts the triumphant reassertion of control over the West by the eastern court after years of animosity. It is in this context that both the history's geographical restriction to half the empire and its chronological limits start to make sense. So too that this history was written by an author whose acquaintance with the West only seems to have started in 424/425[22] (when Olympiodorus might have been on Helion's staff). Whilst he clearly had access to information about the West, Olympiodorus can be shown systematically to project an eastern, ideological perspective on the

---

[19] Soc. 7.44.
[20] Olymp. 43; according to Soc. 7.24.4–5, Theodosius wished to come to Rome, but only made it as far as Thessalonica; see Lee p. 96, this volume.
[21] Soc. 7.21.7–10.
[22] It could be argued that Olympiodorus' acquaintance with western officials goes back further in time. In fact, most of the individuals cited as possible eyewitness sources for Olympiodorus – *PLRE* II 645 (Iustianianus 2); *PLRE* I 459 (Iohannes 2); *PLRE* II 822–4 (Palladius 19), 530 (Heliocrates 1), 622 (Iovius 1); cf. Matthews 1970: 89–90; Treadgold 2004: 725 – could still have been around in 424/425 and do not support the idea of an earlier visit to the West.

events his history describes. In what follows, I argue that the historian highlights as failures in the West precisely those aspects which the East considered its strengths, namely stability in the imperial family, exclusion of outsiders and success in dealing with barbarians. Olympiodorus clearly allowed the self-image of the eastern court to set the standard in his history. Read in this way, Olympiodorus' representation of events sheds more light on eastern elite self-understanding than on western views of recent events. It illustrates the extent to which relations between East and West had been marred by personal animosities, but also the confidence of the East that it had made the right choices. There is a sense of self-congratulation, having won the battle with the West, but also one of superiority. This is brought out in a significant detail: Photius records that Olympiodorus dedicated his history to Theodosius, 'the nephew of Honorius and Placidia, and the son of Arcadius'.[23] This emphasis on family ties would normally be odd, especially since Theodosius had been emperor for almost twenty years at the time of publication, but not in the context in which Olympiodorus wrote. It signals at once the reconciliation between West and East by its inclusion of Galla Placidia and a recognition of Theodosius' superiority: Honorius and Arcadius are both dead and he is the heir to both their realms. In addition, Olympiodorus' self-presentation as a travelling historian, ambassador to the barbarians and lobbyist for the family of the empress underscores his ties with that policy and that successful dynasty.

The context for Olympiodorus' history is thus not the innate desire of a bureaucrat to advise his political superiors nor the result of a life-long commitment to write a history. This chapter does not argue against using Olympiodorus to reconstruct the turbulent history of the West from 407 to 425, nor does it dispute that he may offer reliable and important information. But the image of Olympiodorus as an objective bureaucrat faithfully reporting the views of the West with the interests of the empire in mind should be laid to rest. Instead, he should be seen as reflecting the triumphalism that marked the eastern court in 425. In such an atmosphere,

---

[23] Phot. *Bibl.* 80 (56b.27–9): ὃς ἀνεψιὸς ἐχρημάτιζεν Ὁνωρίου καὶ Πλακιδίας, Ἀρκαδίου δὲ παῖς, πρὸς τοῦτον τὴν ἱστορίαν ἀναφωνεῖ.

it does not matter much whether one wrote on imperial order or spontaneously: all participated in the celebration of triumph.

Closing off the dynasty

The conventional image of the court and family of Theodosius II is decisively coloured by its depiction in the church historians as a quasi-monastic institution. Theodosius' three sisters had embraced perpetual virginity and Theodosius himself is said to have turned the palace into a monastery. In fact – as Sozomen conceded – the decision was not just a matter of pious resolve. In Sozomen's panegyrical account, Pulcheria's asceticism was linked to more mundane concerns: she imposed virginity on herself and her two sisters Arcadia and Marina 'to avoid introducing another man into the palace and so remove all cause for jealousy and intrigue'.[24] The fact that Sozomen can make this statement in a work probably intended to attract the emperor's attention[25] suggests there was no problem in treating virginity as part of dynastic policy. Whatever the precise occasion for the decision,[26] it came to be seen as a cornerstone of the Theodosian dynasty, and Pulcheria's later rejection of her virginity to marry Marcian was regarded as a betrayal of that tradition.[27]

---

[24] Soz. 9.1.3: ὅπως μὴ ἄλλον ἄνδρα ἐπεισαγάγῃ τοῖς βασιλείοις καὶ ζήλου καὶ ἐπιβουλῆς πᾶσαν ἀνέλῃ ἀφορμήν; and see Harries pp. 67–70, this volume.

[25] Van Nuffelen 2004a: 53–61.

[26] Based on the coincidence of Pulcheria's proclamation as Augusta (4 July 414) and the disappearance of the erstwhile strong man Anthemius (last attested 18 April 414), Kenneth Holum argued that Anthemius had proposed that Pulcheria marry his son, Fl. Anthemius Isidorus (*PLRE* II 631–3 [Isidorus 9]). In Holum's view, the proclamation of Pulcheria's virginity and the removal of Anthemius and his family from power communicated the message that no one was to be permitted to break into the imperial family (Holum 1982: 93–7). This speculative argument is decisively weakened by the fact that Anthemius' family continued to be important, even in the period of Pulcheria's supposed ascendency at court. Anthemius' son, Isidorus, would climb to be praetorian prefect of Illyricum in 424, praetorian prefect of the East in 435 and consul in 436. Another member of the family, Procopius (Anthemius' son-in-law), played a key role in the campaign against Persia in 422 (which was, to quote Holum 1977, 'Pulcheria's crusade') and was rewarded with the title of *patricius* (*PLRE* II 920 [Procopius 2]). For a critique of other aspects of Holum's view of the Theodosian court, see Averil Cameron 1994: 10; Price 1994; Cooper 2004.

[27] Burgess 1993–4.

Another important aspect of the dynastic policy of the eastern court has received rather less attention: Theodosius' decision to choose a wife outside the established elite. Athenais, the future empress Eudocia, the daughter of a professor of rhetoric in Athens, was hardly a suitable match for an emperor. Again it is hard to probe beneath the romantic accounts of later Byzantine histories,[28] but the implications of the emperor's decision are important. Theodosius could have married anybody he wished, and a marriage alliance with the imperial house was pursued by many a court grandee. The story of how Rufinus was tricked by Eutropius when he thought his daughter was about to become empress is well known.[29] The Isaurian general Zeno became emperor by marrying Ariadne, the daughter of Leo I. In contrast then with these earlier and later rulers, Theodosius II consciously closed himself and his family off from alliances with the nobility. His virgin sisters were not available, and he himself married a complete outsider.

For some of the possible reasons for this strategic decision, we can turn to Olympiodorus. His account of the complicated family arrangements at the court of Honorius and the tensions and feuds they caused can be understood as implicitly contrasting the wise decisions of the East with the foolish and dangerous ones of the West. The historian recounts too much of this for it to be entirely without point, and the theme surfaces right at the beginning of the work. Two chapters into the section of his narrative that derives from Olympiodorus, Zosimus describes the marriage between Honorius and Thermantia (in 408), the daughter of Stilicho and Serena and the sister of Honorius' first wife. He reports the attraction that Honorius felt for Thermantia and Stilicho's lack of enthusiasm, and then suggests that Serena was actually the driving force behind the match.[30] In Zosimus' version, Serena is a dubious character: when Honorius was about to marry her first daughter Maria, Serena wished the match to take place because

---

[28] Malalas 14.4–5; *Chron. Pasch.* 420 (I 575.4–578.8); Zonaras 13.22 (III 236–7); it is not necessary to substitute for the Byzantine flights of fantasy the hypothesis that Pulcheria's pagan enemies contrived the marriage, so Holum 1982: 120–1.

[29] Zos. 5.1.

[30] Olymp. 3, extracted from Photius' summary (*Bibl.* 80 [56b.34–7]), gives Stilicho the initiative, but that may be the result of extreme abbreviation; on this passage, see Paschoud 1986: 210.

of the influence it would bring her, but also dreaded it because of the young age of her daughter. Serena therefore had recourse to a witch to ensure that Honorius could not 'deprive Maria of her virginity'.[31] This story picks up specific elements of the Theodosian dynastic ideology. Rather than using the death of his wife to distance himself from Stilicho, Honorius reinforces his ties with this general by marrying another of his daughters. (And, as suggested below, in Olympiodorus' eyes Stilicho always pursued his own agenda, weakening the position of the emperor.) Serena's use of a witch also provides an instructive contrast with the high value set on virginity in Theodosian court ideology. Whereas Pulcheria and her sisters voluntarily choose virginity for religious and dynastic reasons, Serena resorts to magic in an attempt to create a virgin wife.

The theme of dynastic tension as the result of marriage is also present in Olympiodorus' treatment of another important female character: Galla Placidia, the daughter of Theodosius I. Her love life was complicated, but not always of her own making. From the beginning, Olympiodorus presents her as torn between the Gothic leader, Athaulf, and the future emperor Constantius III, neither of whom she liked. Captured by the Goths, she was forced to marry Athaulf in an attempt to strengthen the Goths' ties with the Romans. Constantius, then still a general, is depicted as repeatedly urging Athaulf to hand Galla back.[32] After her release, Honorius forced her to marry Constantius (in 417); he had repeatedly asked for her hand and her rejections had already caused tension at court.[33] In a significant remark that may well derive from Olympiodorus, Philostorgius notes that Honorius elevated Constantius to the rank of Augustus 'out of respect for his familial relationship'.[34] In Photius' summary, Olympiodorus notes that Honorius did so unwillingly.[35] Marriage with a sister of the emperor, Olympiodorus suggests, inevitably leads to pressure

---

[31] Zos. 5.28.2: τὸν δὲ μήτε ἐθέλειν μήτε δύνασθαι τὰ τῷ γάμῳ προσήκοντα πράττειν.
[32] Olymp. 22, 24, 26; on Constantius III, see Lütkenhaus 1998; on Galla Placidia, Oost 1968; Demougeot 1985; Sivan 2011.
[33] Olymp. 33.1.1–7.
[34] Philostorgius 12.12 = Olymp. 33.2.1–2: κατὰ τιμὴν τοῦ κήδους.
[35] Olymp. 33.1.14: ἀλλὰ σχεδόν τι ἄκοντος.

by the new in-law to be raised in status. Theodosius II, however, refused to recognise Constantius (who is reported to have planned a military expedition to Constantinople to obtain recognition). Again the contrast is instructive: none of this wrangling was possible in the East as no member of the imperial family was available for marriage.

Olympiodorus' depiction of Constantius III was regarded as ambivalent by John Matthews, who pointed out that he was portrayed as a capable general and a pleasant man who regretted his elevation to the imperial throne and who became greedy once he had assumed the purple.[36] I would rather argue that Constantius appears as a figure of contrast, showing the superiority of the East. Olympiodorus certainly shows Constantius as the stalwart defender of the ruling house, and especially of Galla Placidia, against the Goths.[37] But this attitude was not disinterested, as Philostorgius notes: 'Constantius, cherishing the hope that if he conquered Athaulf in war, he would marry Placidia'.[38] Olympiodorus' portrait of Constantius III was, in fact, ambivalent even before he married Galla and became Augustus. The passage in which Constantius' appearance during public processions is said to have betrayed a 'tyrant's demeanour' reports events of 414, three years before the marriage.[39] Rather than seeing this as representing western attitudes,[40] it can be read as a commentary on the dangers of an imperial marital policy that embraced outsiders: a capable general such as Constantius is allowed to set his eyes on a princess and the title of Augustus, letting his ambition run unchecked. Undoubtedly a man of virtue, he is not capable of self-control. Once he has gained what he desires, he turns into a greedy tyrant. This is a not uncommon depiction in ancient historiography: once someone achieves high station, he is unable to 'bear his fortune' and his morals start to slip. Diodorus Siculus

---

[36] Olymp. 37 with Matthews 1970: 91–2; a more nuanced approach in Baldwin 1980: 224.
[37] Olymp. 22, 37.
[38] Philostorgius 12.4 = Olymp. 26.2.1–2: ἐλπίδας τρέφων, ὡς αὐτὸς καταπολεμήσας Ἀδαοῦλφον τὴν Πλακιδίαν νυμφεύσαιτο.
[39] Olymp. 23.14: εἶδος ἄξιον τυραννίδος.
[40] Matthews 1970: 91.

explains in this way, for example, the blasphemy of Tantalus and Cambyses' assault on the Apis bull.[41] Seen in this light, the portrait of Constantius is both a confirmation of the wisdom of the eastern ruling family in closing itself off, and an implicit contention that the virtues required to be an emperor are not easily found outside that family.

The death of Constantius in 421 did not mark a turn for the better at the western court. In another example of the strategic use of gossip, Olympiodorus records how Honorius grew so fond of Galla Placidia that they kissed each other on the mouth, sparking off rumours of an incestuous relationship. The court made sure that this intense love turned into fierce hatred, causing Placidia to be exiled to Constantinople.[42] The depiction of Honorius is remarkably negative throughout Olympiodorus' history. Bad judgement is the least of the vices conveyed by the narrative: Zosimus reports that at one point Honorius proposed to share the empire with Attalus, the usurper put on the throne by Alaric in 409, thus revealing his lack of stamina.[43] Add to that the emperor's weak moral sense and an inability to control his lusts. This portrayal is remarkable in a work dedicated to Theodosius II, who for fifteen years shared power (and repeated consulates) with Honorius, his imperial nephew, and even more so when contrasted with the way the church historian Sozomen (writing slightly later in the 440s) deals with material drawn from Olympiodorus. Systematically omitting everything that could possibly be read as criticism of the imperial house, Sozomen's version of Honorius verges on the standard image of the providential ruler.[44] In my view, this is an indication that Sozomen was not in any way close to the court; just like Olympiodorus, he dedicated his history to Theodosius, but he had no real sense about what he could or could not say about the imperial family. He therefore decided to stick to a safe representation of events that would absolve all of them of any blame. But Olympiodorus clearly had no qualms about depicting Honorius very badly and criticising Galla Placidia, the mother of the ruling

---

[41] Diod. Sic. 4.74.2, 10.14.2 with Hau 2009; see also Soc. 2.34.1, 3.1.35–7, 4.35.1, 7.10.1, 7.23.3; Zos. 2.55.1.
[42] Olymp. 38.   [43] Zos. 6 8.1.
[44] Alan Cameron 1982: 265–6; Leppin 1996: 129–30; Van Nuffelen 2004b.

emperor in the West. Appeals to Olympiodorus' 'independent judgement' will hardly do: if the eastern court was unwilling to accept such a hostile version of the western imperial family, it seems unlikely that it would have been included in a work dedicated to Theodosius. Olympiodorus must thus have been confident that he was striking the right chord.

The ideal of virginity was a crucial element of imperial self-presentation at the Theodosian court. While eastern church historians made themselves spokesmen for the religious side of this ideology, Olympiodorus can be seen as focusing mainly on its dynastic implications. These were equally important, especially when combined with Theodosius' rejection of any marriage alliance with a court grandee. Taking both sides together, one can discern a conscious policy, designed to close the dynasty off from outsiders. It helped to rule out the destabilising potential of marriage alliances with non-imperial court grandees. Drawing on this ideology, Olympiodorus offers a view on the western court that undoubtedly would find favour in Constantinople. He highlights episodes that show how the western court systematically made the opposite choices to its eastern counterpart, and draws attention to the dire consequences of this, not only internally for western politics but also for the relation between the two branches of the Theodosian dynasty. The extent to which Olympiodorus dared to criticise even Honorius and Galla Placidia shows that he was confident that these views would not displease his intended readers – first and foremost Theodosius himself. In the light of the persistent emphasis on the self-generated nature of the problems in the West, the conclusion of Olympiodorus' history is significant. The triumphant return of Valentinian III to the western imperial throne, engineered by eastern generals, and his betrothal to Theodosius' daughter, are clear signs that the eastern way of doing things was now to be imposed on the West.

Systemic failure

According to Photius, Olympiodorus divided his history into twenty-two books. Fragment 20, stating that 'the second part starts here',⁴⁵ hints at another dividing principle. The first part (Books 1–10) – aside from Olympiodorus' account of his own embassy to the Hun leader Donatus – concluded in 412 with the death of the Gothic general Sarus at the hand of Athaulf. The second part then opened with Athaulf's decision to abandon the usurper Jovinus (and his brother Sebastianus) and establish an alliance with Honorius. That point marked the beginning of the end for most of the usurpers who had seized control in the West in the preceding years.⁴⁶ Olympiodorus then draws attention to Rome's rapid recovery after the sack of 410⁴⁷ and to the rise of Constantius III – a figure whose military effectiveness he recognises. But the second part of Olympiodorus' history is not a rosy counterpart to a gloomy predecessor. Rather, the disappearance of the Goths from their central place in the narrative allows Olympiodorus to focus more closely on the internal problems of the western court: Constantius III's ambitions and tyrannical inclinations, and Galla Placidia and Honorius' *liaisons dangereuses*. In fact, the two parts can be seen as mirroring each other in one important respect: just as Stilicho had planned an expedition against the East,⁴⁸ so now did Constantius. His death, however, marks a real turning point: with Constantius III, western hostility against the East also died.⁴⁹ Indeed, Olympiodorus' history concludes with its reverse: the successful installation of Valentinian III on the western throne by eastern forces. The division of the work into two parts can hardly have been determined by chronological considerations, as the first half only deals with one-third of the total span covered by the history. The division was therefore intentional: to draw attention to the parallels between the two towering individuals which dominate each half – Stilicho and Constantius. It suggests that for Olympiodorus, Stilicho was as ambiguous an individual as Constantius, and one who pursued his own plans while acting as a defender of the empire and marrying into the ruling house.

---

[45] Olymp. 20.1: ἄρχεται δὲ ἡ δευτέρα ὧδε.
[46] That this was a turning point for Olympiodorus is confirmed by Soz. 9.15.3 = Olymp. 20.2.
[47] Olymp. 25, 26.2.8–10.
[48] Olymp. 5.2; cf. Zos. 5.30–5.
[49] Olymp. 33.1.24–5: συντελευτησάσης αὐτῷ καὶ τῆς κατὰ τὴν ἀνατολὴν ὀργῆς καὶ ὁρμῆς ἣν ὤδινεν.

OLYMPIODORUS OF THEBES AND EASTERN TRIUMPHALISM

Olympiodorus does not side with one of the many warring factions at the court of Honorius. Rather, all his leading characters display a moral ambiguity, thus suggesting that the decline of the West was not so much due to (for example) the execution of Stilicho, but rather to a general failure of the entire elite. It is the plotting, infighting and disloyalty towards the emperor by Stilicho and his successors that caused a systemic failure in the West.

Photius' summary says even less about Stilicho than it does about Constantius, but Zosimus' account is preserved up until the sack of Rome and will inform most of the following discussion. In the extant fragments, Olympiodorus made two points about Stilicho right from the outset: that he was married to Serena, and hence connected to the house of Theodosius, and that he had designs on the eastern empire.[50] His desire to add the Illyrican provinces to Honorius' realm is confirmed by Zosimus,[51] who describes Stilicho's intrigues in detail. In this version of events, the Goth Alaric was hired to invade Illyricum in 407 – an event that apparently opened Olympiodorus' history. Yet the expedition was called off: rumours circulated that Alaric had died, and a usurper, Constantine, had been proclaimed in Britain. The cancellation of the expedition greatly annoyed Alaric, who moved from Epirus into Noricum and demanded payments. In the Senate, Stilicho still stuck to his alliance with Alaric, and persuaded the senators to follow suit. Zosimus' narrative makes it clear that Stilicho's behaviour was at the very least awkward: some of the support he received was as a result of the fear he provoked,[52] and one senator who refused to yield, Lampadius, was forced to flee. Moreover, Stilicho shifted the blame on to the imperial house: 'While saying this, Stilicho showed the letter [from the emperor] and said that Serena was the cause, wishing to maintain the harmony of both emperors intact.'[53] Olympiodorus had first introduced Stilicho as the guardian of both Honorius and Arcadius[54] – a remarkable

---

[50] Olymp. 1.1 and 1.2 = Soz. 9.4.2–4.
[51] Zos. 5.26–7, 5.29.7.   [52] Zos. 5.29.6.
[53] Zos. 5.29.8: καὶ ταῦτα λέγων ὁ Στελίχων ἅμα καὶ τὴν ἐπιστολὴν ἐδείκνυ, καὶ τὴν Σερῆναν αἰτίαν ἔλεγεν εἶναι τὴν ἀμφοτέρων τῶν βασιλέων ὁμόνοιαν ἀδιάφθορον φυλάττεσθαι βουλομένην.
[54] Olymp. 1.1.

characterisation, as it seems to imply that Olympiodorus was prepared to endorse Stilicho's doubtful claims.[55] Yet in the events narrated immediately afterwards, Stilicho appears not so much as the guardian of both emperors, but as the person who wishes to make war on the East in order to promote the West. It is rather Serena, the adopted daughter of Theodosius I, who is represented as caring for the unity of the empire. In another episode, she is shown as acting responsibly to secure Honorius' safety. When the second expedition against the East was being prepared in 408, Honorius – on the advice of Serena who feared for his life – decided to follow the preparations closely from Ravenna.[56] To prevent the emperor from monitoring his plans, Stilicho even went so far as to incite Sarus to raise a brief rebellion in Ravenna – but to no avail. As we have seen above (in the account of her daughter, Maria), Serena also receives her share of criticism in Olympiodorus' account, but, crucially, in these episodes she is depicted as putting family above marriage – a significant message in the light of the implications of the family-focused ideology of Theodosius II traced in the previous section.

Stilicho's untrustworthiness in his dealings with Honorius is again underlined in the context of the planned expedition to the East to claim guardianship of the seven-year-old Theodosius II after the death of Arcadius in 408. Honorius wished to join the expedition himself, but was dissuaded by Stilicho who advanced political and financial reasons.[57] Some scholars have tended to believe Stilicho's arguments were correct and truthful[58] but Zosimus' vocabulary suggests insincerity (5.30.3: ἐπενόειτο πολλὰ ταύτης κωλύματα), hinting that Stilicho had his own agenda. Strangely, however, having got Honorius out of the way, Stilicho then did nothing.[59] Zosimus (and one supposes his source Olympiodorus too) does not offer any explanation. It has been suggested that Stilicho realised he could not leave the court where his position

---

[55] This is puzzling; Olympiodorus may mention it in order to show how Stilicho actually failed in his task by continuously plotting against the East; on Stilicho's regency, see in particular Alan Cameron 1969.
[56] Zos. 5.30.1–2.
[57] Zos. 5.31.4; cf. Soz. 9.4.4–8 = Olymp. 5.2.
[58] Matthews 1975: 280; Paschoud 1986: 227.
[59] Zos. 5.31.6.

was being undermined by his enemy Olympius[60] or that he waited for Alaric.[61] It is hard to distil any coherent plan from this episode. Zosimus is in no doubt that Stilicho wished to act as guardian to Theodosius II,[62] and his plotting to keep Honorius away from the East suggests, if not a desire to become emperor himself (as his enemy Olympius shortly afterwards alleged), then at least a wish for unfettered control over the imperial princeling.[63] But Stilicho's sudden and unexplained inactivity makes one wonder if Olympiodorus had any detailed information at all about Stilicho's precise intentions.[64] More important for present purposes is to set this entire episode against the eastern narrative of the succession to Arcadius. Theodosius II's accession was an obvious cause for concern: not only was he just seven years old, but the eastern empire was entangled in a long-running conflict with the West. In origin political, in recent years the dispute over Illyricum had become ecclesiastical, with the jurisdiction of the diocese being disputed between Rome and Constantinople. In addition, Innocent I in Rome was exerting pressure for the restoration of John Chrysostom who had been expelled from Constantinople in 404 – a decision in which Arcadius and Eudoxia had been very much involved.[65] The much later story of the eunuch Antiochus being sent at this point to take care of the young Theodosius II can also be read as a distant reflection of that concern.[66] By the time Constantinopolitan authors start to write about this period, that uncertainty had been transformed into self-congratulation: Socrates praises the Praetorian Prefect Anthemius for his wise rule, while Sozomen highlights the role played by Pulcheria.[67] This attitude need not surprise: in comparison with the West, the East had performed remarkably well. Although run by an emperor

---

[60] Mazzarino 1942: 288–92; Matthews 1975: 280; on this episode, see also Drinkwater 1998: 281.
[61] Burns 1994: 217.   [62] Zos. 5.31.3.
[63] Most modern assessments absolve Stilicho of all blame, see Mazzarino 1942: 288–92; O'Flynn 1983: 56–7.
[64] Cf. Kulikowski 2000a: 329–30.
[65] J. N. D. Kelly 1995: 272–85; Tiersch 2002: 369–423. For a detailed discussion of the relations between Innocent and the East, see Dunn 2005, 2007, 2009 and 2010.
[66] *PLRE* II 101–2 (Antiochus 5) with Greatrex and Bardill 1996; and see Traina pp. 161–2, this volume.
[67] Soc. 7.1; Soz. 9.1.

in his minority, it had not succumbed either to infighting or to external enemies, be they Huns or Romans from the West.

Olympiodorus' portrait of Stilicho has been said to betray a 'strong favour',[68] and indeed Zosimus praises him in a concluding assessment after his death as 'the most moderate and just of all the men who possessed great authority in his time'.[69] The story of the last days of Stilicho is marked by the opposition between barbarians and Romans, with the barbarians repeatedly willing to turn on the Romans. Stilicho, however, is depicted as trying to avoid a clash between the two groups and as prepared to risk his life for that.[70] Indeed, Stilicho appears as prescient: after his death his friends and allies are sought out, the Romans attack the barbarians and Alaric turns on Rome. The precarious balance he had struck was lost. It is probably the contrast with the tragic events after his death, the long series of usurpers and the sack of Rome, that generates such a positive image. Yet the course of events also underlines that impression that Stilicho was as much the last bulwark against the barbarians as the individual who had allowed them to enter the power game in the first place. Zosimus points out that Alaric was willing to make peace because of his previous alliance with Stilicho, but that Honorius, encouraged by Olympius, declined the proposal.[71] Alaric owed much of his status to Stilicho's willingness to use him, but, so at least Zosimus seems to suggest, Stilicho had also been able to restrain him. When Stilicho fell to the plotting of Olympius, the Goths became a force of their own and one that was prepared to turn against the hand that had fed them.[72]

Zosimus' sometimes puzzling account does not permit a clear picture of Stilicho nor of his enemies. Some of this opacity may be due to his desire to paint Stilicho in much brighter colours than Honorius, who was, after all, one of Zosimus' maligned Christian

---

[68] Matthews 1970: 90; see too Maisano 1979: 10; Blockley 1981: 44.
[69] Zos. 5.34.5: πάντων ὡς εἰπεῖν τῶν ἐν ἐκείνῳ δυναστευσάντων τῷ χρόνῳ γεγονὼς μετριώτερος.
[70] Zos. 5.33; Olymp. 5.   [71] Zos. 5.36.
[72] For other negative views of Stilicho, see Eunapius 72.3–4; Orosius 7.38; Rut. Nam. *de red. suo* 2.41–60; Jerome, *Ep.* 123.16 (ed. I. Hilberg, *CSEL* 56, Vienna, 1996). The latter emphasises his links with the barbarians; on Stilicho in general, see Mazzarino 1942; Janssen 2004.

emperors.[73] Yet, as the first plotter against the East, Stilicho was in many respects similar to Constantius III, the later one: both surely had virtues, but they also pursued their own interests, and whilst serving the empire, they also grievously harmed it. Both married into the imperial family, but did not act as loyal servants. They fostered disunity both at their own courts and between both parts of the empire. Indeed, one thing which is clear from Zosimus' account is that the first books of Olympiodorus' history were focused on plans to invade the East, with other events subordinated to this main theme. In a comforting act of retribution, at least for an eastern audience, it was Alaric – Stilicho's tool for the planned expedition against the East in 407 – who took Rome three years later.

The general ambivalence noted above in Olympiodorus' assessment of individual actors in his history should encourage us to shy away from any analysis that attempts to discover his views by compiling an inventory of his likes and dislikes. Rather, Olympiodorus highlights the general failure of the leading personnel in the West, not just of his two main characters, Stilicho and Constantius III, but also of the even less successful and talented individuals in between these two: the *magister officiorum* Olympius, who sidelined Stilicho, was himself severely criticised and was pushed aside in 409, before being killed a year later after a brief return to favour.[74] His successor, who also kept Honorius in close check, was Jovius, who had conspired against Olympius and who would later desert to Attalus, the puppet emperor set up by Alaric in 409.[75] After earlier criticism, Jovius is, however, later commended.[76] Olympiodorus was thus capable of recognising individual merit in those who otherwise were contributing to the decline of the western empire. Indeed, Alaric – like Stilicho – is praised for his moderation,[77] praise which makes the earlier positive assessment

---

[73] Wirbelauer 2011: 234–5; this goes against Paschoud's axiom that Zosimus faithfully transcribes his sources, but that view has been challenged before and is, in fact, untenable: see Van Nuffelen 2004b: 96–7; Alan Cameron 2011: 644.

[74] *PLRE* II 801–2 (Olympius 2); one wonders to what extent the criticism of Olympius as *magister officiorum* is meant to highlight the virtues of Helion (*PLRE* II 533 [Helion 1]), who had occupied that post in the East since 414, and was in 425 at the height of his power.

[75] *PLRE* II 623–4 (Iovius 3).   [76] Zos. 6.1.1.   [77] Zos. 5.51.1.

of the latter lose some of its apparently unique flavour. Rather, Olympiodorus points to a systemic failure of imperial leadership in the West, and from the top down. This allows him to see some positive aspects in individuals, but also provides a justification for the eastern decision to replace senior personnel. Valentinian III and Galla Placidia would be the figureheads, but power was entrusted to someone new, Fl. Constantius Felix (*magister militum* 425–430 and *patricius*). Unmentioned in the sources before 425, he clearly owed his position to the eastern armies.[78]

Ending the *Historiae*

Olympiodorus' history builds to a climax: the control established by the East over the West through the restoration of Valentinian III. The campaign against the usurper John was evidently recounted in considerable detail, as is still evident in Photius' summary.[79] Significantly, Valentinian III was crowned in Rome, and not in Ravenna where both Honorius' court and the usurper John had resided. Unsurprisingly, therefore, Olympiodorus prefixed a description of Rome to his concluding narrative. It clearly was very detailed, noting the income of Roman households, how much praetors spend on games and the size of the baths and the walls.[80] This level of detail is usually taken to betray a personal visit, presumably as a follower of Helion.

Yet we should avoid reading the passage as merely a down-to-earth eyewitness report. In the narrative the passage clearly functioned as a digression that set the scene for Valentinian's elevation, and underlined how a grand city had now returned to imperial control. Indeed, the choice to crown Valentinian in Rome can be understood as a symbol of the restoration of ancestral glory that Theodosius II pretended to accomplish. It was as much a negative as a positive choice: Ravenna, where Honorius had spent many of his days, was avoided, and Rome, which only fifteen years ago had been sacked by the Goths, was to be the seat of

---

[78] *PLRE* II 461–2 (Felix 14).
[79] Olymp. 43.1; see also Philostorgius 12.13–14 = Olymp. 43.2.
[80] Olymp. 41.

imperial government again.[81] The choice for Rome also restored the parallelism with the 'second' or 'new' Rome in the East,[82] and showed how the younger sister guaranteed the well-being of its older sibling.

Against this background, the lavish praise of Rome can be read as implicit praise of Constantinople too. Indeed, the eastern capital had long sought to rival its western sister, spending money on building projects designed to rival the old Rome. Impressive new walls protected Constantinople, and the city's elite emulated the houses of their aristocratic counterparts in Rome.[83] To the readers of Olympiodorus' history, the display of the riches of Rome, even after the disasters that had struck it in recent years, must have been a powerful reminder of their own wealth. The description of Rome, in combination with the triumphant end of the *Historiae*, thus conjures up the combined idea of a *regeneratio* and a *translatio imperii*: it reminds the reader of the reviving grandeur of the traditional capital of the empire whilst also suggesting that the East now protects its majesty.

As we have seen, the very description of the eastern campaign against John was meant to underscore the imposition of eastern tutelage on the West. Yet the ideological message of this ending of the *Historiae* is not only evident from what Olympiodorus narrated, but also from what he left out. In fragment 39, Olympiodorus claims that the usurper John seized power while letters announcing the death of Honorius were still en route to Constantinople. His action, Olympiodorus suggests, forced the East to intervene and install Valentinian. It is the classic story of a usurper being deposed by a righteous emperor. Yet events probably were not that simple. In 424, after Honorius' death, the western *patricius* Castinus was appointed as consul with Victor for the East. This suggests that, at first, Theodosius did not intend to replace Honorius but had planned to rule alone. As the promulgation of both consuls also happened in the East, Theodosius must have

---

[81] On Valentinian III and Rome, see Humphries 2012.
[82] Julian, *Or.* 1.6b–c; Greg. Naz. *Carm.* 2.1.11.15 (ed. C. Jungck, Heidelberg, 1974) on Constantinople as a second Rome. For the mainly ecclesiastical use of 'New Rome', see Canon 3 of the Council of Constantinople (381) with the discussion by McLynn 2012.
[83] Machado 2012; Ward-Perkins 2012: 62–4, 71–4.

accepted Castinus at least as an interlocutor and possibly as his representative in the West.[84] The deal broke down very quickly: Castinus proved dissatisfied and aided John's usurpation, which in turn convinced Theodosius that a member of the imperial family was needed in Italy. Adding this story to the history – and, in so doing, suggesting that Theodosius had actively pursued an alternative strategy – would have marred the grandiose and morally unambiguous finale, in which the Theodosian dynasty returns to the western throne under eastern guidance. Even if Theodosius simply acquiesced in the name proposed to him as western consul for 424, it still does not generate the image of an emperor acting quickly and decisively – precisely the image that Olympiodorus projects for the events of 424/425. By 425, these hesitations and accommodations had been tactfully obliterated from historical memory and substituted by a story of triumph. Instead, Olympiodorus concluded his narrative on the peace treaty between Aetius and the western court.[85] With his Hun mercenaries, Aetius represented indeed a potential threat to the new regime, which was now removed. Olympiodorus' history was clearly triumphalist, justifying the newly established eastern dominance over the West and advertising the stability it promised. Yet, western stability was a mirage. The new strongman behind the throne, Felix, failed to constrain Romans and barbarians alike: in 427 Bonifatius clashed with Aetius and the court, and was declared a public enemy, in 429 the Vandals invaded Africa and in 430 Aetius had Felix killed.[86] Triumphalism has a short life expectancy.

The historian and his history

At first sight, the numerous digressions in which Olympiodorus narrated his travels in the East do not seem to fulfil any specific purpose beyond establishing his credentials as a historian. But set against the ideological background that the previous sections have established for his history, they take on additional meaning. The

---

[84] Seeck 1919: 348–9; Oost 1968: 179; Stickler 2002: 27.
[85] Philostorgius 12.14 = Olymp. 43.2.30–4.
[86] Stickler 2002: 35–9.

digression on university life in Athens claims credit for getting Leontius a 'sophistic chair'.[87] Crucially, Leontius was the father of the empress. By flaunting his relationship with the empress, Olympiodorus flags his allegiance to the wise eastern marriage policy as it is implicitly depicted in his history. The other digressions often refer to embassies that Olympiodorus undertook for the eastern court,[88] and in which he was successful, notwithstanding difficulties and the occasional danger. As we have seen in the context of his portrait of Stilicho, Olympiodorus suggests that the West succumbed to the barbarians because it failed to keep them in check and even used them in its internal power games. The East, by contrast, was spared this fate, and could congratulate itself on its continued stability. That Olympiodorus was not a lover of barbarians is clear from more than one anecdote surviving in the fragments.[89] The way he highlights the success of his embassies again associates him closely with a successful feature of eastern policy. Olympiodorus was an astute enough author to situate these digressions at key points in his narrative: the embassy to Donatus comes just before the end of the first part, and most of the others cluster towards the end of the history.[90]

The privileged social position that is revealed in the digressions is also confirmed by the rest of the narrative. The level of detail of his history would have been impossible to achieve without access to official documents and witnesses.[91] The criticism of a recently deceased emperor, Honorius, and a recently raised Augusta, Galla Placidia (at a time when historians either stayed silent on contemporary events or embraced panegyric)[92] is hard to explain unless one accepts that Olympiodorus knew this criticism was shared by the court. The digressions are, therefore, much more than entertaining rhetorical set pieces: they establish Olympiodorus not only as a true, inquiring historian, but, crucially, also as a collaborator in the

---

[87] Olymp. 28.3 εἰς τὸν σοφιστικὸν θρόνον.
[88] Olymp. 19, 35.2.
[89] Olymp. 27, 40; Zecchini 1983: 25; Van Nuffelen 2004b: 93–5.
[90] Baldwin 1980: 218.
[91] Eunapius (50, 66) apologises to his readers for failing to give any details on Stilicho. As a sophist in a provincial town, he was unable to get access to high-level informants and official correspondence. Olympiodorus is clearly different.
[92] Paschoud 2005; cf. Maisano 1979: 26.

success story that was the eastern empire and of which he set out a mirror image in his description of the West. That Olympiodorus' paganism does not seem to have held him back from embracing eastern triumphalism only illustrates the integrative power of the ideology that pervaded the East in the years after 425.

PART III

PAST AND PRESENT

CHAPTER 6

MAPPING THE WORLD UNDER THEODOSIUS II

Giusto Traina

Under the Emperor Augustus and his successors, the Romans advanced the study of geography in order to create both a practical and a mental map of their imperial world, that is – to quote the striking expression of the late Claude Nicolet – to construct an 'inventaire du monde'.[1] Although evidence for similar activities in late antiquity appears (at least at first sight) scant, the elaboration of Roman geographical knowledge seems to have been a matter of some concern: in part, as a result of what might be termed a 'democratization of culture'[2] and, in part, as a result of the progress of information systems which allowed a deeper sensitivity to geographical and human landscapes.[3]

Geographical texts and maps could also be used for educational purposes. In a speech delivered in 297/298 in support of the restoration of the *Maenianae* (the rhetorical schools in Autun destroyed when the city was sacked in 270 by the usurper Tetricus) the ora-

---

I would like to thank Anca Dan, Patrick Gautier Dalché, Klaus Geus, Christopher Kelly, David Konstan and Amity Law for their valuable comments.

[1] See Nicolet 1991, whose original French title was self-evidently inspired by Conte 1982. The notion of 'cosmic knowledge' – ill-suited to ancient Rome – has been suggested by König and Whitmarsh 2007b: 18–20, who also speak of '"mapping" knowledge' (at 35); see too, the important considerations of Murphy 2004: 131–64, on the 'triumphal geography' of Pliny's encyclopaedia: 'the eye that reads the orbis terrarum is the eye of its ruler' (at 164).

[2] Traina 1998: 87, 2007: 21; the expression 'la democratizzazione della cultura' was coined by Santo Mazzarino in his seminal article of 1960, for discussion see Carrié 2001 and Averil Cameron 2004.

[3] On the sophistication of late-antique geographical information, see Lee 1993: 81–90; Graham 2006: 35–40; for a general survey, see Humphries 2007; see also Maas 2007 on the ethnographic material in Procopius, and note too the *Ethnika*, compiled under Justinian by Stephanus of Byzantium (ed. Billerbeck 2006). A sensitivity to landscape is clearly apparent, for example, in the fragments of the historian Priscus of Panium: see Traina 1993: 286–9.

155

tor Eumenius offered a vivid picture of the schools' porticoes decorated with a map of the *oikoumene*.

> Further, in its porticoes let the young men see and contemplate daily every land and all the seas and whatever cities, peoples, nations the unconquered rulers restore by affection or conquer by valour or restrain by fear. Since for the purpose of instructing the youth, to have them learn more clearly with their eyes what they comprehend less readily by their ears, there are pictured in that place, as I believe you have seen yourself, the sites of all locations with their names, their extent, and the distances between them, the sources and terminations of all the rivers, the curves of all the shores, and the Ocean, both where its circuit girds the earth and where its pressure breaks into it.[4]

This famous description is not necessarily late-antique evidence for the so-called Augustan Map of Agrippa (associated by some modern scholars with the topographic lists of the later *Diuisio orbis terrarum*),[5] but it is clearly a valuable witness of 'the map as expression of imperial power',[6] and also of the pedagogic use of maps in the Roman empire. In the following passage, which closes his speech, Eumenius evokes the representations of 'separate regions':

> Here let the most noblest accomplishments of the bravest Emperors be recalled through representations of the separate regions [*per diuersa regionum argumenta*], while the twin rivers of Persia and the thirsty fields of Libya and the recurved horns of the Rhine and the many-cleft mouth of the Nile are seen again as eager messengers constantly arrive. Meanwhile the minds of the people gazing upon each of these

---

[4] *Pan. Lat.* 9.20.2 (trans. Nixon and Rodgers 1994: 171): *uideat praeterea in illis porticibus iuuentus et cotidie spectet omnes terras et cuncta maria et quidquid inuictissimi principes urbium gentium nationum aut pietate restituunt aut uirtute deuincunt aut terrore deuinciunt. siquidem illic, ut ipse uidisti, credo, instruendae pueritiae causa, quo manifestius oculis discernentur quae difficilius percipiuntur auditu, omnium cum nominibus suis locorum situs spatia interualla descripta sunt, quidquid ubique fluminum oritur et conditur, quacumque se litorum sinus flectunt, qua uel ambitu cingit orbem uel impetu inrupit Oceanus.* On the historical context of this passage, see Traina (in press); and generally on Eumenius' speech, Hostein 2012: 177–250.

[5] For the possible connections: Salway 2001: 29; Whittaker 2002: 86–7; Gautier Dalché 2008: 39. On the Map of Agrippa displayed in the *Porticus Vipsania*, see the contrasting views of Salway 2001: 28–9 – pictorial map with accompanying inscribed text – and Brodersen 1995: 268–87 (with his rebuttal of Salway at 2001: 20 n. 29) – unillustrated collection of *commentarii* on regions of the inhabited world. More generally, see the useful discussion in Arnaud 2007–8 (with sizeable bibliography at 124–6) and the cautious remarks of Whittaker 2002: 85–7: 'many details were transmitted not from the map [of Agrippa] itself but from the written *commentarii* that accompanied it. These were plausibly the origin of the topographic lists … [in the works called the] *Divisio Orbis Terrarum*' (at 86).

[6] Clarke 2008: 210.

places will imagine Egypt, its madness given over, peacefully subject to your clemency, Diocletian Augustus, or you, invincible Maximian, hurling lightning upon the smitten hordes of the Moors, or beneath your light hand, lord Constantius, Batavia and Britannia raising up their muddied heads from woods and waves [*squalidum caput siluis et fluctibus exserentem*], or you, Maximian Caesar, trampling upon Persian bows and quivers. For now, at last it is a delight to see a picture of the world, since we see nothing in it which is not ours.[7]

In their detailed commentary on the *Panegyrici Latini*, Ted Nixon and Barbara Rodgers have suggested that these *diuersa argumenta regionum* alluded to separate maps.[8] But these images might also have represented personifications of provinces and peoples – a long-established iconography with its origin in the tradition of Roman triumphal pictures. Eumenius' description may also allude to commemorative paintings of military campaigns, for which there are some useful third-century parallels: the γραφαί depicting the Parthian war of Septimius Severus (possibly the same images as those on the arch in the Roman Forum) and the *tabulae* of the German campaigns that Maximinus Thrax ordered to be displayed in front of the Roman senate-house. These huge paintings (the third-century historian Herodian describes them as μέγισται εἰκόνες) showed the emperor fighting in the swamps of the North, a landscape not too different from the muddy woods in which Constantius Chlorus fought.[9] Whatever the actual nature of the images displayed in the rhetorical schools of Autun, they formed part of an elaborate programme: the image of the *oikoumene* and the pictures of the Tetrarchic campaigns provided students, teachers and local notables with the necessary data to figure out a mental map of the empire.[10] Although the pictures of

---

[7] *Pan. Lat.* 9.21 (trans. Nixon and Rodgers 1994: 172–7).

[8] Nixon and Rodgers 1994: 172–3 nn. 80–1. More recently, La Bua 2010: 314 has argued that 'the maps posted along the porticoes, politically and ideologically oriented, exemplify the methodological and pedagogical importance of figurative arts and imagery to the educational system'.

[9] Septimius Severus: Herodian 3.9.12; see also Lusnia 2006: especially 276–86; and for the origin of this genre of 'continuous narrative', Holliday 1997: 140–1. According to the *Historia Augusta*, Caracalla built a *porticus* which displayed a painting of his father's exploits (*Sev.* 21.12; *M. Ant.* 9.6–7). Maximinus: Herodian 7.2.8; *SHA Max.* 12.5–11. See too Traina 1986: 725; for a helpful discussion of this material, Östenberg 2009: 192–9 and 219–61.

[10] On the concept of a 'mental map', see Whittaker 2002; and for its application in understanding Jerome's worldview, see Weingarten 2005: 197–208.

the 'separate regions' were not (at least technically) geographical maps, they were nonetheless important examples of topographical illustration. They may properly be regarded as 'landmarks' of an imperial geography structured according to Ptolemy's careful distinction between topography, chorography and geography; in that sense, they constituted a mental map of the *oikoumene* on different scales.[11]

It is tempting to suppose that a similar purpose was intended for the illustrations transmitted by the medieval tradition of the *notitia omnium dignitatum et administrationum tam ciuilium quam militarium*. Several pictures in the *Notitia Dignitatum* (to use its convenient short title) can be considered as maps, at least in a broad sense:[12] these 'pseudo-maps' were rightly included in an account of late-antique cartography written by O. A. W. Dilke for *The History of Cartography* (edited by J. B. Harley and D. Woodward). Dilke highlighted the 'shortcomings' of the *Notitia* and concluded that although it was not 'a useless document ... the useful information would have had to be gathered from the text rather than from the maps'.[13] In Dilke's opinion, 'while the Byzantine emperors retained maps for propaganda and ... religious purposes, the many practical uses for mapping so characteristic of the western empire steadily declined'.[14]

These conclusions were founded on the conventional view that regarded both the western and eastern portions of the *Notitia* as official documents.[15] Thanks to the valuable contribution of Peter Brennan, they can now be thought of rather as 'pseudo-administrative' texts, with more of an ideological than a practical purpose.[16] Brennan may perhaps be pushing his reading

---

[11] Ptol. *Geog.* 1.1.1–6; on the landmark in representations of ancient geography, see Brodersen 1995: 111–37.

[12] Arnaud 1990: 30; Brodersen 1995: 148. Some pictures in the *Notitia* appear in medieval T-O 'Sallust maps': for example, Vienna, Nationalbibliothek, Cod. 160 f° 100 (thirteenth century). For a general introduction to the *Notitia*, see C. M. Kelly 1998: 163–9.

[13] Dilke 1987b: 245.

[14] Dilke 1987a: 259. On the shortcomings of Dilke's contributions to Harley and Woodward 1987, especially the chapter on Byzantine cartography, see the review by Podossinov and Chekin 1991.

[15] Dilke 1987b: 244: 'the official list was kept by the head of the civil service in the West, though it is disputed whether the extant work is governmental or an amateur's copy.'

[16] Brennan 1996: 152.

too far in arguing for a 'composite *Notitia* [which] was certainly like the *Saturnalia* of Macrobius in one way; it created a world that never existed via materials and people who did exist'.[17] But his paper should be welcomed as a salutary reaction against a minimalist approach to the *Notitia*, a text too long regarded more as a 'document' than a 'monument'.[18] And Brennan is absolutely right to call attention to the ideological dimension of the *Notitia*: a representation of a 'new mode of constructing power, a new way to create, encode and maintain a hierarchy of dominance and deference'.[19] Certainly, Michael Kulikowski's defence of the historical value of the *Notitia* (in part written in reaction to Brennan) sounds like a warning against throwing the baby out with the bathwater.[20] But – as Kulikowski rightly affirms – Brennan's paper, although revisionist, does not necessarily devalue the importance of the *Notitia* for a reconstruction of late Roman civil and military institutions. In any case, both the western and the eastern *Notitiae* are more readily understandable as texts framed by a strong ideological expression of concern for the unity of the empire, rather than as official documents primarily intended for administrative purposes.[21]

From the fifth to the eighth century, the texts of the eastern and western *Notitiae* were put together and copied as part of a larger collection, reflected at its best by the *Codex Spirensis*. This is a lavishly illustrated Carolingian manuscript, which in the fifteenth century belonged to the cathedral library of Speyer, and in the next century (before 1566) was owned by Count Palatine Ottheinrich von der Pfalz-Neuburg. The *Spirensis* was unfortunately dismembered by the count's heirs: a fragmentary bifolium

---

[17] Brennan 1996: 168.
[18] The traditional view is still repeated by specialists in late Roman law and administration: see, for example, Purpura 1995; Lee 1998: 211 regards the *Notitia* as an 'administrative document'.
[19] Brennan 1996: 155.
[20] Kulikowski 2000b: 359–60: 'Even if we admit an originally ideological impetus, however, we do not thereby throw up our hands and abandon the *Notitia*'s contents' (at 360).
[21] Zuckerman 1998: 147, 'faute de pouvoir restaurer l'unité politique de l'Empire sur le terrain, c'est sur le papier qu'on tente de recoller les morceaux'; see also Kulikowski 2000b: 359. On concern for the *orbis totus* in *The Gallic Chronicle of 452*, see Molè Ventura 1992: 228–30.

now in Augsburg, and containing part of the *Itinerarium Antonini*, seems to be its only recognisable relic.[22] The texts assembled in the *Spirensis* provided the Carolingian court with valuable materials for an empire patently taking its inspiration from the Roman model. To quote John Mann:

> when Charlemagne was crowned emperor in AD 800, he was faced with the question, not merely 'how does one run an empire?' (he was already doing that), but 'how does one run a *Roman* empire?' In these circumstances the associates and supporters of the Carolingian emperors will no doubt have been interested in any information to be found on the way that the Romans had governed ... Some of the varied documents that were thus collected will have gone to form the *codex Spirensis*.[23]

The core of the *Codex Spirensis* was formed by the '*Notitia*-group': a set of late-antique texts including the *Notitia Dignitatum*.[24] It is generally assumed that this *Ur*-collection of texts included at least the western and the eastern parts of the *Notitia*, the urban *notitiae* of Rome and Constantinople, the *Altercatio Hadriani Augusti et Epicteti philosophi* (from the third century?), and the *Tractatus de gradibus cognationum*, a treatise on various degrees of kinship.[25] This first group of texts, which formed the basis of the later *Spirensis*, seems to have been assembled in the first half of the fifth century. In the running order, the eastern *Notitia* (dated to 401) precedes the western one (updated in the 420s), thus implying the primacy of Constantinople – which, in turn, indicates that the '*Notitia*-group' was first assembled in the eastern empire.[26] This collection was most likely transmitted to the *Spirensis* through a 'proto-*Spirensis*' insular manuscript. This miscellaneous collection then took its place alongside later

---

[22] On the *Codex Spirensis*, see the brief notice at Reeve 1983, and most recently Neira Faleiro 2005: 47–67 (with some bibliographical inaccuracies).
[23] Mann 1991: 219.
[24] Ireland 1979: 53–4 and, before him, Schnabel 1926: 254–7; according to Schnabel, the *Notitia Dignitatum* and both urban *Notitiae* should 'zu einem einheitlichen Ganzen ebenfalls unter Theodosius II. anzusetzen haben' (at 254); see now Brennan 1996: 167.
[25] On the later Byzantine development of this literature, see the fundamental article by Patlagean 1966.
[26] On the date of the eastern *Notitia*, see Zuckerman 1998, overlooked by Kulikowski 2000b: 360 who assumes that 'despite these eastern origins, however, the copy we possess is western, and its eastern portion ceased to be updated after the final division of the empire in 395'. For a useful review of recent discussion, see Wheeler 2012: 621–30; on the *Notitia Urbis Constantinopolitanae*, see now Matthews 2012.

geographical texts such as the seventh-century *Cosmographia* of Pseudo Aethicus Ister and the ninth-century *Liber de mensura terrae* of Dicuil. At some point, the *Itinerarium Antonini*, the anonymous treatise *de rebus bellicis* and the *Laterculus* of Polemius Silvius were also added.

On the face of it, the '*Notitia*-group' may appear as rather an odd set.[27] After all, what relationship was there between the *Notitiae* and an intellectualising text such as the *Altercatio*, or with a description of the degrees of kinship, a treatise most likely originating in a law school? Yet although miscellaneous, this group was not so heterogeneous, for its texts responded to a tradition firmly grounded in the connection between imperial power and control of the whole *oikoumene* – a reasonable subject for both ancient and medieval monarchs. As Michael Kulikowski notes, the texts of the *Notitia*-group 'have in common the goal of constructing an ordered world where none necessarily exists, or imposing a shape on disordered reality'.[28] From that point of view, the *Notitia Dignitatum* is the best surviving evidence illustrating – in both iconographic and literary terms – the world of Theodosius II.

It is not unlikely that the '*Notitia*-group' might have been conceived as a schoolbook. During his long reign, Theodosius II was deeply concerned with culture and education. In 425, he founded a public university in Constantinople.[29] According to later Byzantine tradition, the emperor was also very fond of manuscripts: Michael Glykas (in the thirteenth century) noted that Theodosius was 'also a calligrapher', and Nicephorus Callistus (in the fourteenth century) praised the Gospels with golden letters that Theodosius had copied in his own hand.[30] This interest in manuscripts and their production was the result of an education designed for the *princeps puer*. As a young child, Theodosius was entrusted to Antiochus, a Christian eunuch expressly sent

---

[27] Kulikowski 2000b: 358 (in a rather minimalist way) refers to 'an odd set of texts with a primarily antiquarian interest'.
[28] Kulikowski 2000b: 359.
[29] Lemerle 1971: 63–4 (in the English translation, he responds to the criticism of Speck 1974 at Lemerle 1986: 66 n. 51bis).
[30] Glykas, *Annales* 4.260–1 (*PG* 158: 488C); Nicephorus Callistus, *HE* 14.3 (*PG* 146: 1064B); see now Alan Cameron 2011: 434; Ronconi 2012: 633. On the emperor's involvement in a copy of Solinus' *Collectanea*, see below p. 169.

as ἐπίτροπος by the Sasanian emperor Yazdegerd, possibly on the occasion of the proclamation of the imperial infant as Augustus in January 402.[31] Antiochus was much more than a tutor: in effect, the ἐπίτροπος of an imperial prince was his political guardian. (For example, the Emperor Arcadius – the father of Theodosius II – had been entrusted to Rufinus, the praetorian prefect of the East; Rufinus' rival, Stilicho, claimed to have been appointed ἐπίτροπος of both the western emperor Honorius and his brother Arcadius by their father Theodosius I.[32]) It seems that Antiochus was dismissed in 413 or 414, when Pulcheria took control of her younger brother's education – and with ramifications for the relations between the Roman empire and Iran. Undoubtedly the eunuch Antiochus played a role in the development of Theodosius' concern with the East and the shaping of his policy towards the Sassanian empire. There are certainly some close connections between Constantinople and Ctesiphon – for example, in the elaboration of ideas of astral kingship.[33]

If the *Notitia* had a pedagogic function, the meaning of the 'pseudo-maps' incorporated in this 'pseudo-administrative' text can easily be understood. A first version of the text might have been assembled for the education of Theodosius II (born in 401). Since the western *Notitia* was updated in the 420s, perhaps after the coronation of the young Valentinian III in Rome in 425, it is tempting to suppose that the corrections might then have been added at the initiative of Petronius Maximus, who acted as tutor to the new emperor.[34] The pedagogic aims of the '*Notitia*-group' aside, this

---

[31] Malalas 361; and see, in particular, Greatrex and Bardill 1996. According to Procopius (*Pers.* 1.2.1–10), the Sasanian emperor asserted his claim to have been appointed by Arcadius as the ἐπίτροπος of his son; the claim was viewed sceptically by Agathias 4.26.6–7 (ed. R. Keydell, CFHB 2, 1967). This anecdote has prompted some discussion (useful summary in Mazza 2004: 45–8); but, in fact, Yazdegerd's claim was a diplomatic device (so Averil Cameron 1969–70: 149, with useful bibliography of earlier views; Canepa 2009: 126). What is at stake here is a particular use of the term ἐπίτροπος, reflecting the Persian institution of 'guardianship', known in Armenia as *dayeakut'iwn*, see Traina 2004.
[32] Eunapius 62 and 64; John of Antioch 281–2 with Mazza 2004: 47.
[33] Panaino 2004; Canepa 2009: 100–6.
[34] See Panciera 1996; the suggestion of the *Notitia* as a schoolbook for Valentinian III is made by Zuckerman 1998: 147 n. 79.

collection of texts also offers evidence of a clear concern for imperial unity under Theodosius II. Indeed, the '*Notitia*-group' may be thought of as a sort of Theodosian 'inventaire du monde'. The medieval success of this collection, updated with the geographical compilations of Pseudo-Aethicus Ister and Dicuil, underscores a drive towards geographical systematisation, expressed by both the imperial and the urban *Notitiae*.[35] This interest in systematisation may also be found in some of the most important Latin scholars of this period: Macrobius, Martianus Capella and Orosius – all deeply concerned with geography. In the mid fifth century, Macrobius himself developed several diagrammatic maps to illustrate his commentary on the *Somnium Scipionis*, and Orosius' geographical table is likely to have been *mis en carte* (not necessarily by the author) by the first half of the fifth century. (Martianus Capella's map is more problematic.[36]) All these works were long enjoyed and recopied in the medieval West, and inspired early medieval Latin cartographers, but during the fifth and the sixth centuries they also circulated in the eastern empire whose government still operated (at least internally) in Latin.[37] This tradition was widely accepted, and these authors contributed to the transmission of the basics of classical geography in a Christianised world. After all, the demarcation between 'pagans' and 'Christians' no longer had any force, and this (in turn) may explain why the transformation of classical geography was not so radical.[38]

On the other hand, securely datable evidence from the first half of the fifth century for 'official' descriptive geography written in Greek is more scanty: a register drawn up in the reign of Theodosius II appears to be the chief source of Hierokles' *Synekdemos*.[39] Yet

[35] Lozofsky 2008: 179.
[36] On Macrobius' maps, see Hiatt 2007; Gautier Dalché 2008: 36; on Macrobius more generally, Alan Cameron 2011: 231–72; on Orosius, see Janvier 1982: 59–270 (at 145–69 for the geographical table); Merrills 2005: 35–99; Edson 2008; Fear 2010: 16, 25 for geography; on Martianus Capella, the bibliography in Gautier Dalché 2008: 33–4 with 34 n. 8, 43–4 with 44 n. 34.
[37] Millar 2006: 84–93.
[38] This is the central and important argument of Alan Cameron 2011; more specifically for geography, see Lozofsky 2000. Christian authors undoubtedly contributed to the Christianisation of the Roman mental map: see Inglebert 2001: 99–104; Gautier Dalché 2003 and 2008: esp. 31–2, 52–66; Weingarten 2005: 37–42, 193–264. (Cosmas Indicopleustes' *Christian Topography* is an exception, although its 'transcultural' role must not be overlooked: see Faller 2011.)
[39] Jones 1971: 514–21.

geography was not neglected by the philosophical schools, witness the collection of Greek chorographic texts elaborated by Marcian of Heraclea, an important source for Stephanus of Byzantium. Marcian – the author of a *Periplus of the Outer Sea* – also epitomised Artemidorus' *Geography* and the *Periplus* of Menippus of Pergamum. Although there is no strong evidence for dating, Marcian has been identified with the philosopher Marcianus, who corresponded from Constantinople with Synesius of Cyrene in 406 and 411, and was formerly governor of Paphlagonia.[40]

From the point of view of cartography, there are some indications of the (re)drawing of new maps in the fifth century. A cross-comparison of medieval Latin manuscripts shows the development of this tradition between the fifth and the eighth century.[41] Patrick Gautier Dalché has drawn attention to some analogies between the geographical names in the so-called maps of St Jerome (found in a manuscript written in Tournai, dating from the twelfth century and representing Asia Minor and Palestine) and the text of the *Descriptio totius mundi*.[42] As the limits of neighbouring regions can be seen on the borders of both maps, it is possible to argue that the original model was a larger fifth-century *mappa mundi*, which was very likely related to the text of the *Descriptio totius mundi*. Gautier Dalché has proposed crediting the archetype – which he envisages as a broader fifth-century *mappa mundi* – to Eucherius, bishop of Lyons. The cultural connection ran through the monastery at Lérins in southern France, one of the most important centres of diffusion of eastern culture to western Europe.[43]

The only certain evidence of a map dated to the reign of Theodosius II is found in a Latin poem in twelve hexameter verses,

---

[40] On Marcian of Heraclea (*Geographi Graeci minores*, ed. C. Müller, Paris, 1855, 515–76) and his collection of chorographical tracts, preserved in Parisin. Suppl. Gr. 443 (thirteenth century); Syn. *Ep.* 101, 119 (ed. A. Garzya, Paris, 2000) with Marcotte 2007: 172.
[41] Gautier Dalché 2008: 36–53.
[42] Gautier Dalché 2010; the attribution to Jerome was wrongly proposed by Miller 1895: 1–21, and uncritically followed by later scholars.
[43] Gautier Dalché 2010.

preserved in two medieval manuscripts and in Dicuil's *Liber de mensura terrae*, completed in 825.

> Hoc opus egregium, quo mundi summa tenetur,
> aequora quo, montes, fluuii, portus, freta et urbes
> signantur, cunctis ut sit cognoscere promptum,
> quicquid ubique latet, clemens genus, inclita proles
> ac per saecla pius, totus quem uix capit orbis,
> Theodosius princeps uenerando iussit ab ore
> confici, ter quinis aperit cum fascibus annum.
> Supplices hoc famuli, dum scribit pingit et alter,
> Mensibus exiguis ueterum monimenta secuti
> in melius reparemus opus culpamque priorem
> tollimus ac totum breuiter comprendimus orbem:
> Sed tamen hoc tua nos docuit sapientia, princeps.

> This famous work – including the entire world,
> seas, mountains, rivers, harbours, straits and towns,
> uncharted areas – so that all might know,
> our famous, noble, pious Theodosius
> most venerably ordered when the year
> was opened by his fifteenth consulship.
> We servants of the emperors (as one wrote,
> the other painted) following the work
> of ancient mappers, in not many months
> revised and bettered theirs, within short space
> embracing the entire world. Your wisdom, sire,
> it was which taught us to achieve that task.[44]

This piece of court poetry celebrates the achievement of an annotated map of the world: a *summa mundi* presenting geographical realities together with *urbes* (lines 1–3, *Hoc opus egregium, quo mundi summa tenetur | aequora quo, montes, fluuii, portus, freta et urbes | signantur, cunctis ut sit cognoscere promptum*). The map was prepared on the instruction of the Emperor Theodosius in the year of his fifteenth consulate (lines 6–7, *Theodosius princeps*

---

[44] The poem (= *Anth. Lat. Suppl.* 724) is preserved in two manuscripts of the *Diuisio orbis*: one in the Vatican, Vat. Lat. 642 (twelfth century); the second in Leiden, Leid. Scaliger 39 (seventeenth century). The *Diuisio orbis* was used as a source by Dicuil for his *De mensura orbis terrae*. For the text of the poem, see Dicuil 5.4 (ed. Tierney 1967: 56–8, correcting *tollimus* to *tullimus* in line 11) with Alan Cameron 2002: 125–6, followed by Salway 2005: 134 n. 57. Translation: Dilke 1987a: 259 (slightly modified); also translated Salway 2005: 128 (English) and Wolska-Conus 1973: 275 n. 8 (French). On the influence of this poem on medieval culture, see the useful bibliography in Lozofsky 2008: 172 n. 10.

uenerando iussit ab orbe | confici, ter quinis aperit cum fascibus annum).⁴⁵ It was undertaken by two 'humble servants' of the emperor: one wrote the text, the other painted it (line 8, *supplices hoc famuli, dum scribit pingit et alter*). As Theodosius I held only three consulates, the emperor must be Theodosius II, who was consul for the fifteenth time in 435.⁴⁶ According to Alan Cameron, the copyist implied in the work was Aemilius Probus, who copied a text of Cornelius Nepos for the emperor, and, as it seems, also produced a copy of Proba's *Cento*.⁴⁷

Possibly mistaking Theodosius II for the pious and glorious Theodosius I, the clerics of the Carolingian renaissance contributed to the memory of a geographical *opus Theodosii imperatoris*.⁴⁸ In his introduction, Dicuil notes that the work is preceded by 'a twelve-line poem written by the aforementioned *missi* on the subject of Theodosius' instruction that they should undertake this task'.⁴⁹ Dicuil here attributes to the imperial *missi* (an obviously anachronistic retrojection of the Carolingian *missi dominici*) the redaction of a text he calls *Mensuratio orbis terrae*, but which actually corresponds to a late-antique geographical work. (This text is usually considered as a later development of the so-called Map of Agrippa.⁵⁰) A further difficulty may result from the fact that Macrobius Ambrosius Theodosius – who, as noted above, illustrated his commentary on the *Somnium Scipionis* with diagrammatic maps – known as (the now familiar) 'Macrobius' in the Middle Ages, was known to his contemporaries as 'Theodosius'.⁵¹ Some confusion in the early medieval tradition between Macrobius/Theodosius and the Emperors Theodosius I and II should not be excluded.

---

⁴⁵ Dicuil 1.1 (ed. Tierney 1967: 44) misunderstood the consular date for the regnal year: IN QUINTODECIMO ANNO REGNI IMPERATORIS THEODOSII PRAECEPIT ILLE SUIS MISSIS PROVINTIAS ORBIS TERRAE IN LONGITUDINEM ET LATITU(DI)NEM MENSURARI.
⁴⁶ Wrongly Lozofsky 2008: 173: 'the poem does not specify whether it means Theodosius the Great (379–395) or Theodosius II (408–450)'.
⁴⁷ Alan Cameron 2002: 124–6, 2011: 434, suggesting that Theodosius' map was a copy of the Map of Agrippa; Weber 1976: 22 that the poem introduced a forerunner of the *Tabula Peutingeriana*.
⁴⁸ See the synthesis of Gautier Dalché 2008: 64–5.
⁴⁹ Dicuil 5.4 (ed. Tierney 1967: 56): *duodecim uersus praedictorum missorum de imperante Theodosio hoc opus fieri incipiunt*.
⁵⁰ For the relationship between the *Mensuratio* and the Map of Agrippa, see Nicolet and Gautier Dalché 1986, with further bibliography in Arnaud 2007–8.
⁵¹ Alan Cameron 2011: 233–9; on Macrobius' maps, n. 36 above.

Further evidence of a 'Theodosian' map can be detected in a Carolingian *mappa mundi* of the T–O type (the 'O' representing the encircling ocean and the 'T' dividing the earth into three continents). The earlier of the two manuscripts preserving the map (illustrated overleaf) bears the title *Divisio orbis terrarum Theodosiana*.[52] Patrick Gautier Dalché, its most recent editor, prefers to remain cautious, as this title might be the invention of an anonymous copyist, although he admits, 'On a là, peut-être, l'écho très affaibli d'une entreprise cartographique de Théodose II, qui se serait transmise essentiellement en des régions périphériques de l'Empire d'occident'.[53] In fact, some elements of this map do not correspond to the usual style of Latin geographers: for example, the use of Greek names (*oecumene*, *Libya* instead of *Africa*, and Oriental toponyms such as *Parth[i]ene* and *Drybruce*). Moreover, the size of the regions is not calculated by length and breadth, but by measuring their circuit. Of course, these maps were made more for contemplation than for practical use. A map was primarily a piece of art, meant to summarise the *orbis terrarum* in a limited space (line 11, *totum breuiter comprendimus orbem*).[54] Although it is not clear whether maps always accompanied the publication of a geographical text,[55] they could be sent as a valuable appendix, like the πινάκιον (containing διαγράμματα) sent to the Emperor Julian in 358/359 by the *uicarius Britanniarum* Alypius, jointly with a γεωγραφία, that is a geographical work.[56] Perhaps Theodosius' map was placed in a hall or a portico of the imperial palace, whose iconographic programme reflected what Matthew Canepa has attractively called 'a global visual culture of kingship'.[57]

[52] Vat. Regin. Lat. 123 (1055 or 1056, from Santa María de Ripoll); see the edition of Gautier Dalché 1994–5: 105–8.
[53] Gautier Dalché 1994–5: 96, 103.
[54] There is some evidence of 'thumbnail' late-antique Greek maps, see Marcotte 2010: 642; Pontani 2010.
[55] See for example Orosius, above n. 36.
[56] Julian, *Ep.* 10 (ed. Bidez 1926: 16–17) with Arnaud 1990: 546. Bidez thought of a map of Britain, but a *mappa mundi* seems more appropriate for the preparation of an eastern campaign. Millar 1982: 17 cautiously suggests that the term γεωγραφία might allude to a map, and also notes the well-known description of Vegetius, *Epitoma rei militaris* 3.6 (ed. L. F. Stelten, New York, 1990) of *itineraria ... non tantum adnotata, sed etiam picta*; but see on this difficult passage the important reservations of Janni 1984: 31–2, 39 n. 55.
[57] Canepa 2009: 188.

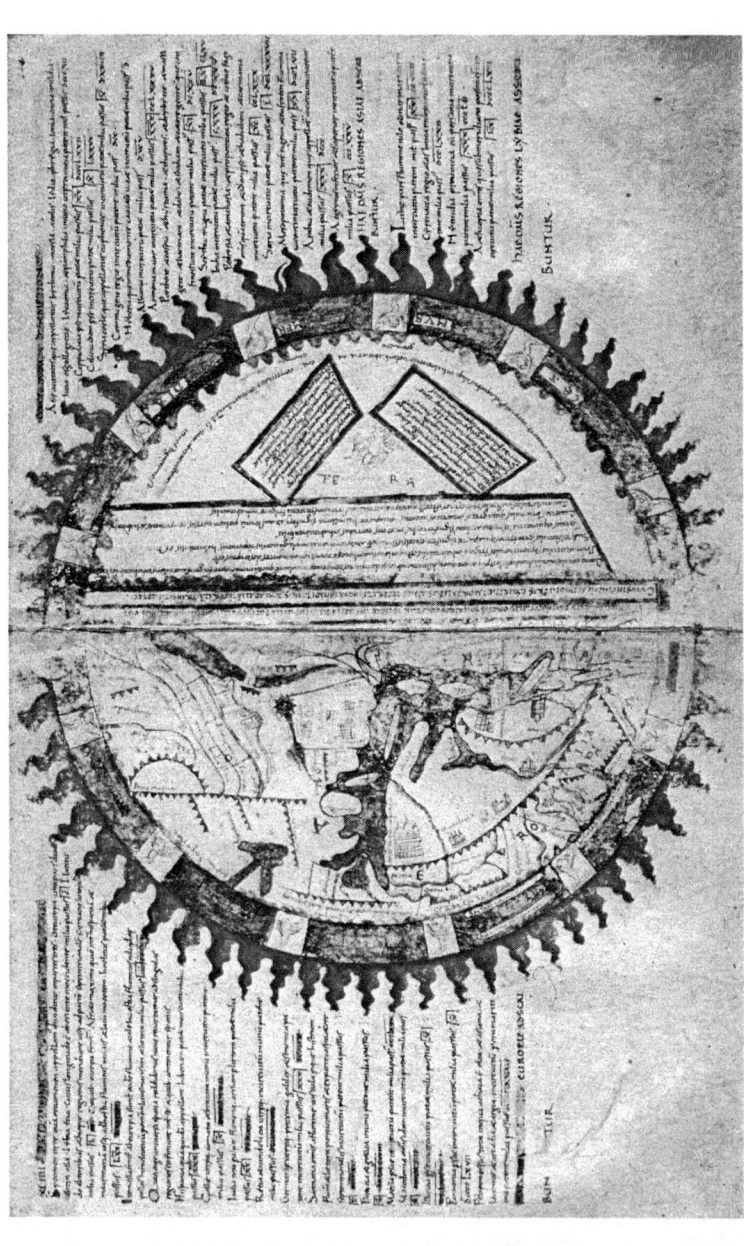

Mid-eleventh-century 'Map of Theodosius': *Vat. Regin. Lat.* 123. f. 143v–144r (from Santa María de Ripoll in Catalonia). © 2013 Biblioteca Apostolica Vaticana.

It has been claimed that an ambitious enterprise such as Theodosius' map, at least as it is grandly described in the poem, could have been placed in a portico of the so-called State University in Constantinople, just like the Map of Agrippa displayed in the *porticus Vipsania* in Rome.[58] But further discussion of the purpose and the whereabouts of Theodosius' map is idle speculation. That said, the poem on Theodosius' map offers good evidence of a systematisation of geographical knowledge under Theodosius II and its connection with an ideological programme that embraced a long-standing Roman tradition linking imperial power firmly with geography. This may help to explain the *explicit* preserved in some manuscripts of Iulius Solinus' *Collectanea rerum memorabilium* (compiled most probably in the third century largely from Pliny's *Natural History* and Pomponius Mela): *feliciter studio et diligentia domni Theodosii inuictissimi principis*.[59] Since, as noted above, the emperor was fond of manuscripts and was apparently a reputed calligrapher, it is not unreasonable to accept Bernard Hemmerdinger's suggestion of Theodosius' personal implication in the redaction of a fifth-century codex of the *Collectanea*, which was very likely provided with topographic pictures.[60] This redaction may be partly traced back from the fourteenth-century *Ambrosianus C 164 inf.*, containing both Solinus' *Collectanea* and the *Cosmographia* of Pseudo Aethicus Ister. As some of its pictures recall the illustrations of the *Notitia Dignitatum*, it is not impossible to imagine that the fifth-century original could have been copied in the Great Palace at Constantinople.[61]

Under Theodosius II, while the status of geography within education does not seem to have changed, a new picture of the geographical reality of the empire was taking shape. It was the result

---

[58] Wolska-Conus 1973: 276: 'le style pompeux et solennel des "douze vers" offre toutes les caractéristiques d'une inscription dédicatoire glorifiant une œuvre – mosaïque ou peinture – destinée à une fondation publique, accessible à un grand nombre de personnes.'
[59] Alan Cameron 2011: 434.
[60] Hemmerdinger 1966: 175: 'Le scribe de cet exemplaire perdu n'est autre que l'empereur Théodose II.'
[61] Revelli 1927: 625; more cautiously, Levi and Levi 1974: 568 n. 1, 573, and 576: 'we think it a justifiable conclusion that the artist who worked on these miniatures was

of the policy of an emperor who ruled in a new Rome when the western part of the empire was dramatically losing its prestige. To quote Gilbert Dagron:

il est révélateur que cette refonte ou réédition d'une œuvre qui marquait la fondation de l'Empire soit ordonnée par le premier empereur qui, après la quasi-disparition de Rome et l'effacement de l'institution impériale en Occident, incarne à Constantinople, où il réside et d'où il ne bouge plus, la romanité tout entière.[62]

It makes good sense that the starting point of Fergus Millar's book on Theodosius' 'Greek Roman Empire' is the key law of 447 in which the emperor clearly expressed his (rather wishful) thinking on the unity of the empire. Millar rightly points to 'a separate "Greek Roman Empire," twinned with its western, Latin-speaking, counterpart – but separate all the same'.[63] This is certainly an important insight. But the world of Theodosius II was not limited to the administrative *realia* of the twin empires: the emperor's geopolitical horizon was clearly wider. And if anxiety was increasing in those parts of the empire increasingly disrupted by barbarian invasion and settlement, Theodosius II was no less concerned with the unity of the East and West.[64] This is one of the most important reasons for the elaboration of the *Theodosian Code*. Jill Harries has highlighted the ideological meaning of *NTh* 1 (15 February 438), confirming the *auctoritas* of the Code and dispelling 'the thick cloud of obscurity' formed by the sizeable weight of legal writings accumulated in the past.[65] Harries also points out the 'language of contrasts' in the *Novella*: 'light and dark, clarity and mist, simplicity and confusion, brevity and prolixity'.[66] Later on, a similar quest for κόσμος will be expressed in Justinian's *Novellae*.[67]

Did this interest in geography help Theodosius improve his control of imperial geopolitics? Certainly, the wars against Iran were not exactly successful, for Roman aggression against Persia

inspired by an illustrated manuscript of Solinus's *Collectanea* dating to late classical times'; see too Gautier Dalché 2008: 38 and 45–6, where he proposes a gradual elaboration of Solinus' map; on Solinus' geography, see now Brodersen 2011.
[62] Dagron 1974b: 67.   [63] Millar 2006: 7; *NTh* 2.
[64] See my observations in Traina 2007: xvi, 41–8.
[65] *NTh* 1.1.   [66] Harries 1999: 60.
[67] Lanata 1994: 34–9.

was discouraged in 422 by an invasion of the Huns. Meanwhile, far more striking events were taking shape in the Mediterranean: the sack of Rome and the Vandal invasion of Africa.[68] The imperial response to military crises reveals deep political and diplomatic knowledge, although some moves were dictated by sheer necessity:[69] in 428, for example, Theodosius was forced to remove Roman protection from the Christian kingdom of Armenia, which then lost its independence.[70] But the sacrifice of Armenia was necessary to check, at least temporarily, a growing military crisis. Needless to say, this setback was not reflected in cartography, nor in commemorative paintings.

Such concerns matched the times: in the face of a major political crisis and the threatened break-up of the empire, both Roman officials and citizens resorted to expressions of the unity of the Mediterranean world as a psychological antidote for their increasing anxieties. Similar feelings may have stimulated Polemius Silvius, a retired official in Gaul, to compile his odd *Laterculus* towards the end of Theodosius' reign.[71] Polemius Silvius was considered 'mentally disturbed' by the redactor of *The Gallic Chronicle of 452*.[72] But this did not prevent medieval copyists from adding his peculiar 'inventaire du monde' to the collection of texts destined to transfer to the Carolingian court the late-antique mapping of the world, as it was elaborated under Theodosius II.

---

[68] See now Roberto 2012: 45–127.
[69] Kaegi 1968: 16–29; Howard-Johnston 1995: 162–3.
[70] Traina 2007: 1–6.
[71] On the *Laterculus*, see Wesch-Klein 2002.
[72] *Chron. Gall. a. CCCCLII*, ed. T. Mommsen *MGH (AA)* IX: 660: *Siluius turbatae admodum mentis*.

CHAPTER 7

'THE INSANITY OF HERETICS
MUST BE RESTRAINED': HERESIOLOGY
IN THE *THEODOSIAN CODE*

Richard Flower

Despite the opening up of many new avenues in the study of late antiquity, heresiology – the quasi-scientific classification and cataloguing of heresies – remains a form of literature that is relatively little studied, with its texts mostly either mined for historical details about poorly understood sects or dismissed as tendentious and ill informed.[1] This form of writing flourished from the late fourth century onwards, with each author building upon the work of his predecessors, adding in the latest enemies of the true faith who had arisen to entrap the unwary. Yet, despite its popularity, heresiology is rarely awarded sufficient importance, either as a tool in the religious controversies of the time or as a dynamic form of literary innovation and experimentation. As Averil Cameron has lamented, these texts are often too easily dismissed 'as sterile or boring, as mere scholastic exercises',[2] copying and collecting material from earlier writings without any innovations or new contributions to knowledge. This is, however, to underestimate both their influence and their originality. As Judith McClure has demonstrated in a brief and extremely useful article, such texts functioned as vital, and respected, repositories of knowledge in late antiquity and the early Middle Ages, even for well-informed theologians such as Gregory the

---

I would like to thank the editor, Christopher Kelly, for his excellent and invaluable advice, as well as the other participants at the conference, particularly Jill Harries, for their constructive feedback.

[1] On this neglect and hostility, see Averil Cameron 2003: 471. Averil Cameron 2008: 105–6 notes approvingly some recent studies seeking to shed new light on the subject: see, in particular, Inglebert 2001: 393–461; Boyarin 2004: 1–27.
[2] Averil Cameron 2003: 484.

Great.³ After all, even the most knowledgeable person has need of an encyclopaedia. Yet, to sideline heresiologies as utilitarian, but uninteresting, assemblages of material would be to misunderstand their importance for the study of late-antique history and literature. Rather than being mere confections of simplified and polemical condemnations, these texts engaged with the methodologies of classical technical and encyclopaedic writing, setting themselves up as catalogues, genealogies and taxonomies of heresy. In part, this was achieved through their form, in which a great variety of different beliefs and groups were arranged into a well-ordered, systematic guidebook. The very appearance and structure of a heresiology, which mirrored other, less controversial branches of knowledge, reassured readers of its reliability and imbued the text with authority as a new late-antique form of technical literature.⁴ Such writings in the Roman world, for example the *Natural History* of Pliny the Elder or the medical treatises of Galen, claimed to provide complete and secure information, guaranteed by the author's learning and experience.⁵ Yet, as Jason König and Tim Whitmarsh remark in their introduction to a volume of essays on the ordering of Roman knowledge, 'the world of knowledge – comprising both the institutions defining it and the texts embodying it – is never neutral, detached, objective. The assumption that the textual compilation of knowledge is a practice distinct from political power will not stand.'⁶ Heresiologies, as carefully ordered catalogues of a new form of religious knowledge, need to be approached in the same manner. The processes of selection, arrangement and editing deserve to be recognised as productive, and often complex, enterprises in their own right. Furthermore, late-antique heresiologies were no mere repetitive catalogues, but were instead characterised by continual innovation, as authors sought not only to conceive of heresy in a variety

---

³ McClure 1979: 186–7.
⁴ On heresiology as technical literature, see, more generally, Flower 2011.
⁵ On Pliny, see below p. 176; on similarities between the approaches of Epiphanius and Galen, see Flower 2011: 79–86.
⁶ König and Whitmarsh 2007b: 7.

of different ways, but also to construct their own authority as heresiologists.

In exploring both the formulations of heresiology and the status of the heresiologist under Theodosius II, this chapter will focus on an example from the very centre of imperial power: a pronouncement of Theodosius issued in 428, and preserved under the title *De haereticis* at 16.5.65 in the *Theodosian Code*.[7] This ruling, aimed at a large range of different heretical groups, represents an engagement with heresiological literature and its growing authority. While the classificatory model used in this text has been seen as foreshadowing Theodosius' great codification project, this 'legal' reading of the law needs to be balanced with a 'heresiological' approach, examining its selection, ordering and pigeon-holing of different heretical groups within the context of the wider development of heresiology.[8] The descriptions of heretics within *CTh* 16.5.65 should be read within prevailing trends for the condemnation of theological opponents and the creation of religious authority during the reign of Theodosius II. I do not mean to say that this text should be 'rescued' from the clutches of 'secular' legal historians and claimed by scholars of religion as their rightful property, but rather that our understanding of it is enriched by seeing it as the product of multiple systematising attitudes towards the collection, arrangement and dissemination of knowledge.

In order to contextualise this law, it is important first to examine the presence and functions of classificatory practices in two prominent heresiologies from the preceding fifty years: the *Panarion* of Epiphanius of Salamis (written in the late 370s) and the *De haeresibus* of Augustine of Hippo (closely contemporary with the law of 428). Epiphanius, by employing a systematic and taxonomising approach to heresy, positioned himself and his text within a long classical tradition of technical writings. In the decades that

---

[7] I have used the terms 'pronouncement' and 'ruling' to avoid giving an anachronistic sense of this statement's initiative, promulgation and enforcement. Throughout this piece, however, *CTh* 16.5.65 and other texts preserved in the *Theodosian Code* will be referred to as 'laws', usually without quotation marks, for the sake of convenience and convention; this should not, however, be taken to imply that they formed part of a planned programme of imperial 'legislation'. On this issue, see Millar 2006: 7–13, 43–4, 207–14.

[8] On the relationship between *CTh* 16.5.65 and the compilation of the *Theodosian Code*, see below pp. 184–92.

followed, others built upon this precedent, creating their own, individual engagements with the developing concept of heresiology as a branch of knowledge. By the 420s, Augustine and the author(s) of *CTh* 16.5.65 were not writing, in the manner of Epiphanius, to establish heresiology as a secure and reliable form of religious scholarship. Instead, they were positioning themselves and their views within this recognised intellectual discipline, constructing their texts as authoritative guides to heresy and, conversely, to orthodoxy. Moreover, they built upon Epiphanius' work by asserting their heresiological authority through additional, individual characteristics of their writings: for Augustine it was the persona of the scholarly, orthodox bishop who consulted and improved upon other scholarly, orthodox bishops, rooting his text firmly in ecclesiastical teachings; in the law of 428, the learning of the well-informed heresiologist was united with the force of imperial pronouncements, past and present.

These heresiological texts were, therefore, certainly not identical. For example, while Epiphanius, Augustine and *CTh* 16.5.65 all discussed the Manichaeans, the treatment of this group varied with the authors' particular concerns. Epiphanius provided a very extensive description and refutation of Manichaean beliefs, including the supposed text of a letter by their founder Mani, but the group was not presented as anything other than simply one of the *Panarion*'s eighty heresies that opposed the true faith.[9] When Augustine described them, he wrote by far the longest chapter in his work, drawing on his own experience and firmly disassociating himself from his former co-religionists.[10] In the law of 428, the Manichaeans were classified and set apart as the worst of all heretics, worthy of being placed in a separate category of villainy.[11] Similarly, the list of heresies in each of these texts was not identical. This should not, however, obscure the fact that they shared a set of fundamental organisational and rhetorical structures. What links and unites these works is their conception of heresiology as an encyclopaedic and thorough account of wrong belief, providing

---

[9] *Panarion* 66 (for edn, see below, n. 14).
[10] Augustine, *De haeresibus ad Quodvultdeum liber* 46 (ed. R. Vander Plaetse and C. Beukers, *CCSL* 46, Turnhout, 1969: 283–345).
[11] *CTh* 16.5.65.2.

them with an air of scholarly objectivity. An encyclopaedia offers a structured and authorised account of the world, purporting to be neutral and descriptive, while actually being subtly prescriptive. The encyclopaedist creates both the contours and the contents of knowledge through the selection and organisation of material, not simply presenting 'facts' to the reader, but judging which pieces of information are worthy of the status of 'facts', approved as suitable subjects for objective study and explication. Moreover, the rhetoric of complete information was an integral feature of ancient encyclopaedic literature, particularly the work of Pliny the Elder from the first century AD, which implicitly proclaimed its ability to make sense of the world.[12] As Trevor Murphy remarks in his study of Pliny's *Natural History*: 'the tacit promise of the encyclopedia is completeness, reliability, and authority: that is, the authorized version of knowledge.'[13]

So, although the texts discussed here are not identical in content or structure, they all shared a conception of the heresiologist as an established form of religious expert, and of heresiology as the authorised version of heresy. By showing off their learning and skill in carefully classifying different heresies, heresiologies homogenised them, to a large extent characterising them as similar and interlinked, standing in clear opposition to orthodoxy. Like encyclopaedic and other technical writings, they presented their readers with a supposedly objective and complete account of their subject, drawing a detailed picture of the heretical landscape that invited the audience to stand in the same vantage point and thus to accept the orthodoxy of the author's position.

Although a number of earlier books had been written with the specific purpose of refuting all heresies – for example the works of Irenaeus of Lyons in the second century and Hippolytus of Rome in the third – most scholars identify a significant watershed in

---

[12] I have referred to such ancient texts using the adjective 'encyclopaedic', rather than terming any of them as an 'encyclopaedia', in an attempt to avoid anachronism. On this issue of terminology, see Doody 2010: especially 40–58.
[13] Murphy 2004: 1–18 quoting 14. On Pliny's authorial practice and ancient 'encyclopaedias' in general, see also Grimal 1966; Howe 1985; Citroni Marchetti 1991; Beagon 1992; Riggsby 2007; Doody 2010.

heresiological literature in the late 370s, with the composition of the highly influential *Panarion*, or *Medicine Chest*, by Epiphanius, bishop of Salamis in Cyprus.[14] As the title suggests, Epiphanius presented his composition as an antidote for heresy, describing it as a collection of 'remedies for those bitten, preventatives for those who will be exposed'.[15] The *Panarion* consisted of eighty chapters, each one covering a different heresy, corresponding to the number of concubines in Song of Songs, who stood in opposition to the single dove, the perfect one.[16] Starting from the Creation itself, Epiphanius ordered his eighty sects in a chronological progression, opening with the tetrad of Barbarism, Scythianism, Hellenism and Judaism.[17] In beginning with the story of the Creation and Fall, and thus equating his history of orthodoxy and heresy with a history of humanity, Epiphanius, like an encyclopaedist, claimed to provide a complete and comprehensive account of all errors of faith that had ever arisen.[18]

The *Panarion*'s first twenty chapters were taken up with pre-Christian heresies, while the other sixty described those devised since the Incarnation, beginning with Simon Magus, who had tried to buy magical powers from the Apostles in Acts, and running through a great range of different sects, both famous and obscure.[19] This exhaustive list was concluded with the contemporary threats of the Apollinarians, Collyridians and Massalians/

---

[14] Epiphanius, *Panarion* (1-33, ed. K. Holl, *GCS* 25, Berlin, 1915; 34-64, ed. K. Holl and J. Dummer, *GCS* 31, 2nd edn, Berlin, 1980; 65-80, *De fide*, ed. K. Holl and J. Dummer, *GCS* 37, 2nd edn, Berlin, 1985). For the significance of Epiphanius, see Bonner 1999: 67-72; Averil Cameron 2003: 475-7. For a useful earlier heresiological writings, see Inglebert 2001: 401; on Epiphanius more generally, see Pourkier 1992; Flower 2011; and also the English translation in F. Williams 2009 and 2012, with an informative introduction to the author and his text at 2009: xi-xxxiii.

[15] *Panarion* Pr. 1.1.2.

[16] Song of Songs 6.8-9; *Panarion* 80.11.5-6, *De fide* 2.1-9.1.

[17] These four 'heresies' occupy *Panarion* 1-4, as well as being listed at 1.1.9 and 8.3.3. The selection of this quartet draws upon Colossians 3.11.

[18] In contrast, Eusebius of Caesarea's presentation of dateable time in his *Chronological Tables* began with Abraham, although the patriarch was described as having been born in the forty-third year of the reign of the Assyrian king Ninus and the twenty-second year of the reign of Europs, king of Sicyon. Epiphanius made his claim to chronological comprehensiveness explicit in his proem, stating that he would provide an account of all heretical error 'from when man was formed on earth until our own time, that is the eleventh year of the reign of Valentinian and Valens and the seventh of Gratian' – *Panarion* Pr. 2.2.3. For a perceptive reading of the *Panarion* as a 'universal history', see Schott 2006.

[19] Simon Magus: *Panarion* 21; Acts 8.9-24.

Messalians, followed by Epiphanius' own statement of faith, the *De fide*, which corresponded to the 'perfect dove' of Song of Songs.[20] What marked out the *Panarion* as different from its heresiological predecessors was not only the enormous scale of the enterprise, but also the systematic way in which Epiphanius approached and presented his task. Despite being a staunchly Nicene work composed in the East under the Homoian emperor Valens, the *Panarion* contains no hint of insecurity or explicit theological defence.[21] Epiphanius presented himself not as a theological polemicist, battling to explain his point of view against competing claims to orthodoxy, but as a reliable guide to a stable subject, explicating secure information in a detached, scholarly and authoritative fashion.

Epiphanius did not, however, merely assemble material from earlier written sources and his own experiences; he marshalled it into an encyclopaedic account of heresy, structuring his text carefully, almost like a natural scientist, in order to present it as a clear, thorough and reliable account of his subject.[22] One prominent feature of this systematisation of heresy was the consistency of the terminology and phrases employed by Epiphanius. While there are significant differences in the lengths of the *Panarion*'s eighty chapters, they share several common features, particularly in the structure and wording of their introductions and conclusions.[23] Most chapters open with a description of the relationship of this particular sect to the preceding one, often as an offshoot from it.

---

[20] At *Panarion De fide* 4.1–6 and 9.1–13.9, Epiphanius also sought to explain the 'threescore queens' and 'virgins without number' of Song of Songs 6.8 as, respectively, the sixty (or sixty-two) generations from Adam to the Incarnation and the multiplicity of pagan philosophical and religious groups. His own brief statement of faith appears at *Panarion De fide* 14.1–18.6, followed by an exposition of church practice and discipline.

[21] 'Nicene' denotes the theological position affirmed at the Council of Nicaea in 325, particularly the use of the term 'homoousios' ('of the same substance') to describe the relationship between the Father and the Son. In 360, under Constantius II, a 'Homoian' creed was agreed, so named because it employed the term 'homoios' ('like') for this relationship. On 'Homoian' Christology and its exponents, often branded as 'Arian' heretics by their opponents, see J. N. D. Kelly 1972: 290–5; Brennecke 1988; Hanson 1988: 557–97; Lenski 2002: 242–61.

[22] See Averil Cameron 2003: 477; Flower 2011; on Epiphanius' sources, Pourkier 1992: 53–75, F. Williams 2009: xxv–xxvii.

[23] On this standard structure, see Pourkier 1992.

Epiphanius then regularly detailed the sect's origins and development, before the main body of the chapter provided an outline and refutation of the group's beliefs. This was often supported by quotations from Scripture and other Christian writings, including both the works of earlier heresiologists, such as Irenaeus, and the sect's own 'heretical' literature, such as Ptolemy's *Letter to Flora*.[24]

Similarly, there is also consistency in the chapter conclusions: Epiphanius declared that he had now sufficiently refuted the heresy's dangerous teachings, that through the power and teaching of God and Scripture he had defeated this enemy and that it was, therefore, time to progress to the next sect. In addition, he frequently compared individual nefarious heresies to particular dangerous and venomous wild animals, especially snakes.[25] On many occasions, Epiphanius declared that, through his careful discovery, explanation and neutralisation of each heresy's doctrines, his *Medicine Chest* had provided the antidote to a heresy's poisonous threat and so given his readers the protection (or cure) that they required. This consistency of phrasing across the many chapters of the *Panarion* should not, however, be dismissed as a sign of the text's literary failure, or as a marker of the 'stale' or 'sterile' nature of heresiology in general. In fact, such repetition played a major role in establishing the authority of the text and the 'heresy' of the groups described within it. This almost formulaic rhetoric stressed the similarity between each group, placing them securely within a genealogy of heresy: every sect was described in the same manner and then assigned its rightful chronological position within a catalogue of heterodoxy, stressing its connection to other heresies and the unbridgeable gulf that lay between it and Epiphanius' own

---

[24] For example, *Panarion* 31.9–32 (Irenaeus against Valentinians/Gnostics); 33.3–7 (*Letter to Flora*).

[25] See Dummer 1973; Pourkier 1992: 78–81; Lyman 1999: 189–90, 2000: 154–7; Averil Cameron 2003: 176; Flower 2011: 82–6. While some animals appeared in more than one chapter, Epiphanius made many comparisons between specific animals and certain heretical groups. See, for example, his statement (at 66.88.2–3) about the similarity between the 'millet serpent' (κεγχρῖτις) and Mani: 'This amphisbaena and deadly beast, the millet serpent, is decorated with many camouflage patterns to trick onlookers, and possesses a sting and a source of poison hidden underneath ... He [Mani] merely makes a show of the name of Christ in his speech, just as the millet serpent hides its poison and tricks people with its decoration by entering dense woods and imitating its surroundings.'

orthodoxy. For example, despite not being widely regarded as heretical in the 370s, the third-century theologian Origen was placed in chapter 64, sandwiched neatly between Sabellius and Paul of Samosata.²⁶ Origen was thus cast as the successor of Manichaeans, Marcionites/Marcianists and Hellenic pagans, as well as the direct ancestor of Arius, Paul of Samosata and the Anomoeans.²⁷ By creating this encyclopaedic account of heresy, which included many groups and doctrines commonly accepted as heretical, Epiphanius thus sought both to label his theological opponents as outside the ranks of the true Christians and, simultaneously, to prove his own orthodoxy. By classifying and taxonomising heresy, Epiphanius created for himself the persona of the expert in a new scholarly field. His *Panarion* was therefore an important milestone in establishing heresiology as an ordered form of religious knowledge, an idea which could then be adopted and developed by his successors.²⁸

After Epiphanius, subsequent heresiologies engaged with the literary form established by the *Panarion*, often employing its structural model and, to varying degrees, its content. These projects were, however, also presented as improvements on, rather than mere additions to, earlier writings, reacting to other heresiologies critically and adapting their methods to suit different circumstances. In particular, a concern with forming a heresiological persona is evident in the *De haeresibus* of Augustine of Hippo, a catalogue of eighty-eight heretical sects which he produced near the end of his life, probably around 428 or 429, at the behest of the deacon Quodvultdeus.²⁹ In composing this text, Augustine made extensive use of both Epiphanius' work

---

[26] For Epiphanius' treatment of Origen, see Young 1983: 141–2; Dechow 1988; Clark 1992: 86–104; Lyman 1997, 1999, 2000; Flower 2011: 76–7.
[27] *Panarion* 64.65.5, 64.71.14, 64.72.9, 64.4.1–2, 65.1.1, 76.3.5.
[28] On the links between the *Panarion* and classical encyclopaedic and technical literature, see Flower 2011: 77–87.
[29] On the text's composition and the role of Quodvultdeus, see Bardy 1931: 397–8; Müller 1956: 2–6; Inglebert 2001: 450; Shaw 2004: 237–8, 2011: 310–11. At 2011: 310, Shaw presents a minimalist view of both Augustine's enthusiasm for the project and its originality: 'Very much against his will, Augustine was persuaded, albeit with considerable

and another similar, chronologically arranged heresiology written by one of his immediate successors, Filastrius, bishop of Brescia in northern Italy, in the 380s or early 390s.[30] Like the *Panarion*, Filastrius' (much briefer) work took the form of a repetitive catalogue, with each of his 156 groups being introduced either by stating that this particular sect was the successor of the previous, or with a simple phrase, such as *alia est heresis* or *alii sunt qui*, that stressed the similarities between the various heretics. Filastrius also arranged his text roughly chronologically, at least when dealing with named groups, working, like Epiphanius, with a conception of the history of humanity and heresy that stretched back to the Creation, and so incorporating twenty-eight pre-Christian sects. Within these, he listed as 'heresies' an extensive number of deviations from pious behaviour related in the Old Testament, such as King Ahaziah of Israel consulting the god of Ekron after falling through the palace roof, and Ahab and Jezebel making offerings to Baal.[31] In addition to Filastrius, Augustine also used a late fourth- or early fifth-century work now conventionally known as the *Indiculus de haeresibus*, which later came to be falsely attributed to Jerome, although the version used by Augustine was anonymous.[32] This text listed forty-seven named heretical individuals and sects (ten pre-Christian, thirty-seven post-Incarnation), together with brief accounts of their origins and beliefs.

Augustine had intended to follow *De haeresibus* with a much lengthier work defining the nature of heresy itself, but never

---

pressure, to produce a typical Mediterranean handbook of heresies at the very end of his life.' – see also Shaw 2004: 238 for a more negative judgement. Augustine's correspondence with Quodvultdeus concerning the work is preserved as *Ep.* 221–4 (ed. R. Vander Plaetse and C. Beukers, *CCSL* 46, Turnhout, 1969: 273–81).

[30] Filastrius Brixiensis, *Diuersarum hereseon liber* (ed. Heylen 1957); for a brief introduction to this text, see Heylen 1957: 209–12; on Augustine's sources, see Jannaccone 1952: especially 12–32.

[31] Ahaziah: Filastrius 13; 2 Kings 1.2. Ahab and Jezebel: Filastrius 16; 1 Kings 16.31.

[32] F. Oehler, *Corpus Haereseologicum* 1, Berlin, 1856, 283–97; there are fifty-five sects listed in the *Indiculus*, although the final eight are evidently a later addition; on this text, see Morin 1907: 450–3; Bardy 1929, 1931: 407–11; Chadwick 1976: 203; McClure 1979: 190; Shaw 2004: 235 n. 24. *De haeresibus* 81, which uses *Indiculus* for information on the Luciferians, remarks that this text is anonymous. See also *De haeresibus Epilogue* 2, where Augustine states that he has heard of a work on heresies by Jerome, but has not been able to acquire it.

realised his aim.³³ In the preface to *De haeresibus*, he complained that Epiphanius, in describing eighty heresies in six very short books, had not provided any refutation of the groups or a positive definition of the faith, and that his own work would be much more satisfactory.³⁴ It is very likely that Augustine was here referring not to the *Panarion* itself, but to an epitome of it known as the *Anacephalaeoses*, which provided merely a list of heresies and short statements about their origins and beliefs.³⁵ The *Anacephalaeoses* appears to have been composed shortly after the *Panarion* and, being much shorter, could have circulated more easily than the full text.³⁶ Its author condensed Epiphanius' arguments into brief notices on salient points, such as a group's origins, its relationship to earlier heresies and an outline of its beliefs and practices.³⁷ Augustine similarly did not actually engage in refutation of the heresies that he described, instead informing Quodvultdeus that such an enterprise was not required: 'Although you thought I ought to relate it, it is unnecessary to ask what the Catholic Church believes in opposition to these ideas, since it is sufficient to know that she does oppose them and that no one ought to put faith in any of them.'³⁸ While Epiphanius and Filastrius had provided detailed remedies for heretical belief, Augustine's book, like the *Anacephalaeoses*, was therefore more like a field guide, allowing the reader to identify the many different forms of heresy. Instead of arguing extensively from Scripture or quotations from earlier authors, *De haeresibus* simply reassured its readers that

---

[33] McClure 1979: 191–2.   [34] *De haeresibus Pr.* 6.
[35] On this issue, see Bardy 1931: 401–4; Jannaccone 1952: 23–6; F. Williams 2009: xxii.
[36] The *Anacephalaeoses* sometimes displays small differences with the *Panarion*, for instance in the order of the sects: the *Panarion* lists the Stoics, Platonists and Pythagoreans as numbers 5, 6 and 7 respectively, while the *Anacephalaeoses* switches the positions of the Stoics and Pythagoreans. For this reason, the *Anacephalaeoses* is usually regarded as not being by Epiphanius – see F. Williams 2009: xxii. (For the text, see Holl and Dummer edn of the *Panarion*, above n. 14.)
[37] See, for example, the description of the Cerdonians at *Anacephalaeoses* 41: 'The Cerdonians are from Cerdo, who received a share of error from Heracleon and added to the deceit. Having emigrated from Syria to Rome, he expounded his preaching in the time of the bishop Hyginus. He preaches that there are two first principles in mutual opposition, and that Christ was not begotten. Similarly, he denies the resurrection of the dead and the Old Testament.'
[38] *De haeresibus Epilogue* 3.

all its listed heresies were undoubtedly beyond the boundaries of orthodoxy, as clearly defined by both Church and bishop. Moreover, Augustine's work is particularly notable for the self-conscious way in which it defined its own place within a heresiological literary tradition. Epiphanius and Filastrius had both sought to establish heresiology as a new branch of scholarly study; Augustine built upon this to construct the status of his text, and of himself as a heresiologist, in relation to his predecessors. When Quodvultdeus had first asked him to write the *De haeresibus*, he had demurred, referring the deacon to the *Anacephalaeoses* and Filastrius' catalogue.[39] Later on, Augustine presented his heresiology as a contribution to the highly specialised and established field of technical expertise represented by these texts, but he also based his authority on his engagement with, and professed superiority over, them. He relied extensively on Epiphanius for his first fifty-seven heresies, sometimes supplementing this information from other sources, for instance incorporating Filastrius' views on the Sabellians, or adding in extra knowledge from his own experiences, as in his lengthy chapter on the Manichaeans.[40] At the end of chapter 57, Augustine declared that he had finished with Epiphanius, having omitted his pre-Christian heresies and altered some of the others, 'recording two in one where I was able to find no difference between them; and similarly, when he wished to make one from two, I placed them individually under their own numbers'.[41] Augustine informed his readers that, while he used Epiphanius as a major source, he would employ his own knowledge and analysis to reclassify the heresies more accurately.

For chapters 58 to 80, Augustine moved on to relate the heresies which he had found in Filastrius, but not Epiphanius, before rounding off the work with groups drawn from two other texts and from his own experience, concluding with the Pelagians.[42]

---

[39] Aug. *Ep.* 222.2 (ed. R. Vander Plaetse and C. Beukers, *CCSL* 46, Turnhout, 1969: 276–7); Bardy 1931: 397–8.
[40] *De haeresibus* 41, 46.
[41] *De haeresibus* 57; on Augustine's treatment of material from Epiphanius, see also Bardy 1931: 399–401.
[42] In chapter 80, Augustine stated his method of critical engagement with Filastrius' text: 'I decided that these heresies ought to be transferred from the work of Filastrius into my own. Certainly, he also recorded some others, but it seems to me that they ought not to be

Having completed the eighty-eighth chapter, Augustine concluded his work with an epilogue, in which he differed from Epiphanius and Filastrius by rejecting the notion of the complete heresiology, not only because new heresies would arise in the future, but also because great difficulties faced anyone who sought to gain thorough information about existing groups.[43] There was, however, hope for the reader, thanks to Augustine's skill in research.

> No one of those whose works on this subject I read listed all heresies. For I found some in one which I did not find in another, and again some in the second which the first did not list. But I listed more than them because I collected from all of them, although I did not find all heresies in each one, and I even added to them those which I recalled, but did not find in any of the books.[44]

Even though heresiology was an ongoing quest for knowledge, Augustine reassured his readers that his own book was superior to all its predecessors: he had read as widely as he possibly could and, after consulting the best authorities and finding them to be incomplete, he had drawn them all together, corrected the errors in their classification and supplemented them with material from his own experience. The message was clear: Augustine had created the most authoritative heresiology yet and could thus, by virtue of his methodology and achievement, be regarded as the greatest heresiologist.

At the same time as Augustine was preparing his catalogue, over a thousand miles away at Constantinople, the text that is preserved as *CTh* 16.5.65 was being written. While this differed from the projects of Epiphanius, Filastrius or Augustine, as it was a pronouncement by the imperial government, it made use of the same

---

termed heresies. Whichever ones I have set down without names, he did not record names for either.' Chapters 81 (Luciferians) and 82 (Jovinianists) were drawn from *Indiculus*. The Arabici in chapter 83 were said to have been identified 'after having scrutinised the history of Eusebius' (in which they appear at Eus. *HE* 6.37). Augustine stated that he had used Rufinus' Latin translation and continuation of Eusebius' *Ecclesiastical History*.

[43] On the difficulty of attaining complete information on heresies and, even more, of knowing whether one has attained comprehensiveness, see *De haeresibus Epilogue* 1.

[44] *De haeresibus Epilogue* 1. The claim that the works of Epiphanius and Filastrius would not be detailed, comprehensive or brief enough, compared to a work by Augustine, is also made by Quodvultdeus at *Ep.* 223.2 (ed. R. Vander Plaetse and C. Beukers, *CCSL* 46, Turnhout, 1969: 278–9).

HERESIOLOGY IN THE *THEODOSIAN CODE*

classificatory approach visible in these other heresiologies. As such, the law's claim to be an authoritative explication of orthodoxy and heresy was staked on its detailed religious knowledge as well as its status as an imperial command. It was issued on 30 May 428 in the imperial capital in the names of the Emperors Theodosius II and Valentinian III, and addressed to the praetorian prefect of the East, Flavius Florentius.[45] The text, as transmitted in the *Theodosian Code*, opens with the characteristically forthright statement that 'the insanity of heretics must be restrained', before declaring that heretics had to return any churches taken from the orthodox and would be subject to financial penalties if they ordained any new priests. What comes next, however, is the most interesting part of the surviving text:

> Next, because they do not all deserve to be punished with the same severity, the Arians certainly, and the Macedonians and Apollinarians, whose crime is to believe lies about the source of truth, having been misled by harmful speculation, are not permitted to have a church within any city; but from the Novatians and Sabbatians all freedom of renewal is removed, if they might happen to attempt any;[46] the Eunomians certainly, the Valentinians, the Montanists or Priscillianists, the Phrygians, the Marcianists, the Borboriani, the Messalians, Euchitae or Enthusiastae, the Donatists, the Audians, the Hydroparastatae, the Tascodrogitae, the Photinians, the Paulians, the Marcellians, and those who have sunk all the way to the lowest villainy of crimes, the Manichaeans, are not to have the means of assembling anywhere on Roman soil; and the Manichaeans are even to be expelled from the cities, since no place must be left to any of them where injury might even befall the elements themselves.[47]

After specifying particular punishments for the Manichaeans, *CTh* 16.5.65 goes on to state that, in addition to its own prescriptions, 'all the laws, which have been issued and promulgated at

---

[45] *CTh* 16.5.65; see *PLRE* II 478–80 (Florentius 7).

[46] This rather opaque statement may mean that the Novatians and Sabbatians were not allowed to build new churches, but could keep those they had.

[47] *CTh* 16.5.65.2: *post haec, quoniam non omnes eadem austeritate plectendi sunt, Arrianis quidem, Macedonianis et Apollinarianis, quorum hoc est facinus, quod nocenti meditatione decepti credunt de ueritatis fonte mendacia, intra nullam ciuitatem ecclesiam habere liceat; Nouatianis autem et Sabbatianis omnis innouationis adimatur licentia, si quam forte temptauerint; Eunomiani uero, Valentiniani, Montanistae seu Priscillianistae, Fryges, Marcianistae, Borboriani, Messaliani, Euchitae siue Enthusiastae, Donatistae, Audiani, Hydroparastatae, Tascodrogitae, Fotiniani, Pauliani, Marcelliani et qui ad imam usque scelerum nequitiam peruenerunt Manichaei nusquam in Romano solo conueniendi orandique habeant facultatem; Manichaeis etiam de ciuitatibus expellendis, quoniam nihil his omnibus relinquendum loci est, in quo ipsis etiam elementis fiat iniuria.*

different times against these and the others who oppose our faith, are to remain valid through eternal and vigorous observance'.[48] This was a law that spoke to earlier laws, drawing them together into a clearly defined attempt to name and catalogue heretical beliefs. While there are many earlier statements directed against 'all heresies' without specification, or to 'those inimical to the Catholic community',[49] this is the first to be heresiological, in the sense of providing a list of those groups deemed to be outside the orthodox faith – without, of course, claiming that no other heresies could exist or might arise over time. All the different heretical groups were united in their opposition to the true faith and were therefore all to be subject to the prohibitions of the imperial government.

This is the largest collection of heretical groups to be named in any single surviving law up to this point. The rationale for the inclusion of these particular sects is not easy to reconstruct. Many of them can be found in the main heresiological works, but the selection is never the same from text to text, and no one heresiology contains them all. Furthermore, the list is certainly nowhere near as extensive as the catalogue of eighty sects in Epiphanius' *Panarion* or *Anacephalaeoses*, let alone the 156 groups described by Filastrius. It is clear that this law is not drawing directly for its content on any individual heresiology, nor does it seem to be using the method employed by Augustine, in which earlier catalogues were compared, combined and supplemented. Also, some of the groups, such as the Tascodrogitae, are not well represented in surviving earlier heresiologies, and the Sabbatiani do not appear in any of them.[50] One notable aspect of the list is that it overwhelmingly represents eastern concerns. There are only three heresies described here which could be said to be predominantly western: Novatians, Donatists and Priscillianists. The Novatians were, however, well established at Constantinople and the inclusion of

---

[48] *CTh* 16.5.65.3.
[49] *CTh* 16.5.42 (November 408). For a reference to 'all heresies', see, for example, *CTh* 16.5.5 (August 379).
[50] The Tascodrogitae appear in *Panarion* 48.14.4 (as well as in the *Anacephalaeoses*) as an alternative name for the Montanists. They also appear as 'Ascodrugitae' in Filastrius 75 and as the 'Ascodrogi' in *NTh*. 3.9 (January 438).

Sabbatians alongside them in this law demonstrates the influence of local concerns on this comprehensive catalogue, since the latter were schismatics who are reported as having split from the Novatian community in the eastern capital during the reign of Theodosius I.[51] The Donatists had already appeared regularly in western laws during the preceding three decades and had even received a brief notice in Epiphanius.[52] In addition, the Priscillianists listed here with the description *Montanistae seu Priscillianistae* are almost certainly to be identified as Montanists who revered Montanus' associate, the charismatic prophetess Priscilla, as was suggested by A. H. M. Jones, rather than followers of the Spanish ascetic Priscillian, as Clyde Pharr assumes in his translation of the *Code*.[53]

Moreover, several, although certainly not all, of the sects listed in this law are to be found in earlier laws preserved in the *Code* under the heading *De haereticis*.[54] A number of them, including the Manichaeans and the Eunomians, appear frequently; some more unusual ones appear only once, such as the Tascodrogitae in a law of 383 or the Sabbatians in one from 423.[55] What is particularly notable,

---

[51] Soc. 5.21; Soz. 7.18; on the Novatian schism of the mid third century, see Cyprian, *Ep.* 40–51 (ed. G. F. Diercks, CCSL 3B, Turnhout, 1994); *Panarion* 59.1.1; Filastrius 82; *Indiculus* 33; *De haeresibus* 38; Jerome, *De uiris illustr.* 70 (ed. E. C. Richardson, TU 14.1a, Leipzig, 1896); Vogt 1968; Frend 1984: 351–7; Pourkier 1992: 381–414; Chadwick 2001: 153–4.

[52] *Panarion* 59.13.6–8 (as a subgroup of the Cathari, or 'Purists', which was Epiphanius' term for the Novatians, although he also regarded the Donatists as tainted with Arianism as well). On Donatism, see, for example, Greenslade 1964: especially 42–8, 58–61, 117–20, 129–43, 192–4, 225–6; Frend 1985; Tilley 1996: xi–xvii, 1997; Gaddis 2005: 49–58, 103–30; Shaw 2011: especially 66–145, 307–47, 490–586. The Donatists had already appeared in a series of laws issued between 405 and 414: *CTh* 16.6.4–5, 16.5.37, 38, 39, 40, 41, 43, 44, 46, 52, 54, 55.

[53] Jones 1964: III 323–4 n. 33; Pharr 1952: 583–4; see also Rougé and Delmaire 2005: 484 for a clear explication of the confusion caused by the term 'Priscillianists'. On the Montanists, also known as Phrygians or followers of the New Prophecy, whose members included Tertullian, see Hippol. *Haer.* 8.19, 10.25 (ed. P. Wendland, GCS 26, Berlin, 1916); Eus. *HE* 5.16–18; Labriolle 1913; Frend 1984: 253–6; Trevett 1996; Chadwick 2001: 114–22. Priscillianists had been bracketed together with Montanists in earlier condemnations: see *CTh* 16.5.40.pr. (February 407), 16.5.48 (February 410), 16.5.59 (April 423).

[54] Valentinians, Marcianists, Borboriani, Messalians, Euchitae, Enthusiastae, Audians, Paulians and Marcellians are all previously unattested in imperial laws in *CTh*, although Valentinians, Marcianists and Paulians (alongside Phrygians/Cataphrygians) are denied the right of assembly in a letter of Constantine quoted in Eus. *V. Const.* 5.64–5.

[55] *CTh* 16.5.10 (June 383) (Tascodrogitae), 16.5.59 (April 423) (Sabbatians); in the earlier rulings preserved under the heading *De haereticis*, the Manichaeans appear in a total of thirteen laws, both eastern and western, issued between 372 and 425 (16.5.3, 7, 9, 11,

however, is that, with the exception of the Encratites, Apotactites and Saccophori, who appear bracketed with the Hydroparastatae in three surviving laws from the early 380s (and of the Caelicolae, who were probably regarded as a Jewish sect, rather than as heterodox Christians) all the heretical groups named in the first sixty-four laws in this chapter of the *Code* also appear in the sixty-fifth.[56] Of course, the process of compilation means that the laws included in chapter 16.5 of the *Code* are unlikely to encompass the full extent of imperial legislation against heretics, yet it would appear that this particular text, *CTh* 16.5.65, represents a novelty within imperial pronouncements on the subject of heretical groups.[57]

In all sixty-four preceding laws preserved under this heading in the *Code*, an individual heretical sect, or small group of sects,

18, 35, 38, 40, 41, 43, 59, 62, 64), as well as having previously been condemned in a Tetrarchic rescript from around 302, transmitted in the *Collatio legum Mosaicarum et Romanarum* 15.3 (ed. R. Frakes, Oxford, 2011); the Eunomians appear in seventeen laws issued between 381 and 423 (16.5.6, 8, 11, 12, 13, 17, 23, 25, 27, 32, 34, 36, 49, 58, 59, 60, 61), all eastern, with the exception of *CTh* 16.5.17, issued at Milan in May 389, when the eastern emperor Theodosius I and his court were present in the West, and addressed to Flavius Eutolmius Tatianus, praetorian prefect of the East – see *PLRE* I 876–8 (Tatianus 5).

[56] Encratites, Apotactites and Saccophori appear alongside the Hydroparastatae in *CTh* 16.5.7.3 (May 381), 16.5.9 (March 382 – this time without the Apotactites) and 16.5.11 (July 383). The Caelicolae make a brief appearance in *CTh* 16.5.43 (November 407), which was issued at Rome and addressed to Curtius, praetorian prefect of Italy and Africa: *PLRE* II 331. In this law, they are described as people 'who hold gatherings of a new and unknown dogma' [*qui nescio cuius dogmatis noui conuentus habent*]. They also appear in *CTh* 16.8.19 (April 409), issued at Ravenna to Jovius, praetorian prefect of Italy: *PLRE* II 623–4 (Jovius 3). This ruling, which also describes the Caelicolae as novel, complains that this sect is turning Christians into Jews. It is likely then that if the Caelicolae were known to the author(s) of *CTh* 16.5.65, they were simply understood to be Jews rather than heretics. This is how they are treated in the *Theodosian Code*, where 16.8 is titled 'On Jews, Caelicolae and Samaritans' [*De Iudaeis, Caelicolis et Samaritanis*]. The fact that they also appear in *CTh* 16.5.43, under the title *De haereticis*, is probably because the majority of that statement concerns Donatists, Manichaeans and 'Priscillianists'. On the Caelicolae, see also Shaw 2011: 277–9. It is also possible, of course, that they were simply unknown at Constantinople in 428. The Pneumatomachi, who appear in *CTh* 16.5.11 (July 383), were also known as Macedonians, under which name they appear both in that imperial ruling and in *CTh* 16.5.65. The Pepyzitae, who appear in *CTh* 16.5.59 (April 423), are glossed there as an alternative name for the Phrygians/Montanists.

[57] On the compilation of the *Code* and the question of omissions from it, see Matthews 1993: 32, 2000: 290, arguing that any absences are the result of the inability of commissioners to find laws; in contrast, Sirks 2007: 147–8 holds that most laws were found, but that the editors omitted obsolete legislation. Honoré 1998: 146 suggests that absences may have been due to difficulties faced by the editors in finding material, but also notes that 'we cannot rule out the possibility that they deliberately omitted some laws which had been repealed'.

had been targeted with specific legal disabilities or punishments, probably usually in response to a question or petition from an official or community. The closest that any preceding law had come to this sort of extensive listing was *CTh* 16.5.59 of 423, which was concerned with 'Manichaeans and Phrygians, whom they call Pepyzitae or Priscillianists or by some other more hidden title, and similarly Arians, and Macedonians and Eunomians, Novatians and Sabbatians and the other heretics'.[58] Even this group of seven sects (together with the two alternative names for Phrygians/Montanists) did not, however, resemble the cataloguing approach taken in *CTh* 16.5.65, either in terms of the number of groups listed or in the sense that the law might be giving a complete roll call of heresies, as seen in the vague reference to 'the other heretics' at the end of its brief list. In contrast, *CTh* 16.5.65 brings together all the heretical groups who had appeared in earlier surviving pronouncements, along with several others, which were either being specifically condemned in law for the first time or had already been mentioned in earlier rulings which are no longer extant. Even though we cannot know whether groups such as the Borboriani had already been the subject of imperial censure, this law of 428 represents a form of 'legislative heresiology', a compilation of all heterodox groups whose names were of concern or interest to those who drafted it.

The classification of this imperial heresiological enterprise, however, differed from that of Epiphanius, Filastrius and Augustine, since the sects were not listed in chronological order, but rather were assigned to four different groups, each subject to different punishments. The Novatians and Sabbatians, who could easily be regarded as schismatics rather than heretics, received the most lenient punishment.[59] Similarly, the Arians, Macedonians and Apollinarians, who had appeared together as a trio in two earlier laws,[60] were explicitly grouped together on account of the

---

[58] *Manichaei et Fryges, quos Pepyzitas siue Priscillianistas uel alio latentiore uocabulo appellant, Arriani itidem Macedonianique et Eunomiani, Nouatiani ac Sabbatiani ceterique haeretici. CTh* 16.5.11 (July 383) listed nine groups, if the Encratites, Apotactites, Saccophori and Hydroparastatae are counted separately.
[59] See also *CTh* 16.5.2 (September 326).
[60] See too *CTh* 16.5.12 (December 383), 16.5.13 (January 384).

nature of their heresy; moreover, they were also deemed worthy of the same punishment on account of this. After the third and largest group of heretics had been listed, the Manichaeans were singled out for special condemnation and punishment, before a number of restrictions were placed on the behaviour and rights of all heretics. Of course, variation in the treatment of sects was not a legal novelty: earlier laws had individually prescribed a great range of prohibitions and penalties for many of these groups. This had, however, taken place in a piecemeal fashion, with each law attacking one heresy or collection of heresies in a similar way. No earlier law had sought to condemn heretics in a manner that was both comprehensive and differentiating.[61]

In one sense, therefore, this text performed a key function already recognisable from earlier heresiologies: it collected together differing theological views and presented them as essentially the same, creating damnation by association. While it did not follow the practice of Epiphanius, Filastrius and Augustine in employing a largely chronological structure for its catalogue, it nonetheless engaged in heresiological classification by splitting the sects into four groups. The reader was presented with a guiding rationale for this thematic division, based on the natures of the individual heresies, which could be identified, classified and pigeon holed.

Within the individual groups therefore, there was a second level of heretical association: by being put together in the first section and deprived of their churches within cities, the Macedonians and Apollinarians had their link with the Arians clearly formalised, turning them into a family of cognate heresies based on the fact that their 'crime is to believe lies about the source of truth'.[62]

---

[61] *CTh* 16.5.9 (March 382) had devoted separate rulings to the testamentory rights of Manichaean anchorite monks, the judicial punishments for Encratites, Saccophori and Hydroparastatae, and also the problem of disagreements over the date of Easter. These decisions, however, appear to be a combination of answers to different questions, rather than an attempt to consider the broad range of heretical opinions as part of a coherent strategy.

[62] *CTh* 16.5.65.2 (May 428); this may be a reference to the views of these heresies concerning Christ, although if Christological error were the only criterion for inclusion in the law's second group of sects then one would expect to see them joined by some of the others, including Eunomians, Paulians and Marcellians. Pharr 1952: 462 n. 150 glosses 'the source of truth' as Christ. Another problem is caused by the fact that the chief heresy of the Macedonians, also known as 'Pneumatomachi', concerned the Godhead of the

Caroline Humfress has usefully suggested that this law should be seen as a resolutely imperial measure, and notes that it was followed shortly afterwards by the announcement of Theodosius' great codification project.[63] It is, however, notable that this law is neither a compilation nor a consolidation of earlier rulings. While it does bring together a number of previously condemned groups, it does not codify the punishments that had been prescribed in the preceding laws. Instead, it imposes its own original structure, classification and judgement on an unprecedented number of heretical groups, without explicitly seeking either to collect or to supplant earlier imperial pronouncements.

This law should, therefore, be read in the context of both the concerns and the practices of other imperial rulings against heresy and also the growing prominence of heresiological literature. By producing an extensive catalogue of heretical sects, it engaged with the model of the heresiology as a form of technical literature and thus a source of secure and reliable knowledge. The authority of this law cannot therefore be neatly pigeon holed as 'imperial', in the way that one might treat a ruling concerning the use of purple dye or the promotions of junior officials under the *consularis aquarum*: rather, it married its status as the emperor's divine words with its recognisably heresiological treatment of its material. Moreover, through its division of different sects into groups and the imposition of a range of punishments based on this separation

---

Holy Spirit, rather than of Christ. The grouping of these three heresies together in this law may be based either on their appearance together in earlier laws (see above n. 47) or on a contemporary view of their relationship which influenced both the preceding laws and this one.

[63] Humfress 2000: 140–1; at 141, Humfress sees an inversion of the heresiological approach in *CTh* 16.5.65, since 'the Emperors ended where the theologians' lists of heretics began'. By this, she means that the list of heretics in this law ends with the Manichaeans, who practised magic, just as heresiological catalogues started their lists of post-Incarnation heresies with Simon Magus – see *Panarion* 21; Filastrius 29; *Indiculus* 1; *De haeresibus* 1. Humfress also notes (at 141–2) that Nestorius was associated with Simon Magus and his followers termed *Simoniani* in *CTh* 16.5.66 (August 435). It seems unlikely, however, that the position of the Manichaeans in *CTh* 16.5.65 represents a subtle allusion to the Simonians, especially as the accusation of magical practices was not limited to these two groups. Honoré 1998: 117–18 argues that the broader structure of the text is similar to the original directive which set in motion the compilation of the *Code*; see below pp. 192–3 for Honoré's suggestions on the authorship of *CTh* 16.5.65.

and labelling, the reader was reassured, just as in the heresiologies of Epiphanius, Filastrius and Augustine, that the work represented a stable and uncontentious outline of heretical belief. By engaging with the classificatory practices of heresiology in its differentiating and cataloguing structure, this text thus arrogated to itself the growing authority of this new form of technical literature.[64]

Unlike the other heresiologies discussed here, however, the authorship of, or initiative behind, this law is not easy to identify. It has been suggested that it was at least heavily influenced, and possibly even drafted, by Nestorius, the recently installed bishop of Constantinople, who then embarked on a campaign against heretical groups in the eastern capital and its surrounding territories, supported by this ruling. Nestorius himself made the claim that he was responsible, in the early days of his episcopate, for a law which targeted not only those who denied the divinity of Christ, but also other heretics: 'for indeed, during the first stages of my ordination, I devised a law against those who say that Christ is wholly human, as well as against the other heresies'.[65] This statement, together with the testimony of Socrates' *Ecclesiastical History* concerning Nestorius' anti-heretical crusade, has persuaded some historians to attribute the law to Nestorius' pen.[66] This attribution does, however, rely on accepting that the bishop of Constantinople could have taken the leading role in dictating a late Roman law, a role usually seen as the highly specialised and closely guarded domain of the *quaestor sacri palatii*.[67] Tony Honoré, in his study

---

[64] When this law appeared in the *Justinianic Code* a century later (*CJ* 1.5.5), not only had it been edited and expanded to include a range of new heretical sects, but the distinctions between the groups had been abandoned, resulting in a longer, but undifferentiated, list of heresies. The only aspect of the original law's classification to survive was the specific condemnation and penalties for Manichaeans.

[65] *Nestoriana* B11 = Loofs 1905: 205.3–5: *certe legem inter ipsa meae ordinationis initia contra eos, qui Christum purum hominem dicunt, et contra reliquas haereses innouaui*.

[66] Soc. 7.29.5; Holum 1982: 150–1; an implicit link between Nestorius (as presented by Socrates) and *CTh* 16.5.65 is also drawn in Lee 2000: 37. Millar 2006: 151–7 discusses both this law and the 'anti-heretical crusade' (154) of Nestorius, but presents the law as an imperial initiative that highlights religious divisions and the need for unity within Christianity. As such Millar sees it as being at odds with Theodosius' choice of the obscure presbyter Nestorius as bishop of his capital; see Gardiner p. 264, this volume.

[67] On the *quaestor sacri palatii*, see Harries 1988.

of the quaestors of the Theodosian dynasty, attributes the drafting of this law to Antiochus Chuzon, a correspondent of Nestorius who treated the bishop kindly after his defeat at the Council of Ephesus in 431, but suggests that it was 'inspired by Nestorius'.[68] Jean Rougé and Roland Delmaire in their *Sources Chrétiennes* edition of Book 16 of the *Code* remain agnostic, reporting the traditional attribution of the law to Nestorius, but noting that it cannot be proven.[69]

If Nestorius is credited with significant involvement in its creation, then this law can be seen not merely as a statement of imperial will and orthodoxy, but also as an affirmation of the authority and expertise of the controversial new bishop. The careful division and grouping of heresies in this text was a strong statement of authorial control, displaying the bishop's heresiological skill and knowledge, while also bolstering it with the support of both earlier imperial pronouncements and the current emperor's mandate. Yet, even if Nestorius did not play a major role in influencing the content of *CTh* 16.5.65, it is notable that, through his claim to authorship of an imperial ruling against heresies, he sought to arrogate to himself the authority of the orthodox, expert heresiologist. The fact that Nestorius was keen to promulgate the belief that he was responsible for this law during the early days of his episcopacy is another indication of how demonstrations of heresiological skill and practical action helped individuals to promote themselves as authoritative voices in the theological disputes of the period. Both Epiphanius and Augustine had presented themselves as active opponents of heresy, not only through their own campaigns against particular heresiarchs and heretical sects, but also through their composition of handbooks which allowed the orthodox to protect themselves against heretical doctrines and to root out dangerous beliefs within their communities. Similarly, Nestorius' statement quoted above, in which he made his claim that 'I devised a law' against all heretics, formed part of a longer attempt to refute the charges of heresy that were levelled against him. In order to defend his own theological position, he argued

---

[68] Honoré 1998: 115–16, 118; on Antiochus Chuzon, see *PLRE* II 103–4 (Antiochus 7).
[69] Rougé and Delmaire 2005: 336.

that his orthodoxy was not in doubt precisely because he had been an enemy of heretics, rooting them out through the medium of an imperial ruling. All three of these bishops presented themselves as tireless enemies of heterodox beliefs and practices, studying their enemies, building up reliable and stable knowledge about their many and varied sects and then deploying this information through texts in order to save the unwary from diabolical snares. While posterity ultimately assigned Nestorius to the ranks of the heretics (and to the pages of heresiologies), his claims to heresiological expertise bear many similarities to those of the saints Epiphanius and Augustine.

CHAPTER 8

WRITING IN GREEK: CLASSICISM AND COMPILATION, INTERACTION AND TRANSFORMATION

Mary Whitby

Theodosius II's reign is framed by literary giants. The closing decades of the fourth century saw the deaths of two: Libanius (314–c. 393) and Gregory of Nazianzus (329–389), the former based in Antioch, staunchly pagan and allied to the Hellenic tradition of the schools, a teacher, practising orator and voluminous letter-writer, Gregory an equally prolific Christian Hellenist, educated at Athens, briefly bishop of Constantinople before retiring to his native Cappadocia. Gregory's writing is dedicated to expounding Scripture and the Christian way of life through sermons, exegesis and a varied corpus of poetry that has only recently begun to receive due attention.[1] In addition, 407 – the year before Theodosius II's accession as sole Augustus – marked the death of another prodigious Antiochene, pupil of Libanius and Christian Hellenist, John Chrysostom, also briefly (398–403/404) bishop of Constantinople before his banishment and death in exile. At the end of the reign, Theodosius' death in 450 approximately marks what was once called the 'Nonnian revolution', that is the appearance of two massive, but very different, hexameter epic poems that were undoubtedly the work of one mind,[2] a forty-eight-book *Dionysiaca* that charts the career of the god Dionysus and a twenty-one-book *Paraphrase* of St John's Gospel. Their author

---

I am grateful to Christopher Kelly for inviting me to write this chapter and for astute advice on improving it, and to Claudia Rapp for bibliography and for making time to read an earlier version.

[1] For example, Alan Cameron 2004: 333–49; McLynn 2006; Demoen 2009.
[2] Vian 1976: ix–lv, 1997; Alan Cameron 1982: 236–9; Shorrock 2011: 49–52.

195

Nonnus was an Egyptian from Panopolis of whom virtually nothing is known.[3]

This snapshot foregrounds the immense fertility and continuing innovativeness of writing in Greek. It also highlights sharp contrasts as well as interactions. The great figures of the fourth century, with a few honourable exceptions (like Claudian), were rhetoricians for whom prose was the natural medium of communication, whereas Nonnus' *oeuvre* is entirely in verse. Secondly, while for the most part fourth-century writers in Greek ally themselves either with secular Hellenism or with Christian polemic and theology, Nonnus moves comfortably between the two and even highlights the affinities of Hellenic and Christian deities:[4] does this reflect a broader assimilation of Hellenic styles to Christian themes under Theodosius II? And how widespread is the use of the classical hexameter for Christian themes? Then again, although Libanius, Gregory and John Chrysostom each spent a brief period in Constantinople, none is strongly linked to the city and only a limited proportion of their literary output is associated with it. To what extent, then, should literary developments in Theodosius II's reign be directly associated with emperor and capital? Certainly some writers have strong associations with the court – notably the Empress Eudocia, Cyrus of Panopolis and Olympiodorus; on the other hand, there is no known link between Nonnus and Constantinople. Finally, while all writers draw consciously or unconsciously upon their predecessors, in Nonnus it is worth emphasising the transformation into verse of an underlying prose account: incorporation of city *patria* in the *Dionysiaca*, while in his *Paraphrase* Nonnus not only elevates the simple *koine* of John's Gospel into epic hexameters, but also draws on the recently completed commentary of Cyril of Alexandria to create an original and polemical work. The interaction of prose and verse and these processes of consolidation deserve further investigation.

Ruth Webb has observed that in the ancient world 'literature' is generally not disengaged like later novels or poetry in the sense

---

[3] *Anth. Gr.* 9.198 (ed. H. Beckby, 4 vols., Munich, 1965) is a short autobiographical epigram which suggests that Nonnus wrote the *Dionysiaca* in Alexandria; cf. *Dion.* 1.13 where Pharos is designated 'a neighbouring island' (γείτονι νήσῳ).

[4] For example, Spanoudakis 2007; Shorrock 2011: 79–115.

of creating an unreal, fictional world or a world of poetic imagination.[5] It is firmly embedded in its contemporary historical context. Writers of the Theodosian period reacted to the exile and death of John Chrysostom, the Christological controversies that generated a series of church councils, the differing paradigms for the ideal life represented by Christianity and Neoplatonism and, within Christianity, between ascetic and philanthropic ideals, as well as to historical events such as wars, rebellions and celebratory and threnodic occasions. In the following discussion I draw in particular on recent scholarship to consider a – far from exhaustive[6] – range of material illustrating the development of, and response to, classical genres as well as new literary trends linked to the increasing prominence of Christianity.

Polemicising Lives

John Chrysostom

A number of broadly biographical works from the period are linked by their polemical purpose. One such cluster focuses on John Chrysostom, whose death in exile in September 407 generated a sequence of apologetic texts that were fundamental in establishing his subsequent saintly status. The earliest, the *Funeral Oration on the death of John Chrysostom*, dates to late 407 or spring 408, soon after news of John's death reached the capital.[7] The author's precise identity is uncertain: the text's editor Martin Wallraff proposed Philip of Side,[8] whereas T. D. Barnes favours a contemporary of John named Cosmas.[9] This long tribute (144 sections) is presented from the beginning as a substitute for a funeral oration; it alludes to topics of classical encomium, such as the author's inadequacy for the task, and conventional themes, like

---

[5] Webb 2006: 107–9.
[6] History-writing, especially ecclesiastical historiography, was the most prominent genre of the time, but I mention it only briefly, since Socrates (Gardiner) and Olympiodorus (Van Nuffelen) are treated elsewhere in this volume.
[7] Wallraff 2005, 2008: 26 dates the oration to autumn 407; Barnes and Bevan (in press) prefer 408.
[8] Wallraff 2005: 47–9, 2007: 17; on Philip, see further below pp. 204–5.
[9] Barnes 2001: 332–4; Barnes and Bevan (in press).

ancestry, native city and education, but these are rejected in favour of an account of John's life in Christ after he became a monk. From section 27, the focus is on John's opponents following his election to the see of Constantinople in 397 and the details of his downfall: he is presented as both saint and martyr.[10] Although the author draws on familiar classicising imagery, biblical allusion is more prominent.[11] Here, then, the classical funeral oration is adapted for the celebration of a revered Christian – amongst well-known antecedents are the fourth-century memorial works by the Cappadocians, Gregory of Nazianzus for Basil and Gregory of Nyssa on Macrina – but with the added agenda of rehabilitation of a highly controversial figure, over whom the Church was for a period in schism.[12]

A related and contemporary text, the *Dialogue on the death of John Chrysostom*, is now confidently attributed to Palladius who, after a period of asceticism in Palestine and Egypt, was by 400 in Constantinople and an associate of John, who may have ordained him bishop of Helenopolis in Bithynia.[13] Palladius too faced charges at the so-called Synod of the Oak in Constantinople which deposed John in September 403 and, after travelling to Rome and soliciting an unsuccessful protest from Pope Innocent I, was exiled to Syene in Egypt. On learning of John's death and that John's enemy, Theophilus of Alexandria, had composed a hostile pamphlet (now lost), Palladius responded in 407/408 with a dialogue set in Rome between an unnamed bishop and a deacon called Theodore that gives an account and defence of John's life.[14] The dialogue form allows a sophisticated non-chronological arrangement in which the deacon in Rome first recounts the facts that have reached him – including the visit of Palladius and his fellow clerics – while the bishop's narrative is preceded by an exposition on the priesthood (1–4). The core falls into two roughly equal parts, first an account of John's life and death, focusing like the *Funeral Oration* on the

---

[10] For example 40, 51, 56 (saint); 133, 144 (martyr) (ed. Wallraff 2007).
[11] For example, classical imagery of the helmsman at 9, 24; biblical allusions at 2, 3.
[12] See Wallraff 2008 on the role of this work in the formation of a 'Johannite opposition' to the ecclesiastical establishment in Constantinople.
[13] Pall. *Dial.* (ed. A.-M. Malingrey, SC 341–2, Paris, 1988); on Palladius and his works: Rapp 2001; Katos 2011.
[14] Details in Katos 2011: 9–32.

adversities of his period in Constantinople and subsequent exile (5–11). There follows a defence of specific aspects of John's lifestyle, in which the dialogue form is fully exploited (12–19). A final brief recapitulation leads into a pitiful account of the fate of John's followers, invective against his opponents and a concluding assertion that God will punish the wicked (20). Demetrios Katos has recently argued that this structure follows the principles of judicial rhetoric: a proem elicits audience goodwill, a persuasive case is presented through a (selective) factual narrative, then a series of proofs and an emotional epilogue.[15] This analysis accounts for the arrangement of the core material in two sections and vindicates the dialogue element, since the deacon's queries strengthen the arguments of the proof section. The appeal targets a Roman audience to continue their early support for John. Yet dialogue remains unusual in a judicial defence; earlier critics observed that it is indelibly associated with Plato's presentation and exoneration of Socrates,[16] who, not unlike John, was condemned to death by the Athenian people for his lifestyle[17] and for his outspokenness (*parrhesia*) as well as for his religious views. This paradigm adds *gravitas* to the glorification of Chrysostom, further enhanced by Christian imagery and biblical allusion.[18]

In addition to their testimony on the events surrounding Chrysostom's deposition, exile and death, these two texts illustrate how classical forms could be adapted to present an apologetic Christian biography. Celebratory funerary oration for an outstanding civic leader and law court defence linked to Platonic dialogue are the foundation for a rehabilitation of John Chrysostom that gathered momentum during Theodosius' reign, key moments being the restoration of his name to the Constantinopolitan diptychs during the patriarchate of Atticus[19] and the interment of his

---

[15] Katos 2007, 2011: 33–97.
[16] Links between Palladius' *Dialogue* and Plato were highlighted by Paolo Ubaldi in 1906 and taken up by later commentators: see Katos 2011: 36–8. While I would agree with Katos that specific links with the *Phaedo* should not be pushed too far, he is in my opinion too dismissive of the broader analogy between John Chrysostom and Socrates.
[17] A number of the charges brought against John at the Synod of the Oak related to his lifestyle, as well as his conduct towards individuals and his handling of church affairs: see Photius' summary *Bibl.* 59.
[18] Rapp 2005: 128.
[19] Katos 2011: 99; the exact date (417/418?) is unknown.

relics in the Church of the Holy Apostles in Constantinople in 438. The latter event generated other laudatory texts: an encomium by Proclus (patriarch of Constantinople, 434–446), extant only in Latin, Armenian and Old Slavonic, is plausibly associated with the restoration of John's relics.[20] And Photius details five lost orations of Theodoret of Cyrrhus following the transfer of the relics, the last of which was delivered in the Church of the Apostles; Photius quotes the proem which indicates that Theodoret was but one contributer in a larger celebration of John.[21] This vindication of John is also apparent in the historians' accounts, which move from a negative portrayal in Socrates to a more partial view in Sozomen and culminate in Theodoret's 'entirely partisan' version.[22]

Collective biography

Twenty years ago Averil Cameron spoke of a 'war of biography' between Christians and Neoplatonists, each of whom produced exemplary *Lives* of great figures from their past from the fourth century on.[23] Plutarch had created a secular model both for collective *Lives* and for focusing on the virtues and vices of his eminent Greeks and Romans, while his successors Diogenes Laertius, Philostratus and Eunapius turned the lens upon philosophers and sophists. Eunapius' *Lives of the Sophists* (c. 396) is roughly contemporary with the anonymous *History of the monks* (or *Lives of the desert fathers*) and shares its personal involvement and idealisation of its subjects. Although there is no evidence that they were consciously opposed, these represent the rival aspirations of Christians and Neoplatonists to define the authentic human being.[24] A later work by Palladius, the *Lausiac History*, dated by its prologue to 419/420, takes up this tradition,[25] but with a new orientation. In the preface, Palladius presents his subjects as role models for anyone aspiring to the Christian life, but in particular

---

[20] *Hom. 20 in Joh. Chrys.* (*CPG* 5819; *PG* 65: 827–34).
[21] Phot. *Bibl.* 273, proem at 509a.26–33.
[22] Mayer 2008 quoting 47; cf. Mayer 2004.
[23] Averil Cameron 1995: 145.
[24] Cox Miller 2000.
[25] Useful discussion with bibliography of the *Lausiac History* and *History of the monks*: Harmless 2004: 275–308.

for Lausus who requested the work and to whom it is dedicated. The *Lausiac History* is a revision of a *monobiblion* mentioned by the historian Socrates which was composed during Palladius' early years as an ascetic in Egypt.[26] The second half of the work (sections 40–70) extends the geographical scope to Syria, Palestine, Asia Minor and Italy and includes female and aristocratic models such as Melania the Elder as well as ascetics.[27] The key to this reworking lies in the dedicatee and the historical context: Claudia Rapp has argued that a clear political agenda can be identified.[28] Lausus, whom Palladius had first met in Egypt, was at this time *praepositus sacri cubiculi* (head of the imperial bedchamber)[29] at the court of Theodosius II, so the invitation from a key official to produce the *Lausiac History* close on fifteen years after Palladius' banishment was an olive branch in the reconciliation of supporters of John. Palladius' role models include wealthy aristocrats like Lausus himself, as well as pious women, such as Pulcheria and her sisters who, until Theodosius' marriage to Eudocia in 421, dominated the imperial court.[30] More recently Katos has identified covert polemic against Jerome and promotion of Origenist sympathisers.[31] In the *Lausiac History*, then, polemic is not directed against Neoplatonic ideals, but rather reflects divisions among Christians and contemporary imperial Constantinopolitan politics, in this latter respect linking desert and capital in a new way.

A rather different agenda may underlie a second collective hagiography of thirty ascetics – ten of them, including the great Simeon Stylites, still living – the *Religious History*, written twenty years later (*c.* 440), by Theodoret of Cyrrhus, who lived from *c.* 393 to *c.* 460, making him a close contemporary of Theodosius. Theresa Urbainczyk has argued that Theodoret consciously set out to foreground the ascetics of the Syrian desert, many of whom he knew, as opposed to the Egyptians who had received more

---

[26] Soc. 4.23.78–9; Pall. *Hist. Laus. pr.* 2 (ed. E. C. Butler, Texts and studies: contributions to biblical and patristic literature 6, 2 vols., Cambridge, 1898–1904).
[27] Rapp 2001; Katos 2011: 102–5.
[28] Rapp 2001.
[29] *PLRE* II 660 (Lausus 1); Pall. *Hist. Laus.* 71.
[30] Pall. *Hist. Laus. Pr.* 3 urges Lausus to become a guide to 'the most pious rulers'.
[31] Katos 2011: 110–23.

attention.³² The deference of these Syrians to Theodoret himself was intended to buttress the Antiochene position, and hence Antiochene theology, against the powerful Cyril of Alexandria. This thesis, though attractive, may be over-stated: Adam Becker has questioned the straightforward equation of Egyptian monks with Cyrilline theology and suggested that Theodoret may have been targeting Cyrilline converts closer to home, such as Rabbula, bishop of Edessa,³³ but the proposal that this collection, like the *Lausiac History*, was assembled for a particular – even polemical – reason, is persuasive.

Manipulating knowledge: florilegia, dialogue, encyclopaedism

The dialogue form exploited by Palladius in the *Lausiac History*, together with the florilegium, or collection of proof-texts, proved particularly fruitful in the disputation so prominent in this period, whether between Hellene and Christian or between differing Christological groups. The versatile and learned Theodoret is a key player in the development of these techniques for didactic purposes. Dialogue and florilegium are united in his *Eranistes*, written in 447/448 to promote his Christological views against those of Dioscorus of Alexandria.³⁴ The core of this highly original work comprises three separate discussions on aspects of the nature of Christ between 'Orthodox' and 'Eranistes': the latter term designates Theodoret's interlocutor who 'collects' diverse opposing doctrines to form a ragbag heresy.³⁵ Each dialogue concludes with a florilegium of texts in support of the point at issue. Cyril of Alexandria had earlier used such dogmatic florilegia in the dispute with Nestorius, establishing the principle of citing the 'fathers' (eminent deceased bishops) in defence of Nicene orthodoxy. In addition, in countering the views of Nestorius at the first Council of Ephesus in 431, Cyril quoted his adversary's writings in order

[32] Theod. *Historia Religiosa* (ed. P. Canivet and A. Leroy-Molinghen, *SC* 234, 257, Paris, 1977–9); Urbainczyk 2002.
[33] Becker 2003.   [34] Ettlinger 2003: 9–10.
[35] Theod. *Eranistes Pr.* (62.5–7) (ed. Ettlinger 1975) with Ettlinger 2003: 2–3.

to disprove them, thus exploiting the florilegium for polemical as opposed to dogmatic purposes.[36] In the *Eranistes*, Theodoret refined this technique by extending the range of authors cited to pre-Nicene fathers and also by including quotations from heretical authors like Apollinarius not for refutation but in dogmatic proof of the point at issue, arguing that their doctrines were the same as his own and the more persuasive since they were derived from the opponents' corpus.[37] He had already used a similar method in a much earlier work, *On the cure of Greek maladies*, which may well date from before he became bishop of Cyrrhus in 431.[38] In twelve discourses intended to vindicate Christianity, Theodoret argues through citations from non-Christian authors, for example Socrates in Plato's *Apology* in connection with the apostles' lack of education in the first discourse, 'On Faith'.[39] In his construction of patristic florilegia, Theodoret was both extraordinarily original and influential: Ettlinger has demonstrated that the florilegium of the *Eranistes* was based entirely on his own research, drawing on an earlier lost work the *Pentalogos*, compiled in connection with pro-Nestorian documentation produced by the eastern bishops, while many later florilegia drew on the *Eranistes*, for example that included in the 'Address to Marcian', attached to the *Acts of the Council of Chalcedon*.[40]

This originality is also manifest in the use of the dialogue form in *Eranistes*: Theodoret explains in his prologue that he will indicate the name of the speaker clearly in the margin, rather than the body, of the text. His objective is to make the work easily intelligible to readers who may be unacquainted with verbal disputation.[41] In *On the cure of Greek maladies* Theodoret adopted a plain style as being the most useful for teaching,[42] but in *Eranistes* he extends the question and answer format, a well-established

---

[36] Ettlinger 1975: 24–5; details of Cyril's extant florilegia at 24 n. 2.
[37] Ettlinger 1975: 25–6.
[38] Pásztori-Kupán 2006: 86 citing Canivet 2000: 28–31 on the date.
[39] Theod. *Graecarum affectionum curatio* 1.30 (ed. Canivet 2000) quoting Plato, *Apology* 17b–c, 18a; partial translation in Pásztori-Kupán 2006: 85–108.
[40] Ettlinger 1975: 23–30, 2003: 3–4; *Actio* 20 (*ACO* II 1.3, pp. 114–16) with Price and Gaddis 2005: III 106–7, 117–20.
[41] Theod. *Eranistes* Pr. (62.10–17) with Lim 1991 on the indication of the speaker.
[42] Theod. *Graec. aff. cur.* Pr. 3.

didactic method, to the more esoteric arena of theological disputation.[43] His *Questions on the Octateuch*, although not a dialogue, is organised around giving an extended answer to questions like, 'Why did God command the offering of sacrifices?' (Question 1 on Leviticus) and, 'What is the meaning of "His glory is like the unicorn's"?' (Question 43 on Numbers).[44] Finally, Theodoret's profound knowledge of contemporary theological issues as well as his didactic purpose are further illustrated by an encyclopaedic work dated after the Council of Chalcedon. His *Compendium of heretical mythification* (αἱρετικῆς κακομυθίας ἐπιτομή) devotes four books to a survey of Christian heretics from Simon Magus, culminating in the major heresies, then, in a final fifth book, a *Compendium of divine doctrines*, longer than the combined length of the other four, presents in counterbalance a systematic analysis of Greek patristic theology.[45]

With Theodoret's archive of heresy and theology we may contrast a very different encyclopaedic work written between 434 and 439 by Philip of Side, a relative of the influential sophist Troilus[46] and a deacon and protégé of John Chrysostom. His *Christian History*, now lost but for a few possible extracts,[47] ran to thirty-six books in nearly one thousand volumes (τόμοι) and was heavily criticised by both Socrates and Photius.[48] Unlike his contemporary ecclesiastical historians, Philip did not pick up where predecessors had left off, but started from Creation like a chronicler with an echo of the opening verse of Genesis (quoted by Photius). Thereafter the work was a repository of all knowledge, including the scientific and mathematical, philosophical, musical, astronomical and geographical in – at least according to its detractors – a pretentious

---

[43] Lim 1991: 182; cf. Papadoyannakis 2006 on instruction by question-and-answer, stressing that the technique spans secular and Christian material, and noting the analogy with our FAQs.

[44] Theod. *Quaestiones in Octateuchum* (ed. J. F. Petruccione, Library of Early Christianity 1–2, 2 vols., Washington, DC, 2007).

[45] Theod. *Haereticarum fabularum compendium* (*PG* 83: 335–556); partial translation in Pásztori-Kupán 2006: 198–220.

[46] Friend and adviser to Anthemius, praetorian prefect of the East in the early years of Theodosius II's reign: *PLRE* II 1128 (Troilus 1).

[47] Winkelmann 1966: 57; Fournet 2003: 521–3; Leppin 2003b: 249–50; for the fragments, see Heyden 2006.

[48] Soc. 7.26–7; Phot. *Bibl.* 35 (7a.31–9).

style and without due regard for chronology. The motivation for this massive project is unknown: it may perhaps have helped console Philip for an unsuccessful career in the church – he came close to being elected bishop of Constantinople on three occasions[49] – or he may have seen it as an alternative route to esteem in the eyes of the scholarly Theodosius.

(Re)casting text

Stylistic levels

Although the florilegium and the instinct for encyclopaedism are primarily late-antique phenomena, the works so far discussed also develop for new purposes essentially classical forms – encomium, judicial defence, dialogue, collective biography. A further response to the classical past is sensitivity to levels of style, which is particularly manifest in Theodoret's careful tailoring of his text to suit his readership, in stark contrast to the flamboyant language of Philip of Side's lost work. Photius, in discussing Theodoret's *Commentary on the Book of Daniel*, describes his style as particularly suited to commentaries since he reveals the meaning of what is obscure through plain and lucid language.[50] So too the ecclesiastical histories are differentiated not only by their various theological stances – Socrates' Novatian sympathies, the Eunomian Philostorgius, Theodoret's opposition to Arianism – but by their conscious adoption of different stylistic levels. Socrates eschews the grand style as inaccessible to the common man, while doubting if he could match the heights of the historians of antiquity, though of course such polemic demonstrates his own firm grounding in classical culture:[51] he was educated in Constantinople by the pagan grammarians Ammonius and Helladius who had fled from Alexandria in 391/392.[52] Sozomen's reworking of Socrates entails not only the addition of new sources – monastic and, especially, legal material – but also a grander style: his work begins

---

[49] Soc. 7.26.1 with Phot. *Bibl.* 35 (7a.39–7b.5); Soc. 7.29.1, 7.35.1.
[50] Phot. *Bibl.* 203 (164a.23–6).
[51] Soc. 6.*pr.*1–4; Leppin 2003b: 251.
[52] Soc. 5.16.9.

with an elaborate panegyrical address to Theodosius, rich in allusions to the relationship of literary men of the past to their patrons, while Book 9 opens with a panegyric of the pious Pulcheria. Like classical historians, Sozomen is prepared to summarise, rather than quoting, documents,[53] and he expresses his allegiances by opening his work with an allusion to the beginning of Xenophon's *Cyropaedia*.[54] As for Philostorgius, while fiercely condemning his theology, Photius commends at some length his elegant style, tempering his comments with criticism of overbold use of ornament.[55] But for Theodoret, whom he mentions at the end of a sequence of ecclesiastical historians, Photius reserves the accolade of the style best suited for history of all the writers mentioned.[56] A modern critic, Hartmut Leppin, identifies a debt to the principles of rhetoricians in the artful construction of Theodoret's five-book work, in which the central chapter of each book has special significance and is thematically linked to a corresponding book in a ring structure – Book 1 linked to Book 5 and Book 2 to Book 4.[57]

Paraphrase and cento

While Theodoret in particular often tailors his style to maximise accessibility, other writers consciously upgrade earlier texts by paraphrasing them in a grander style. So, at one level, Sozomen's *Ecclesiastical History* resembles a *metaphrasis* or paraphrase of the work of Socrates,[58] in that it draws heavily upon Socrates, but uses more elevated language, while also adding new material. The rewriting of a core text in a higher literary register is widespread,

---

[53] Soz. 1.1.14.
[54] Soz. 1.1.1: ἔννοια μοί ποτε ἐγένετο; cf. Xen. *Cyr.* 1.1.1 ἔννοιά ποθ' ἡμῖν ἐγένετο, noted by Leppin 2003b: 252.
[55] Phot. *Bibl.* 40 (8a.37–8b.3).
[56] Phot. *Bibl.* 31; Photius adds: 'It is generally clear, dignified and free from redundancies, although he sometimes employs metaphors that are too bold, almost insipid' (6b.4–6). *Bibl.* 27–30 cover respectively the *Ecclesiastical Histories* of Eusebius, Socrates, Evagrius and Sozomen.
[57] Leppin 2003b: 251–2.
[58] I use the terms interchangeably, adopting whichever is conventional for a particular text. Byzantine theorists attempted to distinguish between *metaphrasis* and *paraphrasis*, but modern critics argue that the distinction does not hold up in practice: Roberts 1985: 25–6. Faulkner (in press) notes that Philo distinguished the two, but that there is no clear difference between them as regards degree of literalness in rendering.

particularly amongst Jewish and Christian biblical exegetes in late antiquity, who used it as a didactic tool.[59] Rewriting often involves expansion, not of an arbitrary or redundant nature, but to incorporate exegesis or to change the orientation of a text. Scott Johnson observes that, while the habit of rewriting was endemic in Christian literature, especially Greek Christian literature, from the earliest times, for example in the rewriting of Mark's Gospel by Matthew and Luke, the mid fifth century saw a particular florescence, in part because of the atmosphere at court, but also because of 'the germination of a Christian self-consciousness at this time' that grew out of shifting patterns of education.[60] The context of these comments is Johnson's study of the *Life and Miracles of Thecla* of which the first recension dates to 444–448, while two further recensions were made in the third quarter of the fifth century.[61] The original *Acts of Paul and Thecla* belong to the second century, but against the background of the growing cult of Thecla at Seleucia in Isauria the *Acts* were rewritten in a grander style that played down the theme of sexual renunciation, while the end was changed so that Thecla did not die but disappeared alive, thus enabling her to work the miracles detailed in new material in the second half of the text, which was several times expanded.

In another paraphrase, an original prose hagiography was reworked in hexameters, the only such work to survive from late antiquity.[62] It was written by no less a person than Theodosius II's wife, the Empress Eudocia, a remarkable woman of whom a good deal is known. Born Athenais, daughter of an Athenian sophist Leontius who gave her a good education partly in Alexandria, she was baptised and married to Theodosius in 421. For twenty years she was an influential figure at court before she retired to Jerusalem after falling from favour, dying there in 460.[63] Her

---

[59] Johnson 2006c: 10–11.
[60] Johnson 2006c: 86–112 quoting 99. The fourth-century sequence of Christian poems in the Bodmer papyrus known as the *Codex Visionum* is an early example of the use of the rhetorical structures of pagan education for Christian themes: Agosti 2009a.
[61] Dagron 1978; Johnson 2006c: especially 5–6 with n. 18.
[62] Phot. *Bibl.* 168 (116b.1–3) alludes to a verse paraphrase of the *Acts of Thecla* by Basil of Seleucia (d. 468). However Dagron 1974a, 1978: 13–15 has shown that the prose *Life and Miracles of Thecla* attributed to Basil is not his work.
[63] *PLRE* II 408–9 (Eudocia 2); Alan Cameron 1982: especially 254–79; Holum 1982: 112–30, 176–94.

paraphrase – perhaps composed in 438–439[64] – deals with Cyprian of Antioch, a magician who converted to Christianity and was martyred along with his fellow-Antiochene Justina in the late third century under Diocletian and Maximian. Photius gives a detailed synopsis of the three-book work, of which the first and part of the second books are extant (900 lines).[65] The opening ninety-nine lines of the poem have now been restored, following the recognition that a fragment in the University Library in Leiden is the missing opening folio of the sole eleventh-century Laurentian manuscript.[66] The first book describes Cyprian's unsuccessful attempt to persuade the Christian Justina to care for her rejected lover, leading to his own eventual conversion. Book 2 details the earlier career of Cyprian and his extensive and exotic travels in the pursuit and practice of magic (an early prototype for the Faust story),[67] until his encounter with Justina made him see the error of his ways. The last book described the joint martyrdom, in which, after surviving being boiled in pitch, the couple were eventually beheaded. The poem brings together three independent prose texts, dating at least from the later fourth century, the *Conversion of Cyprian*, *Confession of Cyprian* and the *Passion of Cyprian and Justina*. Bevegni's analysis has shown that while Eudocia closely followed the prose models (which can sometimes be used to improve the transmitted text), she does not consistently follow any one of the various extant recensions. She also elaborates with new details, for example a passage in praise of Antioch at the beginning.[68] The whole is in Homerising language, with all kinds of metrical licence, but also a sophisticated

---

[64] Livrea 1998 suggests that the relics of Cyprian and Justina were moved to Sixtus III's new Lateran Baptistery and Eudocia's poem composed in connection with the proclamation of her daughter Eudoxia as Augusta in 439, following her marriage to Valentinian III in 437.
[65] Phot. *Bibl.* 184 (128a.36–129b.11); Photius' summary is translated by Wilson 1994: 174–6, who incorrectly describes this work as a cento.
[66] Leid. BPG [= Leiden: Bibliotheca Publica Graeca] 95 with Bevegni 1982, 2004. Bevegni 2006a has an introduction and Italian translation with notes, but regrettably does not print the Greek text which has to be read in Bevegni 1982 and Ludwich 1897: 16–79; further analysis in Bevegni 2006b and 2006/2007.
[67] See Wilson's appendix to Bevegni 2006a (at 173–207).
[68] 1.11–14; see further Livrea 1998: 80–2; Bevegni 2006a: 33–4; and below p. 213 on Eudocia and Antioch.

resemanticisation of Homer, and linguistic affiliation with a wide range of classical, Hellenistic and late-antique authors, as well as extensive neologism.[69] In addition to hagiographical paraphrase, Eudocia wrote Homeric centos that survive in several distinct recensions.[70] In an apologetic epigram, preserved with the centos in several manuscripts, Eudocia explains that she reworked centos begun by an unknown bishop, Patricius, of whose work she makes a number of criticisms, at the same time defending her own technique.[71] As Enrico Livrea has noted, this apologia attests the seriousness of Eudocia's intellectual commitment and her understanding of theoretical issues.[72] Cento composition is no longer a dilettante intellectual occupation, as it was for Ausonius, but a serious medium for conveying the Christian story.[73] The centos first delineate God's plan for mankind using material from the Old Testament and then articulate a selection of stories from the gospels in lines and half-lines lifted from Homer, a programme remarkably similar to that of a Virgilian cento by the aristocratic Proba, written in the mid fourth century.[74] Nor will it surprise that the cultured Eudocia read Latin.[75] Eudocia also turned her hand to biblical paraphrase, though this does not survive: Photius read an eight-book hexameter paraphrase of the Octateuch and of the prophets Zachariah and Daniel. He commends the closeness of Eudocia's version to

---

[69] See especially Bevegni 2006a: 34–48.
[70] Schembra 2007a is the definitive edition. The recensions are of different length: a long version (2,354 lines with Italian translation and commentary: Schembra 2006), a shorter second version (1,948 lines, ed. A.-L. Rey, *SC* 437, Paris, 1998; Italian translation and commentary in Schembra 2007b) and three short recensions (622, 653 and 738 lines respectively). Schembra argues that the short recensions are the work of a single author who had the other two recensions before him; that the second recension is based on the first and that the longest version is Eudocia's; see further Mary Whitby 2009. Mary Whitby 2007: 209–16 compares the treatment of the story of Doubting Thomas in the two longer recensions.
[71] Analysed by Agosti 2001: 74–85; also Livrea 1998: 70–2.
[72] Livrea 1998: 70.
[73] For a brief survey of cento composition with bibliography, see Mary Whitby 2007: 197–9.
[74] See the useful discussion in Curran 2012.
[75] Agosti 2004: 71–2 cites the early fourteenth-century Nicephorus Callistus, *Historia ecclesiastica* 14.23 (*PG* 146: 1129B) which says that Eudocia was educated by her father in Latin as well as Greek. Agosti suggests that Eudocia's metrical habits may reflect the influence of Latin verse.

the original, to the extent that the reader has no need of the base text.⁷⁶ As noted above, her poem on St Cyprian shared this characteristic, although that did not preclude elaborative excursuses or sophisticated refashioning of secular poetic models.

A similar faithfulness has been identified in the roughly contemporary surviving anonymous verse paraphrase of the Psalms, which follows the Septuagint model line by line.⁷⁷ However, a recent study argues that the programme outlined in the prologue permits some freedom since, whereas the prose translation commissioned by Ptolemy required exactitude, that was achieved at the expense of the grace (χάρις) of poetry which this new version aims to restore, relying on divine inspiration. Moreover, since the Septuagint psalms were in stichic form and their text known to many by heart, other poets also remain close to the model in rendering them.⁷⁸ This poet too responds linguistically to the hexameter tradition from Homer to late antiquity in a sensitive and meaningful adaptation of his model. For stylistic and theological reasons it is clear that the work belongs between 450 and 470 (and is not by the fourth-century Apollinarius of Laodicea as was once thought). More precise dating hinges on identification of the Marcian addressed in the prologue (4), now usually thought to be the *oikonomos* of St Sophia under Patriarch Gennadius. Golega dated the work to 457–460, arguing on the basis of allusions in the prologue (36–47) that it was written for a Constantinopolitan patron by an author who originated from Egypt.⁷⁹

Nonnus' *Paraphrase* of the Gospel of John was also composed in Egypt, probably in Alexandria, a decade or two earlier, after the completion in 428 of Cyril of Alexandria's commentary on John which Nonnus used⁸⁰ and perhaps after the first Council of Ephesus in 431, but probably before Chalcedon in 451.⁸¹ This

---

⁷⁶ Phot. *Bibl.* 183–4 (128a.16–17 on closeness to original).
⁷⁷ *Metaphrasis Psalmorum* (ed. A. Ludwich, Leipzig, 1912); Golega 1960: especially 25–44; Agosti 2001: 85–92; Mary Whitby 2007: 196 with further bibliography.
⁷⁸ Faulkner (in press), arguing also that ancient notions of 'word for word' translation were less rigorous than is often supposed. Faulkner is preparing a new edition and study of the Psalm paraphrase.
⁷⁹ Golega 1939; Golega 1960: 32–5, 169–77; succinct discussion: Gonnelli 1989: 51–2 n. 2.
⁸⁰ Livrea 1989: 25, 2000: 53; complete text ed. A. Scheindler, Leipzig, 1881.
⁸¹ The term θεητόκος is applied to the Virgin Mary at *Paraphrase* 2.9 (ed. Livrea: 2000), 19.135; the first Council of Ephesus formally recognised her title θεοτόκος, but it

poem, which has received extensive scholarly attention thanks to Livrea and his students, is consistently more expansive than the works of Eudocia and the Psalm paraphrase in its elaborative exegesis of the Gospel, not only drawing on Cyril, but also incorporating material from the synoptic gospels.[82] It may be that the gospel texts, which were also freely treated in Latin at this time in Sedulius' *Carmen Paschale*,[83] were felt to be more fluid than the Septuagint, since individual gospels vary in content and detail.

The reason for the sudden explosion of Greek biblical poetry has been much debated.[84] The view that it responds to Julian's so-called Edict on Education almost a century earlier by providing an alternative Christian literature for school use is now rightly discredited: these are sophisticated works intended for a sophisticated audience. The precise background of each individual composition may be hard to recover – Nonnus' *Paraphrase* has no explanatory prologue analogous to that of the Psalm paraphrast or Eudocia. But it is attractive to relate these texts more broadly to what is now seen as a dialogue between educated Christians and pagans, maybe in part to offer Christians a high-brow literature or to win new converts,[85] but primarily to enrich Christian texts for an educated mixed pagan and Christian audience to whom Hellenic poetry was a *lingua franca* and who were deeply conscious of shared culture and ideals. So, for example, it has recently been argued that the verse *Lives* of Christ – both Nonnus' *Paraphrase* and Eudocia's centos – should be read in counterpoint to contemporary Neoplatonic hagiography as part of an intercultural debate between pagan and Christian intellectuals on the ideal holy man.[86]

---

was also in use earlier: Livrea 2000: 167–8. Alan Cameron 2000: 182 is sceptical of Chalcedon as a *terminus ante quem*.

[82] For example, Greco 2008; further examples collected by Faulkner (in press), and see now Shorrock 2011: especially 49–78 on Nonnus' *Paraphrase*, stressing intertextuality with the *Dionysiaca*.

[83] On Sedulius see Green 2006: 135–250; interestingly, Sedulius later composed a prose version (the *Opus Paschale*) of his poem: Green 2006: 157–60; see also Roberts 1985: 76–86; Agosti 2009a: 327. Green 2006: 150–2 discusses other Latin Christian poems from the early fifth century.

[84] Agosti 2001 is an excellent survey.

[85] A proselytising sentiment is expressed in the phrase from the anonymous *Metaphrasis Psalmorum Pr.* 32: ἵνα γνώωσι καὶ ἄλλοι ('that others too may learn').

[86] Agosti 2009b, drawing attention, for example, to similarities between miracles performed by Christ and miracles attributed to Proclus.

Averil Cameron's 'war of biography' has swung now towards a view of constructive interaction between Hellenic and Christian culture, that is exemplified at its most extreme in the irrepressible 'biculturalité' of Nonnus, whose talent extended also to the forty-eight-book *Dionysiaca*.[87] Within this larger perspective individual texts must be differentiated. Eudocia and the Psalm paraphrase have long been undervalued, chiefly because of their lax technique by comparison with the metrical rigour and ingenuity of Nonnus.[88] But recent scholarship foregrounds their sophistication and originality and it is doubtless unjust to judge success or failure by the yardstick of Nonnus alone.[89]

Patria

As an Egyptian writing for a Chalcedonian church patron in the capital, the Psalm paraphrast is 'una sorta di religioso "wandering poet"'.[90] Alan Cameron demonstrated that several of his late-antique 'wandering poets' made a living not only by writing encomia and other occasional pieces for wealthy patrons, but also by composing works known as *patria* on the antiquities of various cities that they visited.[91] These works do not survive, but they typically drew on mythological material to add kudos to accounts of a city's origins, incorporating traditions preserved in prose in local histories. Similar source material has now been seen to underlie accounts of the origins of Berytus, Tarsus and Nicaea in Nonnus' *Dionysiaca*.[92] A substantial lost hexameter poem from Alexandria may also belong to this tradition. A fragment, perhaps from Philip of Side, refers to a poem by an Alexandrian lawyer Theodore which in its thirteenth book mentioned the martyrs Pierius and Isidore and the large church dedicated to them in Alexandria. This scant information leaves much uncertainty, but Theodore's profession

---

[87] Fournet's term (2003: 521); and further below pp. 216–18.
[88] For detailed and fundamental analysis, see Agosti and Gonnelli 1995.
[89] See Alan Cameron 2004: 333–9, rehabilitating the poetry of Gregory of Nazianzus.
[90] Gonnelli 1989: 150 n. 24.
[91] Alan Cameron 1965: 489–90, citing evidence for Claudian and Christodorus.
[92] Chuvin 1991; cf. Alan Cameron 2007: 32; on Berytus, see further Hadjittofi 2011: 35–7.

of lawyer links him to other literary *scholastici*, such as the church historian Sozomen and (later) Agathias. And with at least thirteen books his poem was clearly substantial, on the scale of Nonnus' *Paraphrase*. Fournet suggests that it might have been a verse *patria*.[93] If this is right, the poem would represent a work with roots in the city histories of the classical past, but now accommodated to the Christian heritage of Alexandria. Alternatively, it may have been a cycle of martyr *Passions*, a verse counterpart to Palladius' *Lausiac History*, a thesis that is given some support by Photius' mention that Eudocia ended her hexameter poem on Cyprian with a reference to the church of Justina and Cyprian in Rome.[94] In either case the work connects with other substantial Christian hexameter poems from the mid fifth century and is linked, like Nonnus, to Alexandria.

Theodosius and the world of Theodosius

Eudocia, however, belonged at the heart of the Theodosian court. Although surviving evidence for occasional works from the period is limited, poetry holds a prominent position. This empress had the rhetorical skills of an itinerant sophist: she composed verse panegyrics on Theodosius' Persian victory in 422,[95] and the church historian Evagrius records that while visiting his native Antioch on one of her two journeys to Jerusalem (respectively in 438 and the early 440s) she gave a public address (δημηγορήσασα) which concluded with a line adapted from Homer that asserted her kinship with the Antiochenes.[96] Livrea suggested that the whole address was a hexameter *patria*, connecting it with her poem on the Antiochene martyrs Cyprian and Justina.[97] In addition, there are two verse inscriptions linked to Eudocia, one written by her in praise of the baths at Hammat Gader in the Yarmuk valley in

---

[93] Fournet 2003: 534–5.
[94] Phot. *Bibl.* 184 (129b.7–10). [95] Soc. 7.21.8: ἡρωικῷ μέτρῳ ποιήματα.
[96] Evagrius 1.20: ὑμετέρης γενεῆς τε καὶ αἵματος εὔχομαι εἶναι ('I boast that I am of your race and blood'), cf. *Il.* 6.211, 20.241 with Michael Whitby 2000: 48 n. 172 for discussion.
[97] Livrea 1998: 80–1, discussed by Fournet 2003: 535 n. 62.

Palestine,[98] and an epigram in her honour found on a statue base in the Athenian agora.[99] The career of the Egyptian Cyrus of Panopolis is contemporaneous with the rise and fall of the empress: the *Suda* records that Eudocia was Cyrus' patron and that his fall occurred during her absence in Jerusalem.[100] Cyrus became hugely powerful in the capital where in 439 he was simultaneously urban prefect and praetorian prefect of the East. In 441 he became consul, before his great popularity, due in particular to his building works, led to sudden exile to a bishopric in Cotyaeum, where after winning over his flock by a short but topical sermon, he remained until after Theodosius' death.[101] And yet it was as a poet that Cyrus was chiefly remembered.[102] Regrettably only a handful of sophisticated occasional poems survive in the *Anthologia Graeca*.[103] But it was perhaps Cyrus' ability to coin memorable lines apposite to a specific occasion that elicited acclaim: Friedländer argued that Cyrus was 'the great poet' in the sense of being *the* poet of his day.[104] One poem is an extract from a panegyric of Theodosius II in which he is credited with the virtues – but not the vices – of Homeric heroes (Achilles, Teucer, Agamemnon, Odysseus, Nestor). The prominence of Teucer the bowman doubtless compliments Theodosius' love of hunting. Alan Cameron cleverly argued that this poem can be dated before 437/438;[105] it would thus predate Cyrus' rise to power and may have been instrumental in bringing him to the emperor's attention. A second remarkable piece, described in the lemma as a 'dirge' (θρῆνος) marks the moment of Cyrus' exile. The poet assumes bucolic mode for political comment

---

[98] Green and Tsafir 1982: 77–91; Habas 1996.
[99] Sironen 1990. Mango 2004 demonstrates that an iambic inscription from Paphlagonia also attributed to Eudocia is a fake.
[100] Suda K 2776; Alan Cameron 1982: especially 256–63 on chronology.
[101] Whitby and Whitby 1989: 78–9; Alan Cameron 1982: especially 221–5, 243–5, 256–70 correcting *PLRE* II 336–9 (Cyrus 7).
[102] For example, Evagrius 1.19; further citations: Alan Cameron 1982: 225 with Tissoni 2008: 69 n. 7.
[103] For the identification of poems that belong to this Cyrus, see Alan Cameron 1982: 225–39; Tissoni 2008.
[104] Friedländer 1912: 49.
[105] *Anth. Gr.* 15.9; Alan Cameron 1982: 228–30.

in the manner of Virgil's shepherds in *Eclogue* 1 while simultaneously evoking lines from Nonnus' *Dionsyiaca* to lament his inexperience in pasturing flocks – alluding to his new role as bishop of Cotyaeum – and the need to flee the 'well-built' city of Constantinople (the carefully-chosen Homeric epithet εὐκτιμένην draws attention to Cyrus' own building achievements) and seek a new homeland, driven out by the drones, identified with Cyrus' enemy the eunuch Chrysaphius.[106] The authenticity of *Anth. Gr.* 9.808, which praises the fine Constantinopolitan house of a certain Maximinus, is less secure, though a good case can be made for identifying Maximinus with an official under Theodosius.[107] Alan Cameron's masterly discussion of *Anth. Gr.* 1.99, which was inscribed on the column of Daniel the Stylite, ties it indubitably to Cyrus' building work and theology, but Tissoni has now astutely observed that the first line μεσσηγὺς γαίης τε καὶ οὐρανοῦ ἵσταται ἀνήρ ('Between earth and heaven stands a man') combines a Homeric cento (*Il.* 5.769, al.) with a line-end from Nonnus' *Paraphrase* (*Par.* 19.25 and 69).[108] These remnants are our best evidence for high-quality occasional poetry closely linked to the career of a talented Egyptian immigrant.

The work of another talented and well-travelled Egyptian closely associated with Theodosius' court has fared less well. Olympiodorus of Thebes served as a diplomat in the early years of Theodosius' reign, and his twenty-two-book *Material for History*, the only secular history from the period, was dedicated to the emperor.[109] But Photius criticised its careless and vulgar style and it survives only through his substantial summary and other historians' use of it.[110] However, Olympiodorus declared himself a 'poet by profession'[111] and, as with Cyrus, this may initially have brought him to attention.[112] His one surviving line wittily wonders

---

[106] *Anth. Gr.* 9.136 with detailed discussion of the rich literary allusions in Alan Cameron 1982: 230–5; Tissoni 2008: 76–81.
[107] Tissoni 2008: 72–6 with Mary Whitby 2011: 456–7.
[108] Alan Cameron 1982: 239–54; Tissoni 2008: 76.
[109] See also Van Nuffelen in this volume.
[110] Phot. *Bibl.* 80 (56b).
[111] Phot. *Bibl.* 80 (56b.13–14): ποιητής, ὡς αὐτός φησι, τὸ ἐπιτήδευμα.
[112] Alan Cameron 1965: 490–1, 497.

at the magnificence of buildings in Rome and may draw on the Latin poet Ovid.[113] Olympiodorus has been proposed as the author of a historical Homerising epic about a successful Roman campaign against the Blemyes that survives on a papyrus dated around 400 from Egyptian Thebes, his birthplace.[114] Olympiodorus mentions in his history that the Blemyes acted as guides when he was exploring the region for research,[115] but this casts no light on the authorship of the poem. The surviving fragments, however, show little interest in the artistic crafting evident in Olympiodorus' one authentic verse,[116] and it is perhaps more likely that the epic was a local production for a Theban audience.[117] Papyrus fragments indicate that there was plenty of local occasional poetry, but little can be dated or contextualised with precision[118] and doubtless much more has not survived.

This account has focused on a few conspicuous elements in the literary activity of the first half of the fifth century. Scant attention has been paid to inscriptions and none to epistolography, represented, for example, by Theodoret of Cyrrhus, Synesius and his correspondent, the shadowy Troilus of Side.[119] I have considered only Theodoret among theological writers and said nothing of the writings of the Neoplatonist Proclus in Athens. In addition it is artificial to frame within the reign of Theodosius II trends – the evolution of hexameter poetry, for example – that are part of a much larger picture. But on the other hand this limited time scale does illuminate some themes.

The most striking single feature of the majority of the works considered here is experimentation across boundaries: church history

[113] Olymp. 41.1.5: εἷς δόμος ἄστυ πέλει· πόλις ἄστεα μυρία κεύθει ('one house is a town; the city hides countless towns'); Alan Cameron 1982: 233–4 compares Ovid, *Fasti* 6.641–2.
[114] Livrea 1978: 23–31; for further details Miguélez Cavero 2008: 59–61.
[115] Olymp. 35.2.
[116] Mary Whitby 1994: 128–9 on the *Blemyomachia*.
[117] For a succinct account of the Blemyes' threat in this period, see Palme 2007: 257.
[118] Miguélez Cavero 2008: 383–90 has a useful catalogue. Note, however, that other scholars date the works contained in the important Bodmer papyri *Codex Visionum* (cat. no. 40) to the mid fourth century: for example, Agosti 2009a: 321 (and see above n. 60).
[119] See above n. 46.

is extended to include secular material; prose hagiographies, biblical texts and *patria* are recast in verse. The impetus of Christianity inspires creativity – in ecclesiastical history, in Eudocia's deployment of the classical hexameter and in Theodoret's adoption of the dialogue for theological debate. There is a self-consciousness about levels of style: Sozomen's literary upgrading of Socrates, Philip of Side's baroque aspirations, use of classical forms for hagiographic celebration of John Chrysostom, Theodoret's careful selection of appropriate stylistic level. Small-scale occasional pieces do not disappear, but large-scale undertakings, especially works of compilation, abound: Philip of Side's all-encompassing *Christian History*, collected exemplary *Lives*, Theodoret's florilegia and compendia of heresies and patristic theology, Nonnus' *Paraphrase* and *Dionysiaca*, the poem of the Alexandrian lawyer Theodore. They parallel contemporary civic compilations – the *Notitia of Constantinople*[120] and the great legal project of the *Theodosian Code*[121] – and the acts of church councils.

How much of the literary output of the reign is closely linked to the emperor himself? The historians are clearest in their allegiance, with explicit dedications by Olympiodorus and Sozomen and flattering laudation by Socrates and Theodoret,[122] as well as by poets like Eudocia and Cyrus of Panopolis. The *Lausiac History* appears to have been instrumental in the reconciliation of supporters of John Chrysostom. But some worked in the capital for other patrons, perhaps clerics such as the Theodore who urged Socrates to write[123] and the Marcian who prompted the Psalm paraphrase. Talented writers were attracted to the capital from all corners – Sozomen, Philostorgius, Philip of Side, Cyrus, Olympiodorus, Eudocia herself – but in no case is it clear that literary aspirations alone brought them: where there is evidence it suggests the contrary. Others remained independent and firmly attached to their preferred location – Theodoret in Antioch and Cyrrhus, Nonnus in Alexandria. For most, literature was not their main occupation. Egypt, above all Panopolis, produced the most accomplished poets,

---

[120] Jones 1964: II 689; Matthews 2012.
[121] Harries and Wood 1993; Matthews 2000.
[122] Phot. *Bibl.* 80 (56b.26–9) (Olympiodorus); Soz. *Pr.*; Soc. 7.42; Theod. *HE* 5.36.
[123] Soc. 2.1.6, 6.*pr.*1, 7.48.7.

and Eudocia may have been inspired to her own poetic endeavours by her early education in Alexandria or by learning of Nonnus from Cyrus or Olympiodorus. Antioch and Constantinople above all fostered explicitly Christian writing. In Alexandria, arguably the most exciting forum for exchange between Hellenes and Christians, Nonnus experimented in cross-cultural dialogue: the lynching of the Neoplatonist mathematician and teacher Hypatia in 415 was an extremity unrepresentative of the more enlightened encounters suggested by the majority of evidence.[124]

Alan Cameron has mapped our understanding of poetry in the fourth and fifth centuries in a series of seminal writings.[125] Recently he has come to reject early suggestions of tension between Hellenic and Christian culture in favour of the view that Hellenic modes, acquired through the continuing traditional educational system, were for the well-educated both the natural means of expression and the best way of reaching an appreciative audience.[126] Hence there is no need to assume, to take an obvious example, that Nonnus was pagan when he wrote the *Dionysiaca*. Cameron's point applies to prose as well as poetry: in this period the church historians experiment with the stylistic level and content of historiography, while biographers and hagiographers draw on classical precedent to set up models for the ideal life and Theodoret exploits his Hellenic education to engage with contemporary theological debate. Far from oppressive piety, the literature of the Theodosian era suggests an imaginative flexibility, interaction and integration in a world that is essentially comfortable with its Christianity.

---

[124] Dzielska 1995; Watts 2006: 187–203.
[125] Alan Cameron 1965, 1982, 2004, 2007, 2011, especially 226–30, 353–98.
[126] Alan Cameron 2007; cf. Agosti 2009a.

PART IV

PIUS PRINCEPS

CHAPTER 9

STOOPING TO CONQUER: THE POWER OF IMPERIAL HUMILITY

Christopher Kelly

On 26 January 447, the Emperor Theodosius II refused to wear his glittering imperial regalia. He put aside his heavy purple robes, bejewelled diadem, pearl earrings and gem-encrusted shoes. He dismissed his golden carriage and his bodyguards in their scarlet uniforms and shining parade armour. Instead, the emperor set out into the city barefoot. His feet bleeding and his forehead glistening with sweat, he walked the seven miles along the hard, marble-paved streets of Constantinople from the Great Palace to the military parade-ground at the Hebdomon on the shores of the Propontis (the Sea of Marmara), beyond the Theodosian Walls. The emperor was followed by high-ranking dignitaries, priests and a great throng of citizens. At the Hebdomon, the crowd gathered: perhaps near the tall granite column erected some twenty-five years earlier to celebrate Theodosius as *perennis et ubique uictor* – 'forever and everywhere victorious'; perhaps flanked by the church of John the Baptist (about 300 feet away from the column) built by the emperor's grandfather, Theodosius I, to house a precious relic of the saint's head. Prayers, which lasted several days, are likely to have included the *Trisagion* – 'Holy God, Holy Mighty One, Holy Immortal One, have mercy upon us' – an invocation that was said to have been revealed to the people of Constantinople at the Hebdomon by angels a decade before. (But that, of course, is another story.)

The normally prosperous and self-confident residents of the imperial capital – who assumed, as a matter of course, that God was on their side – were in penitent mood. In the dark hours of the early morning of 26 January, a severe earthquake had shaken the city.¹ On the way to the Hebdomon, the scale of the destruction was clearly visible. The recently completed sea walls along the Propontis were severely damaged. The Theodosian Walls had been breached. The Walls, completed at the beginning of Theodosius' reign, were intended to guarantee Constantinople's security. They were one of the most formidable military structures ever built in the Roman empire.² Perhaps as many as sixty towers were now heaps of rubble. The damage may have been widespread – both the inner and the outer walls were fortified with just under a hundred towers each – or perhaps concentrated in the southern section towards the Propontis.³ To be sure, educated persons in the mid fifth century knew how earthquakes happened (that had been explained long ago by the Greek philosopher Aristotle): they resulted from the sudden movement of vast bodies of air in huge voids deep underground.⁴ Aristotle might have explained what caused the earth to shake, but not what caused the air to move in the first place. For many late-antique Christians, these tremors were in accordance with the will of God who sought to turn sinners to repentance. An earthquake was a warning from heaven. The sight of a barefoot emperor walking painfully through the city was an indication of how seriously God's purpose was to be taken.

The possibility of another earthquake was not the only threat faced by the citizens of Constantinople. Two years previously Attila, following the assassination of his brother Bleda, had become sole ruler of the Huns. From the heartland of their empire on the Great

---

¹ The earthquake in January 447 is reported in Marcell. com. 447.1 (fifty-seven towers destroyed); the earthquake and the imperial response in *Chron. Pasch.* 447 (1 586.6–14) and 450 (1 589.6–16), John of Nikiu, *Chronicle* 84.39 (trans. Charles 1916: 95) and Malalas 14.22: ὅστις βασιλεὺς ἐλιτάνευσεν μετὰ τῆς συγκλήτου καὶ τοῦ ὄχλου καὶ τοῦ κλήρου ἀνυπόδητος ἐπὶ ἡμέρας πολλάς (see Baldovin 1987: 206–7 on λιτανεύειν). I follow the understanding of these compact, and sometimes contradictory, versions as resolved in an elegant essay by Brian Croke 1981: 131–44; see too Croke 1978: 7–8; Harries 1994: 39; Diefenbach 2002: 25; Meier 2007: 147; Van Nuffelen 2012: 186–7. Theophanes 5930 (93.5–20) (with Croke 1981: 126–31; Mango and Scott 1997: 145 n. 4) explains the origins of the *Trisagion*. The victory column at the Hebdomon was topped by a statue of Theodosius, the quotation is from the heavily restored inscription on its base: see Demangel 1945: 33–40; Croke 1977: 365–6. For the church of John the Baptist, see Demangel 1945: 28–30; Janin 1969: 413–15; Croke 2010: 255–6, 260.
² Ward-Perkins 2012: 62–4.
³ Croke 1981: 133–5 (suggesting a concentration of damage in the southern part of the Theodosian Walls), 135–6 (damage to the sea walls).
⁴ Aristotle, *Meteorologica* 2.7–8; Croke 1981: 122–5.

Hungarian Plain, the Huns pursued an effective strategy of opportunism. In 441, in apparent disregard of a treaty negotiated with the eastern imperial government two years previously, the Huns pushed into the Balkans sacking almost all the major cities on the middle Danube (including Sirmium, Singidunum, Margum and Viminacium) and south-east along the Morava river valley as far as Naissus and Serdica. It seems likely that this attack was timed to take advantage of the absence of a major expeditionary force which left Constantinople in spring 441 with the aim of regaining Carthage seized by the Vandals in late 439. The Roman army made it only as far as Sicily; it was recalled in spring 442, a threat sufficient to ensure the Huns' withdrawal. Certainly by late 446 (a few months before the earthquake), Theodosius and his advisers were sufficiently confident in the Balkan defences not to accede to Attila's demands that the terms of the treaty negotiated in 439 should be enforced. Attila rejected outright Theodosius' move to negotiate. At the beginning of 447, the Huns opened their offensive by taking forts along the frontier, including Ratiaria, the headquarters of the Danube fleet. With Attila's army advancing, Theodosius might still have been prepared to chance outright war, or he might now have preferred to offer concessions in return for peace. Whatever the emperor's plans, they were wrecked by the earthquake. Theodosius' barefoot penitence through the streets of the imperial capital and the prayers of the crowd assembled at the Hebdomon were a dramatic response both to the breaches in the city's walls and to the possibility of attack by Attila and his Huns.[5]

Theodosius' spectacular act of public humility had its memorable antecedents. Sometime between 400 and early 402, relics were moved from Hagia Sophia to a small martyr-shrine dedicated to St Thomas, on the seashore at Drypia about nine miles along the coast south-west of the city.[6] The night-time procession that accompanied the translation was a splendid sight. The flickering

---

[5] The details of this summary account are fully argued in C. M. Kelly 2009: 119–33, 308–11, following the chronology proposed in Zuckerman 1994: 159–68. Importantly, Zuckerman (at 167–8, 180) places Priscus 9.1 (the rejection of Attila's demands and the attack on Ratiaria) at the beginning of 447; for further discussion, see Blockley 1981: 168–9 n. 48; Croke 1981: 138–9.

[6] Janin 1966: 70; Holum 1982: 56–8; Diefenbach 1996: 46, 2002: 31; Groß-Albenhausen 1999: 184–7; Mayer and Allen 2000: 85–6; Tiersch 2002: 213–15; Meier 2003: 146,

brands lit up the faces of the crowd more brightly than the stars. Reflected in the Propontis, the torchlight turned the sea into a moving river of fire. Even more remarkable, at the centre of this great crowd walked the Empress Eudoxia. Preaching at Drypia as a cold dawn broke, John Chrysostom, the newly installed bishop of Constantinople, professed himself amazed. 'What shall I say? of what shall I speak? I spring up ... I fly and dance and I am raised aloft; and, more besides, I am drunk with this spiritual joy.'[7] The chief cause of Chrysostom's inebriation was the empress herself. No praise was too great for this public performance of humility. Eudoxia's concern to distance herself from the trappings of power was underlined by the absence of her husband, the Emperor Arcadius, whose presence was promised for the dedication of the relics the following day, but whose ceremonial panoply – 'the press of horses and the clash of armed soldiers'[8] – would have turned the procession into a conventional display of imperial authority. By contrast, Eudoxia's faith, proclaimed John, had caused her to reveal her devotion to the holy martyrs. Laying aside her purple robes, removing her diadem and dismissing her bodyguard she had followed the martyrs' reliquary like a maidservant.

> Like a maidservant she walked close behind the holy relics, touching the casket and its linen covering. Quashing all human vanity, in the midst of this great spectacle she was seen by the people [καὶ ἐν μέσῳ θεάτρῳ τοσούτῳ φαινομένη δήμῳ] – she whom all the eunuchs who skulk in the halls of the imperial palace are forbidden to see.[9]

Anyone who had been present on this most glorious of nights, who had seen the empress so openly dressed-down, so publicly *déshabillé*, would never be able to forget it. 'Instead of purple she wore a robe of humility – and because of it she was all the more resplendent.'[10]

For emperors and emperor-watchers in the Roman empire, dramatic displays of imperial humility always posed difficulties of

---

2007: 145–6; Van Nuffelen 2012: 197. For St Thomas' at Drypia, see Janin 1969: 251–2; for the martyr relics, below n. 38.

[7] Joh. Chrys. *Hom.* 2 (*cum imperatrix media nocte in magnam ecclesiam uenisset ...*) *PG* 63: 467–72 at 467.1–4, 470.18–22 (river of fire), 31–3 (faces brighter than stars). There is a useful English translation in Mayer and Allen 2000: 86–92.

[8] *PG* 63: 472.20–1. [9] *PG* 63: 469.8–13. [10] *PG* 63: 470.60–2.

interpretation. A decade before Eudoxia was so enthusiastically celebrated by John Chrysostom, the historian Ammianus Marcellinus noted that the Emperor Julian's refusal to be constrained by court protocol while discharging his imperial duties in Constantinople had not been universally applauded. In his enthusiasm to greet his old teacher, the philosopher Maximus, Julian 'leapt up in an inappropriate manner and forgetting who he was [*exsiluit indecore: et qui esset oblitus*]' rushed out of the senate-house and into the square.[11] For the orator Libanius (a staunch defender of Julian's religious and political reforms), this was the mark of a wise monarch deserving of undiluted praise: the emperor in welcoming Maximus 'had demonstrated to the world, and proclaimed by his actions, that wisdom is to be held in higher esteem than royalty'.[12] On New Year's Day 362, Julian's decision to walk to the installation of the consuls was, again according to Ammianus, approved of by some; others regarded it as 'cheap affectation [*affectatum et uile*]'.[13] For the newly invested consul, Claudius Mamertinus (whose inauguration speech survives as one of the exemplars of fourth-century oratory), Julian's rejection of the 'haughty conceit of the purple [*purpuratorum ... fastidia*]' was the crowning proof – at the end of a lengthy oration – of a ruler who, by accompanying the consuls on foot, could be seen publicly to have restored ancient freedoms. 'It may perhaps seem unnecessary to repeat what you have seen yourselves ... but these marvels – scarcely to be credited – must be committed to writing, affixed to monuments, handed down to posterity for generations to come.'[14]

For Mamertinus, such memorable actions were the proof of Julian's *ciuilitas* – 'This very day, I say, this very day has provided a sufficiently clear example of his citizen-like disposition.'[15] To appeal to *ciuilitas* as a key imperial virtue was to echo a speech – also in thanks for a consulship – delivered in Rome in September 100 by the politician Pliny the Younger before the Emperor Trajan.

[11] Amm. 22.7.3 with Matthews 1989: 236; Pazdernik 2009: 79.
[12] Lib. *Or.* 18.155 with a useful discussion of both accounts in den Boeft *et al.* 1995: 74–7.
[13] Amm. 22.7.1.
[14] *Pan. Lat.* 3.30.1 and 3; again on both accounts, den Boeft *et al.* 1995: 69–71.
[15] *Pan. Lat.* 3.28.1; see too Blockley 1972: 444–5; Browning 1975: 131–2; Rees 2012a: 214–15.

(It was a connection made explicit by the set of twelve model speeches: the so-called *Panegyrici Latini*. The collection as it is presented in the surviving manuscripts opened with Pliny, followed by Drepanius Pacatus' speech before Theodosius I in Rome in 389 and then moved on to Mamertinus on Julian.[16]) Pliny's panegyric pivots on a paradox. At the centre of his speech is a ruler whose supreme power he celebrates; but no more so than when the emperor refrains from its exercise.[17] Of Trajan's superiority there should be no doubt: here is an emperor who fully merits his official title of *Optimus* and – even like Jupiter himself – to be known first and foremost as 'the best'. 'Just as the father of gods and men is worshipped first as *Optimus* and then *Maximus*, so your renown is celebrated all the more as it is clear that you are no less the best than the greatest.'[18]

Pliny is also clear that Trajan is deserving of praise because he behaves (to quote Andrew Wallace-Hadrill) like 'a ruler who is still a citizen in a society of citizens, where the freedom and standing of the individual citizen is protected by law, not the whim of an autocrat'.[19] This delicate tension is one of the key themes of Pliny's speech. What distinguishes Trajan is not only his possession of a god-like authority, but also his studied reluctance to act like an emperor: his moderation (*modestia*), his restraint (*moderatio*) and his concern to elide the all too obvious differences that inevitably and indelibly separate a ruler (*princeps*) from a private citizen (*priuatus*).[20] For Pliny, this combination of apparently antithetical traits was most clearly evident in Trajan's assumption of a third consulship (no different from his first, held before he became emperor): 'What praise can adequately capture the fact that a consul for the third time acted as he did the first time, a ruler the same as a private citizen, an emperor the same as someone subordinate to an emperor [*ullane satis digna praedicatio est idem tertio consulem fecisse quod*

---

[16] See the brief and useful summaries in Rees 2012a: 203–8, 2012b: 23–8.
[17] Key discussions in Wallace-Hadrill 1982: 41–8; Braund 1998: 58–65.
[18] Plin. *Pan.* 88.8 with Braund 1998: 63 and Gibson 2010: 130–4.
[19] Wallace-Hadrill 1982: 42 here defining *ciuilitas*, an abstract noun not used by Pliny (it is first attested in Suet. *Aug.* 51) nor anywhere else in the *Panegyrici Latini*, but which usefully crystallises one of Pliny's central ethical concerns.
[20] Rees 1998: 79–83, 2001: 156–60; Noreña 2011: 36–8; Roche 2011b: 8.

primo, idem principem quod priuatum, idem imperatorem quod sub imperatore].'[21] By crossing that divide, Trajan underscored his own superior status. To quote Roger Rees: 'Like any oxymoron, *privatus princeps* is an arresting collocation of seemingly incompatible ideas.' The tight juxtaposition of Pliny's carefully chosen phrases (*principem/priuatum, imperatorem/sub imperatore*) underlines Trajan's achievement in realising the literally unattainable.[22] In the shimmering glitter of Pliny's words, it is almost possible to forget — at least for a moment — that a monarch cannot also be a private citizen. 'For when a man can advance no further than the highest rank, the only way he can go even higher is by stepping down.'[23]

Pliny's presentation of Trajan's *ciuilitas* offers an attractive framework for understanding acts of imperial humility. The patterns are strikingly similar; to quote Steffen Diefenbach: 'Das Besondere des *civilitas*-Zeremoniells besteht darin, daß der Prinzeps durch den Gestus der *recusatio* und des Verzichts auf seine herausragende Stellung eben diese unterstreicht: Nur dem, der sich in einer herausragenden Position befindet, ist es überhaupt möglich, sich herabzuneigen.'[24] Central to Pliny's version of Trajan is the idea that humility — the public refusal of an emperor to behave like a ruler — might underline the power of a monarch, rather than indicate an absence of authority. By offering to act like a citizen, to bridge the gap between himself and his subjects, Trajan emphasised the distance that lay between them. Anthropologists have long recognised that in the display of power by its apparent disregard (to quote Victor Turner),

the system of social positions is not challenged. The gaps between the positions, the interstices, are necessary to the structure. If there were no intervals, there would be no structure, and it is precisely the gaps that are reaffirmed in this kind of liminality.

---

[21] Plin. *Pan.* 64.4.
[22] Rees 2001: 159–60 quoting 160. [23] Plin. *Pan.* 71.4.
[24] Diefenbach 2002: 33 (see too 39) and generally the important discussion on 31–9 (thoughtfully developing 1996: 51–2). I have learned much from this paper; particularly valuable is Diefenbach's suggestion, key to this study, that Eudoxia's dancing might be understood in terms of *ciuilitas* (at 31–2). Diefenbach's principal argument on the relationship between *ciuilitas* and Christian humility runs in a different direction to that sketched out here, see below n. 28.

CHRISTOPHER KELLY

The structure of the whole equation depends on its negative as well as its positive signs. Thus humility reinforces a just pride in position, poverty affirms wealth.[25]

In such a perspective, Theodosius and Eudoxia may also usefully be viewed. Most immediately, their parades through the streets of Constantinople allowed them to display their closeness to the citizens of the capital and the orthodoxy of their faith.[26] They also made visible the assertion of imperial claims to holiness – here demonstrably not the exclusive preserve of the bishop or the holy man. But, above all, these 'zeremonielle Gesten des Herabneigens' (to borrow a phrase from Diefenbach[27]) were statements of power and position: no less for being a public presentation of piety rather than an exhibition of the virtues of a citizen in a society of citizens. Of course, there is a self-evident distance between *ciuilitas* and Christian humility, but what connects them is that both these dramatic and highly ritualised expressions of imperial condescension turn on the same paradox: the assertion of superior position through its abdication. The point was crisply made – and without the help of anthropology – in an imperial ruling issued by Theodosius II (at Constantinople in March 431) regulating the right to asylum in churches. Those seeking sanctuary were not to be armed,

for we, whom, as is proper, the weapons of sovereignty always encircle, and whom it is not right to be without bodyguards, when entering God's church, we leave the weapons outside, removing our diadem, and by the appearance of a lesser majesty assure all the more for ourselves the reverence due to majesty.[28]

John Chrysostom's account of Eudoxia's participation in the translation of the martyr relics is somewhat unusual in mapping (and thinking through) the complete U-curve of imperial

---

[25] Turner 1969: 201; see too Brown 1992: 75 quoting Chakrabarty 1989: 152.
[26] Diefenbach 1996: especially 52–63, 2002: 39–44; Meier 2003: 144–6, 2007: 150–2.
[27] Diefenbach 2002: 33.
[28] καὶ γὰρ ἡμεῖς, οὓς ἀεὶ τῷ δικαίῳ τῆς ἡγημονίας περιστοιχίζει τὰ ὅπλα καὶ οὓς οὐ πρέπει δίχα δορυφόρων εἶναι, τῷ τοῦ θεοῦ ναῷ προσιόντες ἔξω τὰ ὅπλα καταλιμπάνομεν, ἀποτιθέμενοι τὸ διάδημα, καὶ τῇ τῆς βασιλείας ἐλαττώσεως εἰκόνι μᾶλλον ἡμῖν τὸ τῆς βασιλείας σέβας ἐπαγγέλλεται: *Coll. Vat.* 137.7 (*ACO* I 1.4, p. 64.8–11) with Brown 2002: 99–100; McLynn 2004: 270. The full Greek text of this ruling was included in the records of the Council of Ephesus; edited versions were included (in Latin) in *CTh*

condescension: from the repudiation to the resumption of authority. Perhaps unsurprisingly, the focus of these narratives (as in Theodosius' walk to the Hebdomon) is on the moment of stepping down; that the emperor will return to his conventional position at the apex of court society may be safely assumed. So, for example, in Pliny's version of Trajan, illustrations of the emperor's *moderatio*, *modestia* and laudable actions as *priuatus* and *ciuilis princeps* are juxtaposed with his equitable administration of justice, his generosity to the genuinely deserving, his fiscal prudence, his careful management of his household, his triumphant military exploits, his intelligent deployment of the resources of empire, his unswerving dedication to the best interests of the state and his determination to right past wrongs. As suggested above, the key to Pliny's praise is precisely the apparent paradox of an extensive

9.45.4 and (in Greek) in *CJ* 1.12.3. On the law itself, see Harries p. 75, this volume. For a somewhat different approach to the material discussed above, pressing the contrast between Theodosius' Christian humility and Trajan's civic virtue, see Alan Cameron 1976: 176–8 (for a strong statement of difference); Brown 1992: 157; Diefenbach 2002: 38–9 (with a slightly softer formulation at 46); Meier 2003: 147, 2007: 148–52 especially 151–2; Van Nuffelen 2012: 188. For Peter Van Nuffelen (here following a different strand of Turner's thinking on ritual), the contrast is between an 'ancient ideal of *civilitas*, whereby the emperor would behave as being an equal to his citizens' and rituals of collective repentance where 'the emperor was made equal to his subjects in their shared human frailty and not in their common citizenship; they all collectively dropped to the lowest rank of humankind. Rather than celebrating the emperor's elevation, they reestablished a sense of community' (2012: 188). This seems to me to risk downplaying how these moments are framed. I take my lead from re-evaluations of Theodosius I before Ambrose which have been concerned to emphasise that the emperor's submission in church at Milan should be understood in a much wider political and ritual context; see especially, Brown 1992: 112; McLynn 1994: 323–30, 2004: 262–5 (and particularly the subtle discussion of Theod. *HE* 5.18 at 268–70). Nor am I certain that representations of autocracy in the early empire can be so quickly emptied of their religious content (or *ciuilitas* so easily isolated) to allow a workable distinction between 'civic' and 'Christian' virtue. (That somehow seems an all too convenient late-antique perspective on a pagan Principate.) My starting point is that performances of imperial power, *ciuilitas* and humility were ringed by similar paradoxes. Nor were these confined to problems of how emperors should be represented and their legitimacy affirmed. Crucial to fifth-century Christology was the difficulty of understanding how the Incarnation (the ultimate act of divine humility) could be reconciled with an omnipotent deity. As Pope Leo made clear in his statement read out at the Council of Chalcedon, it was incumbent on all Christians to think of ways of conceiving the joining of the divine and human in the person of Christ so that the Incarnation – that extraordinary *inclinatio miserationis* – did not in any way imply that the Godhead had suffered any *defectio potestatis*: *Coll. Nov.* 5.3 (*ACO* II 2.1, p. 27.14) with Brown 1992: 155, 2002: 97 and the fundamental discussion of these themes in relation to poverty, compassion and charity in Brown 1992: 154–7, 2002: 98–108; see too Rapp 2009: 80–7.

collection of examples of imperial power 'equal to that of the immortal gods'[29] juxtaposed with lengthy descriptions of Trajan's studied reluctance to act like an emperor. This productive tension between the sweeping exercise of absolutist power and the self-restraint of the autocrat is also an important strand in the contemporary church historian Socrates' presentation of Theodosius II. Of course – as with the transition from *ciuilitas* to humility – some of the key terms of reference have significantly shifted: most obviously, Socrates is concerned to interrogate the piety, orthodoxy and Christian commitment of the emperor.[30] In Socrates' account (to quote Luke Gardiner in this volume), the emperor 'appears vigorously active, combining a range of scholarly or contemplative religious pursuits with undeniable acts of leadership, in spheres from imperial defence to religious policy'.[31] Nor, as Gardiner suggests, should the line be drawn too firmly between contemplative pursuits and leadership. For Socrates, the emperor's piety, most clearly evidenced by his private conduct in the seclusion of the imperial palace, was also a virtue worthy of public celebration. Theodosius' prayers guaranteed the safety of the state. In 425, they secured the defeat of the usurper John in Ravenna;[32] once in Constantinople they protected the crowd in the Hippodrome during a heavy and unexpected snowstorm.

> Then the emperor made it clear how his thoughts had turned to God. Communicating with the people through heralds he said: 'It is much better to spurn the show and for all to offer prayers together to God that we may be shielded, secure from the impending storm.' And even before this proclamation was completely finished, those in the Hippodrome – with the greatest joy and all in unison – were offering up prayers and hymns to God. And the whole city was transformed into a single church, and the emperor in the guise of a private person walked into the middle and started the hymn-singing [καὶ ὅλη μὲν ἡ πόλις μία ἐκκλησία ἐγένετο, βασιλεὺς δὲ μέσος ἐξῆρχετο τῶν ὕμνων ἐν ἰδιωτικῷ σχήματι πορευόμενος].[33]

The emperor is at the centre of this story. It is his decision to suspend the races and to direct the people in prayer. It is an

---

[29] Plin. *Pan.* 4.4.
[30] Urbainczyk 1997: 143–6; see too the excellent discussions in Leppin 1996: 160–6; Wallraff 1997: 99–110.
[31] Gardiner p. 247, this volume.
[32] Soc. 7.22.21, 7.23.9–10; see Gardiner p. 263, this volume.
[33] Soc. 7.22.15–17 quoting 16–17; see Gardiner pp. 259–60, 262–3, this volume.

illustration of Theodosius' Christian faith and his ability to control a frightened crowd that only a little while earlier had been divided into rival sporting factions eager to cheer on favoured charioteers. In the midst of a now unified multitude, whose raucous competitive barracking has been transposed into harmonious community hymn-singing, stands an emperor who appears ἐν ἰδιωτικῷ σχήματι – 'in the guise of a private person'. Socrates' careful choice of language connects this public performance of imperial piety with the tradition of praiseworthy emperors who were applauded for appearing as no more than private individuals; and in so doing, underlined their power by a display of its rejection through their own self-restraint: *idem principem quod priuatum, idem imperatorem quod sub imperatore*.[34]

The sheer difficulty of holding these self-evidently antithetical representations of imperial power in play also shapes John Chrysostom's praise of Eudoxia. No empress had ever demonstrated such piety: 'she alone of empresses has escorted martyrs with such great honour, with such great zeal and reverence, mixing with the crowd, completely dispensing with her bodyguard.'[35] It was a mark of the empress' position that, when she chose to humble herself, her achievement exceeded even biblical exempla. 'Miriam too, following the bones of Joseph, once led forth the people, and sang a song ... She did this sounding cymbals; you have accomplished it with your mind and soul sounding louder than a trumpet.'[36] For Chrysostom, it is also important that Eudoxia's actions should be framed by a wider ceremonial setting. It mattered that Arcadius and the imperial bodyguard were absent (a decision which Chrysostom diplomatically attributed to

---

[34] See especially Diefenbach 1996: 51, 2002: 38; Brown 2002: 99; Meier 2007: 146–7; Van Nuffelen 2012: 190. The phrase ἐν ἰδιωτικῷ σχήματι is ambiguous. It does not straightforwardly mean 'as a private person' (that is, without imperial regalia), but carries the indelible sense of appearance/show/pretence – language peculiarly appropriate to the sheer theatricality of these moments. Note too Chrysostom's θέατρον (*PG* 63: 469.11; above n. 9); and usefully on late-antique ceremonial as theatre, MacCormack 1981: 8–14; Matthews 1989: 231–8.

[35] *PG* 63: 471.2–5; for 'mixing with the crowd' as part of the conventional language of *ciuilitas*, see Diefenbach 2002: 35–6.

[36] *PG* 63: 472.1–2, 6–7. For the presentation of imperial piety in Davidic terms, see the valuable discussions in Meier 2007: 145, 154–8; Rapp 2010: 184; Dagron 1996: 129–38 (for some of its longer-term implications).

Eudoxia's foresight), but also that the emperor's arrival was always expected: 'she has divided this duty with him and, while today she is present, she has told us that he will be present tomorrow.'[37] The sermon delivered by Chrysostom the day after the translation of the relics underlined the point in its opening paragraph: yesterday an empress surrounded by citizens, today an emperor screened by his troops. As an example of imperial condescension, Eudoxia's night-time parade before the martyr relics eclipsed Arcadius' brief morning appearance at the shrine without his diadem and with his bodyguard unarmed.[38]

Even so, however fulsome the bishop's praise, neither Eudoxia – who did not tarry at Drypia to hear Chrysostom's second sermon – nor Theodosius, on the long, hard road to the Hebdomon, had any intention of sacrificing their position for more than a strikingly memorable moment. Eudoxia's presence alongside her husband, surrounded by their courtly retinue in all its splendour, only served to emphasise that her exhibition of humility was to be set firmly in the context of her (equally ceremonial) demonstration of imperial authority. The empress may have danced her way to Drypia, but she should perhaps be imagined as returning to the Great Palace in the gilded imperial carriage drawn by snow-white mules.[39] Certainly too, Theodosius' swift and memorable interventions could fairly be judged a success. After the unseasonal snowstorm, there was a bumper harvest.[40] After the earthquake in January 447, the damage

---

[37] *PG* 63: 472.28–30 with Holum 1982: 58.
[38] Joh. Chrys. *Hom.* 3 (*insequenti die adueniente imperatore in martyrium* ...) *PG* 63: 473–8 at 473.11–18. The element of competition between empress and bishop at Drypia is underscored if John Vanderspoel's tentative suggestion (1986: 247–9) on the identity of the relics is accepted: the martyrs of Anaunia, three missionary clerics burned alive by hostile pagans in the Val di Non in northern Italy in 397 (see Gaddis: 2005: 173). The relics were brought (probably from Milan) by Jacobus, a ranking Christian army officer, most likely as part of a diplomatic mission to Constantinople. What was at stake in their public translation to Drypia was a claim to the active promotion of Christianity and to the management of high-level contacts with the West. Chrysostom's apparent praise of Eudoxia might then be read in that more tense, competitive context: that is her demonstration of humility (while undoubted) was properly to be seen as framed (defined, constrained) by her majesty. For an even sharper reading of John's first sermon as offering an implicit critique of Eudoxia's imperial position as a women exercising worldly power, see Tiersch 2002: 213–18.
[39] Joh. Chrys. *Hom. in Rom.* 14.10 (*PG* 60: 537.47–8) with C. M. Kelly 1998: 142; see too, McCormick 2000: 158.
[40] Soc. 7.22.18.

to the Theodosian Walls was repaired in sixty days. The threat of attack was removed as Attila and the Huns turned back towards the Danube, unwilling to risk a lengthy siege of one of the best defended cities in the Mediterranean.[41] There is no record of what happened after Theodosius had prayed with the people (the vigil is said to have lasted several days), but it seems unlikely that he retraced his steps, trudging barefoot and bleeding the seven miles back from the Hebdomon to the Great Palace.[42]

Autocrats rarely appear surprised. The sheer formality of court society is intended to suffocate the unpredictable. The regulation of imperial ceremony aims to ensure that a ruler is rarely caught off guard. John Rufus' *Plerophoriae* (or *Fulfilments*), written in Palestine in the early sixth century, tells the story of the monk Basil and his dramatic intervention in the complex theological wrangling of the 430s which, at least in part, focused on the disputed Christology of Nestorius, bishop of Constantinople from April 428. In Lycia (in south-eastern Turkey), Basil had pursued a life of ascetic rigour alone in cave by the sea-shore until persuaded to found a convent and a monastery. Ordered by a heavenly voice to counter the 'blasphemies of Nestorius', he hurried to Constantinople and confronted Theodosius II in person, shouting as the emperor passed by: "Emperor why do you not confess the Trinity since you were baptised in the name of the Trinity? For the teaching of Nestorius is opposed to the Trinity." Basil was dragged from the imperial presence, arrested, flogged and condemned to exile. A few days later when Theodosius came near a church filled with Basil's supporters the emperor was nearly killed – hit hard on the head by a brick which suddenly dropped out of the sky. The result was a vision in which the emperor was commanded to release Basil who (unstinting in his cause) then demanded the calling of a church council and the deposition of Nestorius.[43]

---

[41] For the details, see C. M. Kelly 2009: 136–9.
[42] Perhaps Theodosius returned on horseback; later specified for certain occasions in the *Book of ceremonies*, see Berger 2002: 16–17.
[43] John Rufus, *Pler.* 35 (*PO* 8.1: 78–81) with Watts pp. 271–2, this volume; for an apparently 'real' Basil, see Caner 2002: 216; Millar 2006: 133, 155–7.

Even without such heavy-handed heavenly help, emperors were often well informed of opposing views. 'Despite the grim impression left by many contemporary accounts, good counsel was never lacking in the higher reaches of the government.'[44] Certainly the detailed dossiers of the church councils of the 430s and 440s (among the most extensive sets of documents to have survived from the Roman empire) show that the emperor and his advisers could in some cases have access to a wide range of reports and be presented with – and be prepared to listen to – sharply conflicting opinions. Perhaps unsurprisingly, the imagination of contemporaries was not caught by this steady accumulation of administrative paperwork (however ultimately important in forming policy), but preferred to dwell on more dramatic moments: the memorable confrontations between emperors and noble-minded courtiers, plain-speaking bishops and heroic holy men.

In late June 431, in the immediate and disputed aftermath of the Council of Ephesus, the archimandrite Dalmatius left his monastery in Constantinople for the first time in forty-eight years (that is since early in the reign of Theodosius I) to confront the emperor and insist that he withdraw his support for Nestorius and back the bishops led by Cyril of Alexandria. According to a brief memorandum written by anti-Nestorian bishops in Constantinople, and entered into the records of the Council of Ephesus, Dalmatius led a crowd of chanting monks to the Great Palace, was granted an audience and emerged with the other archimandrites shouting to the crowd, 'The commands of the emperor'.[45] A further report (also included in the conciliar *acta*) gives more detail on what was said to have happened as the emperor gave way in the face of the holy man's tough talk. Dalmatius had insisted that Nestorius and his partisans had blocked the free flow of information to the capital on the disputed events at Ephesus. Dalmatius presented Theodosius with a letter (said to have been smuggled into the city) in which Cyril

---

[44] Brown 1992: 66.
[45] *Coll. Vat.* 66 (*ACO* I 1.2, pp. 65.11–66.9, especially 66.1–3). For the setting of this incident in the complex circumstances (here only lightly sketched in) surrounding the Council of Ephesus, see helpfully Dagron 1970: 267–8; Holum 1982: 165–73; Caner 2002: 212–23; Wessel 2004: 162–8.

set out his account of the Council's proceedings and his claim to majority support. The emperor paused to read Cyril's letter and – in Dalmatius' view – found it persuasive. Seizing the moment to censure Nestorius, 'in front of all who were present, I said to the emperor, "To whom would you rather listen, six hundred bishops or one impious man?"', Theodosius politely and briefly conceded the point: '"καλῶς ἐζήτησας· εὔχεσθε ὑπὲρ ἐμοῦ – You have looked into things thoroughly. Pray for me."'[46]

Nestorius – nearly two decades later, now in exile in Egypt and still seeking to justify his actions – offered a longer and much sharper account of this confrontation. The framework in *The Book of Heraclides* is the same: 'When the Emperor saw Dalmatius he shook his head and put up his hand as one who is in astonishment at the sight of a person.' The challenge was direct (again in Driver and Hodgson's archaising translation): '"But now God has commanded me, [even] me, to counsel thy Majesty, and I have been commanded to bear thee witness that thou transgresses against thyself in transgressing against the Council and perverting its judgement."'[47] In place of the laconic emperor of Dalmatius' report, Nestorius' account included an extensive imperial response, running to over three pages in translation. Dalmatius pressured an ineffectual (if now surprisingly loquacious) emperor who finally caved in when the monk agreed to absolve him of any guilt. '"On me let this impiety be, O Emperor; I rebuke thee and thine on account of these things."' Nestorius' acid tale ends with Dalmatius so elated by the success of his imperial audience, and so careless of proper protocol (for both holy men and emperors), that on leaving the Great Palace he allowed monks to carry him in a victory procession around the city, shoulder high on a couch covered with rich fabrics.[48] The whole incident was neither an affirmation of Dalmatius' holiness (Nestorius scorned claims to prophetic

---

[46] In the conciliar *acta*, the second part of the account of Dalmatius' activities is (somewhat abruptly) appended to a copy of Cyril's smuggled letter: *Coll. Vat.* 67 (*ACO* 1 1.2, pp. 66.11–68.11 for Cyril's letter = *CPG* 8681; *ACO* 1 1.2, pp. 68. 12–69.6 for Dalmatius' report = *CPG* 5778 quoting p. 69.2-4).
[47] Nestorius, *Heraclides* 375 (ed. P. Bedjan, Paris, 1910) (trans. Driver and Hodgson 1925: 273).
[48] Nestorius, *Heraclides* 382 (trans. Driver and Hodgson 1925: 277).

visions) nor of imperial power (here was an emperor whose mind was clearly agitated).[49]

But for Cyril and his supporters – in their version of the story – Theodosius' willingness to yield to Dalmatius was not the result of indecisiveness or weakness of character, but rather a model instance of proper imperial deportment in the face of exemplary holiness. In late antiquity, those who dared to exercise *parrhesia* – free speech – before emperors were justly praised for their philosophic virtue, virtue (as Peter Brown has persuasively suggested) which increasingly also marked out bishops and holy men in their dealings with imperial authority.[50] Yet these men – like Dalmatius and the senior monks who filled Theodosius' audience chamber in Constantinople – were also successful because the emperor was prepared to listen. One should not be too beguiled by stories of imperial ambush; as Hugh Elton has observed, 'such performances had to be orchestrated and were probably not seen as spontaneous by any of the actors'.[51] Within the ceremonial world of late Roman autocracy, these apparent moments of transgression could paradoxically be presented (and understood) as the proper exercise of imperial power rather than debilitating deviations from it. These were brief encounters with their own etiquette, most evidently on those occasions when shaggy, sharp-eyed ascetics, still ostentatiously clad in their stinking animal skins, were admitted to the silk-draped splendour of the Great Palace.[52] According to his hagiographer (Cyril of Scythopolis), the great early sixth-century Palestinian holy man, St Sabas, almost missed his audience with an emperor. In Constantinople to lobby Anastasius, Sabas was denied admittance by the *silentarii* (the court functionaries who regulated access to the imperial presence) 'since he looked like the meanest of beggars … wearing

---

[49] Nestorius, *Heraclides* 373–4 (trans. Driver and Hodgson 1925: 271–2) with Caner 2002: 217. The alternative was to deny Dalmatius any impact at all. In the late sixth-century account of the incident by the pro-Nestorian Barhadbeshabba, Dalmatius' forthright challenge to Theodosius is curtly dismissed by a shake of the imperial robe: *Historia ecclesiastica* 27 (ed. F. Nau, *PO* 9.5, Paris, 1913, 567). For this gesture of imperial displeasure, see also *Coll. Ath.* 66 (*ACO* 11.7, p. 77.24–6).
[50] Brown 1992: 61–70, 106–17; Rapp 2005: 260–73, especially 267–8.
[51] Elton 2009: 139; see too Caner 2002: 220.
[52] On the 'ascetic look', see Rapp 2005: 269–70.

filthy and much patched rags'. A search, at the emperor's insistence, found the holy man standing in a corner reciting psalms. As Sabas was brought before him, the emperor – in a vision of ceremonial order properly restored – seemed to see an angelic figure leading the way. Of this man's holiness there could be no doubt. A carefully modulated discussion followed (the first of three) in which Sabas set out his case on behalf of Elias, bishop of Jerusalem, who had been severely pressured by the emperor in a divisive doctrinal dispute, and for an end to the aggressive collection of land tax in Palestine. Nor did Sabas' presentation of these difficult issues lack diplomatic courtesy: the holy man insisted that the first object of his visit to the capital was 'to venerate the feet of Your Piety'. Anastasius gave way. Elias' position was confirmed, the tax remitted and generous gifts made to the Palestinian monasteries. In return, like (the pithy version of) Theodosius II, the emperor asked only of the holy man: "εὔχου ὑπὲρ ἡμῶν – Pray for me."[53]

Both emperor and holy man acted out their pre-scripted roles in the successful execution of these zeremonielle Gesten des Herabneigens. Whatever the political or theological complexities, these were moments, rather than the endless back-and-forth of debate, when the protracted process of imperial decision-making could be seen to crystallise. Staged – or, perhaps better, ceremonial – capitulations in the face of manifest holiness allowed emperors to combine opportunities both to alter existing policy and to offer a justification that reached beyond factional court politics, cutting through the complex networks of persuasion and influence that sought to channel or constrain imperial action. In accepting the holy man's admonition, an emperor yielded in a momentary suspension of superiority which confirmed his own religious credentials and his willingness to accept advice and demonstrated his fitness to rule. Parading his piety, the holy man 'acted as the privileged counterpoint' to those who exercised worldly power.

---

[53] Cyr. Scyth. *V. Sabae* 50–4 (quoting 142.7–9, 142.28–143.1, 143.9) with Rapp 2005: 270–2; Pazdernik 2009: 76–8; see too the similar imperial vision of Justinian when Sabas jouneyed to court in 530, *V. Sabae* 71. For the difficulties in Jerusalem, see Binns 1994: 174–82 with Jones 1964: II 814 and Festugière 1962: 72–3 n. 139 (on the land tax).

His was 'a walk-on part'[54] in a complex courtly drama. Despite his bold exercise of *parrhesia*, the monk Basil's initial failure to engage Theodosius on the streets of Constantinople underscores Dalmatius' success in the audience hall of the Great Palace. In a properly choreographed confrontation, an emperor did not need to be brought to his senses by falling masonry.

So too, in the grand demonstrations of imperial humility on the streets of Constantinople, it might be a misstep to think – at least without some important caveats – of these public performances as either 'spontaneous' or 'improvised'.[55] Set-pieces such as Eudoxia's dancing before the martyrs' relics in the arranged absence of Arcadius were carefully orchestrated. Equally, John Chrysostom's surprise and delight were heavily scripted. Certainly, Theodosius' barefoot walk to the Hebdomon was unplanned in that it took place only a few hours after the earthquake had struck the city. But it was not improvised, save in a very narrow sense that it drew on the limited and well-rehearsed repertoire of imperial public ritual.[56] As the largest open space near the city, the Hebdomon was a key part of Constantinople's ceremonial landscape:[57] here emperors were proclaimed; here, before departing for Italy, Theodosius I had prayed at the church of John the Baptist for the defeat of the western usurper, Eugenius; here victorious emperors and troops gathered before processing in triumph through the Golden Gate (the most imposing in the Theodosian Walls) and down the Mese (the 'Middle Avenue') to the ceremonial centre of

---

[54] Brown 1992: 62 and 1998: 611 (on the role of the philosopher in the early empire); see too 1971: 92–3 (on Daniel the Stylite).
[55] Diefenbach 1996: 47, 52; Meier 2007: 146; Van Nuffelen 2012: 185, 187, 189.
[56] Behind this suggestion lies the important discussion in Dagron 1996: 99–100, 118–19 arguing for a more fluid sense of imperial ceremony (even when planned well in advance): a set of key 'structural elements' assembled according to circumstance and choice; see too McCormick 1986: 208–10. The grand set-pieces detailed in the tenth-century compilation, *De ceremoniis*, should be read less as straightforward descriptions than as model ceremonies, part of an imaginary, cryogenic world of court protocol that was never so fixed or tightly prescribed; see McCormick 1985: 2–9, 1986: 175–6; Averil Cameron 1987: 118–19; and similarly for early imperial triumphs, Beard 2007: 80–106.
[57] Dagron 1974b: 100–1; Diefenbach 1996: 45, 48, 2002: 28.

the city: Hagia Sophia, the Hippodrome and the Great Palace.[58] To quote Michael McCormick: the 'population could not but have been aware of the great portico-lined boulevard of triumphal tradition, the lower and central Middle Avenue, which stretched from the city's ceremonial entrance at the Golden Gate to its monumental heart, via the major public squares'.[59] However quickly organised or hurriedly put together (as a grey winter dawn on 26 January 447 revealed the severity of the earthquake damage to the city and its fortifications), Theodosius' slow and painful progress took place along familiar and well-trodden streets. It was another flamboyant ceremonial gesture acted out in a capital city built to form a brilliant backdrop to staged displays of imperial power. For an emperor to walk barefoot from the Great Palace to the Hebdomon was (literally) to enact a triumph in reverse.[60]

Theodosius' barefoot procession was remembered annually for at least another five centuries. The *Typicon of Hagia Sophia* (a tenth-century liturgical calendar detailing the processions through the city by the clergy of the patriarchate) specified a procession on 26 January 'in commemoration of the great earthquake which happened towards the end of the reign of Theodosius the Younger'. It began with an *orthros* (a daybreak service) in Hagia Sophia, then clergy and people processed to the Forum of Constantine and next further west along the Mese first to the Exakionion (the monument marking the site of the main gate of the old Constantinian city walls) and finally to the church of the Virgin in the Helenianai quarter. At least until the seventh century the procession had continued to the Hebdomon.[61] In January 457, exactly a decade after Theodosius' progress, the Emperor

---

[58] Croke 2010: 250–1; *Chron. Pasch.* 402 (1 568.5–8); Marcell. com. 402.2 (on imperial proclamation); Glück 1920: 18–24; McCormick 1986: 208–20; Dagron 1996: 81–5, 90–5; Canepa 2009: 8–11; Soz. 7.24.8 with above n. 1 (on Theodosius).
[59] McCormick 1986: 209.
[60] Diefenbach 2002: 26–7; Meier 2003: 146.
[61] *Typicon of Hagia Sophia* I 212.1–14 quoting 1–2 (ed. J. Mateos, 2 vols., Rome, 1962–3); *Chron. Pasch.* 447 (1 586.6–14) and 450 (1 589.6–16) with Croke 1978: 7–8, 1981: 139–44; for the topography, see Janin 1966: 77, 1969: 177–8; Bauer 1996: 243–5. The route to the Hebdomon was the longest walked by the Constantinopolitan clergy in the tenth century: on 8 May (Feast of John the Theologian), 5 June (anniversary of the Avar attack on the city in 619) and 25 September (to commemorate the revelation of the *Trisagion*), see Croke 1981: 140 n. 82; Berger 2002: 12.

Marcian joined in the commemoration. Despite suffering from severe inflammation of the feet (probably gout), the emperor insisted on walking the whole way to the Hebdomon. He never made it. Overcome with pain, he returned to the Great Palace and died the following day. In the brief account of Marcian's over-exercise of humility there are two telling details. First, that in this ceremonial re-enactment of Theodosius' original excursion, Anatolius, bishop of Constantinople, was so moved (or shamed) by the sight of a limping emperor that he got down from his litter and continued on foot. Second, that this walk was also an occasion for the distribution of relief to the city's poor: a neat coalition of imperial condescension and charity.[62]

The elaboration within a decade of Theodosius' barefoot walk to the Hebdomon into a complex and carefully organised imperial procession emphasises the importance of public displays of humility. Of course, as Peter Van Nuffelen has argued in a pair of important papers, ceremony is far from predictable or straightforward: 'we have to abandon the idea of representation, implying the absolute control of the ruling power over public ceremonies, and emphasise improvisation, risk, and the struggle for control of the ritual and its meaning.'[63] Like panegyric, ceremony can always be unpicked. It is always open to an unsympathetic reading. It requires continual affirmation by its supporters and those whom it advantages. In 431, Theodosius conducted a formal inspection of Constantinople's public granaries. This was most likely a grand occasion: the elaborate version set out in the tenth-century *Book of ceremonies* prescribes the presence of the emperor and praetorian prefect in a golden chariot surrounded by the imperial bodyguard. In 431, Theodosius was stoned by a hungry crowd angry at the

---

[62] Theophanes 5949 (109.23–30) with Theodore Lector 367 (on Marcian's death the day after setting out to the Hebdomon on 26 January 457) and 365 (Marcian's walk to the Hebdomon, distribution of gifts, Anatolius on foot). I follow Croke 1978 in understanding Theophanes and the two passages from (the seventh-century epitome of the mid sixth-century account of) Theodore Lector to refer to the procession and litany on 26 January 457, and the emperor's death the next day. Malalas 14.34 for Marcian's inflamed feet. For a somewhat different reading, preferring to separate the two passages from Theodore Lector, see Van Nuffelen 2012: 189–90.

[63] Van Nuffelen 2010: 232–4 quoting 232, 2012: 185–6, an approach informed by the important discussion in Buc 2001: especially 254–61; see too Dagron 1996: 68.

shortage of food.⁶⁴ Here the distance between emperor and people was exaggerated by the very magnificence of the ceremony: a ruler in purple and gold hedged round by senior officials and guards. In January 447, in the tense and panic-stricken aftermath of a major earthquake, such a dangerous rift was avoided by a memorable profession of imperial humility.

But such tactics were not always guaranteed success. In winter 602, the Emperor Maurice – in the face of a severe food shortage – led the procession to celebrate the Purification of the Virgin Mary (Candlemas, 2 February). The route most likely led from the Great Palace to the Forum of Constantine, turned north down the so-called Long Portico, and then proceeded along the shore of the Golden Horn to the church of the Virgin at Blachernae.⁶⁵ This church, located just outside the Theodosian Walls, held a relic of the Virgin's robe, one of the most holy objects in the city. On this occasion, at least according to the brief notice in John of Antioch (compiling his chronicle a generation later), the emperor walked barefoot.⁶⁶ But this display of humility was not universally applauded. As Maurice – who suffered from arthritis – came near the end of an uncomfortable walk he was pelted with stones thrown by a hungry and hostile crowd. In a longer account of the same incident, Theophylact Simocatta (John of Antioch's rough contemporary) added that the emperor's son, Theodosius, was hurriedly bundled under a cloak by his father-in-law and led away to safety through the grounds of a nearby aristocratic residence. Maurice (probably now no longer barefoot) completed the route surrounded by his bodyguards brandishing their weapons. After celebrating mass at Blachernae, he returned to the Great Palace – no doubt still under close protection.⁶⁷ The emperor's staged humility had neither strengthened his bond with the people of Constantinople nor underscored his authority. It was perhaps mitigated by the remission of punishment for those who had caused

---

⁶⁴ Marcell. com. 431.3; Const. Porph. *Cer.* 2.51 with Croke 1995: 79; see too McCormick 2000: 158; Van Nuffelen 2012: 192.
⁶⁵ Whitby and Whitby 1986: 215 n. 19; Berger 2002: 17.
⁶⁶ John of Antioch 317; see too Theophanes 6093 (283.12–16).
⁶⁷ Theoph. Sim. 8.4.11–8.5.4 (ed. C. de Boor with P. Wirth, Stuttgart, 1972) and Theophanes 6094 (288.27–9) (arthritis).

the disruption, and the week-long festival (immediately following the Purification) in honour of Theodosius' recent marriage.[68] Even so, for Theophylact – with a historian's clarity of hindsight – the stoning of the emperor was a striking breach of ceremonial protocol indicative of the final stages of a failing reign. It seemed only fitting that, a few months later during a riot in the city, Maurice, rightly fearing a *coup d'état*, should have fled the Great Palace at night 'stripping off his royal robes and throwing on the clothes of a private person' – not to display his humility but (really) to disguise his majesty.[69]

Ruptures in imperial representation are a reminder that ceremony, like panegyric, is best understood as a repetitive and powerful argument for how autocracy might be presented – justified, legitimated, sanctified. The problem (as highlighted above) was how to present these displays of humility which on the face of it ran counter to the unmoved magnificence of autocracy, but which allowed emperors to act quickly and publicly in times of crisis, to assert their own claims to holiness, to be seen to change their minds and (paradoxically in so doing) to underscore their own superiority. What mattered was that a set of protocols should be established and reiterated to explain these actions and – on the most positive of accounts – affirm that these striking gestures of abnegation underscored rather than undermined imperial authority. The orderliness of court ceremony and the annual cycle of commemorative parades through the streets of the capital provided a framework for understanding these apparent renunciations of power. Highly visible rejections of kingly authority, even those which seemed spontaneous or improvised, might then appear not as breaches in 'the vast ceremoniousness'[70] of monarchy, but rather as an integrated part of its representation. To repeat Victor Turner's formulation: 'thus humility reinforces a just pride in position, poverty

---

[68] Theoph. Sim. 8.5.4 (clemency); *Chron. Pasch.* 602 (1 693.3–5) with Whitby and Whitby 1986: 215 nn. 17 and 19 (nuptial festivities).
[69] Theoph. Sim. 8.9.7: τὴν βασίλειον στολὴν ἀποδυσάμενος ὁ Μαυρίκος καὶ ἰδιώτου ἐσθῆτα περιβαλόμενος – Theophanes 6094 (288.21–4) and above n. 34.
[70] MacCormack 1981: 9.

affirms wealth.' To plagiarise Pliny: when a man can advance no further than the highest rank, the only way he can go even higher is by stepping down. Yet Pliny's paradoxes (like Victor Turner's) are no more than that. Moments of imperial condescension – an empress dressed in white dancing before martyrs' relics, a ruler ἐν ἰδιωτικῷ σχήματι leading a hymn-singing crowd, a monarch prepared to listen favourably to the reproaches of a holy man – were never so certain in their interpretation. Setting these affirmations of imperial humility securely 'in the cliff face of majesty'[71] helped to reduce (to adopt Van Nuffelen's terms) the risk that they might be misunderstood or deliberately misread. But for those prepared to read across the grain of imperial ceremonial, it was only a short step from condescension to weakness and vacillation. Not every emperor who gave way to a holy man was certain to be applauded for his humility. Not every emperor who walked barefoot through Constantinople was sure to be surrounded by awestruck crowds.

[71] Brown 1992: 157.

CHAPTER 10

THE IMPERIAL SUBJECT: THEODOSIUS II AND PANEGYRIC IN SOCRATES' *CHURCH HISTORY*

Luke Gardiner

Writing history under autocratic rule is always a dangerous undertaking. The risks are magnified when considering how – if at all – to recount contemporary events. This problem was strikingly articulated by the late fourth-century historian, Ammianus Marcellinus. Concluding his *Res Gestae* (and ostensibly abstaining from any assessment of the reigning monarch, Theodosius I) Ammianus offered tart advice for his successors: *quod id, si libuerit, aggressuros, procudere linguas ad maiores moneo stilos*.[1] Was this an exhortation to imitate Ammianus and write up contemporary events in the 'same grandiose and allusive manner'? Or is it 'a warning that events after Theodosius' accession can only be narrated in the medium of panegyric ... a genre with an uneasy relationship with the truth?'[2] This is, as Gavin Kelly has persuasively suggested, a purposeful ambiguity, perhaps best glossed as: 'my successors *should* write grand history as I have done (but perhaps would find it advantageous to adopt the "higher style" of panegyric).'[3]

That the reign of Theodosius I would not in reality match the closure and timeless perfection of panegyric is clear from Ammianus' proleptic hints at the travails that lie beyond the

---

This chapter has been greatly improved thanks to the efforts of a number people, both at the original conference and in the intervening period. I would particularly like to thank, in this respect, Jill Harries, Peter Van Nuffelen and Robin Whelan. Above all, I am deeply indebted to Christopher Kelly for his tireless support and incisive editorial advice.

[1] Amm. 31.16.9.
[2] G. A. J. Kelly 2007a: 219.
[3] G. A. J. Kelly 2007a: 230; see also 2007b.

ostensible terminus of his work (Valens' death at Adrianople). They give the lie to any sense of serene closure or resolution offered in the concluding lines quoted above.[4] Ammianus seemed sceptical that these messy realities would be revealed in any contemporary historical narrative. Rather, they would be cloaked in panegyric by writers concerned with preferment – or merely survival. Many of Ammianus' modern interpreters share such scepticism, reviewing witheringly the historical output of his literary successors. So Gavin Kelly: 'to the detriment of his own narrative, Gibbon, like Roman historians since, had to rely on the later church historians and their equally partisan pagan counterpart Zosimus, on fragments and chronicles, and on Theodosius' panegyrists.'[5]

As regards the church historians, this is a mightily unfair judgement. In Socrates Scholasticus, Ammianus found a worthy heir, and a historian who, at least in one significant respect, surpassed him. For Socrates offered – unlike his near contemporaries, Sozomen and Theodoret – a detailed and even pointed account of the rule of a reigning emperor: Theodosius II. Socrates' monumental *Church History* was published around 440.[6] Relatively little is known concerning his background. From certain textual inferences, Socrates is generally thought to have been born between 380 and 390.[7] He gestures towards his own education under pagan grammarians who had fled Alexandria for Constantinople following the fall of the Serapaeum 391/392.[8] His association with the circle of the sophist Troilus can be inferred from his text,[9] as can his confessional sympathies – at least to some extent. Socrates was certainly

---

[4] On such hints, see G. A. J. Kelly 2007a: 231–9, 2008: 26–8. Ammianus would refuse, however, to continue his historical narrative into this period: to depict 'the current reign ... could not be done without telling lies or omitting truths' (2008: 320).

[5] G. A. J. Kelly 2007a: 241.

[6] See Van Nuffelen 2004a: 10–14; Wallraff 1997: 211–12 n. 14 rightly rejects the publication date of 444–446, suggested in Leppin 1996: 274–8. Caution suggests a date late in 440 or early 441. Socrates claims to offer a full history down to, and including, 439 (7.48.8); accordingly, the possibility of late developments that year requiring consideration, and the general need for revision (cf. 2.1.6.), especially given the text's politically charged message, would argue against swift publication.

[7] See, for example, Wallraff 1997: 209–10 and Leppin 2003b: 221. Nothing is known of Socrates' death.

[8] Soc. 5.16.9; on the dating of the Serapaeum's destruction, Hahn 2008: 340–5; see Urbainczyk 1997: 13–14 on the erroneous depiction of Socrates as a lawyer.

[9] Van Nuffelen 2004a: 18–36.

LUKE GARDINER

a Nicene Christian (possibly a Novatian schismatic[10]) who lived and worked primarily in Constantinople.

The bulk of Socrates' account of Theodosius II – and the text on which I shall focus primarily in this chapter – is set into the seventh and final book of his *Church History*, and may be summarised as follows:

7.18–21:	(422–423) Theodosius' victories in Persia and peace negotiations;
7.22:	Disquisition on Theodosius' virtues and virtuous actions;
7.23–4:	(423–425) Theodosius' victories over the usurper John in the West; thanksgiving ceremonies to God; Valentinian III's installation as western emperor;
7.25–8:	(417?–428) Internal affairs, elections and careers of leading figures in the Constantinopolitan church;
7.29–34:	(428–431) Nestorius' career as bishop of Constantinople; sectarian conflict in Constantinople; Christological controversies and their resolution with Nestorius' deposition;
7.35–40:	(431–434) The career of Nestorius' successor, Maximian; miscellaneous matters concerning the orthodox and Novatian churches in Constantinople and beyond; election of Proclus, Maximian's successor;
7.41–2:	Account of Proclus' virtues, entwined with another encomiastic discussion of Theodosius;
7.43:	(435?) Defeat of barbarians; sermon of Proclus;
7.44–8:	(436–439) Final events, both secular and ecclesiastical; closing review of the *Church History*.

While 7.29–34 and 43–8 present a more conventionally historical – and more critical – approach to Theodosius' reign, 7.18–23 and 41–2 have, wholly or in part, been recognised by a number of scholars as clearly and eruditely panegyrical (or influenced by

---

[10] The evidence for this remains, in my opinion, inconclusive, but see Wallraff 1997: 235–57.

panegyric) in form, content and tone, and in their favourable treatment of the emperor's virtues and feats. As Pierre Maraval has noted, 'leur caractère encomiastique n'est pas douteux'.[11] Here Socrates' Theodosius appears neither the degenerate, indolent monarch, 'neglecting the essential duties of his high office', portrayed by Edward Gibbon, nor quite the harassed and hen-pecked autocrat of Kenneth Holum.[12] Instead, he seems vigorously active, combining a range of scholarly or contemplative religious pursuits with undeniable acts of leadership, in spheres ranging from imperial defence to religious policy. A key difference in modern approaches to Socrates' account has centred on how to reconcile – or even acknowledge – a number of troubling incongruities of form and content. As I shall suggest, these have too frequently been smoothed over, uneasily subordinated to arguments for Socrates' perceived favour for Theodosius. Alternatively, they have been displaced and considered mainly in light of questions concerning the strength of Socrates' optimism about the possibility of sustaining the idyllic peace that seemingly had descended by the *History*'s conclusion.

This chapter seeks to give deeper consideration to these problems of content and context. It will focus on Socrates' treatment of the internal strictures – and what are framed, arguably, as the internal contradictions – of panegyric in depicting imperial rule. Alongside this, Socrates will be seen partially and subtly to corrode any rigid, idealised visions of Theodosius' character and governance – broadly, the part of his account informed by panegyrical tropes. In doing so, he reveals the limitations of panegyric for conveying these realities – for the rule of emperors currently reigning or otherwise. This strategy (as I shall suggest) is achieved through the juxtaposition of the panegyrical passages with a historical narrative detailing some of the necessary compromises and ill-advised actions of Theodosius' reign. What emerges from Socrates' account is a nuanced assessment of Theodosius II, and an acknowledgement of the limitations of all

---

[11] Maraval 2007: 7; see also Harries 1994: 38–40; Leppin 1996: 132–42, 2003b: 234–5, 241, 248; Wallraff 1997: 106–7; Urbainczyk 1997: 144–7, 1998: 302–6; Van Nuffelen 2004a: 299, 416, 473, 2004c: 232–3.
[12] Gibbon 1781b: 317; Holum 1982: 101, 173.

emperors and imperial power, given the compromises necessary for effective rulership.

The genre of panegyric saw its importance underscored in late antiquity, as a key part of a growing body of imperial ceremony that structured courtly life.[13] Public performances of panegyric at once articulated the haughty majesty of monarchy, whilst (carefully) delineating the limits of imperial power and the expectations incumbent upon an autocrat, binding ruler and ruled together.[14] Panegyrics were not solely a preoccupation of the inhabitants of the imperial capitals, but of citizens and cities across the empire, eager to demonstrate their loyalty, to placate an emperor or simply to get ahead. Indeed, many panegyrical texts from earlier periods are known only from their preservation in late-antique anthologies, such as Pliny's famous *Panegyric* – a speech in thanks for his consulship delivered before the Emperor Trajan in Rome in September 100 – preserved, and given exemplary status (of a sort) by the late fourth-century editor of the *Panegyrici Latini* anthology.[15] These texts deeply influenced the composition of new panegyrics in late antiquity – a process affected also by the growing importance of Christianity, as Scripture offered new points of reference and paradigmatic figures.

Across its long history, panegyric had evolved as an aggregate of the contributions of a number of public and private styles of oration. In the Hellenistic period, eulogies were composed in praise of particular individuals (ἐγκώμιον), originally in funereal settings, and laudatory speeches in praise of monarchs (βασιλικοὶ λόγοι). In the Roman context, these became conflated with speeches of thanksgiving for the consulship (*gratiarum actiones*).[16] For ancient and modern commentators, these kinds of orations became synonymous with panegyric, although such terminological flexibility

---

[13] See especially MacCormack 1975 and 1981; C. M. Kelly 1998: 139–50.
[14] Cf. Flower 2007: 35.
[15] On the *Panegyrici Latini*, see Nixon and Rodgers 1994; Rees 2002, 2012b: 13–33. Pliny's influence on the collection was undoubted, but encouraged 'not ... cloning but ... generic modification' (Rees 2011: 188). See too Kelly pp. 225–7, this volume.
[16] Cf. Innes 2011.

THE IMPERIAL SUBJECT: THEODOSIUS II AND PANEGYRIC

did not prevent attempts at offering more clearly defined schemas of the form and content appropriate for panegyrical speeches. Yet, even rhetorical handbooks – such as the late third-century example by Menander of Laodicea[17] – were not rigidly prescriptive, urging panegyrists to choose wisely from a range of *topoi* as befitted the subject of their panegyric and the circumstances of its delivery.[18] Fundamental, however, to all panegyrics was the emphasis on their subjects' exemplary feats, for example, military victories, and the complementary virtues they displayed, such as bravery, justice, temperance and loyalty.[19]

Socrates praised Theodosius for a number of feats and virtues. As Jill Harries has perceptively noted, many virtues for which Theodosius is lauded, including his capacity for working through sleepless nights, his piety, his association with Moses and his engagement with intellectuals and theologians, 'assimilated Theodosius to the image of the *pius princeps* first formulated by Eusebius and applied to Constantine'.[20] Indeed, Theodosius may even surpass Constantine's record on some of Eusebius' categories, not only lecturing Persian monarchs but triumphing over them in war, while Constantine's campaigns had been permanently postponed.[21] Central to Socrates' portrayal of Theodosius was an emphasis on his φιλανθρωπία – his mercy. Socrates presents multiple examples of Theodosius' mercy at 7.22.

> In clemency and humanity he far surpassed all others … Bidding farewell to Aristotle's syllogisms, he exercised philosophy in deeds, gaining mastery over anger [ὀργῆς τε κρατῶν], grief and pleasure. Never has he revenged himself on anyone by whom he has been injured; nor has anyone ever even seen him irritated [ὅλως … ὀργιζόμενόν]. And when some of his most intimate friends once asked him, why he never inflicted capital punishment upon offenders [μηδένα τῶν ἀδικούντων], his answer was, 'Would that it were even possible to restore to life those that have

---

[17] On Menander, see Russell and Wilson 1981; Heath 2004.
[18] See, for example, Rees 2002 on the tailoring of the *Pan. Lat.* to reflect their respective contexts.
[19] For the use (not always straightforward) of Menander by the orators collected in the *Pan. Lat.*, see the useful discussion in Nixon and Rogers 1994: 10–14. On the role, communication and development of imperial *uirtutes*, see especially Fears 1981; Wallace-Hadrill 1982; Classen 1991; with Noreña 2001 on material representations of *uirtutes*. On reading the influence of contemporary moral discourses on the substance of virtues in panegyric, see Van Nuffelen 2004c: 229–31.
[20] Harries 1994: 38. [21] Eus. *V. Const.* 4.56.

249

died.' To another making a similar inquiry he replied, 'It is neither a great nor a difficult thing for a mortal to be put to death, but it is God only that can resuscitate, on reconsideration, a person that has once died.' So habitually did he practise mercy [ἐκ τῆς φιλανθρωπίας], that if anyone were guilty, and, condemned to death, being conducted towards the place of execution, he never reached the city's gates before a pardon was issued, commanding his immediate return. Having once exhibited a show of hunting wild beasts in the Amphitheatre at Constantinople, the people cried out, 'Let one of the boldest *bestiarii* encounter the enraged animal' But he said to them, 'Do you not know that we ought to view these spectacles humanely [φιλανθρώπως]?' And, after he had said this, he instructed the people in future to spectate humanely [φιλανθρώπως].[22]

That Theodosius was concerned with appearing merciful is plausible (after all, this was an important trope in panegyric and contemporary moral discourse[23]) but the proliferation of examples, and alleged consistency, of Theodosius' mercy suggests in and of itself a degree of exaggeration – an 'extraordinary quality of dubious reality'.[24] Furthermore, the picture painted by Socrates is particularly implausible because, of all imperial virtues, mercy was inherently the most discretionary.[25] After all, an empire could not be administered successfully with its laws continually suspended by imperial pardons, or its spectacles constantly restricted by concerns for 'humanity'.[26] Indeed, in his *Life of Constantine*, Eusebius' uneasily qualified praise of Constantine (without parallel elsewhere in the text) for being 'uniformly inclined to clemency', acknowledged, and weakly dismissed, the suggestions of some that the deterrent effect of criminal punishments had

---

[22] Soc. 7.22.6–12; on the Amphitheatre in Constantinople, see Matthews 2012: 101–3.
[23] On praise for imperial mercy towards criminals and usurpers, see Van Nuffelen 2004c: 233–6. On the origin and intensification in Christian panegyric (and other sources) of moral discourses surrounding mercy, consistent abstention from bloodshed and good governance, see especially Van Nuffelen 2004c; cf. Vanderspoel 1995: 200–2.
[24] Van Nuffelen 2004c: 233.
[25] On the origins and ambiguities of mercy as an imperial virtue, see Braund 2009 (on Seneca); Bauman 1999: 67–86 (spanning Republic and early empire); Braund 1998: 68–74 and Konstan 2005 (on Caesar); Roche 2011b: 9 (on Pliny). See Griffin 2003 on conceptualisations of mercy in the early empire as a consistent disposition towards imposing relatively lighter punishments. On the impact of Christianity on imperial and juridical *clementia*, see Harries 1999: 151–2.
[26] On the (irresolvable) tension between expectations of imperial *iustitia* and *clementia*, see Amm. 16.5.12; cf. Saller 1982: 56–7; Millar 1992: 516–17; Noreña 2001: 157. On criticism of mercy as reflecting arbitrary corruption or favouritism in juridical contexts, see Harries 1999: 115–17, 164–6.

THE IMPERIAL SUBJECT: THEODOSIUS II AND PANEGYRIC

perhaps been undermined by this.[27] Socrates exposes the unreality (and undesirability) of such claims to consistent clemency and the larger inability – of which these claims are symptomatic – of panegyric, with its tendency towards the extreme, to facilitate credible, useful assessments of the exigencies of imperial rule. This is most effectively achieved through Socrates' incorporation into his panegyric of an instance when Theodosius obviates any commitments to mercy, and is to be praised for this.

In 425, the usurper John was defeated by Roman troops in Ravenna. He did not die in battle, but was captured. With a telling ellipse, news reaches Constantinople of his *execution*.

> The news of the usurper's destruction [ἐμηνύθη ἀνῃρῆσθαι ὁ τύραννος] arrived while Theodosius was patronising the sports of the Hippodrome. He immediately said to the people: 'Come now, let us leave these diversions, and proceed to church to offer thanksgiving to God, whose hand has overthrown the usurper' ... The spectacles were immediately forsaken and neglected, the people all passing out of the Hippodrome singing praises together with him, as with one heart and one voice. Arriving at the church, the whole city again became one congregation. (7.23.11–13)

John's execution is not attributed to his soldier-captors' initiative, nor, as in some other accounts, to Theodosius' nephew and western imperial colleague, Valentinian III.[28] Indeed, Socrates depicts Valentinian only being raised to the rank of Caesar and sent to the West following John's death (7.24.3). Executions of usurpers, were, of course, an imperial prerogative (conversely, the pardoning of usurpers could be a praiseworthy act of φιλανθρωπία).[29] Theodosius, depicted as deeply involved in organising this campaign, and clearly remaining in contact with the 'front', is surely here implicated as having authorised John's death.[30] So much for the permanent suspension of capital punishment. Theodosius'

---

[27] Eus. *V. Const.* 4.31, 4.54–55.1 with Speigl 1971, Thornton 1997, Averil Cameron and Hall 1999: 325 and Bleckmann 2010.
[28] For ἀνῃρῆσθαι denoting the imperially ordained execution of usurpers, see, for example, Soc. 1.4.4, 1.25.1. Incidents where (what may be) independent initiative (without the usual imperial authorisation) drive such executions are conspicuously noted by Socrates at 2.5, 2.25.11, 5.25.15. The responsibility is Valentinian's in Philostorgius 12.13; Proc. *BV* 1.3.9.
[29] Soc. 2.28.18 on Constantius and Vetranio.
[30] Cf. Priscus 16 on Theodosius' lack of mercy towards usurpers.

251

commitment to mercy is also violated in another way. The emperor greets the news by directing his subjects away from the games, instructing them to rejoice and to praise God. The episode becomes an inclusive moment of public catharsis, joined to an act of religious thanksgiving and unity, after a period of civil war. It is also a moment of exultation in the death and destruction of a human being. As such, the episode runs contrary to Theodosius' earlier didactic speech at the Amphitheatre – supposedly representative of his thought – evincing profound concern with the coarsening, dehumanising effects on his subjects of exultation before sights of pain and cruelty: 'Do you not know that we ought to view these spectacles with feelings of humanity?' (7.22.12). Despite these contradictions, Theodosius is clearly judged as acting wisely in these incidents: his abandonment of mercy and φιλανθρωπία is not evidence of failings on his part. How, then, are we to understand this contradiction?

Socrates, having exposed this problem, remains silent, making no attempt to reconcile the two. There is no resort to conventional panegyrical attempts to defuse and resolve the problematic, necessary contradictions of imperial rule.[31] Panegyrists could have recourse to the language of paradox.[32] Different contexts, dictating in each situation the correct response, might be foregrounded to explain equal praise for values and actions that might themselves appear contradictory.[33] The only question was, of course, if the subject under scrutiny had made that correct choice.[34] Regarding praise for mercy and punishment, logical contradiction could be avoided, for example, through emphasising a division between times of peace or war, or by resorting to the rhetoric of 'appropriate' punishments to fit different crimes or the need to rehabilitate as well as to punish.[35] Moreover, with contradictions resolved, divergent

---

[31] Cf. Pliny's playful disarming of concerns over Trajan's largesse: Plin. *Pan.* 41.1 with Noreña 2011: 30–1; Roche 2011b: 12–13; cf. *Pan. Lat.* 2.24.2, 10.4.3–4.
[32] Cf. *Pan. Lat.* 12.10.5.
[33] Cf. *Pan. Lat.* 6.12.1–4, 6.20.1–4; 12.8.4, 12.20.4, 12.23.1–3 with Rodgers 1989: 233 n. 2.
[34] On the broader issue of resolving contradictions between diverging virtues, or 'having it both ways' in panegyric, see Maguinness 1933 and Seager 1983. On their complementarity in the person of the emperor, see Roche 2011b: 10.
[35] Van Nuffelen 2004c: 229–33.

values were frequently even repackaged as complementary to one another, and parallel approaches to the same goal, including mercy and severity.[36]

Socrates eschews any such flexibility. Here contradiction is starkly, and mutely, exposed. That it cannot always be resolved, or explained away, is precisely the point. The unrealistic claims of absolute imperial consistency in the pursuit of particular virtues, undergirded by another rhetorical trope, characteristic of panegyric, by which 'a particular event becomes an expression of an imperial characteristic to which general validity is attributed',[37] are intentionally undermined. Equally, attempts in panegyric to resolve the contradictions of imperial rule in terms of complementary, context-specific modulation of behaviour are implicitly found wanting. These episodes reflect the prioritisation of contradictory virtues, whilst also, through their alignment with one another, revealing the difficulties and contingencies of imperial judgement. Read in isolation, Theodosius' actions in both the Hippodrome and the Amphitheatre appear well calibrated, and even the only naturally correct responses to the demands of these particular occasions. Yet read in parallel, each highlights features in the other that reflect the (necessary) sacrifice, compromise or even tension that Theodosius' actions entailed. The emperor's didactic turn in the Amphitheatre appears a humane gesture of leadership, befitting a monarch. Yet, as the rapturous response to Theodosius' actions in the Hippodrome reminds the reader, his lecture in the Amphitheatre was not met with any degree of enthusiasm.[38] Conversely, Theodosius certainly pleases the crowd in the Hippodrome, uniting them in a well-received burst of civic catharsis. But as his speech in the Amphitheatre reminds the reader, such a move risked compromising wider claims to mercy, and coarsening – indeed even, to an extent, dehumanising – his subjects, as they exulted in John's death. As noted above, in panegyric the resolution

---

[36] Cf. *Pan. Lat.* 2.36.4, 2.44.1–45.7 (particularly elegant examples); also 6.20.1, 8.19.3, 12.6.1, 12.11.2.
[37] MacCormack 1972: 722.
[38] Cf. Harries 1994: 39, although 'angry howls' as a reaction are not part of Socrates' account.

of contradiction between virtues could be achieved with recourse to context-specificity – to the notion that a single, specific situation had, or required, a single, natural response. For Socrates, however, each imperial action may be correct. But it is not inherently so. Each is a compromise: a matter of weighing alternatives and painful trade-offs. Context mattered, but there was no one 'natural' choice to be made or missed. Rather, in each situation Socrates implicitly directs the reader's attention to a set of competing, mutually exclusive possibilities. It is towards this type of difficult judgement that the juxtaposition of these two episodes gestures. Here are the realities of imperial rule, and what ought to be the real focal points for fine-grained moral assessment of Theodosius.

The subjects, audiences and authors of panegyric were perennially transfixed by the interplay of sincerity and flattery, criticism and praise, and by the ultimate impossibility of securing any one interpretation of a panegyric to the exclusion of all others. Confronted by this troubling instability of meaning, panegyrists reached for ever more baroque devices to affirm their sincerity, even foregrounding the problem of insincerity itself.[39] Accordingly, panegyrists proved keen to set themselves and their works apart from the sycophantic products of their predecessors, even when using – and precisely because they were using – the same generic models and *topoi*.

In Socrates' case, there are multiple critiques of previous panegyrists, and disavowals of the genre *in toto*. Socrates' *History* begins precisely correcting Eusebius' account of the origins of Arianism in the *Life of Constantine*, because Eusebius was 'more intent – as is the case with works of praise – on eulogising the emperor and on the panegyrical grandiloquence of his composition than on accurately capturing what happened'.[40] Socrates' explanation for Eusebius' disingenuous account is unusual: Eusebius' narrative was distorted because – from honest or

---

[39] See especially Bartsch 1994: 148–87 on Pliny's attempts to claim sincerity.
[40] Soc. I.1.2: τῶν ἐπαίνων τοῦ βασιλέως καὶ τῆς πανηγυρικῆς ὑψηγορίας τῶν λόγων μᾶλλον ὡς ἐν ἐγκωμίῳ φροντίσας ἤπερ τοῦ ἀκριβῶς περιλαβεῖν τὰ γενόμενα.

THE IMPERIAL SUBJECT: THEODOSIUS II AND PANEGYRIC

self-serving intentions – he was writing panegyric,[41] not because of Arian sympathies (although Socrates acknowledges that others see this as the cause). Socrates was as much Eusebius' corrector as his continuator. As with other elements of Socrates' account of Constantine, the elaborate praise of Eusebius is replaced with a rather less grandiloquent account of the emperor.[42] Socrates' engagement with Eusebius elsewhere prompts meditation on the differing subject material and purpose of panegyric from church history, and, importantly, the tendency for material selected (or framed) in panegyric to speak exclusively to imperial glory – to an exaggerated, simplified image of imperial rule. Socrates disavows discussing secular topics such as Constantine's renovations of cities, 'leav[ing] to others more competent to detail such matters, the emperor's glorious achievements, inasmuch as they belong to a different subject, and require a distinct treatise [ἰδίας τε δεόμενα πραγματείας]' (1.18.14). Such concerns chime with the programmatic criticism of panegyric at the start of Book 6, where Socrates contrasts the composition of encomia with 'the bitter truth'. Instead, Socrates proclaims his expectation of criticism for recounting the events 'of our own age' without 'magnifying the deeds' of those that some may admire (6.pr.6). Socrates would instead, he asserted, write a straightforward and faithful narrative, according to the 'laws of history' (6.pr.9).

Theodosius II was, as Socrates alerts the reader, himself the subject of such grandiloquent, self-serving and untrustworthy encomia following his victories over Persia.

> Many ... produced panegyrics [βασιλικοὺς ... λόγους] on this occasion. Some, indeed, were stimulated by the desire of being noticed by the emperor whilst others were anxious to display their talents to the masses, being unwilling that their erudition, acquired with great effort, should remain unknown. (7.21.10)

This account immediately precedes Socrates' own encomium on Theodosius. Socrates' offers a pointedly contrasting programmatic statement, disclaiming imperial favour and wider renown,

---

[41] For a sense of modern arguments over the status of the *Life* as a panegyrical text, see Barnes 1989b; Averil Cameron 1997; and the useful discussion in M. S. Williams 2008: 25–36.
[42] Urbainczyk 1998: 306–10.

255

and desiring only that Theodosius' virtues be preserved for the edification of future generations.[43] Socrates insists upon the distinction of his own praise of Theodosius from all comparable panegyrical writings. Yet Socrates had also criticised the entire genre – contrasting it against sober, reliable historical narrative. Moreover, in panegyric, such phrases of differentiation and disavowal were themselves fundamental *topoi*. If these are not to be read immediately as imbued with (intentionally) self-subverting irony,[44] Socrates, like his fellow panegyrists, would have need of further strategies of authentication.

Between panegyrists – as also between monarchs – loaded comparisons could usefully be deployed.[45] Forensic critiques of the coerced praise of previous, undeserving emperors were invoked as guarantors of the current panegyrist's sincerity. *Now* there was no need for dissimulation, *now* emperors could be assessed properly and *now* criticism of the warped panegyrics of old offered a contrast for present rectitude and was indicative of the current panegyrist's ability and freedom to tell right from wrong, and to discern praiseworthy subject from blameworthy. Favourable comparisons of contemporary monarchs with their predecessors not only served to corroborate the panegyrists' freedom of speech (*parrhesia*) and moral faculties.[46] Such *comparationes* also helped to locate the imperial subject more securely and credibly in the Greco-Roman moral landscape, illuminating his defining virtues: the emperor matched, and indeed surpassed, the achievements of his noble predecessors (and of other figures from the historical or mythical past), whilst gloriously inverting the abysmal *exempla* of notorious tyrants and villains.[47]

---

[43] Note the similarities between this critique of previous panegyrics (Soc. 7.21.10–22.3) and Eusebius' counterpart (*V. Const.* 1.10). These may be intentional, further eliding the distance between Socrates' own work and his disreputable predecessors'.
[44] *Pace* Gelzer 1999: 71–2.
[45] Rapp 1998: 283.
[46] On panegyrical *parrhesia*, see especially Bartsch 1994: 178–80. On *parrhesia* in other contexts, see Brown 1992: especially 61–70, 103–17, 126–46.
[47] On *comparationes* in panegyric, see Nixon 1990; Bartsch 1994: 148–87; Nixon and Rodgers 1994: 23–6; Long 1996a: 36–7; Roche 2011b: 10–14. On *comparationes* with scriptural figures (always complicated by considerations of typology and re-enactment), see Hollerich 1989; Flower 2007: 74–87; Meier 2007: especially 155; M. S. Williams 2008; Rapp 2008, 2010: especially 183–4.

THE IMPERIAL SUBJECT: THEODOSIUS II AND PANEGYRIC

Socrates offers, for Theodosius, such a point of comparison in Julian, alone of Roman emperors. Their differing approaches regarding mercy are explicitly contrasted.

In clemency and humanity he far surpassed all others. For Julian, although professing to be a philosopher, could not moderate his rage [τὴν ὀργήν] against the Antiochenes who derided him, but inflicted upon Theodore the most agonising tortures. Theodosius by contrast, bidding farewell to Aristotle's syllogisms, exercised philosophy in deeds, gaining mastery over anger, grief and pleasure. (7.22.6–8)

In Book 3 of his *History*, Socrates offers an extended account, framed by a critical overview, of Julian's reign (3.1, 3.21–3). This account and critical analysis are the natural reference points for any claims made about Julian during this sketch of Theodosian virtues. Concerning mercy, Julian did indeed have the Christian martyr Theodore tortured at Antioch, angered by his mocking hymns (3.19). Yet Julian's resentment of the inhabitants of Antioch did not always result in violence. When the Antiochenes mocked him on another occasion, Julian composed his *Misopogon* in response (3.17). As Van Hoof and Van Nuffelen astutely note: '[Socrates] reads the *Misopogon* not so much as Julian's punishment of the Antiochenes, but rather as a way of *quenching* his anger.'[48] Instead of violent deeds: 'Julian, abandoning his former purpose of revenging himself on his satirists by injurious deeds, expended his wrath (τὴν ὀργὴν διελύσατο) in reciprocating their abusive taunts; for he wrote a pamphlet against them which he entitled … *Misopogon*' (3.17.9). Like Theodosius, Julian tempers his anger with mercy. This imperfect contrast undermines, rather than confirms, assertions of Theodosius' consistent commitment to mercy.

Socrates' broader understanding of Julian in Book 3 is informed by a prominent critical response to the late fourth-century Antiochene sophist Libanius' laudatory works on Julian. Socrates suggests the sophist favoured Julian as Libanius was 'a co-religionist, a sophist and a friend to the emperor' (3.23.6). Socrates notes:

Had Libanius not been Julian's co-religionist, he would not only have given expression to all that has been said against him by Christians, but would have magnified

---

[48] Van Hoof and Van Nuffelen 2011: 183; cf. Urbainczyk 1998: 314.

every ground of censure as naturally becomes a rhetorician. For while [the Emperor] Constantius was alive, he wrote encomia upon him, but after his death he brought the most insulting and reproachful charges against him. So that, had Porphyry been emperor, Libanius would certainly have preferred his books to Julian's; and had Julian been a mere sophist, he would have termed him a poor one, as he does Ecebolius in his *Epitaph upon Julian*. (3.23.3–5)

Panegyrical writing is understood, independent of any specific sectarian or personal bias, to distort moral assessments of its subjects. Even had Libanius agreed with Julian's Christian opponents, measured criticism would not have been forthcoming: as a rhetorician writing panegyric – or, its converse, invective – only hyperbolic, polarised moral judgements were possible. Libanius' switch between exultant praise and damning criticism of Constantius also exemplifies this, and elucidates further problems with the crude moral framework provided by panegyric.[49] The rapidity and violence of the switch from praise to invective on a monarch's death cheapens any moral judgement made by that author, whilst drawing attention to the role of *comparatio* in articulating the virtues of emperors, and to the dishonest, mutable and intertwined exaggeration of flaws and virtues that such *comparatio* required. Socrates' critique of Libanius, then, foregrounds two interwoven problems of panegyric: that of bias (personal, sectarian or otherwise), and that of generic form (that is, the tendency towards crude and extreme moral judgements).[50]

The virtuous images of Theodosius articulated (partly) through opposition to a demonised Julian emerge, therefore, with credibility compromised. Socrates' focus on *comparatio* with Julian draws attention to a number of Theodosius' other attributes that appear, through thematic parallelism, to be founded and strengthened on implicit contrast with specific claims made about Julian in passages of invective.[51] These passages, too, however, sit uneasily against the nuances of Socrates' wider historical narrative. One seeming opposition that begins decomposing – even at the moment

---

[49] Cf. Julian's besmirching of Constantius' memory at Soc. 3.1.44–8.
[50] Although reading Socrates' panegyric as in many ways conventional, Urbainczyk 1998: 317 notes sensitively that compared with Sozomen, Socrates had little use for the 'outrageous claims' of panegyric.
[51] These include Theodosius' tolerance (Soc. 7.41–2) and his authoritative engagement with Scripture (7.22.5).

of articulation – relates to the personal piety and patronage of the two emperors. Theodosius demonstrated piety by honouring those 'dedicated to God, and especially those whom he recognised as outstanding in piety' (7.22.13), even donning the filthy cassock of a recently deceased bishop, to partake in his sanctity (7.22.14). Socrates' critique of Julian's patronage in Book 3 may offer an implicit contrast: Julian favoured 'professional philosophers; consequently, an abundance of pretenders to learning of this sort resorted to the palace ... wearing their palliums, being more conspicuous for their costume than their erudition' (3.1.56). Both emperors seemingly chose company that suited their nature (and religious affiliations), with diametrically opposing results.

Whilst Julian may have associated with high-living 'philosophers in garb only', in his own behaviour he was rather closer to Theodosius. Wearing his filthy cassock, Theodosius 'rendered his palace little different from a monastery' (7.22.4). Julian curbed the courtly excesses of his imperial predecessor, expelling eunuchs and hairdressers, cutting transport expenditures and bureaucracy, and treated the Senate with an almost republican reverence (3.1.50–2, 3.1.54). As Socrates notes, 'these retrenchments were highly lauded by some few, but strongly criticised by all others, for bringing the imperial dignity into contempt, by stripping it of pomp and magnificence which exercise so powerful an influence over the minds of the vulgar' (3.1.53). Julian's apparent flaw here was his permanent subordination of the needs of kingship to those of philosophy: 'an emperor may be a philosopher in all that regards prudence; but should a philosopher attempt to imitate the attributes of an emperor, he would frequently depart from his own principles' (3.1.59). Julian's philosophical interests outbalanced all else.[52]

For Theodosius there is no comparable rebuke, for he, by contrast, 'exercised philosophy in deeds, by gaining mastery over anger, grief and pleasure' (7.22.8). For him, philosophy offered practical tools or was an exercise to be performed, rather than becoming an all-encompassing identity. Theodosius could, in other words, modulate his behaviour. When required to lead the

---

[52] Cf. Chesnut 1986: 243–51 and Van Nuffelen 2004a: 371.

citizens of Constantinople in supplication before God to avert a storm, Theodosius spontaneously abandoned the trappings of secular majesty and abased himself amongst his people, no longer communicating with them by heralds,[53] but coming among them, and, strikingly, not in purple robe and crown, but 'dressed as a private citizen' (ἐν ἰδιωτικῷ σχήματι) (7.22.17).[54] This act proved successful, suggesting that Theodosius' abandonment of imperial dignity was the correct response to the particular situation. This was a pose, and one used judiciously. It did not become all-encompassing, displacing or undermining displays of majesty when such poses were called for. Rather, the use and renunciation of majesty are reconciled and understood as complementary – and the ability correctly to modulate between such complementary behaviour (monastic, majestic, private) itself becomes a virtue.

The reader, in light of Socrates' subversive account of Theodosius' mercy, would rightly be suspicious of this smooth rhetorical move. Socrates was not denying the possibility of modulating between behaviours and virtues, or that Theodosius was practised at this, but rather that such modulation somehow implied the negation of any contradiction, and that every context was endowed with a single, natural and correct response. The abandonment of imperial robes for a private citizen's appears successful, confirming Theodosius' status and his relationship with his people and God. That this involved any risky trade-offs and necessary compromises remains unmentioned. Elsewhere, Socrates described how imperial abandonment of official garments, and the assumption of inferior garb, could reflect an abdication of power and the acknowledgement of a loss of popular support.[55] The gesture, then, had multiple valences. The risk of Theodosius' action proving counter-productive through being interpreted wrongly or uncharitably in light of this is unmentioned (and unmentionable) in the panegyric. Socrates' broader historical narrative, however, alerts the reader to such possibilities. Moreover, the assertion of Theodosius' judicious flexibility concerning the public exercise of imperial virtues is articulated through implicit *comparatio*

---

[53] Cf. Alan Cameron 1976: 167–8.
[54] See Kelly pp. 230–1, this volume.
[55] Soc. 2.18.18; cf. 7.10.5.

THE IMPERIAL SUBJECT: THEODOSIUS II AND PANEGYRIC

with Julian's rigidity. That such contrasts were repeatedly undermined elsewhere cannot but affect how we view the depiction of Theodosius' competence here.

'I write not from adulation, but truthfully narrate facts well known to everybody' (7.42.5). Such arch appeals to external verification ineluctably invite criticism and counter-examples. Even without this authorial comment, there would have been many aspects of Theodosius' rule well known to a Constantinopolitan audience – and (tellingly) undiscussed in the *Church History* – that would render components of Socrates' panegyric dubious. Socrates' claims of consistent imperial mercy appear particularly vulnerable in this respect. Theodosius famously judged necessary (with, no doubt, some difficulty) the execution of Paulinus, his friend and official, probably on the grounds of adultery with the Empress Eudocia.[56] Nor did Theodosius present an egregiously merciful face to his subjects. Notwithstanding possible lacunae in the *Theodosian Code*, the title on pardons and amnesties is replete with the merciful laws, commuting punishment, of virtually every emperor since Constantine, but records none attributable to Theodosius – despite his having had ample opportunity and cause.[57] Even in times of peace, Theodosius was associated with warlike, bloody imagery on his coinage.[58]

Far more corrosive, for the reception of his panegyrical writing, than appeals to common knowledge was Socrates' placement of his panegyric (7.18–23, 7.41–2) alongside long passages of critical historical narrative concerning the emperor (7.28–34). This destabilises in particular the praise for Theodosius' inclusive

---

[56] The execution may have just preceded the final publication of the *History*. That this would undermine Socrates' claims regarding capital punishment is no argument for seeing publication as necessarily preceding the execution: see Urbainczyk 1997: 35 n. 89; Van Nuffelen 2004a: 10–12 (contra Alan Cameron 1982: 266; Holum 1982: 176–94; Wallraff 1997: 210–11 n. 10).

[57] *CTh* 9.38.11 (February 410), 9.38.12 (August 410), both dating from Theodosius' minority, clearly originate from Honorius' western court.

[58] A favoured motif, which became common in late-antique coinage, was of the emperor, armed, bearing a shield engraved with a mounted horseman spearing a defeated enemy: Kent 1994: 47–8. On this imagery (Kent's 'obverse legend Kfa') in Theodosius' coinage during war and peacetime, see 259 nos. 257–9, 265; and above n. 30.

tolerance. The moment of unifying catharsis and religious celebration in the Hippodrome at the usurper John's death was itself only one of several such pivotal episodes in the panegyrical portion of Socrates' account of the emperor where Theodosius' pious mediating presence was crucial in enabling the empire to overcome adversity. In examples situated in Theodosius' campaigns against Persia, his defeat of John, and his prevention of a disastrous harvest failure, Socrates outlines a loose general pattern of imperial practice. Theodosius perceives a crisis and entrusts the empire's salvation to God, embarking upon striking displays of 'submissive faith'.[59] These displays of piety and submission to God have a heavily performative aspect. Theodosius does not just repeatedly submit himself to God's will in prayer, but his actions, directly or indirectly, unite the people of Constantinople in prayer to God and harmony with one another, ensuring that divine favour is both earned and kept.[60] As Peter Van Nuffelen has noted, such (often spontaneous) moments of humility were also part of an ongoing performance that 'reestablished a sense of community' between city and emperor.[61]

At a critical point during Theodosius' wars against Persia (421–422), with the entire Persian army marshalled against the empire, Theodosius is depicted placing his faith in God for salvation. This act merited divine aid, causing angels to appear to travelling Romans who brought the message of salvation to Constantinople, uniting its populace in relief, and ensuring that they, too, collectively, offered prayers to God in thanks for his providential care. Imperial soldiers also became more courageous at this sign, reversing prior losses, and, with further divine aid, repeatedly triumph, culminating in a successful peace settlement, securing the end of Persian persecution of Christians – the original *casus belli* (7.18.15–18, 7.20.8–13). Regarding the harvest, as discussed above, Theodosius addressed the citizenry in the Hippodrome, directing them away from the current spectacle 'to unite in prayer to God to avert the impending storm' (7.22.16). They unite and do

---

[59] Luibhéid 1965: 38.   [60] Cf. Gelzer 1999: 61–72.
[61] Van Nuffelen 2012: 188. Cf. Diefenbach 1996, 2002: 31–9; Meier 2007: 146–8.

so joyously, singing hymns and 'becoming a single church, with Theodosius leading them' (7.22.17). Accordingly, God held back the bad weather, saving the harvest. That this episode lacks explicit dating or corresponding record elsewhere,[62] and was situated amongst other, thematically similar imperial behaviour, suggests that its inclusion was an attempt to present a representative composite or type of the behaviour exhibited by Theodosius. During John's revolt (423–425), again 'the prayers of the pious emperor prevailed',[63] causing angels to lead Roman troops across marshland to storm John's stronghold at Ravenna, echoing the Israelites' crossing of the Red Sea (7.22.21).[64] As described above, on learning of John's defeat, Theodosius urged his people to thank God for this favour, leading them in prayer to worship together at a single church (ἐκκλησίαν τοῦ Θεοῦ), where they also became, in this instant, metaphorically 'a single church' (μία ἐκκλησία) (7.23.11–12).

In these episodes, Socrates showed Theodosius' alignment of piety with temporal success as characterised by submission to divine will and humility, expressed in a nexus uniting his private prayers with public performance: set-piece, liturgical or ritualistic scenes that saw Theodosius mapping his pious approach on to the people and cityscape of Constantinople. The coalition of emperor and populace, and of the populace with itself, in spiritual submission, underwrites continuing military victories at the periphery of empire, or general providential favour. It was a religious unity – but not one of coerced doctrinal uniformity. Rather, this ritual unity centred around harmonious toleration and coexistence. Theodosius generated unity without demanding religious conformity, and even fought against Persia not to impose Christianity but to end religious persecution there. From these

---

[62] *Pace* Van Nuffelen 2012: 190; freak weather in 408 (*Chron. Pasch.* 408 [1 570.15–17], Philostorgius 12.8) and 443 (Marcell. com. 443.1) may be relevant, though neither matches Socrates' account satisfactorily; furthermore, 443 likely post-dates the *History*, while 408 involves Theodosius as a child. On the (confused) recording in chronicles of such events, associated with imperial involvement in exculpatory or propitiatory rituals, see Croke 1981: 146–7 and Kelly pp. 221–2, this volume.
[63] Soc. 7.23.9.
[64] Rapp 1998: 283–7 and Gelzer 1999: 61–72.

individual episodes Socrates would later abstract inclusive tolerance as a consistent virtue:

> [The emperor] never approved of those who attempted to persecute others. Indeed, I should say in meekness he surpassed all those who have ever faithfully borne the priestly office. What is recorded of Moses in Numbers (12.3): *The man Moses was very meek, above all the men upon the earth* – may most justly be applied today; for the Emperor Theodosius is *meek above all the men upon the earth*. (7.42.1–2)

That such inclusive tolerance was important for Socrates – and that Theodosius had indeed practised it – ought not to be doubted. But to proclaim consistency was to court refutation.

Socrates' unvarnished historical narrative concerning the episcopacy of Nestorius (428–431) in Constantinople (7.29–34), irreparably corrodes this rosy impression of Theodosius' consistent tolerance (whilst still showing the value of tolerance in general). Nestorius – Theodosius' appointee – offered a more aggressive, forceful religious policy to secure divine favour and military success (and even to take the fight to Persia). In modern scholarship on Socrates' portrayal of Nestorius, this central aspect of his early episcopacy has often been overshadowed by Socrates' idiosyncratic account of the bishop's development of controversial Christological theories, and of the resulting Council of Ephesus.[65] Indeed, the persecution Nestorius launched to secure divine approval is sometimes ignored entirely.

In a sermon soon after his election, Socrates records Nestorius' extraordinary offer to Theodosius: 'Give me, my prince, the earth purged of heretics, and I will give you heaven. Assist me in destroying heretics, and I will assist you in vanquishing the Persians' (7.29.5). That persecution ensues soon after this request emphatically reflects Theodosius' assent. Furthermore, the persecution is timed almost exactly contemporaneously with, and embracing the same sort of programme as, intolerant, anti-heretical legislation that Nestorius influenced.[66] Nestorius attempted to seize an Arian church, sparking conflict and causing the Arians, in desperation,

---

[65] For example, Luibhéid 1965; Wessel 2001.
[66] Soc. 7.29.5; *CTh* 16.5.65 (May 428); Nestorius' own suggestion of his influence (*Nestoriana* BII = Loofs 1905: 205.2–5) has generally been followed: for example, Holum 1982: 150; on all this, see Flower pp. 192–4, this volume.

THE IMPERIAL SUBJECT: THEODOSIUS II AND PANEGYRIC

to burn the building, with the resulting conflagration engulfing much of Constantinople (7.29.8–10). Even Theodosius' attempt to mitigate Nestorius' attacks on the Novatian schismatics[67] only highlights his acquiescence in Nestorius' actions against other groups,[68] which received further imperial endorsement.[69] The inclusive μία ἐκκλησία of the Constantinopolitan populace that had, in previous moments of crisis, worshipped together in a single church (εὐκτήριον οἶκον / ἐκκλησίαν τοῦ Θεοῦ), its unity forged by Theodosius, is dissolved. Instead, conflict over the Arians' church (εὐκτήριον τόπον) erupted, bringing neither temporal victories nor converts, turning Constantinople from a site of splendid civic and religious harmony – crucial to imperial relations with God, and thus previous war efforts (to protect Christians from persecution elsewhere) – into a site of distress and conflict itself.

The significance of Socrates' emphasis on this complicity between Theodosius and Nestorius has not been fully recognised. In some modern accounts, this connection is ignored or omitted. Others skirt around or deny imperial support for Nestorius, and misleadingly imply that Socrates' emphasis was on Nestorius' sole culpability for the persecutions.[70] Such collaboration does not 'fit' with an emphasis on Theodosian tolerance. But it cannot be ignored or smoothed over. Inescapably, all attempts to reconcile the panegyrical framework with the historical narrative that Socrates provides, and its subtle moral lessons, must fail – for the irreconcilability of these two features of Socrates' account of Theodosius is intentional. Socrates' Nestorius was not the heretic

---

[67] Perhaps an ironic suggestion, given the Novatians' condemnation in *CTh* 16.5.65 (though being apportioned less severe treatment here than other religious deviants).
[68] Soc. 7.29.11.   [69] Soc. 7.31.4.
[70] Omitted, for example, in Harries 1994; Krivushin 1996; Leppin 2003b; avoided in Liebeschuetz 1993: 159; Urbainczyk 1998; Zecchini 2002; Michael Whitby 2003. Urbainczyk 1997: 35 n. 90 suggests that Socrates wrote evasively of the circumstances of Nestorius' election and episcopacy to absolve the emperor of blame. Leppin 1996: 215, summarising Socrates' account of the persecutions, glosses over Theodosius' complicity: '[Socrates] die durch Nestorius ausgelösten und damit in die Regierungszeit Theodosius' II. fallenden ταραχαί erwähnt'. Van Nuffelen 2004a: 411–12, 420–2 avoids Socrates' emphasis on the alignment of Theodosius and Nestorius at this juncture, focusing more attention on Ephesus. Wallraff 1997: 106–7 n. 376 and Maraval 2007: 144 n. 2 sidestep Socrates' emphasis on Theodosius' collusion with Nestorius, whilst attempting, unconvincingly, to argue for Theodosius' general tolerance with reference to possible non-implementation of anti-heretical legislation (cf. Lippold 1973: 1015–21).

265

of contemporary accounts, nor had he wickedly seized the reins of power for himself.[71] He had acted with Theodosius' endorsement. The adoption of coercion was not understood as rooted in unabashed, self-serving malice: Nestorius' violent hatred of heretics was, ultimately, the product of his fiery zeal for orthodoxy.

The insertion of a subtle, more conventionally historical account of the Nestorian interlude renders panegyric problematic in a number of ways. Narrowly, claims of a consistently tolerant Theodosius are undermined by their juxtaposition with this episode. That the episode has not been incorporated within, and *cannot* be reconciled with, the panegyric reveals, once more, panegyric's inability to capture nuanced or necessarily complicated behaviour within its simplistic moral framework. Importantly too, the worldview engendered by this sort of framework itself produces disaster when invoked to shape policy in the real world. Nestorius had packaged his preferred policy instruments in precisely the sort of stark moral dichotomies beloved of panegyrists: interchangeably, heretics and Persia stood reified as enemies of the Divine and Roman orders.

A seemingly optimistic, resolute concluding statement crowns Socrates' text.

> In such a flourishing condition were the affairs of the Church at this time. But we shall here close our history, praying that the churches everywhere, with the cities and nations, may continue in peace; for with the existence of peace, those who desire to write histories will find no materials for their purpose. (7.48.6–7)

Rightly, aspects of this conclusion have generated unease in some of Socrates' most perceptive readers. For Peter Van Nuffelen, peace and stability may happily be re-established here, but with qualifications.[72] Beneath the triumphalist rhetoric, this account of the Theodosian settlement is – in light of certain events recounted in the *History* and experiences common to all those living in Socrates' milieu – informed by 'une certaine crainte du retour du passé … c'est-à-dire la peur que les vaincus ne reprennent des

---

[71] Cf. Soc. 7.32.
[72] Van Nuffelen 2004a: 407–25; cf. Leppin 2003b: 235.

forces et qu'ils renversent le règne de paix et de foi orthodoxe'.[73] For Martin Wallraff, the historical episodes immediately preceding the conclusion offered insubstantial bases for Socrates' perceived optimism. As explanation, comforting trends and retrenchments in Theodosian political, cultural and religious life beyond the *History* are appealed to.[74] Contemporary perception of such trends could be tempered by an awareness of possible fragility, but the magnitude of the upheavals of the coming decades was, understandably, unknown.

Wallraff is right to question these preceding events. In these episodes, certain disputes are brought to resolution (although others, and the prospect of further disruptions,[75] loom in the background). The task, however, of uniting Constantinople's populace tolerantly as μία ἐκκλησία alongside one another before God is undertaken here primarily by figures other than Theodosius – especially the orthodox bishop of Constantinople, Proclus (7.43, 7.45), and his Novatian counterpart, Paul (7.39, 7.46). In many ways they displace or marginalise Theodosius. Indeed, that such a displacement presented the possibility for considerable friction is reflected in the final incident of the *History*. Proclus ordained one Thalassius as bishop of Caesarea, knowing that Theodosius had been about to appoint him praetorian prefect. This was 'such as none of the ancients had done'.[76] The ordination pointed again towards encroachment into formerly imperial roles by supposed subordinates, and possible conflict to come between an emperor and the bishop of Constantinople. At its close, the reader is thus reminded of both proximate and deeper, structural causes that will, inevitably, generate strife well beyond the terminus of the *History*.

The vision at the *History*'s close of peace under Theodosius, with the resolution of all strife and contradiction, is aligned with the obsolescence of historiography: strife was its *raison d'être*.[77] Yet strife had not ended, nor had history ceased its flow. The rhetoric

[73] Van Nuffelen 2004a: 418; cf. 117.
[74] Wallraff 1997: 177, 282, 291–4; cf. Szidat 2001: 13–14. Wallraff 1997: 282 suggests that Socrates saw the period of peace established at the end of his *History* as less impressive than earlier periods.
[75] Soc. 7.45.5–7.
[76] Soc. 7.48.1–5 quoting 1; *PLRE* II 1060 (Thalassius 1).
[77] Cf. Soc. 7.48.7, 1.18.15–16.

of the establishment of peace – emblematised and safeguarded in the person of the perfect emperor – was but another characteristic feature of panegyrical writing. As such, it was invoked not to confirm its imminence or realisation, but only to reveal its hollowness. Those notes detected by scholars within Socrates' text that jar with the suggestions of the descent of profound peace upon the empire, are not so much submerged, anxious qualifications beneath a claim for the 'end of history', but its deliberate contradiction. They are to be understood through the prism of Socrates' critique of panegyric. Panegyric is too crude a tool for making nuanced judgements about the complex decisions of imperial governance. It offers a timeless framework ill-fitted to aid comprehension of a world inextricably embedded in the onward flow of history and human imperfection. Theodosius' reign heralded not the end of historiography, but its indispensability.

CHAPTER 11

THEODOSIUS II AND HIS LEGACY IN ANTI-CHALCEDONIAN COMMUNAL MEMORY

Edward Watts

Theodosius II is one of the last Roman emperors embraced as orthodox by both Chalcedonian and anti-Chalcedonian Christians.[1] This is in some ways surprising since his reign saw a controversy about the teachings of Nestorius, bishop of Constantinople, develop into a fissure that, two years after the emperor's death, ultimately shattered the unity of the eastern Church.[2] For Chalcedonians, the battle that Theodosius led against Nestorius is celebrated as a victory for orthodoxy, while his sanctioning of the Alexandrian bishop Dioscorus' violent actions at the second Council of Ephesus is downplayed.[3] Anti-Chalcedonians for their part can point to both councils of Ephesus as moments when Theodosius backed their position. Despite this, both groups are handicapped somewhat by a lacuna in the narrative sources describing ecclesiastical affairs in the crucial decade of the 440s. Both sides acknowledge this.

---

[1] With the exception of Marcian, it is not until the reign of Justin I that anti-Chalcedonians begin pointedly attacking the orthodoxy of emperors. Marcian is abused by anti-Chalcedonians and embraced by Chalcedonians (anti-Chalcedonian abuse will be detailed below; for the Chalcedonian embrace see Evagrius 2.1). Although the two Leos and Zeno all accepted Chalcedon, they were much less aggressive in pushing its acceptance and receive the standard respect generally accorded to a legitimate Christian emperor. The two Leos, for example, are endorsed as pious believers by anti-Chalcedonian authors, despite their mildly pro-Chalcedonian positions (for example, Zacharias, *HE* 4.5 [ed. E. W. Brooks, *CSCO* 87–8, Paris, 1919–24]). Zeno too was considered pious (for example, Zacharias, *HE* 5.7 and *Vita Severi* 35 [ed. M.-A. Kugener, *PO* 2.1, Paris, 1903]). Anastasius was, of course, moderately anti-Chalcedonian. He was warmly embraced by anti-Chalcedonians while Chalcedonians treated him with the same respect that anti-Chalcedonians showed Leo I (for example, Evagrius 3.34).

[2] The event that led to this was, of course, the Council of Chalcedon convened by the Emperor Marcian in 451; for Chalcedon, see the important and concise reconstruction of Gaddis 2005: 310–22; note too Price and Gaddis 2005 and the still classic discussion of Frend 1972: 46–50.

[3] Contrast, for example, Evagrius 1.7, 1.12 (on Theodosius' actions against Nestorius) and 1.10 (which seems to place blame for the second Council of Ephesus on Dioscorus and the eunuch-chamberlain Chrysaphius).

From the Chalcedonian perspective, Evagrius Scholasticus notes at the outset of his *Ecclesiastical History* that Eusebius, Sozomen, Theodoret and Socrates have 'produced a most excellent record of the advent of our compassionate God, and ... of whatever events have occurred among us, whether more or less worthy of mention, down to a certain period of the reign of Theodosius'.[4] From the anti-Chalcedonian side, Pseudo-Zacharias notes a similar lacuna in the material available to him[5] and indicates that he will address events in this period 'cursorily, so that the account of the matters in various places ... should not grow too big'.[6] Evidently neither sixth-century author found an authoritative treatment of events that could bridge the gap between the point at which Socrates, Sozomen and Theodoret left off and the one at which Zacharias Scholasticus picked up.

While Theodosius' activities in the 440s are undertreated by ecclesiastical historians like Evagrius and Pseudo-Zacharias, they receive much more attention in other types of texts that come out of later Christian communities. This chapter considers four anti-Chalcedonian textual profiles of Theodosius that arose out of an Egyptian milieu. These narratives date from the fifth to the eighteenth centuries and come from a wide variety of sources, but they all draw upon a similar basic understanding of what Theodosius II represented to Egyptian anti-Chalcedonians. Taken together, these narratives demonstrate that a view of Theodosius took hold quite soon after Chalcedon and, once established, it has lived on in Egyptian anti-Chalcedonian communal memory to this day.

---

[4] Evagrius 1.*pr*.

[5] 'After the *Ecclesiastical [History]* of Eusebius of Caesarea, both Socrates and Theodoret composed histories, down to the 32nd year of the reign of Theodosius the Younger. In these they described, as best as they could, and to serve as a profitable record for discerning (readers), the events and affairs that occurred in different places, about which they strove to learn, basing themselves on documents, letters, records and oral sources that they had investigated' (Ps.-Zacharias, *Miscellaneous History*, 2.Introduction.a, trans. S. Brock in Greatrex 2011: 82). The work of Pseudo-Zacharias is a twelve-book Syriac composite text assembled in the later sixth century. The first two and final six books are made up of materials collected by its unknown compiler. Books 3–6 largely reproduce Zacharias Scholasticus' *Ecclesiastical History*, with a few small additions inserted by the compiler.

[6] Ps.-Zacharias, 2.Introduction.c; in fact, the second book of the work is a collection of miscellaneous materials touching on things as diverse as the Seven Sleepers of Ephesus, the Eutychian question and the return of the body of John Chrysostom to Constantinople.

The earliest of these texts is the *Plerophories* of John Rufus, a work that contains, as its preface claims, 'the witnesses and revelations that God has made to the saints, on the subject of the heresy of the two natures and the prevarications that came about at Chalcedon'.[7] In all, the *Plerophories* describes the context and preserves the content of eighty-nine visions and other forms of divine communication which God granted leading Egyptian and Palestinian ascetics as well as some selected lay associates. Though probably written down in the 510s, much of this material derives from the later fifth-century oral testimony of Peter the Iberian, a member of the Iberian royal family who grew up at Theodosius' court and later founded a monastery outside Gaza. When Juvenal, the bishop of Jerusalem, turned his back on Dioscorus at the Council of Chalcedon, the Palestinian church rebelled. Juvenal was prevented from returning to Palestine and those bishops who remained loyal to him were replaced, often with anti-Chalcedonian ascetics. Peter was chosen as the anti-Chalcedonian bishop of Maiuma and held that position until he was forced into exile following Juvenal's return to Jerusalem in 453. While in exile, Peter helped galvanise Egyptian resistance to Chalcedon. He eventually returned to the ascetic community he founded in Palestine and there served as John Rufus' ascetic mentor.[8]

Theodosius features in four of the eighty-nine visions John recounts. In three of them he plays a similar role, but it is worth considering the outlier first. This vision, the thirty-fifth in the text, offers a pre-Chalcedonian portrait (and one possibly prior to the second Council of Ephesus) of the emperor that derives from a story told to Peter the Iberian by a mentor named Basil.[9] When Nestorius was bishop of Constantinople, Basil claimed to have heard a voice

---

[7] John Rufus, *Pler.* heading (*PO* 8.1: 11); while John was writing in Gaza, the anti-Chalcedonian ascetic community to which he belonged had close ties to Egypt. Timothy Aelurus, patriarch of Alexandria (457–477), was one of John's most important sources for material in the *Plerophories*, a fact that illustrates the text's frequent reflection of Egyptian attitudes.

[8] For discussion of the career of Peter the Iberian, see Horn 2006: 50–111; Steppa 2002: 6–11.

[9] John Rufus, *Pler.* 35 (*PO* 8.1: 78–81); Basil is otherwise unknown, but may be the archimandrite and deacon who upbraided Nestorius at the first Council of Ephesus; for discussion of this passage, see Steppa 2002: 148; and Kelly p. 233, this volume.

in the heavens calling him to hasten to Constantinople and refute the bishop's blasphemy. Basil made this journey and soon crossed paths with Theodosius. Basil called out to the emperor that he too was not following the Trinity. Basil was then arrested and tortured but, while he was being held, the emperor was hit on the head by a falling brick and nearly killed. That evening, a divine figure appeared before the emperor and told Theodosius that he suffered because of his treatment of Basil. Theodosius immediately summoned the saint and asked him what could be done to rectify things. Basil told the emperor to summon a council to investigate the teachings of Nestorius and, John Rufus writes, the first Council of Ephesus was called soon afterwards. Given its source, Vision 35 depends upon oral testimony likely shared with Peter the Iberian in the late 430s or early 440s.[10] It then offers a pre-Chalcedonian narration of Theodosius' gradual evolution from an apparent supporter of Nestorius to a sovereign who completely disavowed Nestorius' teaching.[11] Basil's story not only explains Theodosius' turning away from Nestorianism, but twists the narrative in such a way that the community of monks to which John Rufus belongs can claim credit for the emperor's change of heart by associating it with one of their spiritual ancestors.

Unlike this early tradition, the material dating to the mid to late fifth century offers a very different, less fluid profile of Theodosius. Vision 32, for example, was told to John by Peter the Iberian and concerned a monk who heard a divine voice announce when Theodosius had died.[12] Vision 54, which appeared to Peter the Iberian himself, gives a bit more information about how the significance of Theodosius' death might be understood. At the time of the emperor's departure, Peter saw the cloak of the bishop of Jerusalem going up to heaven, a clear suggestion that the

---

[10] The tradition is likely an early one both because of Basil's relationship to Peter and the focus it places upon Theodosius' relationship with Nestorius. Basil is said by John Rufus to have 'placed [Peter] on the path to salvation when he was a child and found himself in the imperial city' (John Rufus, *Pler.* 35. [*PO* 8.1: 78.4–5]). On Basil's relationship with Peter the Iberian, see Steppa 2002: 97.

[11] Theodosius' moderate attitude towards Nestorius can be seen in his initial complaint that the Council reached its decision too quickly (*Coll. Vat.* 83 [*ACO* 1.1.3, pp. 9–10]; Evagrius 1.5) and also by his apparent hesitance in ratifying Nestorius' expulsion (1.7).

[12] John Rufus, *Pler.* 32 (*PO* 8.1: 75).

God-given legitimacy of the bishop of Jerusalem would be taken back following the Council of Chalcedon.[13] The most interesting vision involving Theodosius, however, is the twenty-seventh. This concerned a soldier named Zeno who served in an Alexandrian military cohort sent to guard Peter the Iberian during the reign of the Emperor Zeno.

> A certain soldier named Zeno, head of the cohort of Dacians encamped in Alexandria, was sent by the *cubicularius* Cosmas to watch, until his arrival, our bishop Peter the Iberian ... When he arrived in Palestine, he recounted to the venerable man, in our presence, the following story (a certain Peter, who was a *scholarius*, recounted to me that which follows): 'I was a great friend of Nestorius, I approved of the Council of Chalcedon and the Emperor Marcian, and many times I raised myself against those who opposed it. I saw, during the night, a man who said to me: "How long will you be in error and refuse to adhere to the truth? Come now and I will show you where you can find the Emperor Theodosius in one place and Marcian in another." And he took me to see, in one place filled with a great and inaccessible light, the venerable Theodosius in an ineffable glory and more brilliant than the sun. Then he guided me to another place full of smoke and obscurity and shadows and he said to me, "Do you see Marcian in the torments in this place?" ... I saw Marcian suspended by hooks of iron in the midst of flames.'[14]

This vision, John Rufus explains, persuaded Zeno to join Peter the Iberian in opposing the creed approved at Chalcedon.

One of the distinguishing features of the *Plerophories* is the way in which John Rufus is able to define the individual character of a large collection of figures while simultaneously preserving for them a coherent identity across the whole text.[15] This is particularly well done for heroic figures like Peter the Iberian and villains like the Emperor Marcian.[16] Theodosius – who is neither a major hero nor a villain – plays a secondary role in the text but, even allowing for his initial turn away from Nestorianism, his profile too is thematically consistent. He belongs to an age when a man of true faith governed the empire, orthodox bishops presided over its most important sees and the twin pillars of political and church power responded to the commands of God communicated

---

[13] John Rufus, *Pler.* 54 (*PO* 8.1: 109).
[14] John Rufus, *Pler.* 27 (*PO* 8.1: 68–9).
[15] On the wider aims of John Rufus, see the thorough discussion of Steppa 2002 as well as Watts 2010: 133–8.
[16] Watts 2010: 134–6.

through pious ascetics. Theodosius then serves as a counterpoint to the post-Chalcedonian order in which the impious Marcian and corrupt bishops like Juvenal of Jerusalem oppressed ascetics like Peter the Iberian and worked to overturn the imperial and ecclesiastical order they inherited.

Pseudo-Theopistus' *History of Dioscorus*, a later sixth-century text, picks up and further develops this characterisation of Theodosius. Dioscorus, the focal point of this text, succeeded Cyril as bishop of Alexandria in 444 and was chosen by Theodosius II to preside over the second Council of Ephesus in 449. He was put on trial at Chalcedon and then exiled to Gangra, where he died in 454. In its current form, the *History* is a Syriac translation of an Egyptian original that contextualises Dioscorus' deposition and exile by showing how they fit into the history of the Egyptian Church. To do this, the *History* introduces a sequence of well-known Egyptian ecclesiastical and ascetic leaders, and speaks about how their examples inspired Dioscorus during the reign of Marcian.[17] The author aims to illustrate the divine inspiration of Dioscorus' rejection of Chalcedon and his unwillingness to respond to Marcian's pressure by showing how revered Egyptian Christians acted similarly in the past and indicated their approval of his current actions.

While Theodosius is not a leading figure in Pseudo-Theopistus' text, the literary character of the emperor again supports crucial elements of its narrative. The *History* begins, for example, by describing the situation in the Roman world during the last moments of Theodosius' life. Although all seemed well, the text claims that the death of Theodosius roughly coincided with the deaths of Cyril, Celestinus, bishop of Rome, Victor, the *koinobiarch*

---

[17] Ps.-Theopistus, *History of Dioscorus* (= *Hist.*) (ed. Nau 1903) has three phases, all of which feature Egyptian exemplars prominently. The first phase describes the lead-up to the Council of Chalcedon. It describes how figures like the apostle Mark and bishops Peter I, Dionysius, Theonas, Athanasius and Cyril all anticipate Dioscorus' resistance. The text's second phase details the events of the Council itself and makes the case that Dioscorus was there following the 'orthodox faith of Nicaea' and the example of Cyril (ch. 12). The third and final phase of the text blends the events of Dioscorus' exile with visions and stories showing how his actions correspond to the models of exemplary Egyptian Christians like the Pachomian monks – Pachomius himself, Petronius and Theodore – as well as bishops like Cyril, Alexander and Athanasius (ch. 19).

of the large Pachomian monastic system, and Shenoute, the archimandrite of a 4,000-person ascetic community.[18] Without these powerful leaders to fight for piety, it continues, 'blasphemies about God' began to 'shake the universe'.[19] After Theodosius' death, his sister Pulcheria assumed effective control of the state and married a handsome 'Nestorian' palace courtier named Marcian. With Satan's help, she contrived to get Marcian recognised as the legitimate emperor.[20] Once enthroned, Marcian called upon his subjects to be instructed in the religious ideas of Theodoret and Ibas, an agenda that Pope Leo reinforced by sending a letter of support. News of these events soon reached Dioscorus and he wrote a response. Marcian then summoned the bishops to Chalcedon in order to suppress the arguments of Dioscorus.[21] This introductory sequence makes clear that Theodosius presided over a golden age in which the Church, the state and the monasteries all supported one another as they upheld orthodoxy.

The fourth chapter of the *History of Dioscorus* characterises the age of Theodosius in the same way. It describes the arrival of a letter sent by Marcian in which the new emperor calls upon his subjects to embrace the teachings of Theodoret and Ibas of Edessa. Dioscorus is informed of Marcian's letter by Theopistus and responds:

> I know this already, my son, so quiet yourself. Did not our father Cyril say to me, 'Rest your spirit and your body during the reign of Theodosius, because after him, death will produce a second Eve, named Pulcheria. For if Eve had hidden her eyes and not looked at the tree of good and evil, death would not have entered into the world. And if Pulcheria had hidden her eyes and not looked at Marcian, the canons and doctrines of the true faith would not be disrupted.'[22]

The text then marks out the reign of Theodosius as a sort of Christian paradise from which the empire was expelled when Pulcheria married Marcian. This is an extremely subtle characterisation of the

---

[18] *Hist.* 1; this is chronologically problematic. Theodosius II died in 450, Cyril in 444, Celestinus in 432 and Shenoute in the later 450s. Nevertheless, this dubious claim does point to the text's interest in tying the events of Dioscorus' career to a broader Christian narrative.
[19] *Hist.* 2 (Nau 1903: 243). [20] *Hist.* 3.
[21] *Hist.* 4–5. [22] *Hist.* 4 (Nau 1903: 250).

Theodosian age that highlights the emperor's support for orthodoxy as well as the importance of Pulcheria's chastity in sustaining divine favour.[23] Like John Rufus in the *Plerophories*, however, the author of the *History of Dioscorus* is interested less in flushing out the details of Theodosius' reign than in establishing its ideal character and emphasising the true horror of the regime that followed it. Indeed, the rhetorical power of this comparison could only diminish if more attention were paid to the actual characteristics of Theodosius. He works much better as a vessel into which the reader can place all the good qualities one might associate with an imperial Eden.

While these fifth- and early sixth-century texts offer a thematically coherent profile of Theodosius, this is a profile that can, to some degree, be explained by the way in which Egyptian anti-Chalcedonians in the period before the reign of Justinian understood their relationship with imperial power: it was in their view overwhelmingly a co-operative one. It is, then, extremely interesting to see that, even as the relationship between the Egyptian Church and the emperor becomes much more adversarial in the late sixth and early seventh centuries, the Egyptian texts continue to present Theodosius as a characteristically pious sovereign.[24] Indeed, John of Nikiu's *Chronicle*, a late seventh-century text, makes the same contrast between the glorious and pious sovereign Theodosius and his horrific successor Marcian. John's treatment of Theodosius is far more developed than the two texts treated above, but the themes he advances are essentially the same. He begins with a story taken from the *Chronicle* of John Malalas about Theodosius, a childhood friend named Paulinus who was serving as his *magister officiorum*, and a magnificent apple that a military officer had given to the emperor.[25] The emperor marvelled

[23] For the importance of Pulcheria's virginity in the Theodosian court, see Holum 1982: 93–6 and Harries pp. 67–70 and Van Nuffelen pp. 136–41, this volume. Sozomen claims that this was done 'to avoid bringing another male into the palace and to remove any opportunity for the plots of ambitious men' (9.1.3). Anti-Chalcedonian authors, of course, were perfectly willing to present Pulcheria's marriage to Marcian as a plot by an ambitious man.

[24] For discussion of these later events and the attitudes they inspired, see Davis 2004: 101–28; Sijpesteijn 2007: 442–3.

[25] John of Nikiu, *Chronicle* (= *Chronicle*) 87.1–13 (trans. Charles 1916: 104–5). The story is first found in Malalas 14.8 and *Chron. Pasch.* 444 (1 584.5–585.23); for Paulinus see *PLRE* II 846–7 (Paulinus 8); for discussion of this incident, see Holum 1982: 176–7.

at the size of the apple and gave it to his wife, Eudocia, who then passed it along to Paulinus. When the emperor learned of this, he became enraged at Eudocia but, John says, they quickly made up. Paulinus was not so lucky. A report was passed to Theodosius that Paulinus was plotting to overthrow him and Theodosius ordered his execution, though he and Eudocia continued to love Paulinus greatly. John of Nikiu concludes his version of this episode by asserting that 'lying historians who are heretics and abide not by the truth have recounted and said that Paulinus was put to death because of the Empress Eudocia. But the Empress Eudocia was wise and chaste, spotless and perfect in all her conduct.'[26]

John's apology for the conduct of the imperial couple in this anecdote helps to set up the next event he recounts. Although he had fathered a daughter, the Emperor Theodosius had difficulty producing a male heir. John records that Theodosius sent a letter to the Egyptian monasteries in Scetis in order to find out what he needed to do to produce male offspring.[27] They replied 'When thou quittest this world, the faith of thy fathers will be changed; for God out of love to thee has not given thee a male offspring lest it should become wicked.'[28] Once he received this response, John continues, 'the Emperor Theodosius and his wife were alike pained by this communication, and they abandoned all conjugal intercourse and lived, by mutual consent, in befitting chastity'.[29] They remained together until they could celebrate the marriage of their daughter to the western emperor Valentinian III. Eudocia then sought permission to go to Jerusalem. In a sign of his respect for orthodoxy, Theodosius asked that Cyril of Alexandria accompany her there. Cyril did as requested and Eudocia 'withdrew from the world and lived in solitude'.[30]

For his part, Theodosius 'also gave himself to fasting and prayer and to the singing of psalms and hymns, and he pursued a virtuous course. And his virgin sisters, who were older than he, the blessed Arcadia and Marina, had died before the empress

---

[26] *Chronicle* 87.13 (trans. Charles 1916: 105).
[27] *Chronicle* 87.14 (trans. Charles 1916: 105).
[28] *Chronicle* 87.15 (trans. Charles 1916: 105).
[29] *Chronicle* 87.16 (trans. Charles 1916: 105).
[30] *Chronicle* 87.17–22 quoting 22 (trans. Charles 1916: 105–6).

quitted the palace.'³¹ Pulcheria, however, began working to protect Nestorians because 'she feared the strength of the empire of the Emperor Theodosius'.³² She first tried to undercut the authority of the emperor and Eudocia by forging a document that made him look weak and incompetent.³³ This ruse failed, however, and she suffered in silence as Theodosius called the second Council of Ephesus and sanctioned the depositions ordered there.³⁴ When Theodosius died, however, John claims that Pulcheria asserted herself immediately. Taking no counsel from the pious Eudocia, Pulcheria 'audaciously promulgated an imperial decree without taking the advice of Valentinian the emperor of Rome or that of the chief officers and Senate, and married Marcian, the commander-in-chief of the army, and placed the imperial crown on his head and made him emperor. And she became his wife and sacrificed her virginity.'³⁵

On the day of his accession, John writes, a prodigy occurred that clearly signified divine disapproval of this course of events:

> And on the day of Marcian's accession, there was darkness over all the earth from the first hour of the day till the evening. And that darkness was like that which had been in the land of Egypt in the days of Moses, the chief of the prophets. And there was great fear and alarm among all the inhabitants of Constantinople. They wept and lamented and raised dirges and cried aloud exceedingly, and imagined that the end of the world was at hand. And the senate, the officers and the soldiers, (even) all the army, small and great, that was in the city were filled with agitation and cried aloud, saying: 'We have never heard nor seen in all the previous reigns of the Roman empire such an event as this.' And they murmured very much, but they did not express themselves openly. And on the following day the Divine love had compassion on mankind, and the sun rose and the light of day reappeared.³⁶

Mention of this prodigy is followed by a discussion of the Council of Chalcedon, the deposition of Dioscorus and 'disturbances that arose in Constantinople and all other places' up until the time of Marcian's death.³⁷

---

[31] *Chronicle* 87.23 (trans. Charles 1916: 106).
[32] *Chronicle* 87.28 (trans. Charles 1916: 106–7).
[33] *Chronicle* 87.29–32 (trans. Charles 1916: 107).
[34] *Chronicle* 87.34–5 (trans. Charles 1916: 107).
[35] *Chronicle* 87.36 (trans. Charles 1916: 107).
[36] *Chronicle* 87.38–41 (trans. Charles 1916: 108).
[37] *Chronicle* 87.42–4 quoting 44 (trans. Charles 1916: 108).

John of Nikiu constructs a narrative of Theodosius' reign that emphasises the piety of the emperor and his wife while simultaneously highlighting the perfidy of Pulcheria and Marcian. John crafts his entire narrative treatment of the reigns of Theodosius and Marcian in such a way that it shows how the piety (and impiety) of these two imperial couples mirrored one another. The chaste Eudocia and Theodosius embodied faithfulness to orthodoxy to the same degree that Marcian and Pulcheria exemplified heresy. John then has not only expanded the traditional anti-Chalcedonian treatment of Theodosius and Marcian to include their empresses, but he actually focuses upon Eudocia and Pulcheria at least as much as he does on their husbands. Despite this expansion, however, the basic characterisations of each emperor remain essentially the same; Theodosius is pious and Marcian is the opposite.

After John of Nikiu, the Egyptian historiographical treatment of its Roman past becomes much less extensive. Liturgy, however, remained an effective and common vehicle through which knowledge of Christian Roman history was communicated to Egyptians. And it is here that traditions about Theodosius II found in the Coptic *Synaxary* provide important additional information on Egyptian Christian views of this emperor. The *Synaxary* (a catalogue listing the saints commemorated on each day of the Egyptian calendar and setting out their achievements) is a complicated text that currently survives as a fifteenth-century Arabic translation of an earlier Coptic original to which small elements have subsequently been added.[38] Despite this late date, the *Synaxary* is extremely useful because it preserves many traditions about the Coptic Church and its history that first appear in late antiquity. The wide circulation and annual recitation of this historical material on the same day across Egypt also seems to have ensured that, once they entered into the liturgical cycle, the historical profiles of figures featured in the *Synaxary* remained relatively stable. In many cases, the material in the *Synaxary* corresponds in detail and theme to both medieval texts like Severus' *History of*

---

[38] The translation was undertaken by Michael, bishop of Athrib and Malig. The textual history of this important document remains woefully understudied, but, as will be shown below, it is clear that material has been added progressively since the initial fifteenth-century translation.

the Patriarchs and late-antique documents like the fifth-century *History of the Church of Alexandria*.[39] This feature of the text makes it extremely useful as a source for the reception of Egyptian Christian commemorations of the Roman period.

Theodosius II appears in the *Synaxary* on fourteen different days, but twelve of these simply use the emperor as a date marker to indicate the time when a person lived or an event occurred. Two appearances, however, provide more substantial indications of how Theodosius is understood within the Coptic community of believers. The shorter of these commemorates the death of the Syrian monk Barsauma.[40] This notice tells us a bit about Barsauma's early life and ascetic practice, mentions that he performed many miracles and indicates that he was once blessed by St Simeon Stylites. The thing that marked his holiness most profoundly, however, was 'his resistance to the heresy of Nestorius and his followers'. This is demonstrated by how Theodosius II and Marcian differed

---

[39] Severus, *History of the Patriarchs of the Coptic Church of Alexandria* (ed. B. T. A. Evetts, *PO* 1.2, 1.4, 5.1, 10.5, Paris, 1904–15); *History of the Church of Alexandria* (ed. T. Orlandi, Studi copti 2, Milan, 1968–70). The thematic overlap with the *Synaxary* occurs in many places. One typical example can be seen by comparing the ways in which Severus' *History of the Patriarchs* and the *Synaxary* treat the figures of Dioscorus and Timothy Aelurus. The *History of the Patriarchs* presents Timothy as the successor of the 'militant Father Dioscorus' and alludes to the hardships he suffered for his faith including 'banishment to the island of Gangra, like Dioscorus, for seven full years' (Severus, *History of the Patriarchs*, Timothy II = 13.445). The *Synaxary* similarly focuses upon the difficulties that Timothy endured. It highlights his exile (Mesori 7) and the political opposition he faced (Mesori 23), as well as his position as the theological and spiritual heir of Dioscorus (Mesori 7, Hathor 2, 30) (ed. R. Basset, *PO* 3.3, Paris, 1909, 246–7, 365 [Hathor], *PO* 17.3, Paris, 1923, 710, 745 [Mesori]). All translations from the Coptic *Synaxarion* are taken from the St George's Orthodox Church, Chicago, translation of the *Synaxarium of the Coptic Church*.

[40] This notice appears on Amshir 9 (ed. R. Basset, *PO* 11.5, Paris, 1915, 806–9): 'I. On this day of the year 458 AD, the blessed father Anba Barsauma, the father of the Syrian monks, departed ... St Barsauma was a contemporary of St Simeon the Stylite. When St Barsauma knew about him, he went to visit him and they blessed each other. He was well known for his resistance to the heresy of Nestorius and his followers. He attended the Universal Council at Ephesus at the invitation of Emperor Theodosius the Younger, who gave him a great honor. Some accused St Barsauma of eating, drinking and living a luxurious life. The Emperor called him and saw for himself St Barsauma's righteousness and his ascetic living. The Emperor vindicated him and allowed him to return to his monastery with great honor. When Emperor Marcian called for the Council at Chalcedon, the fathers asked the Emperor not to call upon St Barsauma, for they knew of the grace that was in him. When the Council agreed on the two natures of Christ, St Barsauma resisted these heretic teachings and he was persecuted by the Chalcedonians.'

THEODOSIUS II AND ANTI-CHALCEDONIAN COMMUNAL MEMORY

in their treatment of him. Theodosius, according to this notice, invited Barsauma to attend the first Council of Ephesus, absolved him of blame when his opponents falsely charged the monk with luxurious living and granted him great honour. Marcian, by contrast, did not invite Barsauma to Chalcedon, 'for he knew of the grace that was in him'. Unsurprisingly, Barsauma fought against Chalcedon until the day he died.

Theodosius here serves as a sort of touchstone for orthodoxy whose blessing legitimates the holiness of Barsauma. The contrast of Theodosius with Marcian further underlines the saint's positive qualities. The text then offers a very deliberate rhetoric that constructs the holiness of Barsauma through his association with the famous fifth-century Syrian pillar-saint Simeon Stylites, certifies it through his interaction with the pious emperor Theodosius and validates it by documenting his resistance to the impiety of Marcian. The success of this profile, however, depends almost entirely upon the audience recognising the significance of the saint's interaction with prototypical heroes like Simeon and Theodosius as well as villains like Marcian.

A more complicated mention of Theodosius appears thirteen days earlier on Tubah 26. This notice commemorates the martyrdom of forty-nine elders of Scetis who died along with an imperial envoy and his son when a group of pagan 'berbers' attacked their monastery. The narration begins with Theodosius writing to Scetis to ask the monks to pray that God grant him a son, an adaptation of a tradition already seen in John of Nikiu. While this was a relatively minor event that John of Nikiu used to explain Eudocia's withdrawal to Jerusalem, the *Synaxary* makes much more of it.[41] When Theodosius' delegation arrives in Scetis, St Isidore, one of the monastic elders, responded that God did not wish Theodosius to have a son who would associate with the heretics who were to come after the emperor's death. Despite this, some palace courtiers advised Theodosius to divorce his wife in the hope that a new wife would produce a male heir. Theodosius, however, refused to do anything other than what the elders of Scetis demanded. He accordingly sent another envoy to ask them for further advice.

[41] *PO* 11.5: 699–703; for discussion of this story in John of Nikiu, see above p. 277.

When the envoy arrived, he learned that Isidore had recently died. The envoy then asked the emperor's question of Isidore's corpse. The corpse responded: 'What I had said before, I also say now. The Lord will never give him a son to participate with the heretics, even if he marries ten women.' Immediately following this miracle, berbers attacked the monastery and killed forty-nine of its monks as well as the imperial envoy and his son.

The second part of the text then discusses the various places to which the relics of these martyrs were taken. In the years following the raid, people from neighboring cities and towns took the bodies away. The remains of the imperial messenger and his son were particularly appealing prizes – their relics appear to have been separated on at least two occasions, only to be brought back together by divine intervention. More interesting is the text's description of the fate of these remains during what the *Synaxary* calls 'the times of persecution'. These refer to the attacks on the Coptic Church launched by the Emperor Justinian in the mid sixth century and, particularly, to the campaigns of Heraclius in the 630s. These often violent assaults targeted both church leadership and, particularly in the case of Heraclius, also church property. The Coptic Church responded by attempting to protect itself and its resources as best it could. Under Justinian the monks built a church for the saints. During the Heraclian persecution, the bodies of the saints were moved there permanently to serve as a focal point for Coptic devotion. They remained important even after Egypt came under Arab control. As Egyptian monasteries and churches gradually declined during the long period of Islamic rule, the relics were moved again – this time to a cell once occupied by a monk at the monastery of St Macarius. Finally, in the eighteenth century, they were moved to their current resting place, a church within that monastery.

It is clear that this notice celebrates the *martyrion* of these saints that exists today at the monastery of St Macarius, but it did not always serve this purpose. This tradition begins with Theodosius II and grows over time to include not only elements derived from the period of anti-Chalcedonian resistance to Justinian and Heraclius, but also medieval and early modern materials. And yet these different components do not hinder the text from functioning as a coherent narrative. To explain the significance of the relics, the holiness of the figures from which they derive must first be established. It is here that the particular anti-Chalcedonian understanding of Theodosius II becomes useful. By consulting the monks of Scetis and refusing to act in any way other than that which they counsel, Theodosius confirms their great authority and holiness. Theodosius' orthodoxy is underlined by the warning that heresy would follow the emperor's death. Theodosius' request for clarification of the initial vision leads not only to the miracle of post-mortem speech, but also to the martyrdom of the monks and his messenger. Each of these components amplifies and further clarifies the holiness of the ascetics.

Although a pious Roman emperor helps define the initial holiness of these saints, their sanctity is not diminished when the Egyptian anti-Chalcedonian Church's relationship with imperial power changes. These same relics – whose power is shown in part by evoking the memory of Theodosius – become treasures hidden by Egyptian bishops resisting the heretical, persecuting emperors of the sixth and seventh centuries. They retain this status after Egypt passes under Islamic rule. Even under these conditions, the legacy of Theodosius continues to be preserved as a narrative core that gave meaning to later events. Theodosius' interaction with the monks then makes it clear why one should care about the various relocations of the martyrs' remains as well as the church that now houses them.

This is by no means an exhaustive survey of anti-Chalcedonian treatments of Theodosius II, but it does point to some important ways that anti-Chalcedonians simultaneously constructed and drew upon this emperor's legacy. Almost immediately after Chalcedon it seems that a general anti-Chalcedonian consensus grew up that Theodosius represented an anti-Marcian figure whose justice and piety could be contrasted in their communal histories with the negative characteristics exhibited by his persecuting successor. As the selections from the *Plerophories* show, this definition levelled out and washed away some of the nuances and characteristics that made up pre-Chalcedonian profiles of the emperor. Compared with Marcian, the reign of Theodosius became a sort of pre-Chalcedonian utopia in which the Church, the Roman empire and the monasteries all supported one another as they upheld orthodoxy. The emperor and the system he created came to be embraced as exemplifying an ideal moment of church–state co-operation. While this is present in sixth- and seventh-century texts, the *Synaxary* reveals the long-term resonance of this idea. The only sovereigns mentioned in the same sort of positive light as Theodosius in the *Synaxary* are a few Old Testament kings from the line of David and the orthodox Roman emperors of the fourth and fifth century. The Christian Roman empire in late antiquity was not just recognised as a part of an anti-Chalcedonian Coptic Christian history. It plays a central role in that history, and the reign of Theodosius II represents the Christian empire's apogee. Once established, Theodosius' example as a generic, pious Christian sovereign remained important in Egypt long after specific memories of the emperor and the empire he ruled had faded.

BIBLIOGRAPHY

Adams, C. and Laurence, R. (eds.) (2001) *Travel and geography in the Roman empire*, London.
Agosti, G. (2001) 'L'epica biblica nella tarda antichità greca. Autori e lettori nel IV e V secolo', in F. Stella (ed.) *La scrittura infinita. Bibbia e poesia in età medievale e umanistica. Atti del convegno di Firenze 26-28 giugno 1997*, Millennio medievale 28, Atti di convegni 8, Florence, 67–104.
(2004) 'Alcuni problemi relativi alla cesura principale nell'esametro greco tardoantico', in F. Spaltenstein and O. Bianchi (eds.) *Autour de la césure. Actes du colloque Damon des 3 et 4 novembre 2000*, Echo (Université de Lausanne. Institut d'archéologie et d'histoire ancienne) 3, Bern, 61–80.
(2009a) 'Cristianizzazione della poesia greca e dialogo interculturale', *Cristianesimo nella storia* 31: 313–35.
(2009b) 'La *Vita di Proclo* di Marino nella sua redazione in versi. Per un'analisi della biografia poetica tardoantica', *CentoPagine* 3: 30–46.
Agosti, G. and Gonnelli, F. (1995) 'Materiali per la storia dell'esametro nei poeti cristiani greci', in M. Fantuzzi and R. Pretagostini (eds.) *Struttura e storia dell'esametro Greco*, Studia di metri classica 10, 2 vols., Rome, 1 289–434.
Archi, G. G. (1976) *Teodosio II e la sua codificazione*, Naples.
Arnaud, P. (1990) 'La cartographie à Rome', PhD thesis, Université de Paris IV.
(2007–8) 'Texte et carte de Marcus Agrippa. Historiographie et données textuelles', *Geographia antiqua* 16–17: 73–126.
Arnaud-Lindet, M.-P. (1990) 'Introduction', in M.-P. Arnaud-Lindet, *Orose, Histoires (contre les païens)*, vol. 1: *Livres I–III*, Paris, v–ciii.
Atzeri, L. (2008) *Gesta senatus Romani de Theodosiano publicando. Il Codice Teodosiano e la sua diffusione ufficiale in Occidente*, Freiburger rechtsgeschichtliche Abhandlungen 58, Berlin.
Audano, S. (ed.) (2008) *Nonno e i suoi lettori*, Hellenica 27, Alessandria.
Azéma, Y. (1964) *Théodoret de Cyr, Correspondance. Introduction, texte critique, traduction et notes, Epist. Sirm. 1–95, SC* 98, Paris.
Bagnall, R. S. (ed.) (2007) *Egypt in the Byzantine world, 300–700*, Cambridge.
Bagnall, R. S., Cameron, Alan, Schwartz, S. R. and Worp, K. A. (1987) *Consuls of the Later Roman Empire*, Philological monographs of the American Philological Association 36, Atlanta, GA.
Baldini, A. (1998) 'Eunapio, Olimpiodoro ed una tradizione occidentale post-flavianea', *RSA* 28: 149–81.
(2000) 'Considerazioni sulla cronologia di Olimpiodoro di Tebe', *Historia* 49: 488–502.

(2004) *Ricerche di tarda storiografia (da Olimpiodoro di Tebe)*, Studi di storia 9, Bologna.
Baldovin, J. F. (1987) *The urban character of Christian worship: the origins, development, and meaning of stational liturgy*, Orientalia Christiana Analecta 228, Rome.
Baldwin, B. (1980) 'Olympiodorus of Thebes', *AC* 49. 212-31.
Bardill, J. (1999) 'The Golden Gate in Constantinople: a triumphal arch of Theodosius I', *AJA* 103: 671-96.
Bardy, G. (1929) 'L'«Indiculus de Haeresibus» de Pesudo-Jérome', *RecSR* 19: 385-405.
— (1931) 'Le "De Haeresibus" et ses sources', in *Miscellanea Agostiniana*, 2 vols, Rome, II 397-416.
Barnes, T. D. (1981) *Constantine and Eusebius*, Cambridge, MA.
— (1989a) 'The baptism of Theodosius II', *Studia Patristica* 19: 8-12.
— (1989b) 'Panegyrics, history and hagiography in Eusebius' *Life of Constantine*', in R. Williams (ed.) *The making of orthodoxy: essays in honour of Henry Chadwick*, Cambridge, 94-123 (repr. in T. D. Barnes, *Eusebius to Augustine: selected papers 1982-1993*, Aldershot, 1994, no. XI).
— (2001) 'The funerary speech for John Chrysostom (*BHG*³ 871 = *CPG* 6517)', *Studia Patristica* 37: 328-45.
— (2006) 'A lost prince in a sermon of Nestorius', *Studia Patristica* 39: 3-5.
— (2007) 'Arcadius the son of the Emperor Theodosius II', in M. Mayer i Olivé, G. Baratta and A. Guzmán Almagro (eds.) *XII Congressus internationalis epigraphiae graecae et latinae: provinciae imperii romani inscriptionibus descriptae, Barcelona, 3-8 Septembris 2002*, 2 vols., I 109-12.
— (2010) *Early Christian hagiography and Roman history*, Tria cordia 5, Tübingen.
Barnes, T. D. and Bevan, G. (in press) *Funerary speech for John Chrysostom*, Translated texts for historians, Liverpool.
Bartsch, S. (1994) *Actors in the audience: theatricality and doublespeak from Nero to Hadrian*, Revealing Antiquity 6, Cambridge, MA.
Bassanelli Sommariva, G. (2003) 'L'uso delle rubriche da parte dei commissari theodosiani', in G. Crifò and S. Giglio (eds.) *Atti dell'Accademia Romanistica Costantiniana. XIV convegno internazionale in memoria di Guglielmo Nocera*, Naples, 197-239.
Bauer, F. A. (1996) *Stadt, Platz und Denkmal in der Spätantike. Untersuchungen zur Ausstattung des öffentlichen Raums in den spätantiken Städten Rom, Konstantinopel und Ephesos*, Mainz.
Bauman, R. A. (1999) *Human rights in ancient Rome*, London.
Beagon, M. (1992) *Roman nature: the thought of Pliny the Elder*, Oxford.
Beard, M. (2007) *The Roman triumph*, Cambridge, MA.
Becker, A. (2003) Review of Urbainczyk 2002, *BMCR* 2003.02.19.
Berger, A. (2002) 'Straßen und Plätze in Konstantinopel als Schauplätze von Liturgie', in Warland, 9-19.

Bevegni, C. (1982) 'Eudociae Augustae *Martyrium S. Cypriani* I 1–99', *Prometheus* 8: 249–62.
  (2004) 'Per una nuova edizione del *De Sancto Cypriano* dell'imperatrice Eudocia. Note testuali ed esegetiche', Νέα Ῥώμη 1: 35–44.
  (2006a) *Eudocia Augusta. Storia di San Cipriano*, Piccola biblioteca Adelphi 541, Milan.
  (2006b) 'Sui modelli del *De sancto Cypriano* dell'imperatrice Eudocia', in E. Amato (ed.) *Approches de la troisième sophistique. Hommages à Jacques Schamp*, Collection Latomus 296, Brussels, 389–405.
  (2006/2007) 'Il *De sancto Cypriano* dell'imperatrice Eudocia. Questioni aperte', *Koinonia* 30/31: 155–68.
Bidez, J. (1926) *L'empereur Julien. Œuvres completes*, vol. II, Paris.
Billerbeck, M. (2006) *Stephani Byzantii Ethnica*, vol. I: Α–Γ, CFHB 43, Berlin.
Binns, J. (1994) *Ascetics and ambassadors of Christ: the monasteries of Palestine, 314–631*, Oxford.
Bleckmann, B. (2010) 'Zwischen Geschichtsschreibung und Panegyric? Das Problem der kritische Passagen zu Konstantin in der *Vita Constantini* des Eusebios', in P.-L. Malosse, M.-P. Noël and B. Schouler (eds.) *Clio sous le regard d'Hermès. L'utilisation de l'histoire dans la rhétorique ancienne de l'époque hellénistique à l'antiquité tardive. Actes du colloque international de Montpellier (18–20 octobre 2007)*, Cardo 8, Alessandria, 231–6.
Blockley, R. C. (1972) 'The Panegyric of Claudius Mamertinus on the Emperor Julian', *AJPh* 93: 437–50.
  (1981) *The fragmentary classicising historians of the later Roman empire: Eunapius, Olympiodorus, Priscus and Malchus*, ARCA, classical and medieval texts, papers and monographs 6, Liverpool.
  (1983) *The fragmentary classicising historians of the later Roman empire: Eunapius, Olympiodorus, Priscus and Malchus*, vol. II: *Text, translation and historiographical notes*, ARCA, classical and medieval texts, papers and monographs 10, Liverpool.
  (1992) *East Roman foreign policy: formation and conduct from Diocletian to Anastasius*, ARCA, classical and medieval texts, papers and monographs 30, Leeds.
  (1998) 'The dynasty of Theodosius', in Cameron and Garnsey, 111–37.
Boak, A. E. R. (1915) 'The Roman *magistri* in the civil and military service of the empire', *HSPh* 26: 73–164.
Boatwright, M. T. (2011) 'Women and gender in the Forum Romanum', *TAPhA* 141: 105–41.
Bonner, G. (1999) '*Dic Christi veritas ubi nunc habitas*: ideas of schism and heresy in the post-Nicene age', in W. E. Klingshirn and M. Vessey (eds.) *The limits of ancient Christianity: essays on late antique thought and culture in honor of R. A. Markus*, Ann Arbor, MI, 63–79.
Boyarin, D. (2004) *Border lines: the partition of Judaeo-Christianity*, Philadelphia, PA.

BIBLIOGRAPHY

Braund, S. (1998) 'Praise and protreptic in early imperial panegyric: Cicero, Seneca, Pliny', in Whitby, 53–76.
(2009) *Seneca, De clementia*, Oxford.
Brennan, P. (1996) 'The *Notitia dignitatum*', in C. Nicolet and P. Gros (eds.) *Les littératures techniques dans l'antiquité romaine. Statut, public et destination, tradition*, Fondation Hardt: Entretiens sur l'antiquité classique 42, Geneva, 147–78.
Brennecke, H. C. (1988) *Studien zur Geschichte der Homöer. Der Osten bis zum Ende der homöischen Reichskirche*, Beiträge zur historichen Theologie 73, Tübingen.
Brodersen, K. (1995) *Terra cognita. Studien zur römischen Raumerfassung*, Spudasmata 59, Hildesheim.
(2001) 'The presentation of geographical knowledge for travel and transport in the Roman world: *itineraria non tantum adnotata sed etiam picta*', in Adams and Laurence, 7–21.
(2011) 'Mapping Pliny's world: the achievement of Solinus', *BICS* 54: 63–88.
Brown, P. (1971) 'The rise and function of the holy man in late antiquity', *JRS* 61: 80–101 (repr. in P. Brown, *Society and the holy in late antiquity*, London, 1982, 103–52).
(1981) *The cult of the saints: its rise and function in Latin Christianity*, London.
(1992) *Power and persuasion in late antiquity: towards a Christian empire*, Madison, WI.
(1998) 'Asceticism: pagan and Christian', in Cameron and Garnsey, 601–31.
(2002) *Poverty and leadership in the later Roman empire*, Hanover, NH.
Browning, R. (1975) *The Emperor Julian*, London.
Brubaker, L. (1997) 'Memories of Helena: patterns in imperial female matronage in the fourth and fifth centuries', in L. James (ed.) *Women, men and eunuchs: gender in Byzantium*, London, 52–75.
Buc, P. (2001) *The dangers of ritual: between early medieval texts and social scientific theory*, Princeton, NJ.
Burgess, R. W. (1993–4) 'The accession of Marcian in the light of Chalcedonian apologetic and Monophysite polemic', *ByzZ* 86/87: 47–68 (repr. in R. W. Burgess, *Chronicles, consuls, and coins: historiography and history in the later Roman empire*, Farnham, 2011, no. XII).
Burns, T. S. (1994) *Barbarians within the gates of Rome: a study of Roman military policy and the barbarians, ca. 375–425 AD*, Bloomington, IN.
Bury, J. B. (1923) *History of the later Roman empire from the death of Theodosius I to the death of Justinian (AD 395 to AD 565)*, vol. I, London.
Cain, A. and Lenski, N. (eds.) (2009) *The power of religion in late antiquity*, Farnham.
Cameron, Alan (1965) 'Wandering poets: a literary movement in Byzantine Egypt', *Historia* 14: 470–509 (repr. in Alan Cameron 1985, no. 1).
(1966) 'The date and identity of Macrobius', *JRS* 56: 25–38.
(1969) 'Theodosius the Great and the regency of Stilico', *HSPh* 73: 247–80.

(1976) *Circus factions: Blues and Greens at Rome and Byzantium*, Oxford.
(1982) 'The empress and the poet: paganism and politics at the court of Theodosius II', in J. J. Winkler and G. Williams (eds.) *Later Greek literature*, Yale Classical Studies 27, 217–89 (repr. in Alan Cameron 1985, no. III).
(1985) *Literature and society in the early Byzantine world*, London.
(2000) 'The poet, the bishop and the harlot', *GRBS* 41: 175–88.
(2002) 'Petronius Probus, Aemilius Probus and the transmission of Nepos: a note on late Roman calligraphers', in J.-M. Carrié and R. Lizzi Testa (eds.) *Humana sapit. Études d'antiquité tardive offertes à Lellia Cracco Ruggini*, Bibliothèque de l'Antiquité tardive 3, Turnhout, 121–30.
(2004) 'Poetry and literary culture in late antiquity', in Swain and Edwards, 327–54.
(2007) 'Poets and pagans in Byzantine Egypt', in Bagnall, 21–46.
(2011) *The last pagans of Rome*, New York/Oxford.
Cameron, Alan and Long, J. (1993) *Barbarians and politics at the court of Arcadius*, The transformation of the classical heritage 19, Berkeley, CA.
Cameron, Averil (1969–70) 'Agathias on the Sassanians', *DOP* 23-4: 68–183.
(1987) 'The construction of court ritual: the Byzantine *Book of Ceremonies*', in D. Cannadine and S. Price (eds.) *Rituals of royalty: power and ceremonial in traditional societies*, Cambridge, 106–36.
(1994) 'The cult of the Virgin in late antiquity: religious development and myth-making', in Swanson, 1–21.
(1995) *Christianity and the rhetoric of empire: the development of Christian discourse*, Sather classical lectures 55, Berkeley, CA.
(1997) 'Eusebius' *Vita Constantini* and the construction of Constantine', in M. J. Edwards and S. Swain (eds.) *Portraits: biographical representation in the Greek and Latin literature of the Roman empire*, Oxford, 145–74.
(2003) 'How to read heresiology', *Journal of Medieval and Early Modern Studies* 33: 471–92 (repr. in D. B. Martin and P. Cox Miller [eds.] *The cultural turn in late ancient studies: gender, asceticism and historiography*, Durham, NC, 2005, 193–212).
(2004) 'Democratization revisited: culture and late antique and early Byzantine elites', in J. Haldon and L. I. Conrad (eds.) *Elites old and new in the Byzantine and early Islamic Near East: papers of the sixth workshop on late antiquity and early Islam*, Studies in late antiquity and early Islam 1, Princeton, NJ, 91–107.
(2008) 'The violence of orthodoxy', in E. Iricinschi and H. M. Zellentin (eds.) *Heresy and identity in late antiquity*, Texte und Studien zum antiken Judentum 119, Tübingen, 102–14.
Cameron, Averil and Garnsey, P. (eds.) (1998) *The Cambridge ancient history*, vol. xiii: *The later Roman empire, AD 337–425*, Cambridge.
Cameron, Averil and Hall, S. G. (1999) *Eusebius' Life of Constantine*, Oxford.

Cameron, Averil, Ward-Perkins, B. and Whitby, Michael (eds.) (2000) *The Cambridge ancient history,* vol. xiv: *Late antiquity: empire and successors,* AD 425–600, Cambridge.

Canepa, M. (2009) *The two eyes of the Earth: art and ritual of kingship between Rome and Sasanian Iran,* The transformation of the classical heritage 45, Berkeley, CA.

Caner, D. (2002) *Wandering, begging monks: spiritual authority and the promotion of monasticism in late antiquity,* The transformation of the classical heritage 33, Berkeley, CA.

Canivet, P. (2000) *Théodoret de Cyr. Thérapeutique des maladies helléniques,* SC 57.1, vol. 1, Paris.

Carrié, J.-M. (2001) 'Antiquité tardive et "démocratisation de la culture". Un paradigme à géométrie variable', *AntTard* 9: 27–46.

Chadwick, H. (1976) *Priscillian of Avila: the occult and the charismatic in the early Church,* Oxford.

(2001) *The Church in ancient society: from Galilee to Gregory the Great,* Oxford.

Chakrabarty, D. (1989) *Rethinking working-class history: Bengal, 1890–1940,* Princeton, NJ.

Charles, R. H. (1916) *The Chronicle of John, Bishop of Nikiu, translated from Zotenberg's Ethiopic text,* London.

Chesnut, G. F. (1986) *The first Christian histories: Eusebius, Socrates, Sozomen, Theodoret, and Evagrius,* 2nd edn, Macon, GA.

Chew, K. (2006) 'Virgins and eunuchs: Pulcheria, politics and the death of Emperor Theodosius II', *Historia* 55: 207–27.

Chin, C. M. (2008) *Grammar and Christianity in the late Roman world,* Philadelphia, PA.

Chrysos, E. (1983) 'Konzilsakten und Konzilsprotokolle vom 4. bis 7. Jahrhundert', *Annuarium Historiae Conciliorum* 15: 30–40.

Chuvin, P. (1991) *Mythologie et géographie dionysiaques. Recherches sur l'oeuvre de Nonnos de Panopolis,* Vates 2, Clermont-Ferrand.

Citroni Marchetti, S. (1991) *Plinio il Vecchio e la tradizione del moralismo romano,* Biblioteca di 'Materiali e discussioni per l'analisi dei testi classici' 9, Pisa.

Clark, E. A. (1992) *The Origenist controversy: the cultural construction of an early Christian debate,* Princeton, NJ.

Clarke, K. (2008) 'Text and image: mapping the Roman world', in F.-H. Mutschler and A. Mittag (eds.) *Conceiving the empire: China and Rome compared,* Oxford, 195–214.

Classen, C. J. (1991) 'Virtutes imperatoriae', *Arctos* 25: 17–39 (repr. in C. J. Classen, *Zur Literatur und Gesellschaft der Römer,* Stuttgart, 1998, 255–71).

Clauss, M. (1980) *Der magister officiorum in der Spätantike (4.–6. Jahrhundert). Das Amt und sein Einfluss auf die kaiserliche Politik,* Vestigia 32, Munich.

BIBLIOGRAPHY

Clemente, G. (2010) 'La *Notitia Dignitatum*. L'immagine e la realtà dell'impero tra IV e V secolo', in G. Bonamente and R. Lizzi Testa (eds.) *Istituzioni, carismi ed esercizio del potere, IV–VI secolo d.C.*, Munera 31, Bari, 117–32.

Clover, F. M. (1983) 'Olympiodorus of Thebes and the *Historia Augusta*', in G. Alföldy and J. Straub (eds.) *Bonner Historia-Augusta-Colloquium 1979–1981*, Antiquitas 4:15, Bonn, 127–56 (repr. in F. M. Clover, *The late Roman West and the Vandals*, Aldershot, 1993, no. XIII).

Conte, G. B. (1982) 'L'inventario del mondo. Ordine e linguaggio della natura nell'opera di Plinio il Vecchio', in A. Barchiesi, R. Centi *et al.* (eds.) *Gaio Plinio Secondo, Storia Naturale i. Cosmologia e geografia, libri 1–6*, Turin, xvii–xlvii (repr. as 'L'inventario del mondo. Forma della natura e progetto enciclopedico nell'opera di Plinio il Vecchio', in G. B. Conte, *Generi e lettori, Lucrezio, l'elegia d'amore, l'enciclopedia di Plinio*, Milan, 1991, 95–144 and G. B. Conte [trans. G. W. Most], *Genres and readers: Lucretius, love elegy, Pliny's Encyclopaedia*, Baltimore, MD, 1994, 67–104).

Cooper, K. (1998) 'Contesting the Nativity: wives, virgins, and Pulcheria's *imitatio Mariae*', *Scottish Journal of Religious Studies* 19: 31–43.

(2004) 'Empress and *Theotokos*: gender and patronage in the Christological controversy', in Swanson, 39–51.

(2009) 'Gender and the fall of Rome', in P. Rousseau (ed.) *A companion to late antiquity*, Chichester, 187–200.

Cox Miller, P. (2000) 'Strategies of representation in collective biography: constructing the subject as holy', in T. Hägg and P. Rousseau (eds.) *Greek biography and panegyric in late antiquity*, The transformation of the classical heritage 31, Berkeley, CA, 209–54.

Croke, B. (1977) 'Evidence for the Hun invasion of Thrace in AD 422', *GRBS* 18: 347–67 (repr. in Croke 1992, no. XII).

(1978) 'The date and circumstances of Marcion's decease', *Byzantion* 58: 5–9 (repr. in Croke 1992, no. VIII).

(1981) 'Two Byzantine earthquakes and their liturgical commemoration', *Byzantion* 51: 122–47 (repr. in Croke 1992, no. IX).

(1992) *Christian chronicles and Byzantine history, 5th–6th centuries*, Aldershot.

(1995) *The Chronicle of Marcellinus: a translation and commentary*, Australian Association for Byzantine Studies, Byzantina Australiensia 7, Sydney.

(2005) 'Dynasty and ethnicity: Emperor Leo I and the eclipse of Aspar', *Chiron* 35: 147–203.

(2010) 'Reinventing Constantinople: Theodosius I's imprint on the imperial city', in S. McGill, C. Sogno and E. Watts (eds.) *From the Tetrarchs to the Theodosians: later Roman history and culture, 284–450 CE*, Yale Classical Studies 34, Cambridge, 241–64.

Curran, J. (2012) 'Virgilizing Christianity in late antique Rome', in Grig and Kelly, 325–44.

Dagron, G. (1970) 'Les moines et la ville. Le monachisme à Constantinople jusqu'au concile de Chalcédoine (451)' *T&M* 4: 229–76.

BIBLIOGRAPHY

(1974a) 'L'auteur des "actes" et des "miracles" de Sainte Thècle', *AB* 92: 5–11.

(1974b) *Naissance d'une capitale. Constantinople et ses institutions de 330 à 451*, Bibliothèque byzantine études 7, Paris.

(1978) *Vie et miracles de Sainte Thècle. Texte grec, traduction et commentaire*, Subsidia Hagiographica 62, Brussels.

(1996) *Empereur et prêtre. Étude sur le «césaropapisme» byzantin*, Paris (trans. J. Birrell, *Emperor and priest: the imperial office in Byzantium*, Cambridge, 2003).

Davis, S. (2004) *The early Coptic Papacy: the Egyptian Church and its leadership in late antiquity*, Popes of Egypt 1, Cairo.

Dechow, J. F. (1988) *Dogma and mysticism in early Christianity: Epiphanius of Cyprus and the legacy of Origen*, Patristic monograph series 13, Macon, GA.

Demandt, A. (1969) 'Der Tod des älteren Theodosius', *Historia* 18: 598–626.

(1970) 'Magister militum', *RE Suppl. Bd* 12: 553–790.

(1980) 'Der spätrömische Militäradel', *Chiron* 10: 609–36.

Demangel, R. (1945) *Contribution à la topographie de l'Hebdomon*, Recherches françaises en Turquie 3, Paris.

Demoen, K. (2009) 'Poétique et rhétorique dans la poésie de Grégoire de Nazianze', in P. Odorico, P. A. Agapitos and M. Hinterberger (eds.) *'Doux remède ...': poésie et poétique à Byzance. Actes du IVe colloque international philologique "EPMHNEIA", Paris 23–24–25 février 2006*, Dossiers byzantins 6, Paris, 47–66.

Demougeot, E. (1985) 'L'évolution politique de Galla Placidia', *Gerión* 3: 183–210.

den Boeft, J., Drijvers, J. W., den Hengst, D. and Teitler, H. C. (1995) *Philological and historical commentary on Ammianus Marcellinus XXII*, Groningen.

Destephen, S. (2008) 'L'idée de représentativité dans les conciles théodosiens', *AntTard* 16: 103–18.

Diefenbach, S. (1996) 'Frömmigkeit und Kaiserakzeptanz im frühen Byzanz', *Saeculum* 47: 35–66.

(2002) 'Zwischen Liturgie und civilitas. Konstantinopel im 5. Jahrhundert und die Etablierung eines städtischen Kaisertums', in Warland, 21–49.

Dilke, O. A. W. (1987a) 'Cartography in the Byzantine empire', in Harley and Woodward, 258–85.

(1987b) 'Itineraries and geographical maps in the early and late Roman empires', in Harley and Woodward, 234–57.

Doody, A. (2010) *Pliny's encyclopaedia: the reception of the Natural History*, Cambridge.

Doran, R. (1992) *The Lives of Simeon Stylites*, Cistercian studies series 112, Kalamazoo, MI.

Dörrie H. and Dörries H. (1966) 'Erotapokriseis', *Reallexikon für Antike und Christentum* 6: 342–70.

BIBLIOGRAPHY

Drijvers, J. W. (1992) *Helena Augusta: the mother of Constantine the Great and the legend of her finding of the True Cross*, Brill's studies in intellectual history 27, Leiden.

(1993) 'Helena Augusta: exemplary Christian empress', *Studia Patristica* 24: 85–90.

Drinkwater, J. F. (1998) 'The usurpers Constantine III (407–411) and Jovinus (411–413)', *Britannia* 29: 269–98.

Driver, G. R. and Hodgson, L. (1925) *The bazaar of Heracleides*, Oxford.

Dummer, J. (1973) 'Ein naturwissenschaftliches Handbuch als Quelle für Epiphanius von Constantia', *Klio* 55: 289–99.

Dunn, G. (2005) 'The date of Innocent I's Epistula 12 and the second exile of John Chrysostom', *GRBS* 45: 155–70.

(2007) 'Innocent I and Anysius of Thessalonica', *Byzantion* 77: 124–48.

(2009) 'Innocent I and Rufus of Thessalonica', *JÖByz* 59: 51–64.

(2010) 'Innocent I, Alaric, and Honorius: church and state in early fifth-century Rome', in Luckensmeyer and Allen, 243–62.

du Plessis, P. J. (2009) 'The structure of the *Theodosian Code*', in J.-J. Aubert and P. Blanchard (eds.) *Droit, religion et société dans le Code Théodosien. Troisièmes journées d'étude sur le Code Théodosien, Neuchâtel, 15–17 février 2007*, Geneva, 3–17.

Dzielska, M. (1995) *Hypatia of Alexandria*, trans. F. Lyra, Revealing Antiquity 8, Cambridge, MA (first published as *Hypatia z Aleksandrii*, Krakow, 1993).

Edson, E. (2008) 'Maps in context: Isidore, Orosius, and the medieval image of the world', in Talbert and Unger, 219–36.

Elm, S., Rebillard, É. and Romano, A. (eds.) (2000) *Orthodoxie, christianisme, histoire*, Collection de l'École française de Rome 270, Rome.

Elton, H. (2009) 'Imperial politics at the court of Theodosius II', in Cain and Lenski, 133–42.

Errington, R. M. (1996) 'The accession of Theodosius I', *Klio* 78: 438–53.

(2006) *Roman imperial policy from Julian to Theodosius*, Chapel Hill, NC.

Ettlinger, G. H. (1975) *Theodoret of Cyrus, Eranistes: critical text and prolegomena*, Oxford.

(2003) *Theodoret of Cyrrhus, Eranistes*, Fathers of the Church 106, Washington, DC.

Evans Grubbs, J. (1995) *Law and family in late antiquity: the Emperor Constantine's marriage legislation*, Oxford.

Fairbairn, D. (2007) 'Allies or merely friends? John of Antioch and Nestorius in the Christological controversy', *JEH* 58: 383–99.

Faller, S. A. (2011) 'The world according to Cosmas Indicopleustes: concepts and illustrations of an Alexandrian merchant and monk', *Transcultural Studies* 2: 193–232.

Faulkner, A. (in press) 'Faith and fidelity in biblical epic: the *Metaphrasis Psalmorum*, Nonnus and the theory of translation', in K. Spanoudakis (ed.)

Nonnus of Panopolis in context: poetry and cultural milieu in late antiquity, Berlin.

Fear, A. T. (2010) *Orosius: Seven books of history against the pagans*, Translated texts for historians 54, Liverpool.

Fears, J. R. (1981) 'The cult of virtues and Roman imperial ideology', *ANRW* 2.17.2, 827–948.

Feissel, D. (1999) 'Deux grandes familles isauriennes du Ve siècle d'après des inscriptions de Cilicie Trachée', *MiChA* 5: 9–17.

Feld, K. (2005) *Barbarische Bürger. Die Isaurier und das Römische Reich*, Millennium-Studien 8, Berlin.

Festugière, A.-J. (1962) *Les moines de Palestine. La vie de saint Sabas* (= *Les moines d'Orient* vol. III.2), Paris.

Flower, R. (2007) 'Polemic and episcopal authority in fourth-century Christianity', PhD thesis, University of Cambridge.

   (2011) 'Genealogies of unbelief: Epiphanius of Salamis and heresiological authority', in C. M. Kelly, R. Flower and M. S. Williams (eds.) *Unclassical Traditions*, vol. II: *Perspectives from East and West in late antiquity, CCJ* supplementary volume 35, Cambridge, 70–87.

Fournet, J.-L. (2003) 'Théodore, un poète chrétien alexandrin oublié. L'hexamètre au service de la cause chrétienne', in D. Accorinti and P. Chuvin (eds.) *Des Géants à Dionysos. Mélanges de mythologie et de poésie grecques offerts à Francis Vian*, Hellenica 10, Alessandria, 521–39.

Fraisse-Coué, C. (1995) 'Le débat théologique au temps de Théodose II. Nestorius', in C. and L. Pietri (eds.) *Histoire du Christianisme des origines à nos jours*, vol. II. *Naissance d'une chrétienté (250–430)*, Paris, 499–550.

Frend, W. H. C. (1972) *The rise of the Monophysite movement*, Cambridge.

   (1984) *The rise of Christianity*, London.

   (1985) *The Donatist Church: a movement of protest in Roman North Africa*, 3rd edn, Oxford.

Friedländer, P. (1912) 'Die Chronologie des Nonnos von Panopolis', *Hermes* 47: 43–59.

Gaddis, M. (2005) *There is no crime for those who have Christ: religious violence in the Christian Roman empire*, The transformation of the classical heritage 39, Berkeley, CA.

Gautier Dalché, P. (1994–5) 'Notes sur la "carte de Théodose II" et sur la "mappemonde de Théodulf d'Orléans"', *Geographia antiqua* 3–4: 91–108 (repr. in Gautier Dalché 1997, no. IX).

   (1997) *Géographie et culture. La representation de l'espace du VIe au XIIe siècle*, Aldershot.

   (2003) 'Principes et modes de la représentation de l'espace géographique durant le Haut Moyen Âge', in *Uomo e spazio nell'alto medioevo*, Settimane di studio del Centro italiano di Studi sull'alto medioevo 50, 2 vols., Spoleto, 1 117–50.

   (2008) 'L'*Héritage* antique de la cartographie médiévale. Les problèmes et les acquis', in Talbert and Unger, 29–66.

BIBLIOGRAPHY

(2010) 'Eucher de Lyon, Iona, Bobbio. Le destin d'une *mappa mundi* de l'antiquité tardive', *Viator* 41.3: 1–22.
Gelzer, T. (1999) 'Das Gebet des Kaisers Theodosius in der Schlacht am Frigidus (Socr. h. e. 5, 25)', in E. Campi, L. Grane and A. M. Ritter (eds.) *Oratio. Das Gebet in patristischer und reformatorischer Sicht*, Forschungen zur Kirchen- und Dogmengeschichte 76, Göttingen, 53–72.
Gibbon, E. (1781a) *The history of the decline and fall of the Roman Empire*, vol. II, London.
(1781b) *The history of the decline and fall of the Roman Empire*, vol. III, London.
Gibson, B. (2010) 'Unending praise: Pliny and ending panegyric', in D. H. Berry and A. Erskine (eds.) *Form and Function in Roman Oratory*, Cambridge, 122–36.
Gillett, A. (1993) 'The date and circumstances of Olympiodorus of Thebes', *Traditio* 48: 1–29.
Glück, H, (1920) *Das Hebdomon und seine Reste in Makriköi. Untersuchungen zur Baukunst und Plastik von Konstantinopel*, Beiträge zur vergleichenden Kunstforschung 1, Vienna.
Golega, J. (1939) 'Verfasser und Zeit der Psalterparaphrase des Apolinarios', *ByzZ* 39: 1–22.
(1960) *Der homerische Psalter. Studien über die dem Apolinarios von Laodikeia zugeschriebene Psalmenparaphrase*, Studia patristica et byzantina 6, Ettal.
Gonnelli, F. (1989) 'Il psalterio esametrico I–II', *Koinonia* 13: 51–9, 127–51.
Graham, M. W. (2006) *News and frontier consciousness in the later Roman empire*, Ann Arbor, MI.
Graumann, T. (2002) *Die Kirche der Väter. Vätertheologie und Väterbeweis in den Kirchen des Ostens bis zum Konzil von Ephesus (431)*, Beiträge zur historischen Theologie 118, Tübingen.
(2007) 'Council proceedings and juridical process: the cases of Aquileia (AD 381) and Ephesus (AD 431)', in K. Cooper and J. Gregory (eds.) *Discipline and Diversity*, Studies in church history 43, Woodbridge, 100–13.
(2010) 'Protokollierung, Aktenerstellung und Dokumentation am Beispiel des Konzils von Ephesus (431)', *Annuarium Historiae Conciliorum* 42: 7–34.
Greatrex, G. (2001) 'Lawyers and historians in late antiquity', in R. Mathisen (ed.) *Law, society, and authority in late antiquity*, Oxford, 148–61.
(ed.) (2011) *The Chronicle of Pseudo-Zachariah Rhetor: church and war in late antiquity*, Translated texts for historians 55, Liverpool.
Greatrex, G. and Bardill, J. (1996) 'Antiochus the *praepositus*: a Persian eunuch at the court of Theodosius II', *DOP* 50: 171–97.
Greco, C. (2008) 'La cena di Betania e l'Ultima Cena. Esegesi cristiana e motivi dionisiaci in *Par*. M 7–16', in Audano, 43–55.
Green, J. A. and Tsafir, T. (1982) 'Greek inscriptions from Hammat Gader: a poem by the Empress Eudocia and two building inscriptions', *IEJ* 32: 77–96.

Green, R. P. H. (1995) 'Proba's Cento: its date, purpose, and reception', *CQ* 45: 551–63.
(1997) 'Proba's introduction to her Cento', *CQ* 47: 548–59.
(2006) *Latin epics of the New Testament: Juvencus, Sedulius, Arator*, Oxford.
Greenslade, S. L. (1964) *Schism in the early Church*, 2nd edn, London.
Grégoire, H. and Kugener, M.-A. (1930) *Marc le Diacre, Vie de Porphyre évêque de Gaza*, Paris.
Gregory, T. (1979) *Vox populi: popular opinion and violence in the religious controversies of the fifth century AD*, Columbus, OH.
Griffin, M. (2003) 'Clementia after Caesar: from politics to philosophy', in F. Cairns and E. Fantham (eds.) *Caesar against liberty? Perspectives on his autocracy*, ARCA, classical and medieval texts, papers and monographs 43, Papers of the Langford Latin Seminar 11, Liverpool, 157–82.
Grig, L. and Kelly, G. A. J. (eds.) (2012) *Two Romes: Rome and Constantinople in late antiquity*, New York/Oxford.
Grimal, P. (1966) 'Encyclopédies antiques', *Journal of World History* 9: 459–82.
Groß-Albenhausen, K. (1999) *Imperator christianissimus. Der christliche Kaiser bei Ambrosius und Johannes Chrysostomus*, Frankfurter althistorische Beiträge 3, Frankfurt.
Habas, E. (1996) 'A poem by the empress Eudocia: a note on the patriarch', *IEJ* 46: 108–19.
Hadjittofi, F. (2011) 'Nonnus' unclassical epic: imaginary geography in the *Dionysiaca*', in C. M. Kelly, R. Flower and M. S. Williams (eds.) *Unclassical traditions*, vol. II: *Perspectives from East and West in late antiquity, CCJ* supplementary volume 35, Cambridge, 29–42.
Hadot, I. (1998) 'Les aspects sociaux et institutionnels des sciences et de la médécine dans l'antiquité tardive', *AntTard* 6: 233–50.
Haedicke, W. (1939) 'Olympiodorus (von Theben)', *RE* 18: 201–7.
Hahn, J. (2008) 'The conversion of the cult statues: the destruction of the Serapeum 392 AD and the transformation of Alexandria into the "Christ-loving" city', in J. Hahn, S. Emmel and U. Gotter (eds.) *From temple to church: destruction and renewal of local cultic topography in late antiquity*, Religions in the Graeco-Roman world 163, Leiden, 335–66.
Hans, L.-M. (1988) 'Der Kaiser als Märchenprinz. Brautschau und Heiratspolitik in Konstantinopel 395–882', *JÖByz* 38: 33–52.
Hanson, R. P. C. (1988) *The search for the Christian doctrine of God: the Arian controversy, 318–381*, Edinburgh.
Harley, J. B. and Woodward, D. (eds.) (1987) *The history of cartography*, vol. I: *Cartography in prehistoric, ancient, and medieval Europe and the Mediterranean*, Chicago, IL.
Harmless, W. (2004) *Desert Christians: an introduction to the literature of early monasticism*, Oxford.
Harries, J. (1986) 'Sozomen and Eusebius: the lawyer as church historian in the fifth century', in C. Holdsworth and T. P. Wiseman (eds.) *The inheritance of historiography 350–900*, Exeter studies in history 12, Exeter, 45–52.

(1988) 'The Roman imperial quaestor from Constantine to Theodosius II', *JRS* 78: 148–72.

(1993) 'Introduction: the background to the Code', in Harries and Wood, 1–16.

(1994) '"Pius princeps": Theodosius II and fifth-century Constantinople', in P. Magdalino (ed.) *New Constantines: the rhythm of imperial renewal in Byzantium, 4th–13th centuries: papers from the twenty-sixth spring symposium of Byzantine studies, St Andrews, March 1992*, Aldershot, 35–44.

(1997) 'Roman law codes and the Roman legal tradition'. in J. W. Cairns and P. J. du Plessis (eds.) *Beyond dogmatics: law and society in the Roman world*, Edinburgh studies in law 3, 85–104.

(1999) *Law and empire in late antiquity*, Cambridge.

Harries, J. and Wood, I. (eds.) (1993) *The Theodosian Code: studies in the imperial law of late antiquity*, London (2nd edn, 2010).

Hau, L. I. (2009) 'The burden of good fortune in Diodoros of Sicily: a case for originality?', *Historia* 58: 171–97.

Heath, M. (2004) *Menander: a rhetor in context*, Oxford.

Hefele, C. J. and Leclercq, H. (1908) *Histoire des conciles d'après les documents originaux*, vol. II.1. Paris.

Hemmerdinger, N. (1966) 'Les lettres latines à Constantinople jusqu'à Justinien', in P. Wirth (ed.) *Polychordia. Festschrift Franz Dölger zum 75. Geburstag*, vol. I (= *Byzantinische Forschungen* I), 174–8.

Herrin, J. (2001) *Women in purple: rulers of medieval Byzantium*, Princeton, NJ.

Heyden, K. (2006) 'Die *Christliche Geschichte* des Philippos von Side. Mit einem kommentierten Katalog der Fragmente', in M. Wallraff (ed.) *Julius Africanus und die christliche Weltchronistik*, Texte und Untersuchungen zur Geschichte der altchristlichen Literatur 157, Berlin, 209–43.

Heylen, F. (1957) *Filastrii episcopi Brixiensis diversarum hereseon liber*, CCSL 9, Turnhout, 207–324.

Hiatt, A. (2007) 'The Map of Macrobius before 1100', *Imago Mundi* 59: 149–76.

Hollerich, M. (1989) 'The comparison of Moses and Constantine in Eusebius' *Life of Constantine*', *Studia Patristica* 19: 80–95.

Holliday, P. J. (1997) 'Roman triumphal painting: its function, development, and reception', *Art Bulletin* 79: 130–47.

Holum, K. G. (1977) 'Pulcheria's crusade AD 421–22 and the ideology of imperial victory', *GRBS* 18: 153–72.

(1982) *Theodosian empresses: women and imperial dominion in late antiquity*, The transformation of the classical heritage 3, Berkeley, CA.

Honoré, T. (1986) 'The making of the Theodosian Code', *ZRG* 103: 133–222.

(1998) *Law in the crisis of empire, 379–455 AD: the Theodosian dynasty and its quaestors*, Oxford.

Horn, C. B. (2006) *Asceticism and Christological controversy in fifth-century Palestine: the career of Peter the Iberian*, Oxford.

BIBLIOGRAPHY

Horn, C. B. and Phenix, R. R. (2008) *John Rufus: the Lives of Peter the Iberian, Theodosius of Jerusalem and the Monk Romanus*, Writings from the Greco-Roman world 24, Leiden.
Hostein, A. (2012) *La cité et l'Empereur. Les Éduens dans l'Empire romain d'après les Panégyriques latins*, Paris.
Howard-Johnston, J. (1995) 'The two great powers in late antiquity: a comparison', in Averil Cameron (ed.) *The Byzantine and early Islamic Near East: papers of the third workshop on late antiquity and early Islam: states, resources and armies*, Studies in late antiquity and early Islam 1, Princeton, NJ, 157–226 (repr. in J. Howard-Johnston, *East Rome, Sasanian Persia and the end of antiquity: historiographical and historical studies*, Aldershot, 2006, no. 1).
Howe, N. P. (1985) 'In defense of the encyclopedic mode: on Pliny's Preface to the Natural History', *Latomus* 44: 561–76.
Humfress, C. (2000) 'Roman law, forensic argument and the formation of Christian orthodoxy (III–VI centuries)', in Elm, Rebillard and Romano, 125–47.
Humphries, M. (2007) 'A new created world: classical geographical texts and Christian contexts in late antiquity', in Scourfield 2007a, 33–67.
  (2012) 'Valentinian III and the city of Rome (425–55): patronage, politics, power', in Grig and Kelly, 161–82.
Hunt, E. D. (1982) *Holy Land pilgrimage in the later Roman empire, AD 312–460*, Oxford.
Ilski, B. K. (2005) 'Der schwache Kaiser Theodosios?', in L. M. Hoffman and A. Monchizadeh (eds.) *Zwischen Polis, Provinz und Peripherie. Beiträge zur byzantinischen Geschichte und Kultur*, Mainzer Veröffentlichungen zur Byzantinistik 7, Wiesbaden, 3–23.
Inglebert, H. (2001) *Interpretatio christiana. Les mutations des savoirs (cosmographie, géographie, ethnographie, histoire) dans l'antiquité chrétienne (30–630 après J.-C.)*, Collection des Études augustiniennes, série antiquité 166, Paris.
Innes, D. C. (2011) 'The *Panegyricus* and rhetorical theory', in Roche 2011a, 67–84.
Ireland, R. (1979) 'The transmission of the text', in R. Ireland (ed.), *De rebus bellicis (papers presented to E. A. Thompson)*, part 2: *The text*, British Archaeological Reports, international series 63, Oxford, 39–78.
Janin, R. (1964) *Constantinople byzantine. Développement urbain et répertoire topographique*, Archives de l'Orient chrétien 4A, 2nd edn, Paris.
  (1966) 'Les processions religieuses à Byzance', *REByz* 24: 69–88.
  (1969) *La géographie ecclésiastique de l'Empire byzantin: première partie, le siège de Constantinople et le patriarcat œcuménique, vol. iii: Les églises et les monastères*, 2nd edn, Paris.
Jannaccone, S. (1952) *La dottrina eresiologica di S. Agostino. Studio di storia letteraria e religiosa a proposito del trattato De Haeresibus*, Raccolta di studi di letteratura cristiana antica 20, Catania.

BIBLIOGRAPHY

Janni, P. (1984) *La mappa e il periplo. Cartografia antica e spazio odologico*, Pubblicazioni della Facoltà di lettere e filosofia, Università di Macerata 19, Rome.
Janssen, T. (2004) *Stilicho. Das weströmische Reich vom Tode des Theodosius bis zur Ermordung Stilichos (395–408)*, Marburg.
Janvier, Y. (1982) *La géographie d'Orose*, Paris.
Johnson, S. F. (ed.) (2006a) *Greek literature in late antiquity: dynamism, didacticism, classicism*, Aldershot.
(2006b) 'Introduction', in Johnson 2006a, 1–8.
(2006c) *The Life and Miracles of Thekla: a literary study*, Hellenic studies 13, Washington, DC.
Jones, A. H. M. (1964) *The later Roman empire, 284–602: a social, economic, and administrative survey*, 3 vols., Oxford.
(1971) *The cities of the eastern Roman provinces*, 2nd edn, Oxford.
Kaegi, W. E. (1968) *Byzantium and the decline of Rome*, Princeton, NJ.
Katos, D. C. (2007) 'Socratic dialogue or forensic debate? Judicial rhetoric and stasis theory in the *Dialogue on the Life of St John Chrysostom*', *VChr* 61: 42–69.
(2011) *Palladius of Helenopolis: the Origenist advocate*, Oxford.
Kelly, C. M. (1998) 'Emperors, government and bureaucracy', in Cameron and Garnsey, 138–83.
(2004) *Ruling the later Roman empire*, Revealing antiquity 15, Cambridge, MA.
(2009) *The end of empire: Attila the Hun and the fall of Rome*, New York.
Kelly, G. A. J. (2007a) 'The sphragis and closure of the *Res gestae*', in J. den Boeft, D. den Hengst, H. C. Teitler and J. W. Drijvers (eds.) *Ammianus after Julian: the reign of Valentinian and Valens in Books 26–31 of the Res gestae*, Mnemosyne supplement 289, Leiden, 219–41.
(2007b) '"To forge their tongues to grander styles": Ammianus' epilogue', in J. Marincola (ed.) *A companion to Greek and Roman historiography*, 2 vols., Oxford, II 474–82.
(2008) *Ammianus Marcellinus: the allusive historian*, Cambridge.
Kelly, J. N. D. (1972) *Early Christian creeds*, 3rd edn, London.
(1995) *Golden mouth: the story of John Chrysostom: ascetic, preacher, bishop*, London.
Kent, J. P. C. (1994) *Roman imperial coinage*, vol. X: *The divided empire and the fall of the western parts, AD 395–491*, London.
Kidd, B. J. (1922) *A history of the Church to AD 461*, vol. III: *AD 408–461*, Oxford.
König, J. and Whitmarsh, T. (eds.) (2007a) *Ordering knowledge in the Roman empire*, Cambridge.
(2007b) 'Ordering knowledge', in König and Whitmarsh 2007a, 3–39.
Konstan, D. (2005) 'Clemency as a virtue', *CPh* 100: 337–46.
Krivushin, I. (1996) 'Socrates Scholasticus' *Church History*: themes, ideas, heroes', *ByzF* 23: 95–107.

BIBLIOGRAPHY

Kulikowski, M. (2000a) 'Barbarians in Gaul, usurpers in Britain', *Britannia* 31: 325–45.
    (2000b) 'The *Notita Dignitatum* as a historical source', *Historia* 49: 358–77.
Labriolle, P. de (1913) *Les sources de l'histoire du montanisme*, Collectanea Friburgensia n.s. 15, Fribourg.
La Bua, G. (2010) 'Patronage and education in third-century Gaul: Eumenius' Panegyric for the Restoration of the Schools', *JLA* 3: 300–15.
Lanata, G. (1994) *Società e diritto nel mondo tardo antico. Sei saggi sulle Novelle giustinianee*, Turin.
Leader-Newby, R. (2004) *Silver and society in late antiquity: functions and meanings of silver plate in the fourth to seventh centuries*, Aldershot.
Lee, A. D. (1993) *Information and frontiers: Roman foreign relations in late antiquity*, Cambridge.
    (1998) 'The army', in Cameron and Garnsey, 211–37.
    (2000) 'The eastern empire: Theodosius to Anastasius', in Cameron, Ward-Perkins and Whitby, 33–62.
    (2002) 'Decoding late Roman law', (review of Harries 1999; Honoré 1998; Matthews 2000) *JRS* 92: 185–93.
    (2007) *War in late antiquity: a social history*, Oxford.
    (in press) 'Emperors and generals from Constantine to Theodosius', in J. Wienand (ed.) *Contested monarchy: integrating the Roman empire in the fourth century AD*, New York/Oxford.
Lemerle, P. (1971) *Le premier humanisme byzantin. Notes et remarques sur enseignement et culture à Byzance des origines au Xe siècle*, Paris.
    (1986) *Byzantine humanism, the first phase: notes and remarks on education and culture in Byzantium from its origins to the 10th century*, trans. H. Lindsay and A. Moffatt, Byzantina Australiensia 3, Canberra (first published as Lemerle 1971).
Lenski, N. (1999) 'Assimilation and revolt in the territory of Isauria, from the 1st century BC to the 6th century AD', *JESHO* 42: 413–65.
    (2002) *Failure of empire: Valens and the Roman state in the fourth century AD*, The transformation of the classical heritage 34, Berkeley, CA.
Leppin, H. (1996) *Von Constantin dem Grossen zu Theodosius II. Das christliche Kaisertum bei den Kirchenhistorikern Socrates, Sozomenus und Theodoret*, Hypomnemata 110, Göttingen.
    (2003a) *Theodosius der Grosse*, Darmstadt.
    (2003b) 'The church historians (1): Socrates, Sozomenus, and Theodoretus', in Marasco, 219–54.
    (2009) 'Power from humility: Justinian and the religious authority of monks', in Cain and Lenski, 155–64.
Levi, M. and Levi, A. (1974) 'The medieval map of Rome in the Ambrosian Library's manuscript of Solinus (C 246 Inf.)', *PAPhS* 118: 567–94.
Levick, B. (1990) *Claudius*, London.
Liebeschuetz, J. H. W. G. (1990) *Barbarians and bishops: army, church, and state in the age of Arcadius and Chrysostom*, Oxford.

(1993) 'Ecclesiastical historians on their own times', *Studia Patristica*, 24: 151–63.
Lim, R. (1991) 'Theodoret of Cyrrhus and the speakers in Greek dialogues', *JHS* 111: 181–2.
(1995) *Public disputation, power, and social order in late antiquity*, The transformation of the classical heritage 23, Berkeley, CA.
Lippold, A. (1973) 'Theodosius II', *RE Suppl.* 13, 961–1044.
Livrea, E. (1978) *Anonymi fortasse Olympiodori Thebani Blemyomachia (P. Berol. 5003)*, Beiträge zur klassischen Philologie 101, Meisenheim am Glan.
(1989) *Nonno di Panopoli, Parafrasi del Vangelo di S. Giovanni, canto XVIII. Introduzione, testo critico, traduzione e commento*, Speculum contribute di filologia classica 9, Naples.
(1998) 'L'imperatrice Eudocia e Roma. Per un datazione del *de S. Cypr.*', *ByzZ* 91: 70–91.
(2000) *Nonno di Panopoli, Parafrasi del Vangelo di S. Giovanni, canto B. Introduzione, testo critico, traduzione e commento*, Biblioteca patristica 36, Bologna.
Long, J. (1996a) *Claudian's In Eutropium: or, how, when, and why to slander a eunuch*, Chapel Hill, NC.
(1996b) 'Juvenal renewed in Claudian's *In Eutropium*', *IJCT* 2: 321–35.
Loofs, F. (ed.) (1905) *Nestoriana: die Fragmente des Nestorius*, Halle.
Lozofsky, N. (2000) *The Earth is our book: geographical knowledge in the Latin West ca. 400–1000*, Ann Arbor, MI.
(2008) 'Maps and panegyrics: Roman geo-ethnographical rhetoric in late antiquity and the middle ages', in Talbert and Unger, 169–88.
Luckensmeyer, D. and Allen, P. (eds.) (2010) *Studies in religion and politics in the early Christian centuries*, Early Christian studies 13, Strathfield, NSW.
Ludwich, A. (1897) *Eudociae Augustae, Procli Lycii, Claudiani carminum graecorum reliquiae, accedunt Blemyomachiae fragmenta*, Leipzig.
Luibhéid, C. (1965) 'Theodosius II and heresy', *JEH* 16: 13–38.
Lusnia, S. S. (2006) 'Battle imagery and politics on the Severan Arch in the Roman Forum', in S. Dillon and K. E. Welch (eds.) *Representations of war in Ancient Rome*, Cambridge, 272–99.
Lütkenhaus, W. (1998) *Constantius III. Studien zu seiner Tätigkeit und Stellung im Westreich 411–421*, Habelts Dissertationsdrucke, Reihe Alte Geschichte 44, Bonn.
Lyman, J. R. (1997) 'The making of a heretic: the life of Origen in Epiphanius, *Panarion* 64', *Studia Patristica* 31: 445–51.
(1999) 'Origen as ascetic theologian: orthodoxy and authority in the fourth-century Church', in W. A. Bienart and U. Kühneweg (eds.) *Origeniana septima. Origenes in den Auseinandersetzungen des 4. Jahrhunderts*, Bibliotheca ephemeridum theologicarum Lovaniensium 137, Leuven, 187–94.

BIBLIOGRAPHY

(2000) 'Ascetics and bishops: Epiphanius on orthodoxy', in Elm, Rebillard and Romano, 149–61.
Maas, M. (2007) 'Strabo and Procopius: classical geography for a Christian empire', in H. Amirav and B. ter Haar Romeny (eds.) *From Rome to Constantinople: studies in honour of Averil Cameron*, Late antique history and religion 1, Leuven, 67–83.
MacCormack, S. (1972) 'Change and continuity in late antiquity: the ceremony of *adventus*', *Historia* 21: 721–52.
(1975) 'Latin prose panegyrics', in T. A. Dorey (ed.) *Empire and aftermath: silver Latin II*, London, 143–205.
(1981) *Art and ceremony in late antiquity*, The transformation of the classical heritage 1, Berkeley, CA.
Machado, C. (2012) 'Aristocratic houses and the making of late antique Rome and Constantinople', in Grig and Kelly, 136–58.
Maenchen-Helfen, O. (1973) *The world of the Huns: studies in their history and culture*, Berkeley, CA.
Maguinness, W. S. (1933) 'Locutions and formulae of the Latin panegyrists', *Hermathena* 48: 117–38.
Maisano, R. (1979) *Olimpiodoro tebano, frammenti storici*, Quaderni di *Koinonia* a cura dell' Associazione di studi tardoantichi 4, Naples.
Malamud, M. A. (1989) *A poetics of transformation: Prudentius and classical mythology*, Cornell studies in classical philology 49, Ithaca, NY.
Mango, C. (2004) 'A fake inscription of the empress Eudocia and Pulcheria's relic of Saint Stephen', Νέα Ῥώμη 1: 23–34.
Mango, C. and Scott, R. (1997) *The Chronicle of Theophanes Confessor: Byzantine and Near Eastern history AD 284–813*, Oxford.
Mann, J. C. (1991) 'The *Notitia Dignitatum*: dating and survival', *Britannia* 22: 215–19 (repr. in J. C. Mann, *Britain and the Roman empire*, Aldershot, 1996, no. XXXVII).
Marasco, G. (ed.) (2003) *Greek and Roman historiography in late antiquity: fourth to sixth century AD*, Leiden.
Maraval, P. and Périchon, P. (2004–7) *Socrate de Constantinople, Histoire ecclésiastique*, 4 vols., SC 477, 493, 506 and 507, Paris.
Marcotte, D. (2007) 'Le corpus géographique d'Heidelberg (*Palat. Heidelb. Gr.* 398) et les origines de la "collection philosophique"', in C. D'Ancona Costa (ed.) *The libraries of the Neoplatonists*, Philosophia antiqua 107, Leiden, 167–75.
(2010) 'Une carte inédite dans les scholies aux *Halieutiques* d'Oppien. Contribution à l'histoire de la géographie sous les premiers Paléologues', *REG* 123: 641–59.
Mastandrea, P. (2001) 'L'epigramma dedicatorio del "Cento Vergilianus" di Proba (*AL* 719d Riese²). Analisi del testo, ipotesi di datazione e identificazione dell'autore', *BStudLat* 31: 565–78.
Matthews, J. F. (1970) 'Olympiodorus of Thebes and the history of the West (AD 407–425)', *JRS* 60: 79–97 (repr. in J. F. Matthews, *Political life and culture in late Roman society*, London, 1985, no. III).

(1975) *Western aristocracies and imperial court AD 364–425*, Oxford (rev. edn 1990).
(1989) *The Roman Empire of Ammianus*, London.
(1993) 'The making of the text', in Harries and Wood, 19–44.
(2000) *Laying down the law: a study of the Theodosian Code*, New Haven, CT.
(2012) 'The *Notitia Urbis Constantinopolitanae*', in Grig and Kelly, 81–115.
Mayer, W. (2004) 'John Chrysostom as bishop: the view from Antioch', *JEH* 55: 455–66.
(2008) 'The making of a saint: John Chrysostom in early historiography', in Wallraff and Brändle, 39–59.
Mayer, W. and Allen, P. (2000) *John Chrysostom*, London.
Mazza, M. (2004) 'Bisanzio e Persia nella tarda antichità. Guerra e diplomazia da Arcadio a Zenone', in *Convegno internazionale: la Persia e Bisanzio (Roma, 14–18 ottobre 2002)*, Atti dei convegni Lincei 201, Rome, 39–76.
Mazzarino, S. (1942) *Stilicone. La crisi imperiale dopo Teodosio*, Studi pubblicati dal R. Istituto italiano per la storia antica 3, Rome.
(1960) 'La democratizzazione della cultura nel "basso impero"', in *Rapports du XIe congrès international des sciences historiques, Stockholm, 21–28 août 1960*, Göteborg, 5 vols., II 35–54 (repr. in S. Mazzarino, *Antico, tardoantico ed èra costantiniana*, vol. I, Storia e civiltà 13, Bari, 1974, 74–98).
McClure, J. (1979) 'Handbooks against heresy in the West, from the late fourth to the late sixth centuries', *JThS* 30: 186–97.
McCormick, M. (1985) 'Analyzing imperial ceremonies', *JÖByz* 35: 1–20.
(1986) *Eternal victory: triumphal rulership in late antiquity, Byzantium and the early medieval West*, Cambridge.
(2000) 'Emperor and court', in Cameron, Ward-Perkins and Whitby, 135–63.
McGill, S. (2005) *Virgil recomposed: the mythological and secular centos in antiquity*, American Philological Association, American classical studies 48, Oxford.
(2007) 'Virgil, Christianity, and the *Cento Probae*', in Scourfield 2007a, 173–93.
McGuckin, J. A. (1994) *St Cyril of Alexandria: the Christological controversy: its history, theology and texts*, Supplements to *Vigiliae Christianae* 23, Leiden.
(1996) 'Nestorius and the political factions of fifth-century Byzantium: factors in his personal downfall', *BRL* 78.3: 7–21.
McLynn, N. B. (1994) *Ambrose of Milan: church and court in a Christian capital*, The transformation of the classical heritage 22, Berkeley, CA.
(2004) 'The transformation of imperial churchgoing in the fourth century', in Swain and Edwards, 235–70 (repr. in McLynn 2009, no. I).
(2006) 'Among the Hellenists: Gregory and the sophists', in J. Børtnes and T. Hägg (eds.) *Gregory of Nazianzus: images and reflections*, Copenhagen, 213–38 (repr. in McLynn 2009, no. VIII).
(2009) *Christian politics and religious culture in late Antiquity*, Farnham.

BIBLIOGRAPHY

(2012) '"Two Romes, beacons of the whole world": canonizing Constantinople', in Grig and Kelly, 345–63.

Meier, M. (2003) 'Göttlicher Kaiser und christlicher Herrscher? Die christlichen Kaiser der Spätantike und ihre Stellung zu Gott', *Das Altertum* 48: 129–60.

(2007) 'Die Demut des Kaisers. Aspekte der religiösen Selbtstinszenierung bei Theodosius II. (408–450 n. Chr.)', in A. Pečar and K. Trampedach (eds.) *Die Bibel als politisches Argument. Voraussetzungen und Folgen biblizistischer Herrschaftslegitimation in der Vormoderne*, Historiche Zeitschrift Beiheft (n.F.) 43, Munich, 135–58.

(2011) '"Ein dogmatischer Streit". Eduard Schwartz (1858–1940) und die "Reichskonzilien" in der Spätantike', *ZAC* 15: 124–39.

Merrills, A. H. (2005) *History and geography in late antiquity*, Cambridge studies in medieval life and thought 64, Cambridge.

Miguélez Cavero, L. (2008) *Poems in context: Greek poetry in the Egyptian Thebaid 200–600 AD*, Sozomena: studies in the recovery of ancient texts 2, Berlin.

Millar, F. (1982) 'Emperors, frontiers and foreign relations 31 BC to AD 378', *Britannia* 13: 1–23 (repr. in *Rome, the Greek world, and the East*, vol. II: *Government, society, and culture in the Roman empire*, ed. H. M. Cotton and G. M. Rodgers, Chapel Hill, NC, 2004, 160–94).

(1992) *The emperor in the Roman world (31 BC–AD 337)*, 2nd edn, London.

(2006) *A Greek Roman empire: power and belief under Theodosius II (408–450)*, Sather classical lectures 64, Berkeley, CA.

Miller, K. (1895) *Mappae mundi. Die ältesten Weltkarten*, vol. III: *Die kleineren Weltkarten*, Stuttgart.

Mitchell, S. (2007) *A history of the later Roman empire, AD 284–641*, Oxford.

Molè Ventura, C. (1992) *Principi fanciulli. Legittimismo costituzionale e storiografia cristiana nella tarda antichità*, Testi e studi di storia antica 2, Catania.

Moorhead, J. (1992) *Theoderic in Italy*, Oxford.

Morin, G. (1907) 'Le *Liber dogmatum* de Gennade de Marseille et problèmes qui s'y rattachent', *RBen* 24: 445–55.

Müller, L. G. (1956) *The De Haeresibus of Saint Augustine: a translation with an introduction and commentary*, The Catholic University of America, Patristic studies 90, Washington, DC.

Murphy, T. M. (2004) *Pliny the Elder's Natural History: the empire in the encyclopedia*, Oxford.

Nau, F. (1903) 'Histoire de Dioscore, patriarche d'Alexandrie', *Journal Asiatique* (10e sér.) 1: 5–108 (introduction and text), 241–310 (trans.).

(1914) 'Résumé de monographies syriaques', *Revue de l'Orient chrétien* 19: 113–24, 279–89.

Neira Faleiro, C. (2005) *La Notitia Dignitatum. Nueva edición crítica y comentario histórico*, Nueva Roma 25, Madrid.

BIBLIOGRAPHY

Nicolet, C. (1991) *Space, geography, and politics in the early Roman empire*, Jerome Lectures 19, trans. H. Leclerc, Ann Arbor, MI (first published as *L'inventaire du monde*. *Géographie et politique aux origines de l'empire romain*, Paris, 1988).

Nicolet, C, and Gautier Dalché, P. (1986) 'Les "quatre sages" de Jules César et la "mesure du monde" selon Julius Honorius. Réalité antique et tradition médiévale', *JS* 157–218 (repr. in Gautier Dalché 1997, no. VIII).

Nixon, C. E. V. (1990) 'The use of the past by the Gallic panegyricists', in G. W. Clarke (ed.) *Reading the past in late antiquity*, Rushcutters Bay, NSW, 1–36.

Nixon, C. E. V. and Rodgers, B. S. (1994) *In praise of later Roman emperors: the Panegyrici Latini: introduction, translation, and historical commentary*, The transformation of the classical heritage 21, Berkeley, CA.

Noreña, C. (2001) 'The communication of the emperor's virtues', *JRS* 91: 146–68.

(2011) 'Self-fashioning in the *Panegyricus*', in Roche 2011a, 29–44.

O'Flynn, J. M. (1983) *Generalissimos of the western Roman empire*, Edmonton.

Ohme, H. (1998) *Kanon ekklesiastikos. Die Bedeutung des altkirchlichen Kanonbegriffs*, Arbeiten zur Kirchengeschichte 67, Berlin.

Oost, S. I. (1968) *Galla Placidia Augusta: a biographical essay*, Chicago.

Östenberg, I. (2009) *Staging the world: spoils, captives and representations in the Roman triumphal procession*, Oxford.

Painter, K. (1991–2) 'The silver dish of Ardabur Aspar', in E. Herring, R. Whitehouse and J. Wilkins (eds.) *Papers of the Fourth Conference of Italian Archaeology*, 4 vols., London, II 73–80.

Palme, B. (2007) 'The imperial presence: government and army', in Bagnall, 244–70.

Panaino, A. (2004) 'Astral characters of kingship in the Sasanian and Byzantine worlds', in *Convegno internazionale, la Persia e Bisanzio (Roma, 14–18 ottobre 2002)*, Atti dei convegni Lincei 201, Rome, 555–94.

Panciera, S. (1996) 'Petronio Massimo precettore di Valentiniano III', in C. Stella and A. Valvo (eds.) *Studi in onore di Albino Garzetti*, Brescia, 277–97 (repr. in S. Panciera, *Epigrafi, epigrafia, epigrafisti. Scritti vari editi e inediti (1956–2005) con note complementari e indici*, 3 vols., Rome 2006, II 1153–66).

Papadoyannakis, Y. (2006) 'Instruction by question and answer: the case of late antique and Byzantine *Eratopokriseis*', in Johnson 2006a, 91–105.

Paschoud, F. (1975) *Cinq études sur Zosime*, Paris.

(1985) 'Le début de l'ouvrage d'Olympiodore', in *Studia in honorem Iiro Kajanto, Arctos*, Acta Philologica Fennica, Supplementa 2, Helsinki, 185–96 (repr. in Paschoud 2006b, 143–51).

(1986) *Zosime, Histoire nouvelle*, vol. III, part 1, Book V, Paris.

(1989) *Zosime, Histoire nouvelle*, vol. III, part 2, Book VI and index, Paris.

BIBLIOGRAPHY

(2005) 'Biographie und Panegyricus: wie spricht man vom lebenden Kaiser?', in K. Vössing (ed.) *Biographie und Prosopographie. Internationales Kolloquium zum 65. Geburtstag von Anthony R. Birley, 28. September 2002, Schloss Mickeln, Düsseldorf, Historia* Einzelschriften 178, Stuttgart, 103–18.

(2006a) 'Cinq études sur Zosime (Paris, 1975)', in Paschoud 2006b, 63–75.

(2006b) *Eunape, Olympiodore, Zosime: scripta minora. Recueil d'articles, avec addenda, corrigenda, mise à jour et indices*, Bari.

Pásztori-Kupán, I. (2006) *Theodoret of Cyrus*, London.

Patlagean, E. (1966) 'Une représentation byzantine de la parenté et ses origines occidentales', *L'homme* 6.4: 59–81 (repr. in E. Patlagean, *Structure sociale, famille, chrétienté à Byzance: IVe au XIe siècle*, London, 1981, no. 1).

Pazdernik, C.F. (2009) 'Paying attention to the man behind the curtain: disclosing and withholding the imperial presence in Justinianic Constantinople', in T. Fögen and M. M. Lee (eds.) *Bodies and boundaries in Graeco-Roman antiquity*, Berlin, 63–85.

(2012) '"How then is it not better to prefer quiet, than the dangers of conflict?": the imperial court as the site of shifting cultural frontiers', in D. Brakke, D. Deliyannis and E. Watts (eds.) *Shifting cultural frontiers in late antiquity*, Farnham, 99–111.

Perrone, L. (1993). 'Da Nicea (325) a Calcedonia (451). I primi quattro concili ecumenici: istituzioni, dottrine, processi di ricezione', in G. Alberigo (ed.) *Storia dei concili ecumenici*, 2nd edn, Brescia, 11–118.

Pharr, C. (1952) *The Theodosian Code and Novels and the Sirmondian Constitutions*, Princeton, NJ.

Pietri, C. (1976) *Roma Christiana. Recherches sur l'Église de Rome, son organisation, sa politique, son idéologie de Miltiade à Sixte III (311–440)*, Bibliothèque des écoles françaises d'Athènes et de Rome, 224, Rome.

Pigani, A. (1985) 'Il modello omerico e la fonte biblica nel centone di Eudocia imperatrice', *Koinonia* 9: 33–41.

Podossinov, A. V. and Chekin, L. S. (1991) review of Harley and Woodward, *Imago Mundi* 43: 112–23.

Pollmann, K. (2004) 'Sex and salvation in the Vergilian *cento* of the fourth century', in R. Rees (ed.) *Romane memento: Vergil in the fourth century*, London, 79–96.

Pontani, F. (2010) 'The world on a fingernail: an unknown Byzantine map, Planudes, and Ptolemy', *Traditio* 65: 177–200.

Pourkier, A. (1992) *L'hérésiologie chez Épiphane de Salamine*, Christianisme antique 4, Paris.

Price, R. M. (1994) 'Marian piety and the Nestorian controversy', in Swanson, 31–8.

Price, R. M. and Gaddis, M. (2005) *The Acts of the Council of Chalcedon*, Translated texts for historians 45, 3 vols., Liverpool.

Purpura, G. (1995) 'Sulle origini della *Notitia dignitatum*', in *Atti dell'Accademia romanistica costantiniana. X convegno internazionale in onore di Arnaldo Biscardi*, Naples, 347–57.

Rapp, C. (1998) 'Comparison, paradigm and the case of Moses in panegyric and hagiography', in Whitby, 277–98.
(2001) 'Palladius, Lausus and the *Historia Lausiaca*', in C. Sode and S. Takács (eds.) *Novum Millennium: studies on Byzantine history and culture dedicated to Paul Speck*, Aldershot, 279–89.
(2005) *Holy bishops in late antiquity: the nature of Christian leadership in an age of transition*, The transformation of the classical heritage 37, Berkeley, CA.
(2009) 'Charity and piety as episcopal and imperial virtues in late antiquity', in M. Frenkel and Y. Lev (eds.) *Charity and giving in monotheistic religions*, Studien zur Geschichte und Kultur des islamischen Orients 22, Berlin, 75–87.
(2010) 'Old Testament models for emperors in early Byzantium', in P. Magdalino and R. Nelson (eds.) *The Old Testament in Byzantium*, Washington, DC, 175–98.
Rees, R. (1998) 'The private lives of public figures in Latin prose panegyric', in Whitby, 77–101.
(2001) 'To be and not to be: Pliny's paradoxical Trajan', *BICS* 45: 149–68.
(2002) *Layers of loyalty in Latin panegyric, AD 289–307*, Oxford.
(2011) 'Afterwords of praise', in Roche 2011a, 175–88.
(2012a) 'Bright lights, big city: Pacatus and the *Panegyrici Latini*', in Grig and Kelly, 203–22.
(2012b) 'The modern history of Latin panegyric', in R. Rees (ed.) *Latin Panegyric*, Oxford, 3–48.
Reeve, M. D. (1983) '*Notitia dignitatum*', in L. D. Reynolds (ed.) *Texts and transmission: a survey of the Latin classics*, Oxford, 253–7.
Revelli, P. (1927) 'Figurazioni cartografiche dell'età imperiale in un codice ambrosiano di Solino del primo trecento', in A. Gemelli (ed.) *Raccolta di scritti in ordine di Felice Ramorino*, Pubblicazioni della Università cattolica del Sacro Cuore, ser. 4, scienze filologiche 7, Milan, 615–26.
Riggsby, A. M. (2007) 'Guides to the wor(l)d', in König and Whitmarsh 2007a, 88–107.
Roberto, U. (2012) *Roma capta. Il sacco della città dai Galli ai Lanzichenecchi*, Rome.
Roberts, M. (1985) *Biblical epic and rhetorical paraphrase in late antiquity*, ARCA, classical and medieval texts, papers and monographs 16, Liverpool.
Roche, P. A. (ed.) (2011a) *Pliny's praise: the Panegyricus in the Roman world*, Cambridge.
(2011b) 'Pliny's thanksgiving: an introduction to the *Panegyricus*', in Roche 2011a: 1–28.
Rodgers, B. S. (1989) 'The metamorphosis of Constantine', *CQ* 39: 233–46.
Ronconi, F. (2012) 'La main insaisissable. Rôle et fonction des copistes byzantins entre réalité et imaginaire', in *Scrivere e leggere nell'alto medioevo*, Settimane di studio della Fondazione Centro italiano di studi sull'alto medioevo 59, Spoleto, 2 vols., II 627–64.

Rougé, J. and Delmaire, R. (2005) *Les lois religieuses des empereurs romains de Constantin à Théodose II (312–438)*, VOL. I: *Code Théodosien livre* XVI, SC 497, Paris.

Russell, D. A. and Wilson, N. G. (eds.) (1981) *Menander Rhetor*, Oxford.

Sabbah, G. (2008) *Sozomène, Histoire ecclésiastique: livres* VII–IX, SC 516, Paris.

Şahin, S. (1991) 'Inschriften aus Seleukeia am Kalykadnos (Silifke)', *Epigraphica anatolica* 17: 139–66.

Saller, R. P. (1982) *Personal patronage under the early empire*, Cambridge.

Salway, B. (2001) 'Travel, *itineraria* and *tabellaria*', in Adams and Laurence, 22–66.

 (2005) 'The nature and genesis of the Peutinger map', *Imago Mundi* 57: 119–35.

Sandnes, K. O. (2011) *The Gospel 'according to Homer and Virgil': cento and canon*. Supplements to *Novum Testamentum* 138, Leiden.

Scharf, R. (1990) 'Die "Apfel-Affäre" oder gab es einem Kaiser Arcadius II', *ByzZ* 83: 435–50.

Schembra, R. (2006) *La prima redazione dei centoni omerici. Traduzione e commento*, Hellenica 21, Alessandria.

 (2007a) *Homerocentones*, CCSG 62, Turnhout.

 (2007b) *La seconda redazione dei centoni omerici. Traduzione e commento*, Hellenica 22, Alessandria.

Schmitt, O. (1994) 'Die *Buccellarii*. Eine Studie zum militärischen Gefolgschaftswesen in der Spätantike', *Tyche* 9: 147–74.

Schnabel, P. (1926) 'Der verlorene Speirer Codex des *Itinerarium Antonini*, der *Notitia Dignitatum* und anderer Schriften', *Sitz. der Preussischen Akademie der Wissenschaften, Phil.-Hist. Klasse* 29: 242–57.

Schnapp, J. T. (1992) 'Reading lessons: Augustine, Proba, and the Christian *détournement* of antiquity', *Stanford Literature Review* 9: 99–123.

Schor, A. (2011) *Theodoret's people: social networks and religious conflict in late Roman Syria*, The transformation of the classical heritage 48, Berkeley, CA.

Schott, J. M. (2006) 'Heresiology as universal history in Epiphanius's *Panarion*', *ZAC* 10: 546–63.

Schwartz, E. (1914) 'Zur Vorgeschichte des ephesinischen Konzils', *HZ* 112: 237–63.

 (1928) *Cyrill und der Mönch Viktor*, Akademie der Wissenschaften in Wien, Philosophisch-historische Klasse, Sitzungsberichte 208.4, Vienna.

Scourfield, J. H. D. (ed.) (2007a) *Texts and culture in late antiquity: inheritance, authority, and change*, Swansea.

 (2007b) 'Textual inheritances and textual relations in late antiquity', in Scourfield 2007a, 1–32.

Seager, R. (1983) 'Some imperial virtues in the Latin prose panegyrics: the demands of propaganda and the dynamics of literary composition', in F. Cairns (ed.) *Papers of the Liverpool Latin Seminar*, vol. IV, ARCA, classical and medieval texts, papers and monographs 11, 129–65.

Seeck, O. (1919) *Regesten der Kaier und Päpste für die Jahre 311 bis 476 n. Chr. Vorarbeit zu einer Prosopographie der christlichen Kaiserzeit*, Stuttgart.
Shaw, B. D. (2004) 'Who were the Circumcellions?', in A. H. Merrills (ed.) *Vandals, Romans and Berbers: new perspectives on late antique North Africa*, Aldershot, 227–58.
  (2011) *Sacred violence: African Christians and sectarian hatred in the age of Augustine*, Cambridge.
Shorrock, R. (2011) *The myth of paganism: Nonnus, Dionysus and the world of late antiquity*, London.
Sijpesteijn, P. M. (2007) 'The Arab conquest of Egypt and the beginning of Muslim rule', in Bagnall, 437–59.
Sirks, A. J. B. (1993) 'The sources of the Code', in Harries and Wood, 45–67.
  (2007) *The Theodosian Code: a study*, Studia Amstelodamensia: studies in ancient law and society 39, Friedrichsdorf.
Sironen, E. (1990) 'An honorary epigram for Empress Eudocia in the Athenian Agora', *Hesperia* 59: 371–4.
Sivan, H. (1993) 'Anician women, the *Cento* of Proba, and aristocratic conversion in the fourth century', *VChr* 47: 140–57.
  (2011) *Galla Placidia: the last Roman empress*, Oxford.
Sogno, C. (2006) *Q. Aurelius Symmachus: a political biography*, Ann Arbor, MI.
Spanoudakis, K. (2007) 'Icarius Jesus Christ? Dionysiac passion and biblical narrative in Nonnus' Icarius episode (*Dion.* 47, 1–264)', *WS* 120: 35–92.
Speck, P. (1974) review of Lemerle 1971, *ByzZ* 76: 385–93 (repr. in P. Speck, *Understanding Byzantium: studies in Byzantine historical sources*, [trans. S. A. Takács], Aldershot, 2003, 6–16).
Speigl, J. (1971) '*Eine Kritik an Kaiser Konstantin in der Vita Constantini des Euseb*', in E. C. Suttner and C. Patock (eds.) *Wegzeichen. Festgabe zum 60. Geburtstag von Prof. Dr. Hermengild M. Biedermann OSA*, Das östliche Christentum (n.s.) 25, Würzburg, 83–94.
Steppa, J.-E. (2002) *John Rufus and the world vision of anti-Chalcedonian culture*, Gorgias dissertations in early Christian studies 1, Piscataway, NJ.
Stickler, T. (2002) *Aëtius. Gestaltungsspielräume eines Heermeisters im ausgehenden Weströmischen Reich*, Vestigia 54, Munich.
Swain, S. and Edwards, M. J. (eds.) (2004) *Approaching late antiquity: the transformation from early to late empire*, Oxford.
Swanson, R. N. (ed.) (1994) *The Church and Mary*, Studies in church history 39, Woodbridge.
Szidat, J. (2001) 'Friede in Kirche und Staat. Zum politischen Ideal des Kirchenhistorikers Sokrates', in B. Bäbler and H.-G. Nesselrath (eds.) *Die Welt des Sokrates von Konstantinopel. Studien zu Politik, Religion und Kultur im späten 4. und frühen 5. Jh. n. Chr. zu Ehren von Christoph Schäublin*, Munich, 1–14.
  (2010) *Usurpator tanti nominis. Kaiser und Usurpator in der Spätantike (337–476 n. Chr.)*, *Historia* Einzelschriften 210, Stuttgart.

Talbert, R. J. A. (2010) *Rome's world: the Peutinger Map reconsidered*, Cambridge.
Talbert, R. J. A. and Unger, R. W. (eds.) (2008) *Cartography in antiquity and the Middle Ages: fresh perspectives, new methods*, Technology and change in history 10, Leiden.
Thompson, E. A. (1944) 'Olympiodorus of Thebes', *CQ* 38: 43–52.
  (1946) 'The Isaurians under Theodosius II', *Hermathena* 68: 18–31.
  (1950) 'The foreign policies of Theodosius II and Marcian', *Hermathena* 76: 58–75.
Thornton, T. C. G. (1997) 'Eusebius of Caesarea, Constantius II and the imperfections of Constantine the Great (*Vita Constantini* 4.31 and 4.54)', *Studia Patristica* 29: 158–63.
Tierney, J. J. (1967) *Dicuil: Liber de mensura orbis terrae*, Scriptores Latini Hiberniae 6, Dublin.
Tiersch, C. (2002) *Johannes Chrysostomus in Konstantinopel (398–404). Weltsicht und Wirken eines Bischofs in der Hauptstadt des Oströmischen Reiches*, Studien und Texte zu Antike und Christentum 6, Tübingen.
Tillemont, Le Nain de, L.-S. (1738) *Histoire des empereurs et des autres princes qui ont regné durant les six premiers siecles de l'Eglise*, vol. VI, Paris.
Tilley, M. (1996) *Donatist martyr stories: the Church in conflict in Roman North Africa*, Translated texts for historians 24, Liverpool.
  (1997) 'Sustaining Donatist self-identity: from the church of the martyrs to the *collecta* of the desert', *JECS* 5: 21–35.
Tissoni, F. (2008) 'Ciro di Panopoli riconsiderato (con alcune ipotesi sulla destinazione delle *Dionisiache*)', in Audano, 67–81.
Tompkins, I. G. (1995) 'Problems of dating and pertinence in some letters of Theodoret of Cyrrhus', *Byzantion* 65: 176–95.
Traina, G. (1986) 'Paesaggio e "decadenza". La palude nella trasformazione del mondo antico', in A. Giardina (ed.) *Società romana e impero tardoantico*, vol. III: *Le merci gli insediamenti*, Rome, 711–30.
  (1993) 'De Synésios à Priscus. Aperçus sur la connaissance de la "barbarie" hunnique (fin du IVe–milieu du Ve siècle)', in F. Vallet and M. Kazanski (eds.) *L'armée romaine et les barbares du IIIe au VIIe siècle*, Mémoires de l'Association française d'archéologie mérovingienne 5, Rouen, 285–90.
  (1998) 'Luoghi della transizione. Appunti sul paesaggio antico', *Comparaison* 2: 79–91.
  (2004) 'Un *dayeak* armeno nell'Iberia precristiana', in V. Calzolari, A. Sirinian and B. Levan Zekiyan (eds.) *Documenta memoriae. Dall'Italia e dall'Armenia, studi in onore di Gabriella Uluhogian*, Bologna, 255–62.
  (2007) *428 dopo Cristo. Storia di un anno*, Rome (trans. Allan Cameron, *428 AD: an ordinary year at the end of the Roman empire*, Princeton, NJ, 2009).
  (in press) 'Geografia dell'impero', in A. Melloni, M. Dissegna and P. Dainese (eds.) *Enciclopedia costantiniana*, vol. I, Rome.
Treadgold, W. (1995) *Byzantium and its army, 284–1081*, Stanford, CA.

(2004) 'The diplomatic career and historical work of Olympiodorus of Thebes', *International History Review* 26: 709–33.

(2007) *The early Byzantine historians*, Basingstoke.

Trevett, C. (1996) *Montanism: gender, authority and the new prophecy*, Cambridge.

Trombley, F. R. (2001) *Hellenic religion and Christianization, c. 370–529*, Religions in the Greco-Roman world 115/2, 2nd edn, 2 vols., Leiden.

Turner, V. W. (1969) *The ritual process: structure and anti-structure*, London.

Ubaldi, P. (1906) 'Appunti sul «Dialogo storico» di Palladio', *Memorie della R. Academia delle Scienze di Torino* 56: 217–96.

Uphus, J. B. (2004) *Der Horos des Zweiten Konzils von Nizäa 787. Interpretation und Kommentar auf der Grundlage der Konzilsakten mit besonderer Berücksichtigung der Bilderfrage*. Konziliengeschichte Reihe B: Untersuchungen, Paderborn.

Urbainczyk, T. (1997) *Socrates of Constantinople: historian of church and state*, Ann Arbor, MI.

(1998) 'Vice and advice in Socrates and Sozomen', in Whitby, 299–319.

(2002) *Theodoret of Cyrrhus: the bishop and the holy man*, Ann Arbor, MI.

Usher, M. D. (1997) 'Prolegomenon to the Homeric Centos', *AJPh* 118: 305–21.

(1998) *Homeric stitchings: the Homeric centos of the Empress Eudocia*, Lanham, MD.

van Bremen, R. (1996) *The limits of participation: women and civic life in the Greek East in the Hellenistic and Roman periods*, Dutch monographs on ancient history and archaeology 15, Amsterdam.

Vanderspoel, J. (1986) 'Claudian, Christ and the cult of the saints', *CQ* 36: 244–55.

(1995) *Themistius and the imperial court: oratory, civic duty and paideia from Constantius to Theodosius*, Ann Arbor, MI.

Van Hoof, L. and Van Nuffelen, P. (2011) 'Monarchy and mass communication: Antioch AD 362/3 revisited', *JRS* 101: 166–84.

Van Nuffelen, P. (2004a) *Un héritage de paix et de piété. Étude sur les histoires ecclésiastiques de Socrate et de Sozomène*, Orientalia Lovaniensia analecta 142, Leuven.

(2004b) 'Sozomenus und Olympiodorus, oder wie man Profangeschichte lesen soll', *JbAC* 47: 81–97.

(2004c) 'The unstained rule of Theodosius II: a late antique panegyrical topos and moral concern', in G. Partoens, G. Roskam and T. Van Houdt (eds.) *Virtutis imago: studies on the conceptualisation and transformation of an ancient ideal*, Collection d'études classiques 19, Leuven, 229–56.

(2010) 'Beyond bureaucracy: ritual mediation in late Antiquity', in M. Kitts, B. Schneidmüller, G. Schwedler *et al.* (eds.) *State, power, and violence*, Ritual dynamics and the science of ritual 3, Wiesbaden, 231–46.

(2012) 'Playing the ritual game in Constantinople (379–457)', in Grig and Kelly, 183–201.

BIBLIOGRAPHY

Vessey, M. (2002) 'The tongue and the book: Erasmus' *Paraphrases on the New Testament* and the arts of Scripture', in H. M. Pabel and M. Vessey (eds.) *Holy Scripture speaks: the production and reception of Erasmus' Paraphrases on the New Testament*, Erasmus Studies 14, Toronto, 29–58.

Vian, F. (1976) *Nonnos de Panopolis, Les Dionsiaques, tome I, chants I–II*, Paris.

(1997) 'Μάρτυς chez Nonnos de Panopolis. Étude de sémantique et de chronologie', *REG* 110: 143–60.

Vinel, F. (1987) 'La *Metaphrasis in Ecclesiasten* de Grégoire le Thaumaturge. Entre traduction et interprétation, une explication de texte', *Cahiers de Biblia Patristica* 1 (*Lectures anciennes de la Bible*): 191–216.

Vogt, H. J. (1968) *Coetus sanctorum. Der Kirchenbegriff des Novatian und die Geschichte seiner Sonderkirche*, Theophaneia. Beiträge zur Religions- und Kirchengeschichte des Altertums 20, Bonn.

Volgers, A. and Zamagni, C. (eds.) (2004) *Erotapokriseis: early Christian question-and-answer literature in context: proceedings of the Utrecht Colloquium, 13–14 October 2003*, Contributions to biblical exegesis and theology 37, Leuven.

Volterra, E. (1983) 'Sulla legge delle citazioni', *Atti della Accademia Nazionale dei Lincei. Memorie. Classe di Scienze morali, storiche e filologiche* 8.27.4: 185–267.

von Haehling, R. (1980) 'Damascius und die heidnische Opposition im 5. Jahrhundert nach Christus. Betrachtungen zu einem Katalog heidnischer Widersacher in der Vita Isidori', *JbAC* 23: 82–95.

(1988) '"Timeo, ne per me consuetudo in regno nascatur." Die Germanen und der römische Kaiserthron', in M. Wissemann (ed.) *Roma Renascens. Beiträge zur Spätantike und Rezeptionsgeschichte*, Frankfurt, 88–113.

Wallace-Hadrill, A. (1982) '*Civilis princeps*: between citizen and king', *JRS* 72: 32–48.

Wallraff, M. (1997) *Der Kirchenhistoriker Sokrates. Untersuchungen zu Geschichtsdarstellung, Methode und Person*, Forschungen zur Kirchen- und Dogmengeschichte 68, Göttingen.

(2005) 'L'epitaffio di un contemporaneo per Giovanni Crisostomo ("Ps.-Martirio"). Inquadramento di una fonte biografica finora trascurata', in *Giovanni Crisostomo. Oriente e Occidente tra IV e V secolo. XXXIII incontro di studiosi dell'antichità cristiana*, Studia ephemeridis augustinianum 93, 2 vols., Rome, 1 37–49.

(2007) *Oratio funebris in laudem Sancti Iohannis Chrysostomi. Epitaffio attribuito a Martirio di Antiochia (BHG 871, CPG 6517)*, with Italian trans. by C. Ricci, Quaderni della *Rivista di bizantinistica* 12, Spoleto.

(2008) 'Tod im Exil. Reaktionen auf die Todesnachricht des Johannes Chrysostomos und Konstituierung einer "johannitischen" Opposition', in Wallraff and Brändle, 23–37.

Wallraff, M. and Brändle, R. (eds.) (2008) *Chrysostomosbilder in 1600 Jahren. Facetten der Wirkungsgeschichte eines Kirchenvaters*, Arbeiten zur Kirchengeschichte 105, Berlin.

BIBLIOGRAPHY

Ward-Perkins, B. (2012) 'Old and New Rome compared: the rise of Constantinople', in Grig and Kelly, 53–78.
Warland, R. (ed.) (2002) *Bildlichkeit und Bildorte von Liturgie*. Schauplätze in Spätantike, Byzanz und Mittelalter, Wiesbaden.
Watts, E. J. (2006) *City and school in late antique Athens and Alexandria*, The transformation of the classical heritage 41, Berkeley, CA.
  (2010) *Riot in Alexandria: tradition and group dynamics in late antique pagan and Christian communities*, The transformation of the classical heritage 46, Berkeley, CA.
Webb, R. (2006) 'Rhetorical and theatrical fictions in Chorikios of Gaza', in Johnson, 2006a: 107–24.
Weber, E. (1976) *Tabula Peutingeriana, Codex Vindobonensis 324. Kommentar*, Graz.
Weingarten, S. (2005) *The saint's saints: hagiography and geography in Jerome*, Ancient Judaism and early Christianity 58, Leiden.
Wesch-Klein, G. (2002) 'Der Laterculus des Polemius Silvius. Überlegungen zu Datierung, Zuverlässigkeit und historischem Aussagewert einer spätantiken Quelle', *Historia* 51: 57–88.
Wessel, S. (2001) 'The ecclesiastical policy of Theodosius II', *Annuarium Historiae Conciliorum* 33: 285–308.
  (2004) *Cyril of Alexandria and the Nestorian controversy: the making of a saint and of a heretic*, Oxford.
Wheeler, E. (2012) '*Notitia Dignitatum, Or.* 38 and Roman deployment in Colchis: assessing recent views', in B. Cabouret, A. Groslambert and C. Wolff (eds.) *Visions de l'Occident romain. Hommages à Yann Le Bohec*, Collection du Centre d'études et de recherches sur l'Occident romain 40, 2 vols., Paris, II 621–76.
Whitby, Mary (1994) 'From Moschus to Nonnus: the evolution of the Nonnian style', in N. Hopkinson (ed.) *Studies in the Dionysiaca of Nonnus*, Cambridge Philological Society supplementary volume 17, Cambridge, 99–155.
  (ed.) (1998) *The propaganda of power: the role of panegyric in late antiquity*, Mnemosyne Supplement 183, Leiden.
  (2007) 'The Bible hellenized: Nonnus' *Paraphrase* of St John's Gospel and "Eudocia's" Homeric centos', in Scourfield 2007a, 195–232.
  (2009) Review of Schembra 2007a, *ByzZ* 101: 811–15.
  (2011) Review of Audano 2008, *Eikasmos* 22: 455–8.
Whitby, Michael (2000) *The Ecclesiastical History of Evagrius Scholasticus*, Translated texts for historians 33, Liverpool.
  (2003) 'The church historians and Chalcedon', in Marasco, 449–95.
Whitby, Michael and Whitby, Mary (1986) *The History of Theophylact Simocatta: an English translation, with introduction and notes*, Oxford.
  (1989) *Chronicon Paschale 284–628 AD*, Translated texts for historians 7, Liverpool.
Whittaker, C. R. (2002) 'Mental maps and frontiers: seeing like a Roman', in P. McKechnie (ed.) *Thinking like a lawyer: essays on legal history and general*

BIBLIOGRAPHY

history for John Crook on his eightieth birthday, Mnemosyne supplement 231, Leiden, 81–112 (repr. in C. R. Whittaker, *Rome and its frontiers: the dynamics of empire*, London, 2004, 63–87).

Wickham, C. (2005) *Framing the early Middle Ages: Europe and the Mediterranean, 400–800*, Oxford.

Williams, F. (2009) *The Panarion of Epiphanius of Salamis: Book I (sects 1–46)*, 2nd edn, Nag Hammadi and Manichaean Studies 63, Leiden.

—— (2012) *The Panarion of Epiphanius of Salamis: Books II and III, De Fide*, 2nd edn, Nag Hammadi and Manichaean Studies 79, Leiden.

Williams, M. S. (2008) *Authorised lives in early Christian biography: between Eusebius and Augustine*, Cambridge.

Wilson, N. G. (1994) *Photius, The Bibliotheca: a selection translated with notes*, London.

Winkelmann, F. (1966) *Untersuchungen zur Kirchengeshichte des Gelasios von Kaisareia*, Sitz. der Deutschen Akademie der Wissenschaften zu Berlin, Klasse für Sprachen, Literatur und Kunst 1965, no. 3, Berlin.

Wirbelauer, E. (2011) 'Die Eroberung Roms in der Darstellung Philostorgs', in D. Meyer (ed.) *Philostorge et l'historiographie de l'antiquité tardive/ Philostorg im Kontext der spätantiken Geschichtsschreibung*, Collegium Beatus Rheanus 3, Stuttgart, 229–45.

Wolska-Conus, W. (1973) 'Deux contributions à l'histoire de la géographie. I La diagnôsis ptoléméenne. II La "Carte de Théodose II"', *T&MByz* 5: 259–79.

Young, F. M. (1983) *From Nicaea to Chalcedon: a guide to the literature and its background*, London.

Zecchini, G. (1983) *Aezio. L'ultima difesa dell'Occidente romano*, Centro ricerche e documentazione sull'antichità classica, monographie 8, Rome.

—— (2002) 'L'immagine di Teodosio II nella storiografia ecclesiastica', *MediterrAnt* 5: 529–46.

Zuckerman, C. (1994) 'L'empire d'orient et les Huns. Notes sur Priscus', *T&MByz* 12: 159–82.

—— (1998) 'Comtes et ducs en Égypte autour de l'an 400 et la date de la *Notitia Dignitatum Orientis*', *AntTard* 6: 137–47.

INDEX

Key to abbreviations used:
mag. off. = *magister officiorum*
MVM = *magister utriusque militiae*
PPO = *praefectus praetorio*
PSC = *praepositus sacri cubiculi*
PVC = *praefectus urbis* (Constantinople)
PVR = *praefectus urbis* (Rome)
QSP = *quaestor sacri palatii*

Aelia Eudocia (Athenais), 58, 60, 131, 133, 278, 279
  alleged adultery, 261, 277
  as another Helena, 53, 71
  children, 54n. 176, 88n. 87
  influence of, 73, 88
  literary work, 31, 34, 35, 63, 196, 207–14, 217
  marriage to Theodosius, 15, 54, 60, 68, 137, 201
  pilgrimage to Jerusalem, 45, 46, 213
  retirement to Jerusalem, 277, 281
Aemilius Probus, 166
Aetius, Fl. (*MVM*), 100, 150
Agathias, 213
agentes in rebus, 80
Agintheus (*MVM*), 93n. 19
Alaric, 99, 101, 140, 143
  established Attalus, 147
  relationship with Stilicho, 145, 146–7
Alexander (bishop of Alexandria), 274n. 17
Alexander (monk), 47
Alexandria, 210, 212, 213, 217, 218, 273
  Serapaeum, 245
Alypius (*vicarius*), 167
Ambrose (bishop of Milan), 229n. 28
Ammianus Marcellinus, 55, 62, 244, 245
Ammonius (grammarian), 205
Anagastes, Fl. (*MVM*), 91n. 5
Anastasius (emperor), 236, 237, 269n. 1

Anatolius (bishop of Constantinople), 240
Anatolius, Fl. (*MVM*), 67, 91, 94, 99, 104, 105n. 70
  acclaimed at Edessa, 94
Anomoeans (heresy), 180
Anthemii, 76
Anthemius (emperor), 72
Anthemius, Fl. (*PPO*), 72, 76n. 42, 86, 136n. 26, 145, 204n. 46
Anthologia Graeca, 214
Antioch, 92, 195, 208, 213, 217, 218, 257
  Daphne, 98
Antiochus (eunuch), 145, 161–2
Antiochus Chuzon (*QSP*), 75, 87, 193
Apollinarians (heresy), 27, 177, 185, 189, 190
Apollinarius (bishop of Laodicea), 203, 210
Apollonius (*MVM*), 91, 94
Apotactites (heresy), 188, 189n. 58
Arbazacius (*comes*), 99n. 45
Arcadia (sister of Theodosius), 136, 277
Arcadius (emperor), 17, 24, 44, 82, 96n. 32, 105, 118n. 32, 224, 232, 238
  death, 6, 135, 144
  exile of John Chrysostom, 46, 118n. 31, 145
  legal reform, 75n. 38, 77
  marriage policy, 88
  petitioned by Porphyry, 3, 50, 51
  received relics of Samuel, 42
  Stilicho's claim to guardianship, 143, 162
Arcadius (son of Theodosius), 54n. 176, 88n. 87
Ardaburii, 71, 98, 99, 101
  marriage alliance with Plinta, 102
Ardaburius the Elder (*MVM*), 71, 99, 105, 134
Arianism, 90

315

INDEX

Ardaburius the Younger (*MVM*), 71, 99
Ariadne (daughter of Leo I), 137
Arianism, 27, 46, 178, 185, 187n. 52, 189, 190, 205, 254, 255
   bar to throne, 107–8
   faith of generals, 12, 72, 90–1
   seizure of churches, 264, 265
Ariobindus, Fl. (*MVM*), 71, 72, 95, 97, 104, 105n. 70
   Arianism, 91
Aristotle, 222, 249, 257
Arius (heretic), 180
Armatius (son of Plinta), 101
Armenia, 26, 171
Arnegisclus, Fl. (*MVM*), 71, 91
Artemidorus (geographer), 164
Asclepiodotus (*PPO*), 74, 80n. 54
Asia Minor, 164, 201
Aspar, Fl. Ardabur (*MVM*), 71, 72, 91, 99, 104n. 65, 134
   Arianism, 107, 108
   letter from Theodoret, 94
   relationship with Leo I, 98, 100, 102, 107
   relationship with Marcian, 95
   retainers, 101
   son Patricius made Caesar, 108
Athanasius (bishop of Alexandria), 13, 118, 274n. 17
Athanasius (bishop of Perrha), 68
Athaulf, 16, 138, 139, 142
Athenais *see* Aelia Eudocia
Athens, 131, 133, 137, 151, 195, 216
Attalus (usurper), 140, 147
Atticus (bishop of Constantinople), 199
Attila, 11, 71, 72, 79, 99, 103, 105, 222, 223, 233
Audians (heresy), 185, 187n. 54
Augustine (bishop of Hippo), 27, 28, 174, 175, 180–4, 189, 190, 192, 193, 194
Augustus (emperor), 155
Aurelianus (*PPO*), 76n. 42
Ausonius, 209
Autun, 155, 157

Balkans, 6, 11, 79, 223
Barsauma (monk), 45, 280–1
Basil (bishop of Caesarea), 198
Basil (monk), 233, 238, 271, 272

Basil of Seleucia, 207n. 62
Baudo (rebel), 92n. 16, 107
beneficia see honours
Bleda (Hunnic leader), 222
Blemyes, 131, 216
Bonifatius (*MVM*), 100, 150
Borboriani (heresy), 27, 185, 187n. 54, 189
Bucellarii, 100–1

Caecilianus (*PPO*), 86n. 82
Caelicolae (heresy), 188, 188n. 56
Candidianus (*comes*), 12, 118, 119, 121, 124, 126
Caracalla (emperor), 157n. 9
Carthage, 223
Castinus (consul), 149, 150
Celestine (bishop of Rome), 113n. 15, 274
Cerdonians (heresy), 182n. 37
Charlemagne, 160
Christodorus (poet), 212n. 91
Chrysaphius (eunuch), 68, 107, 215, 269n. 3
Claudian (poet), 196, 212n. 91
Collyridians (heresy), 177
comes rei priuatae, 82
comitatenses, 97
consistory (*consistorium*), 7–11, 12, 17, 19, 26, 49, 50, 51, 73–7, 85, 88, 103
   imposition of order, 76, 84, 86, 88
   influence of Pulcheria, 15, 73
   legislative function, 73, 75, 78
   membership, 7n. 17, 80, 95
   patronage, 79–81
Constans (*MVM*), 105n. 70, 106
Constantine, 20, 51, 53, 63, 70, 76, 76n. 41, 84, 111n. 6, 128, 250, 255, 261
   constitutions starting point of *Theodosian Code*, 23
Constantine (usurper), 143
Constantinople, 62
   Amphitheatre, 56, 250, 252, 253
   Augusteum, 69
   Blachernae Church, 241
   Church of the Holy Apostles, 200
   defence, 101, 105
   earthquake, 42, 221, 232, 238, 239, 241
   Forum of Constantine, 239, 241
   granaries, 240

INDEX

Great Palace, 4, 43, 44, 46, 47, 58, 61, 221, 238, 239, 241
Hagia Sophia, 45, 46, 54, 69, 239
Hebdomon, 42, 43, 96, 96n. 32, 221, 222, 223, 229, 232–3, 238, 239
Hippodrome, 46, 55, 56, 96, 230, 239, 251, 253, 262
literary centre, 218
Mese, 238, 239
as 'new' Rome, 149
personification, 99
proximity of praesental armies, 11, 93, 97
public disorder, 100, 113, 278
public processions, 42–3, 51, 228
public spectacles, 73, 106
Rufinianae Palace, 7, 9, 19
Senate, 9, 42, 68, 69, 78, 79, 81, 225, 259, 278
Theodosian Walls, 96, 149, 221, 222, 233, 238, 241
'University', 81, 161, 169
Constantinus, Fl. (*PPO*), 67
Constantius I (Chlorus), 157
Constantius II, 76, 178n. 21, 258, 258n. 49
Constantius III, 16, 106, 131, 138–40, 142, 147
consulship, 104–6
Cornelius Nepos, 166
Cosmas (*cubicularius*), 273
Council of Antioch, 68
Council of Chalcedon (451), 204, 210, 229n. 28, 269n. 2, 271, 274n. 17, 278, 281
  acta, 9, 126, 203
  aftermath, 58, 61, 270, 271, 273, 274, 284
Council of Ephesus (431), 109–29, 210, 264, 271n. 9, 272, 281; *see also* Cyril of Alexandria, role at Ephesus; Theodosius II, role in Council of Ephesus 431
  acta, 9, 20, 234
  aftermath, 269
  arguments before Theodosius, 7, 9, 19
  role of Antiochus Chuzon, 75, 193
Council of Ephesus (449), 94, 271; *see also* Theodosius II, role in Council of Ephesus 449

acta, 9
convocation, 112, 114, 122
role of Theodoret, 93
Council of Nicaea (325), 21, 125, 126
court, 6, 20
ceremony, 50, 73, 233
factional struggles, 18, 21, 49, 68, 71, 87, 237
'monastic', 5, 52, 132, 136, 259
sidelining of generals, 11
Ctesiphon, 162
Curtius (*PPO*), 188n. 56
Cyprian (martyr), 213
Cyprian of Antioch, 34, 208
Cyril (bishop of Alexandria), 117n. 29, 202, 234, 235, 236, 274n. 17, 275, 277
  criticised by Theodosius, 13, 14, 18, 115–17, 118, 119
  death, 274
  deposition, 129
  exegetical work, 196, 210
  role at Ephesus, 8, 12, 36, 37, 47, 109, 125, 126, 202
Cyril of Scythopolis, 236
Cyrus of Panopolis (*PPO*), 83n. 68, 84, 87
  literary work, 31, 196, 214–15, 217

Dalmatius (monk), 47, 48, 49, 234–6, 238
Daniel (rebel), 92n. 16
Daniel the Stylite, 215
Danube, 6, 223, 233
decurions, 68, 83
Descriptio totius mundi, 164
Dicuil (geographer), 161, 163, 165, 166
Diocletian, 70, 157, 208
Diogenes Laertius (biographer), 200
Dionysius (bishop of Alexandria), 274n. 17
Dionysius (*MVM*), 91, 105n. 70
Dioscorus (bishop of Alexandria), 14, 128, 202, 269, 271, 274–6, 278, 280n. 39
domestici, 81
Domnus (bishop of Antioch), 68
Donatists (heresy), 185, 186, 187, 188n. 56
Donatus (Hun leader), 130, 142, 151

Ecebolius (philosopher), 258

317

INDEX

education reform in Constantinople, 29, 81
Egypt, 61, 114, 131, 217, 279, 282, 283, 284
Elias (bishop of Jerusalem), 237
Encratites (heresy), 188, 189n. 58, 190n. 61
Enthusiastae (heresy), 185, 187n. 54
Epiphanius (bishop of Salamis), 27, 28, 174, 175, 176–84, 186, 187, 189, 190, 192, 193, 194
Eucherius (bishop of Lyons), 164
Euchitae (heresy), 185, 187n. 54
Eudoxia (wife of Arcadius), 3, 43, 44, 118n. 32, 145, 223–4, 228, 231–2, 238
Eugenius (usurper), 238
Eumenius (orator), 156, 157
Eunapius (biographer), 200
Eunomians (heresy), 27, 185, 187, 189, 190n. 62, 205
Euphratensis (province), 67
Eusebius (bishop of Caesarea), 52, 53, 55, 57, 64, 177n. 18, 249, 250, 254–5, 256n. 43, 270
Eutropius (eunuch), 82, 137
Eutychians (heresy), 270n. 6
Evagrius Scholasticus, 59, 61, 213, 270

Faustus, Anicius Acilius Glabrio (*PPO*), 22, 26
Felix, Fl. Constantius (*MVM*), 148, 150
Filastrius (bishop of Brescia), 181–4, 186, 189, 190, 192
fiscus, 74
Flaccilla (daughter of Theodosius), 54n. 176, 88n. 87
Florentius (*MVM*), 93n. 19, 94
Florentius, Fl. (*PPO*), 80n. 54, 82, 83–4, 85n. 80, 86, 185
Fravitta, Fl. (*MVM*), 105

Gainas (*MVM*), 72
Galen, 173
Galerius (emperor), 70
Galla Placidia, 16, 105n. 70, 131, 134, 135, 148
    depiction by Olympiodorus, 138–41, 151
Gangra, 274, 280n. 39

Gaza, 4, 271
generals, 90–108; *see also* Arianism, faith of generals; honours, granted to generals
    as 'barbarians', 72
    defeats limiting political clout, 11, 103
    made patrician, 104
    personal wealth, 97
    rivalry between generals, 11, 102
    sidelined in imperial rhetoric, 12, 71–2
Gennadius (bishop of Constantinople), 210
Goths, 6, 26, 91, 138, 139, 142, 146, 148
governors, 75, 83, 100
Gregory I (bishop of Rome), 172
Gregory of Nazianzus, 195, 196, 198, 212n. 89
Gregory of Nyssa, 198

Helena (mother of Constantine), 53, 70n. 18
Helion (*mag. off.*), 77n. 44, 80, 134, 147n. 74, 148
Helladius (grammarian), 205
Hellenism *see* pagans
Heraclianus (usurper), 106
Heraclius (emperor), 282
Hierius (*PPO*), 84
Hierokles (geographer), 163
Hippolytus (bishop of Rome), 176
History of the Church of Alexandria, 280
History of the Patriarchs of the Coptic Church of Alexandria, 280
Homer, 31, 32, 33, 34, 63, 209, 210, 213, 214, 216
Homoian *see* Arianism
Honorius (emperor), 6, 16, 24, 86n. 82, 118n. 31, 135, 146, 148
    death, 131, 135, 149
    depiction by Olympiodorus, 141, 151
    depiction by Sozomen, 140
    marriage to Maria, 137
    marriage to Thermantia, 137
    relationship with Constantius, 16, 106
    relationship with Galla Placidia, 138, 140, 142
    relationship with Stilicho, 16, 143, 144, 162
honours (*beneficia*), 80–3

INDEX

granted to generals, 12, 104–6
patricius, 104
Hydroparastatae (heresy), 185, 188, 189n.
  58, 190n. 61
Hypatia (philosopher), 218
Hypatius (*MVM*), 93n. 19

Ibas (bishop of Edessa), 275
Illyricum, 11, 93, 102, 143, 145
imperial women, 14, 20, 69–71, 88
  danger of celibacy, 54, 88
  projection of public piety, 88
  virginity, 33
Innocent I (bishop of Rome), 145
Ioannes (*MVM*), 91, 107
Irenaeus (bishop of Lyons), 176, 179
Isaurians, 100, 101
Isidore (martyr), 212
Isidore (monk), 281, 282
Isidorus, Fl. Anthemius (*PPO*), 72,
  136n. 26
Italy, 150, 201
Iulius Solinus (geographer), 169

Jerome, 164, 181, 201
Jerusalem, 42, 51, 271
Jews, 45, 48, 74, 177
John (bishop of Antioch), 113n. 15, 119n.
  33, 125, 126, 127n. 51, 241
John (bishop of Nikiu), 58, 59, 276–9
John (*comes*), 124n. 43, 127n. 51
John (usurper), 46, 149;
  see also Theodosius II, defeat of
    John
  campaign against, 11, 103, 148, 246
  death, 251, 253, 262
  defeat, 15, 105, 131, 133, 134, 230, 251
  usurpation, 71, 150, 263
John Chrysostom (bishop of
  Constantinople), 13, 47, 118n. 32,
  195, 196, 197–200, 204, 217
  exiled by Arcadius, 46, 118, 145, 197,
    198, 201
  posthumous rehabilitation, 31, 43,
    270n. 6
  praise of Eudoxia, 223–4, 228, 231–2,
    238
John of Lycopolis, 48, 49
John Lydus, 133
John Malalas, 276

John Rufus, 58, 60, 61, 62, 233, 271–4,
  276
Jovinianists (heresy), 184n. 42
Jovinus (usurper), 142
Jovius (*PPO*), 147, 188n. 56
judges, 77
Julian (emperor), 38n. 105, 167, 211, 225,
  257–9, 261
Justin I, 269n. 1
Justinian (emperor), 50, 51, 276, 282
Juvenal (bishop of Jerusalem), 271, 274

Lampadius (senator), 143
Lausus (*PSC*), 201
law, 77, 78, 100; *see also* Theodosian
  Code
  appeals, 78
  *Collatio legum Mosaicarum et
    Romanarum*, 188n. 55
  concerning generals, 94–5
  Corpus Iuris Civilis, 87
  criminal law. 86n. 82
  emperor subject to them, 77
  Justinianic Code, 74
  law of citations, 84
  law of inheritance, 39, 74–5, 85
  law of sanctuary, 40, 75, 86
  laws on right religion, 40, 77
  lex generalis (general law), 39, 41, 77
  marriage law, 85, 85
  Novellae of Theodosius II, 9, 37, 38,
    74, 77
  on heresy, 27–9, 174, 175, 184–94, 264
  pagans banned from civil service, 91n. 6
  Praetorian Edict, 75
  rescripts, 77
  shaped by agendas of officials, 83–4
  shared legal culture, 84
  Sirmondian Constitutions, 38n. 104,
    39n. 109
  Twelve Tables, 23
  use of Greek, 84
Leo I, 71, 96n. 32, 98, 108, 137, 269n. 1,
  269n. 1
  marriage alliance with Aspar, 102
  murder of Aspar, 100, 107
Leo I (bishop of Rome), 229n. 28, 275
Leo II (emperor), 269n. 1
Leontius (father of Aelia Eudocia), 131,
  133, 151, 207

319

INDEX

Libanius, 195, 196, 225, 257, 258
Licinia Eudoxia (daughter of Theodosius), 26, 45, 54n. 176, 88n. 87, 131, 133
Licinius (emperor), 21
limitanei, 94, 97, 103
Luciferians (heresy), 181n. 32, 184n. 42
Lucius (*MVM*), 91, 92
Lupianus (*MVM*), 93n. 19
Lycia (province), 233

Macedonians (heresy), 27, 185, 189, 190
Macedonius (*MVM*), 93n. 19
Macrina (saint), 198
Macrobius (*PSC*), 83
Macrobius Ambrosius Theodosius (*PPO*), 83n. 67, 159, 163, 166
magister militum see generals
magister off., 11, 103
Magnus Maximus, 96n. 30
Mamertinus, Claudius (consul/orator), 225
Manichaeans (heresy), 27, 175, 180, 185, 187, 188n. 56, 189, 190, 191n. 63, 192n. 64
Map of Agrippa, 156, 166, 169
Marcellians (heresy), 185, 187n. 54, 190n. 62
Marcian, 104n. 65, 269n. 1, 269n. 1
  convened Chalcedon, 269n. 2, 275
  death, 240, 240
  depiction by anti-Chalcedonians, 58–62, 273–81, 283, 284
  marriage to Pulcheria, 54, 60, 68, 95, 136, 275, 278
  relationship with Aspar, 95
Marcian of Heraclea (geographer), 164
Marcianists (heresy), 27, 180, 185, 187n. 54
Margum, 223
Maria (first wife of Honorius), 137, 144
Marina (sister of Theodosius), 136, 277
Mark the Deacon, 3
Martianus Capella, 163
Martin (bishop of Tours), 48–9
Martyrius (*QSP*), 87
Maurice (emperor), 50, 241–2
Maxentius (emperor), 53
Maximian (bishop of Constantinople), 246
Maximian (emperor), 157, 208
Maximinus Thrax (emperor), 157

Melania the Elder, 201
Menander (Rhetor) of Laodicea, 249
Menippus of Pergamum (geographer), 164
Messalians (heresy), 178, 185, 187n. 54
Michael (bishop of Athrib and Malig), 279n. 38
Michael Glykas (historian), 161
Montanists (heresy), 27, 185, 186, 187, 188n. 56

Naissus, 223
Neoplatonists, 197, 200, 201, 216
Nestorius (bishop of Constantinople), 76n. 41, 83n. 68, 113n. 15, 114n. 17, 118n. 29, 118n. 32, 119n. 33, 125, 191n. 63, 273
  attacked by Barsauma, 280
  attacked by Basil, 233, 271
  attacked by Cyril, 109, 123, 202
  attacked by Dalmatius, 47, 236
  Christology, 59, 60, 269, 272
  deposition, 129, 233, 246
  persecution of heretics, 264–6
  possible author of law on heresy, 29, 192–4, 264
  relationship with Theodosius, 8, 46, 128
Nicephorus Callistus (historian), 161
Nonnus, 196, 210–13, 215, 217, 218
Noricum (province), 143
Notitia Dignitatum, 24, 25, 29, 97, 101, 158–63
Notitia of Constantinople, 160, 217
Novatians (heresy), 27, 185, 186, 189, 205, 246, 265, 267

Olympiodorus of Thebes, 15, 16, 26, 109–29, 196, 215–16, 217
paganism, 132, 152
Olympius (*mag. off.*), 145, 146, 147
Origen, 180
Orosius, 163

Pacatus, Drepanius (orator), 226
Pachomius (monk), 274n. 17
pagans, 45, 74, 91, 108, 163, 177, 180, 195, 196, 205, 211, 245, 281
Palaestina (province), 103
palatini, 82
Palestine, 164, 201

INDEX

Palladius (bishop of Helenopolis), 198–202, 213
Panegyrici Latini, 157, 248
Panopolis, 217
Paphlagonia, 164
Patricius (bishop), 31
Paul (heretic), 267
Paul of Samosata (heretic), 180
Paulians (heresy), 185, 187n. 54, 190n. 62
Paulina (wife of Zeno), 98
Paulinus (*mag. off.*), 80, 102, 261, 276, 277
Pelagians (heresy), 183
Persian War (421–422), 11, 68, 71, 103, 104, 134, 136n. 26, 170, 213, 246, 255, 262, 263
Peter I (bishop of Alexandria), 274n. 17
Peter the Iberian, 58, 60, 61, 62, 271–4
Petronius (monk), 274n. 17
Petronius Maximus (emperor), 162
Peutinger Map, 25
Philip of Side, 197, 204, 205, 212, 217
Philostorgius, 130, 205, 206, 217
Philostratus (biographer), 200
Photinians (heresy), 185
Photius (bishop of Constantinople), 130–1, 135, 138, 141, 143, 148, 200, 204, 208, 209, 213, 215
Phrygians (heresy), 27, 185, 189
Pierius (martyr), 212
Plato, 199, 203
Platonists, 182n. 36
Plinta, Fl. (*MVM*), 71, 90, 93, 95n. 28, 99, 101, 103, 105
  Arianism, 90
  marriage alliance with Ardaburii, 102
  retainers, 101
Pliny the Elder, 155n. 1, 169, 173, 176
Pliny the Younger, 44, 225–8, 229, 243, 248, 250n. 25, 252n. 31, 254n. 39
Plutarch, 200
Pneumatomachi (heresy) *see* Macedonians
Polemius Silvius (geographer), 161, 171
Pomponius Mela, 169
Porphyry (bishop of Gaza), 3, 50, 51
Porphyry (philosopher), 258
praepositus sacri cubiculi, 82
praetorian prefect
  access to emperor, 79
  control over army provisions, 11, 102
  role as judge, 78
Priscillianists (heresy) *see* Montanists
Proba, Faltonia Betitia (poetess), 32, 33n. 87, 35, 54n. 176, 166, 209
Proclus (bishop of Constantinople), 118n. 32, 200, 246, 267
Proclus (philosopher), 216
Procopius (*MVM*), 72, 104, 136n. 26
Procopius (usurper), 76
Proculus (*PVC*), 80n. 54, 81n. 59
protectores, 81
Pseudo-Aethicus Ister (geographer), 161, 163, 169
Pseudo-Theopistus, 58, 60, 274–6
Pseudo-Zacharias, 270
Ptolemy (geographer), 158, 179
Ptolemy (pharoah), 210
Pulcheria, 43, 47; *see also* Sozomen, depiction of Pulcheria
  access to Theodosius, 74
  depiction by John of Nikiu, 278–9
  education of Theodosius, 88, 162
  influence of, 14, 15, 67–70, 72–3, 145
  marriage to Marcian, 54, 60, 68, 95, 136, 275, 278
  public piety, 44, 54, 70, 201
  received relics of the Forty Martyrs of Sebaste, 45, 53
  role at Ephesus 431, 109n. 2
  role in Theodosius' marriage, 54, 68
  virginity, 5, 15, 45, 54, 69, 70, 89, 136, 137, 138, 276
Pythagoreans, 182n. 36

quaestor sacri palatii, 78, 79, 94, 192
Quodvultdeus (deacon), 180, 182, 183, 184n. 44

Rabbula (bishop of Edessa), 202
Ravenna, 46, 53, 55, 148
registers (*laterculi*), 80
res priuata, 82
Rome, 26, 42, 134, 148
  Church of St Justina and St Cyprian, 213
  description in Olympiodorus, 131, 148
  personification, 99
  sack of, 142, 143, 146, 147, 171

INDEX

Rome (cont.,)
  Senate, 21, 26, 77, 84, 108, 143, 157
Rufinus, Fl. (*PPO*), 162

Sabas (monk), 50, 51, 236, 237
Sabbatians (heresy), 27, 185, 187, 187, 189
Sabellians (heresy), 183
Sabellius (heretic), 180
Saccophori (heresy), 188, 189n. 58, 190n. 61
sacrae largitiones, 82
Sallustius (*QSP*), 80
Samaritans, 45
Sapricius (*MVM*), 93n. 19, 94
Sarus (*MVM*), 142
Scetis, 60, 281, 283
scrinia, 82
Seleucia (Isauria), 98, 102, 207
Senator, Fl. (ex-consul), 67
Septimius Severus (emperor), 157
Serdica, 223
Serena (wife of Stilicho), 137, 138, 143, 144
Sergitheon, 97
Shenoute (archimandrite), 275
Sicily, 223
Simeon Stylites, 48, 49, 280, 281
Simon Magus (heretic), 177, 191n. 63, 204
Simonians (heresy), 76n. 41, 191n. 63
Singidunum, 223
Sirmium, 223
Sixtus III (bishop of Rome), 208n. 64
Socrates (historian), 52, 90, 133, 145, 192, 201, 204, 217, 270;
  see also Sozomen, reworking of Socrates
  depiction of John Chrysostom, 200
  depiction of Theodosius II, 46, 52, 54–8, 230–1, 244–68
  Novatian, 205, 245
Sozomen, 90, 93, 217, 245, 258n. 50, 270
  depiction of Honorius, 140
  depiction of John Chrysostom, 200
  depiction of Pulcheria, 44, 45, 69, 136, 145, 206
  legal education, 213
  reworking of Socrates, 205, 206, 217
  use of Olympius, 130, 140

Stephanus of Byzantium (geographer), 155n. 3, 164
Stilicho (*MVM*), 99, 102, 142, 143, 144, 147, 151, 162
  marriage alliance with Honorius, 16, 137, 138
  marriage to Serena, 102, 143
  plans to control East, 16, 132, 142, 143, 144, 145
  relationship with Alaric, 146–7
  retinue, 100
Stoics, 182n. 36
Syene, 198
Symmachus, Q. Aurelius (*PVR*), 78
Synaxary (Coptic), 58, 59, 60, 61, 281–4
Synesius (bishop of Cyrene), 164, 216
Syria, 94, 201

Tascodrogitae (heresy), 185, 186, 187
Taurus, Fl. (*PPO*), 76, 86
tax, 3, 67, 68, 97
  collectio lustralis, 73
Tetrarchy, 70
Tetricus (usurper), 155
Thalassius (bishop of Caesarea), 267
Theoderic the Ostrogoth, 108n. 79
Theodora (wife of Justinian), 51, 68
Theodore (lawyer), 212, 217
Theodore (martyr), 257
Theodore (monk), 274n. 17
Theodoret (bishop of Cyrrhus), 275
  advocate of Nestorius before Theodosius, 8, 9, 19
  Church History, 206, 217, 245, 270
  depiction of John Chrysostom, 200
  letter to Pulcheria, 67–8
  letters to bishops, 8
  letters to generals, 93, 97
  letters to officials, 71
  literary work, 200, 202–4, 205, 216, 217, 218
Theodosian Code, 9, 10, 14, 17, 25, 29, 64, 74, 86, 88, 217; *see also* law
  arrangement, 22, 40, 86
  aspiration to clarity, completeness and order, 22–3, 27, 36–41, 78, 84–6, 170
  Christianity not a special category, 86
  failure to achieve ambition, 25, 78, 87
  oratio to Roman Senate in 426, 77, 84

INDEX

received by Roman Senate in 438, 21–2, 26
starting point constitutions of Constantine, 10, 22, 27, 41, 85
Theodosius (son of Maurice), 241
Theodosius I, 63, 82, 102, 138, 144, 166, 229n. 28
  compared to Theodosius II, 5, 21, 64, 84
  death, 6
  defeat of Magnus Maximus, 96n. 30
  dynastic policy, 23, 162
  petitioned by John of Lycopolis, 48
  public piety, 51, 238
  received head of John the Baptist, 42, 221
Theodosius II, 8, 58, 63, 145, 148, 149, 150, 223; *see also* Socrates, depiction of Theodosius
  access to, 74
  baptism, 51
  barefoot walk to Hebdomon, 43, 223, 229, 232, 233, 238, 239, 240
  birth, 3
  children, 54n. 176, 88n. 87
  coinage, 261
  commissioning of *mappa mundi*, 25, 26, 164–9
  compared to Constantine, 52, 249
  compared to Moses, 46, 59, 249, 264
  confronted by Basil, 233, 271–2
  criticism of Cyril, 13, 14, 18, 115–17
  death, 6, 54, 68, 88, 91, 95, 195, 214, 272, 274, 275
  defeat of John, 53, 134, 246
    celebratory procession, 56, 96, 251, 263
    resultant triumphalism, 26, 133–6
  delegation of powers as supreme judge, 78, 87
  depiction by Egyptian anti-Chalcedonians, 58–62, 281–4
  depiction in modern scholarship, 5–6, 64
  dynastic ideology, 70, 144
  education, 88, 162
  fear of deposition, 92
  generosity, 81
  hunting, 96n. 32, 214
  inspection of granaries, 240
  interest in education, 81, 161, 205
  lack of ambition, 69, 83, 84
  lack of leadership, 4, 10, 17, 18, 19, 20, 76, 78, 86–8
  lack of military experience, 91, 96
  leading supplication to avert storm, 259–61, 262
  longevity, 6, 11, 19, 76, 86
  marriage to Aelia Eudocia, 15, 68, 137, 141, 201, 207
  personal piety, 52
  petitioned by Dalmatius, 47, 234–6, 238
  petitioned by Porphyry, 3, 50
  petitioned by Simeon Stylites, 48, 49
  philanthropia, 249–54, 257, 261
  received relics of John Chrysostom, 43
  refusal to recognise Constantius III, 139
  relationship with Ardaburii, 71
  relationship with generals, 72, 90–108
  relationship with Honorius, 140
  relationship with Nestorius, 46, 60, 264–6, 269, 272, 280
  removed protection of Armenia, 26, 171
  rhetoric of humility, 51, 52, 71, 243
  rhetoric of imperial unity, 23–7, 170
  rhetoric of learning, 30, 70
  rhetoric of piety, 7, 45, 46, 52, 53, 54, 64, 70, 72, 259
  role in Council of Ephesus 431, 13, 17, 19, 109–29, 269
  role in Council of Ephesus 449, 14, 128, 269, 274, 278
Theodulus (*MVM*), 93n. 19
Theonas (bishop of Alexandria), 274n. 17
Theophilus (bishop of Alexandria), 198
Thermantia (second wife of Honorius), 16, 137
Thessalonica, 96, 133
Thrace, 11, 93, 102
Timothy (bishop of Alexandria), 271n. 7, 280n. 39
Trajan (emperor), 44, 225–8, 229, 248, 252n. 31
Trier, 48
Troilus of Side (philosopher), 204, 216, 245

urban prefect of Constantinople, 78, 79, 81, 82

323

INDEX

urban prefect of Rome, 78

Valens (emperor), 178, 245
Valentinian I, 48, 49
Valentinian III, 25, 88, 105n. 70, 162, 278
   marriage to Licinia Eudoxia, 26, 45, 131, 133, 141, 277
   restoration by Theodosius, 15, 23, 26, 77n. 44, 96, 113n. 15, 131, 134, 141, 142, 148, 246, 251
Valentinians (heresy), 27, 185, 187n. 54
Valerius (*mag. off.*), 74, 79n. 50
Vandals, 6, 11, 71, 95, 103
   capture of Carthage, 223
   invasion of Africa, 26, 150, 171
Varanes (*MVM*), 105n. 70
Victor (consul), 149
Victor (*koinobiarch*), 274
Viminiacum, 223
Virgil, 32, 34, 35, 215

Xenophon, 206

Yazdegerd I (shah), 162

Zacharias Scholasticus, 270, 270n. 5
Zeno (emperor), 137, 269n. 1, 273
Zeno (soldier), 273
Zeno, Fl. (*MVM*), 94, 101, 103, 104n. 65, 105
   bath-house inscription, 98
   paganism, 91, 91n. 8
   plans to overthrow Theodosius, 92
   role in Marcian's accession, 95
Zosimus, 130, 137, 140, 143-7, 245